# RE-EDUCATING THE IMAGINATION

# Re-Educating the Imagination

Toward a Poetics,
Politics, and
Pedagogy of
Literary
Engagement

# Deanne Bogdan

Foreword by
Margaret Meek

BOYNTON/COOK PUBLISHERS
HEINEMANN
Portsmouth, NH

IRWIN
Toronto, Canada

**Boynton/Cook Publishers, Inc.**
A Subsidiary of
**Heinemann Educational Books, Inc.**
361 Hanover Street, Portsmouth, NH 03801
Offices and agents throughout the world

BOYNTON/COOK ISBN : 0-86709-305-6
IRWIN ISBN: 0-7725-1943-9


**Library of Congress Cataloging-in-Publication Data**
Bogdan, Deanne.
     Re-educating the imagination : toward a poetics, politics, and
pedagogy of literary engagement / Deanne Bogdan.
         p.   cm.
     Includes bibliographical references and index.
     ISBN 0-86709-305-6
     1. Literature—Study and teaching (Higher)—United States.
2. Literature—History and criticism—Theory, etc.   3. Politics and
literature.   4. Imagination.   5. Poetics.   I. Title.
     PN70.B6   1991
     807.1'173—dc20                                          91-46519
                                                                CIP


**Canadian Cataloguing in Publication Data**
Bogdan, Deanne Gail, 1938–
     Re-educating the imagination : toward a poetics,
politics, and pedagogy of literary engagement

Includes bibliographical references and index.
ISBN 0–7725–1943–9

1. Literature—Study and teaching (Higher).
2. Literature—History and criticism—Theory, etc.
3. Politics and literature.   4. Imagination.
5. Poetics.   I. Title.

PN59.B64 1992     807'.1'1     C92–094956–8

Cover design by Jenny Jensen Greenleaf
Printed in the United States of America
92   93   94   95   96   9   8   7   6   5   4   3   2   1

*For Joe, Elisabeth, and Stasia*

# Table of Contents

**Foreword**   ix

**Acknowledgments**   xv

**Introduction**   xxi

Prelude   xxi
Overview of the Book   xxxi
The Educated Imagination   xxxv
The Re-Educated Imagination   xxxviii

**Chapter One: Plato and the
   "Uneducated" Imagination**   1
Current Platonic Issues in the Relationship
   Between Word and World   2
Plato, Poetry, and the "Uneducated" Imagination   6
Plato, the Educational Value of Poetry,
   and the Meta-Problem   10
The Censorship Problem   11
The Justification Problem   13
The Response Problem   16
Conclusion   18

**Chapter Two: Sidney and Shelley: The Allegorical
   and Romantic Imagination**   21
Why a Defense of Poetry?   21
Sidney and the Allegorical Imagination   24
Poetry as a "Speaking Picture" and Reader Response   26
Sidney's Defense of Plato and the Meta-Problem   31
Shelley and the Romantic Imagination   34
The Romantic Imagination and the Meta-Problem   37
Conclusion   41

## Chapter Three: The Educated Imagination and the Justification Problem  45

Northrop Frye and the Meta-Problem  47
The Anagogic Worldview of the Educated Imagination:
    The Poetics of Total Form  53
The Educated Imagination and the Justification
    Problem in Language Arts Education  57
The Problem With the Educated Imagination
    and the Justification Problem  63


## Chapter Four: The Educated Imagination and the Censorship Problem  73

The Censorship Situation: Some Assumptions  73
The Case of Peterborough County  78
The Censorship Problem, the Stubborn Structure, and
    the Meta-Problem  85
The Problem with the Educated Imagination
    and the Censorship Problem  92


## Chapter Five: The Educated Imagination and the Response Problem  102

The Response Problem, the Meta-Problem, and
    Educational Policy  102
Literary Response and Frye's Stubborn Structure  109
The Educated Imagination and the Autonomous Reader:
    A Taxonomy of Reader Responses and Respondents  112
Teaching Total Form as Dialectic  120
Some Real Readers Reading  123


## Chapter Six: The Re-Educated Imagination and Literary Literacy  130

The Educated Imagination and Literary Literacy  130
The Re-Educated Imagination and Literary Literacy  135
The Poetics of Pluralism  136
The Poetics of Need  140
The Feeling Problem  140
The Power Problem  143
The Location Problem  147
Pluralism, Need, and the Problem with the Meta-Problem  148

(Dis)Identification, Response Development, and the
Pedagogy of Need     151
The Meta-Problem Expanded: Feeling, Power,  and Location     155

## Chapter Seven: The Re-Educated Imagination and Literary Experience     161

Is There Literary Life After Literary Literacy     161
Transformation and Enculturation:
The Sacred and the Profane of Literary Experience     165
Stasis as Transparency     166
Harmony as the Auditory Ideal     167
Self and Other in Literary Experience     169
Literary Experience as Stereophonic Vision     170
Defining Literature and Aesthetic Experience     170
Literary Experience as a Feeling Behavior     174
Literary Experience as a State of Grace     175
The Recognition Scene, Hegemony, and Ethical Freedom     176
Literary Experience as a Literate Behavior     177
Literary Experience as an Ethical Behavior     179
Literary Experience as Misrecognition     181
Literary Experience as a Ludic Behavior     184
Literary Experience and Literary Literacy as
Cultural Critique     186
Conclusion     190

## Chapter Eight: The Re-Educated Imagination and Embodied Criticism     195

The Re-Educated Imagination and the Power of Horror     195
Literary Response as Embodied Reading: On First Looking Into
Steiner's "Presences"     200
The Poetics of Ordinary Existence: Toward an Ontology of
Literary Subjectivity     206
Coda     210
Reading the Seduction     212
Embodied Criticism: The Scale of Seduction     216
Reflection: Feeling Feeling—The Music of the Spheres
(Tonic Major)     216
Locating Location: Rupture and The God Trick
(Minor Second)     218
(Dis)Empowering Power: Appassionata Furioso
(Diminished Mediant)     220

Reconstruction: Reclaiming Power (Perfect Sub-Dominant)    221
Relocating Identity (Imperfect Dominant)    222
Voicing Voice (Augmented Sub-Mediant)    223
Leading Note (Major Seventh)    224

## Chapter Nine: The Re-Educated Imagination and Embodied Pedagogy    228

First Things First: Passion Without a Victim    230
The Professionalization of Literary Response
    and the Meta-Problem    234
Girls and Boys Together: The Non-Professionalization
    of Literary Response    239
Dissonant/Dissident Behaviors: From Transgression
    to Transfiguration    246
Ways in to William Wordsworth    248
The Singing School    250
The Assignment and the Journals    250

## Chapter Ten: Toward An Alternative Sublime    261

The Poetics of Ordinary Existence and Pure Utterance    261
Double Mirror: Frye, Process, and Embodiment    268
Double Vision, Double-Take: Mythology, Ideology,
    and Gender    273
Literary Convention and Reality    278
The Continuum and the Gap    285
Girls and Boys Together Again? Literary Experience
    and Literary Literacy    289
Can Literature Education Change the World? Woolf and
    Three Guineas    290
Old Myths, New Myths    293
Double Perspective: The Pedagogy of Ordinary Existence    294
Transformations and Transfigurations    295

**Postlude**    303

**Appendix**    307

**Works Cited**    309

**Index**    337

# Foreword

From time to time, and over time, those of us who choose to read in preference to engaging in other activities stop to ask ourselves what, in reading, are we doing? Our reflections explore, casually or more profoundly, the process of reading texts, whether carnal or sacred in Kermode's (1979) terms, and to ask what reading is good for. "What is this writing really about and what difference does it make whether I like it or not?" After these pauses and the grasp of consciousness they produce, the continuity of our reading habits and our discernment of reading as a distinctive kind of experience usually change.

If reading is what we do for a living because we teach it, profess it, count on it as writers, editors, or reviewers, we are almost bound to chase our thinking beyond the level of a common understanding. Our situated perspectives show us reading as a predominantly social activity in a literate culture, related to history and literature. The questions then include: "Why should others read this?" and "What will it do to them, for good or ill, if they think about it?" In all of the forty-five years during which I have taught literature in schools and teachers of literature in universities, I have never ceased to wonder what I am up to, and, what if at all, any good has come of it for others. I firmly know that, if I were now to be deprived of all the understandings I owe to reading, very little would be left in my head. What has grown with the years is a persistent curiosity about how readers become, and how the determined, if halting, attempts of the beginner grow into the serious addiction, pragmatic, aesthetic, or both, of the print-persistent adult. I suspect that, whatever their apologia for their literary self, most teachers of literature know that their recursive experiences of reading have much to do with their impulse to interact with other readers as well as with texts. We need each other in order to describe what we are doing and to justify what, to those outside the reading circle, may seem indolence or self-indulgence.

Some reading experiences have a particular shaking, even shattering, quality: *ébranlement* is the bell-ringing word in my head. When I was an undergraduate, many of my contemporaries were swept away from their studies of French poetry to invade the

Normandy beaches, while I, younger and less fit for non-combatant "war work," was left behind to read philosophy and literature in the company of distinguished scholars of advanced age. (That is, as old as I am now.) They were too revered and honored to be closely interrogated by an inexperienced girl, and they took for granted that their students had read the texts more than once. I doubt if the ancient scholars ever knew the extent of my guilt that I could read Locke, Berkeley, and Hume, as well as Chaucer and Shakespeare, while my friends lurked in foxholes and in shelters or met bombs and bullets. If theirs were the real experiences, what then were mine?

The feeling of inadequacy persisted, not only in response to the texts, until by a series of fortunate accidents of the kind that all readers know about, I read the early published work of Simone Weil, whose strange and tragic death while in exile in England I'd heard about. Here was a philosopher school-teacher for whom reading with students, correcting essays, and working with her hands were integral to the life of the mind. I discovered that her great desire had been to return to France to fight in the Resistance movement. But when she asked her friend Maurice Schumann to use his influence to help her to join the maquis, he told her to leave that to others. Her war work was to prepare a document about the fundamental ideas that would inform the thinking of those who were planning the restoration of French society after the war was over. You can read the result; it's called *l'Enracinement* (Weil, 1949) or *The Need for Roots* (1952b). Imagine *that* as a reading lesson! I discovered that in reading we talk, think, write, yes write. As we recreate the direct experience we have of a text, we are reading like a writer. Reading relates all the functions of language and thought in the ways that David Hume makes plain when he writes of human understanding. We see resemblances, cause, and contiguity. So my reading of literature and philosophy in the context of the sacrificial horrors of war was transformed into work. I had been doing my bit, as far as I was able, at the time.[1]

Comparably, in reading Deanne Bogdan's study, my other readings of the theoretical texts of the last decade or so have been rattled about, fundamentally almost, and put together again, differently. In Barthes' terms, the text of this book has entered the text of my life. In itself the book is a powerful reading lesson which has come at a significant time. Most discussions of education in England are now geared to a pragmatic materialism, a reductive view of what literature is about in a culture that proclaims its tradition but doesn't reread it well enough. In contrast, here is an expansive detailed, fearless philosophical exploration of what literature teaching can be like. The author puts active engagement with reading, readers, and texts at the heart of education and refuses to justify this position for it in terms of anything else. She believes that the "literary imagination" is "as much a condition of the text as a product of it." In dealing with "questions about what, why, and how we teach literature," she sees reading as the process that leads to the answers.

Re-Educating the Imagination explores the layeredness of any construct of literature. It rejoices in the pleasures of the complexity of reading, and the metaphorical relation of texts to musical scores. Those whom the author calls "embodied readers" cannot fail to rediscover the interactive nature of reading, its counterpoint, its way with intertextuality, and its differences for different readers, especially in terms of gender.

Every reader has two histories; both are shared. The first lies in wait for us as we learned our language and enter the history of our culture. As girls and boys we learn the oral texts: rhymes, lore, proverbs which are the bequests of our ancestors. Then we take on the traditional writing system as we learn to read and to make distinctions and choices in the texts and in the world of our own time. We enter our language, are changed by it, and change it. As readers we come to take charge of our individual histories and preferences. Jane Miller (1984) says: "Reading neither gives us reality nor prepares us for it. It does, though, allow us to understand that all our realities are constructions of the imagination and of language." Reading and reality are continuously juxtaposed in the complex interpenetrations of philosophy, literary theory, social awareness, and education, all of which characterize the analytic stance of Re-Educating the Imagination.

As we meet them, Deanne Bogdan's students are reflective, mature adults. We watch them as they read, and as they are encouraged to reflect on their differences and confront what other teachers might call their prejudices, but, here, are characterized as their "direct responses." As they seek out the roots of their understandings and their ethical judgments in the contexts of literature and the "good" life as they perceive it, they discover that, unlike Sidney, Shelley, and Northrop Frye, they cannot assume the consonance of poetry and absolute values. We see them encounter literature as an institution, and watch their teacher as she helps them to discover the nature and worth of their own judgments.

As she does this, Deanne Bogdan also engages in a re-reading and revaluing of her own mentor, Northrop Frye. We are all indebted to those who taught us; then we have to find our own way. (Imagine my dilemma when I saw in a class a teacher who had once been my student. I watched myself when young for fully an hour before I could even begin to "deconstruct" that situation for us both.) Here, the interwoven argument, in all its learned subtlety, is an example of what the book itself exists to demonstrate: that the institution of literature can be explored, resisted, and even refused. Here the Laocoon struggle, the loyalty of the student to the teacher and her need to escape his theoretical thrall, had once its counterpart in the desire of English critics in the late 40s and 50s to slip the coils of Leavis' dominance in decisions about what had to be read in schools and what counted as criticism in the academy. Teachers of my generation have worked to resist the imposition of traditional texts on those who find it difficult to believe they were meant to read them. Now the situation is even more complicated, as parents demand that their children should have the canon of great books which they believe were withheld from them.

Choosing texts for students to read in school or college brings the theoretical strata of this book to the bar of pedagogic practice. Now we see how Deanne Bogdan analyzes the differences, the kind we know we have to learn to live with. Her feminism opens up issues of class as well as those of gender. Her views on censorship depend on contexts with which I am only readerly familiar, but I can replace these with other examples from London which force me to admit my own intolerance. Reading as a transcendental operation has disappeared; it can be relocated only socially and historically. So we must face the inevitability of redescribing it beyond the limitations of what Richard Rorty calls "final vocabularies," the words we use for exercises of this kind, words which we believe we cannot do without (1979, 1982). This is, for me, the central challenge of the book, the way by which I propose to re-educate my imagination.

Imagine, then, a teacher who has been delighted by *Haroun and the Sea of Stories,* a book for children (of about eight or nine) written by the last remaining British hostage, Salman Rushdie. The tale is pure enchantment, spell-binding in the tradition of Sheherezade and as jokey as a slapstick comic. Even the least experienced reader can "get it," as we say. Our good literature teacher becomes aware of it as a "defence of poesie," a challenge to the re-education of the imagination in Bogdan's terms of "direct experience" of the literary. Does she see it in the tradition of Sidney and Shelley? Would a book for children ever be that? If the context of its being read is a multicultural London school, would the enchantment escape the wrath of those who urge on Rushdie (1990a) a more irrevocable doom than Plato ever conjured up for the poets? Deanne Bogdan's book shows us that the construction of that reality takes us to the limits of what we are capable of imagining.

Before they discover literature as an academic institution, children read with the whole of themselves. Their bodies arch over and around the books that help to sort out both language and the world.

Possession, a construct explored by A.S. Byatt at great length in a novel (1990), is something they know as part of the experience of stories. They first come to take it for granted, then lose, and afterwards try to rediscover it as thought and feeling, separately. While they are still able to displace the boundaries of sense and nonsense, to retell the story of Hansel and Gretel as part of the text of their lives, children know that in reading they can make a whole world although they understand it only in part. Perhaps, in seeking to re-educate our imaginations we try to recapture something of this wholeness. But we may have to realize that language too has its limitations, including those we impose on it. Yet, somehow, the poets, back from exile, begin again to dance to the music of time and we gladly join in.

Margaret Meek
School of Education
University of London

## Endnote

1. Part of this understanding came when I was a student of philosophy. It was revived by my reading of Robert Scholes' *Protocols of Reading* (1989).

# Acknowledgments

The idea of a defense of poetry first captured my imagination when Roger Kuin introduced me to Sidney's *Apologie for Poetrie* at the beginning of my graduate studies. I wish to thank him for prodding me into this book, though it is a very different book from the one we originally had in mind. I am also indebted to Walter Pitman, Malcolm Levin, and Dwight Boyd of the Ontario Institute for Studies in Education for the study leave which allowed me to complete this project, and to the Social Sciences and Humanities Research Council of Canada for awarding me a research grant. Particular appreciation is owed to Helene Moglen and Wendy Brown for their support while I was affiliated with the Feminist Studies Focused Research Activity, Kresge College, University of California, Santa Cruz; and to Patricia White, John White, and Graham Heydon, Philosophy of Education Department, and Jane Miller, Department of English and Media Studies, Institute of Education, University of London, where I was Visiting Fellow in 1991.

I am especially grateful to those who read the entire manuscript: David Bleich, Robert Denham, Nan Johnson, Susan Laird, and Margaret Meek; to those who read parts of it: Patricia Brückmann, James Cunningham, Judith Millen, and Alice Pitt, for their comments and suggestions; and to Bob Boynton, for his encouragement and belief in the need for the book. It would not have materialized without the diligence, commitment, and editorial insight of Hilary Davis, whose role far exceeded that of research assistant. I thank Jill Given-King, for her efficiency and remarkable good humor in preparing the manuscript; Margaret Brennan, for her administrative expertise; Stephen Hooker, for his assistance on the bibliography; and Cheryl Kimball, Wendy Burton, and Lisa Panayotidis, for their work in the final stages of production. Other friends and colleagues who have lent support within various contexts are Clive Beck, John Beresford, Jeni de Carlo, Max Dublin, Margaret Early, Jean Hayhoe, Mike Hayhoe, Ursula Kelly, Karen Robinson, Lynda Stone, Barbara Williams, John Willinsky, and Stephen Yeomans. I am also obliged to Jeff Reynolds, Christabelle Sethna, and the members of course 1462, Department of History and Philosophy of Education, Ontario Institute for Studies in Education, for permitting me to excerpt their work.

The contribution of my family has been immeasurable. I thank my daughter Elisabeth, for shared interiorities and giving me direction(s) while I was in London; and my daughter Stasia, for daily commiserations, proof-reading, and quiet strength. My spouse Joseph has remained infinitely patient and selfless in face of the many impositions made by an undertaking of this kind on joined lives. Through it, he has shown me joy in imaginative experience and in ordinary existence.

I offer this book, which is, in large measure, a critique of the work of Northrop Frye, within the spirit of his legacy to criticism and to education—commitment to the Blakean ideal of "mental fight"—and in commemoration of the death on December 6, 1989, in Montreal, of the fourteen female student engineers who were murdered in their classroom.

The following have generously given permission to use quotations from copyrighted works, to republish or adapt previously published material:
From "In the Fall" by Alistair MacLeod. Used by permission of the Canadian Publishers, McClelland and Stewart, Toronto, 1976. "Adolescent," by Joyce Peseroff. Printed in *Harvard Magazine*, July/August, 1988. From "A Moral Drama for our Times Must Never Be Censored" by Peter Peart. Used by permission of *Directions*, Newsletter of the Ontario Council of Teachers of English, *14* (2): 1–2 (1989). Used with permission of *The Whig Standard*, Kingston, Ontario, where the article was first published.

Versions of some of the chapters have been published previously. They are:

*Chapter 3*: Excerpts from "Northrop Frye and the Defence of Literature," *English Studies in Canada, 7* (2): 203–214 (June 1982). Excerpts from "The Justification Question: Why Literature?" *English Education, 17* (4): 238–248 (December 1985). (Copyright 1985 by The National Council of Teachers of English. Reprinted with permission.)

*Chapter 4*: Excerpts from "School Censorship and Learning Values through Literature," by Deanne Bogdan and Stephen Yeomans, *Journal of Moral Education, 15* (3): 197–210 (October 1986). Excerpts from "Literature, Values, and Truth: Why We Could Lose the Censorship Debate," *English Quarterly, 20* (4): 273–284, (1987). Excerpts from "The Censorship of Literature Texts: A Case Study," *Literature in the Classroom: Readers, Texts, and Contexts*, ed. Ben F. Nelms, 1988. (Copyright 1988 by The National Council of Teachers of English. Reprinted with permission.)

*Chapters 4 and 10*: Excerpts "From Stubborn Structure to Double Mirror: The Evolution of Northrop Frye's Theory of Poetic Creation and Response," *The Journal of Aesthetic Education, 23* (2): 33–43 (Summer 1989).

*Chapter 5*: Excerpts from "A Taxonomy of Responses and Respondents to Literature," *Paideusis 1* (1): 13–32 (Fall 1987). Excerpts from "Virtual and Actual Forms of Literary Response," *The Journal of Aesthetic Education, 20* (2): 51–57. Excerpts from "Romancing the Response: Issues of Engagement and Detachment in Reading Literature," *Values and Evaluation: Proceedings of Inkshed V*, ed. Phyliss Artiss et al. St. John's, Newfoundland: Memorial University of Newfoundland, 104–114 (1989).

*Chapter 6*: Excerpts from "Judy and her Sisters: Censorship and the Poetics of Need," *Proceedings of the Forty-Fourth Annual Meeting of the Philosophy of Education Society*, 1988, ed. J. Giarelli. Normal, IL: Philosophy of Education Society, 66–77 (1989). Excerpts from "A Case Study of the Selection/Censorship Problem and the Educational Value of Literature," *Journal of Education, 170* (2): 39–56 (1988). Excerpts from "Censorship, Identification and the Poetics of Need." In *The Right to Literacy*, eds. A. Lunsford, H. Moglen & J. Slevin. NY: The Modern Language Association of America, 128–147 (1990).

*Chapter 8*: Excerpts from "The Re-Educated Imagination and the Power of Literary Engagement," *The Journal of Educational Thought, 24* (3A): 83–109 (1990).

*Chapter 9*: Excerpts from "Joyce, Dorothy and Willie: Literary Literacy as Engaged Reflection," Proceedings of the Forty-fifth Annual Meeting of the *Philosophy of Education Society*, 1989, ed. Ralph Page, Normal, IL: Philospohy of Education Society, 168–182 (1990). Excerpts from "Feminism, Romanticism and the New Literacy in Response Journals." In *Reading and Response*, eds. M. Hayhoe & S. Parker, Buckingham, UK: Open University Press, 62–72 (1990).

Parts of Chapters 1 and 10 have been reworked for an article, "Reading as Seduction: The Censorship Problem and the Educational Value of Literature," *ADE Bulletin*, The Modern Language Association of American, 102 (fall 1992).

# Introduction

## Prelude

This book is a critique and defense of literature education. It attempts both to call into question the humanist underpinnings of the traditional claims of literature to instruct through delight and to incorporate and reconfigure those claims within their social and educational context. It is a book which prods the reader to consider some basic assumptions underlying the profession of teaching literature. At the same time, it tries to make connections and build bridges: between canon and curriculum, among the disciplines, between the schools and the universities. Here it joins the company of other books recently published on the poetics, ethics, and politics of reading, studying, and teaching literature (Bersani, 1990; Booth, 1988a, 1988b; Eldridge, 1989; Poirier, 1987; Watkins, 1989). By participating in the tradition of poetic apologetics, *Re-Educating the Imagination* combines a critique of the premise of Northrop Frye's liberally educated imagination with that of a feminist analysis of literature education, while exploring the possibility that literature can influence for ill as well as for good. What begins as an attempt to argue for a distinctive role for literature in the curriculum ends as the articulation of a neo-Romantic *poetics of ordinary existence*.

The first part of the book, "The Educated Imagination," brings together three current issues concerning literature in the schools: the place and function of literature in the language arts curriculum, school text censorship, and "the response model" in the pedagogy of literature. In undertaking to write such a book, I want to reflect on the impact, now beginning to be felt within literature education, of shifts coming from a number of sectors. These shifts are a result of reader-response theory and poststructuralist criticism having made their way into thinking that informs pedagogy, of revisionist conceptions about the educational function of language, and of the heightened awareness generally, inside and outside the academy, about the power of literature to name, to form attitudes, and to condition behavior. Such a re-formation is manifest among progressives as the need to expand traditional ideas about what is taught in an increasingly pluralist society and among conservatives as the impulse to cleave to fervently-held, traditional values and beliefs, even to the point of censorship and self-censorship. These influences speak to the unpredictable outcomes of psychic transformations and political changes inevitably ensuing from the altered perspective that the reading and study of literature have long purported to bring about in readers.

All of the above powerfully affect that sacred space of the literature classroom, the locus of the imperative to instruct through delight and the awesome burden of responsibility assumed by it. There, literally governed by the mandate and the constraints of state-controlled directives to educate according to both Latin roots of education – *educare*, to bring up, train, rear, produce; and *educere*, to draw out, bring away, raise up, erect—today's teachers of literature are faced with the paradoxical task of conditioning the minds and feelings of the young in two directions at once—that of enculturation into a collective ethos or worldview, on the one hand, and personal growth and development, on the other.

Not so long ago these apparently contradictory goals seemed entirely compatible—that time was as recent as 1963, when Northrop Frye (1963a) published his *The Educated Imagination*, originally aired on radio by the Canadian Broadcasting Corporation. I did not hear those talks; but I do own a hard-cover edition of the book, which I vividly remember ordering from a catalogue the CBC mailed out the year after the programs were first heard. It was the '60s: the world was breaking out, and I had recently arrived in the suburbs of Toronto with my spouse and year-old daughter. Though I had been content teaching secondary school for three years, I very much missed the intensity and excitement of the intellectual life I had just begun to experience as a student, when suddenly it came time to graduate. Now I was a mother in a strange city, trying to establish myself as a substitute teacher, to study Chaucer in an evening course, and to reproduce on my own some semblance of what I had left behind in university life.

The slim volume[1] that arrived in the mail spoke to my spiritual longing for an accessible, synoptic view of answers to questions I had started thinking about as an undergraduate, issues in aesthetics, poetics, philosophy of education, and what is now readily recognized as literary theory, issues which teaching literature to grade nine students had for me made concrete. In 1963 *The Educated Imagination* became a solace for and a gateway to my own intellectual sensibility. When later I returned to the high-school classroom, it had become fashionable to use Frye's book in Ontario grade thirteen English. (It was a fortuitous combination of the essay genre, Canadian content, and the right size.) In probing Frye's thought with my students, I discovered that it was the most perceptive of them who found the ideas in that book the most difficult. Undeceived by his simplicity of language, conversational tone, and directness of expression, my students were consumed with the weighty questions he raised (they complained of being "deep Fryed" and "Bogged Down" by them): questions such as the educational value of literature; the relationship between moral and aesthetic values in literature; among the author, the work, and the reader; between the direct, participating response and the critical response; between literacy and the literary; and the relationship among literature, the arts, education, and culture. In order to pursue those questions to my own satisfaction, I embarked on a program of doctoral studies that culminated in a dissertation on Frye as a kind of archetypal apologist for poetry of the twentieth century, in the tradition of Philip Sidney and Percy Bysshe Shelley, and in response to Plato's banishment of the poets from his Republic (Bogdan, 1980). Since then, my preoccupation with these questions has informed all my writing on theoretical and applied subjects related to literature education.

Why did the educated imagination, as conceptualized by Frye, resonate so sonorously with the dual aims of enculturation and personal development mentioned earlier? One answer might be that there then existed a consensus, in theory and in practice, of the central place of literature in the curriculum; a more or less constant, predictable literary canon; and agreed upon goals for literature education as well as pedagogical approaches to implement those goals. A related answer is that inscribed in the hearts and minds of English teachers, most of whom were steeped in the liberal humanist tradition of Anglo-American letters out of which sprang Frye's fierce commitment to the social value of art, was a dedication to realizing in students' lives the very Blakean ideal that had sustained the literary education of an entire generation—that literature could transform students' lives. Frye's *The Educated Imagination* (1963a) is a synthesis of the implications of that ideal. Intended for the "average" citizen and classroom teacher (Who might that be?), the book was written in a cultural context that affirmed democratic ideals, freedom of inquiry, and the primacy of the individual, as well as structuralist, neo-Romantic conceptions of the text and reader.

Am I suggesting that this has now all changed? Is my impetus to write a book titled *Re-Educating the Imagination* a reflection of my sense that, nearly thirty years later, the case for the educational value of literature bears re-examination? It seems to me that though the tenets of the humanist vision are still intact as primary concerns—life is still more desirable than death, happiness more than misery, satisfaction more than want, love more than hate (Frye, 1990a)—the conditions under which these values are thought to be attained through literary art demand fuller scrutiny than in the past.

This imperative shows up in literature education as what I call a meta-problem: the interdependence of "The Justification Problem," "The Censorship Problem," and "The Response Problem." Each of these "problems" I see as itself problematized; that is, I wish to make both the conceptual framework of each problem and the means of its respective resolution deliberately more complex than I think they were when *The Educated Imagination* (1963a) shored up the values—literary, aesthetic, social, political, and personal—shared by most who professed literature (Graff, 1987).

Today, the censorship problem has proved so thorny that it can no longer be settled by stereotyping censors as the lunatic fringe, as the "other," the "they," the "not one of us," who can be easily warded off by a bag of tricks, a list of political strategies designed to "keep them at bay." Some censors are acutely aware as literary critics (Chapter 4); often the sophistication with which they argue their case prompts those among the profession who repudiate censorship in others and deny it in themselves to think twice about the fine line between censorship and the selection of literary texts in the schools.

The justification problem is no less perplexing. One of the most significant achievements of the ethos of "the educated imagination" was that it demonstrated the logical connection between the literary and literacy (Frye, 1982a, 102–117). My belief is that the validity of this relationship still obtains, but that the case for the literary per se needs to be reopened and remade in the hindsight of poststructuralist theories about the nature of texts and the processes of responding to them (Chapters 7 and 8). With respect to literature education, redefining and re-establishing the literary qua literary is a necessary precondition for drawing up curriculum (what is to be taught) and for devising pedagogy (how it is to be taught). The persuasiveness with which the case for the literary can be made has enormous implications, especially now in a society that values empirical means for measuring the competence of students and teachers. That the literary *is* in fact necessary for literacy is not universally accepted, even by literacy theorists. The actual place of literature in the curriculum is further threatened, ironically, by progressive views about other aspects of language arts, against which literature must compete for time and space. When teachers give more attention to the composing process and to visual and media literacy, then the time previously allotted to educating the verbal imagination is eroded. As Frye (1970) has pointed out, unfortunately "there are no courses in remedial metaphor" (94).

The response problem is perhaps the richest of the three problems of the meta-problem in its implications for literature education, not only because of the exciting possibilities for the classroom generated by reader-response theory, the "response model" of literature education, and the influence of poststructuralism on critical pedagogy, but because theories of response ultimately inform how educators think about the censorship and justification problems, and how they determine the conditions for resolving them. What readers do with texts matters as much as what texts are purported to say. This dictum, more generally accepted in the past decade or so, now becomes a whole new ground for looking at what we teach and why (Bogdan & Straw, 1990; Straw & Bogdan, in press).

All three of the above problems can be said to intersect under a larger rubric—the power of literature and the arts to shape reality positively, but also negatively. The main objective of this book is to examine the assumption that the power of literature is unconditionally benign; its aim is, in effect, to reopen the issues raised by Plato's banishment of the poets. Both inside and outside the schools, some continue to extol the power of literature in traditional ways while others see power within literature as hegemonic (dominant but not overtly controlling). I think it is neither coincidental nor surprising that in my own country the same community that has boasted commitment to its regional culture (Sullivan, 1989b) has been rife with censorship strife in moves to ban "mainstream" literary works, such as Hemingway's "The Killers," for "violent language" (Sullivan, 1989a). On the one hand, some believe Newfoundland art has obvious educational power and should thus be supported by government funding to bring local artists into the schools. On the other, the power of the expressly literary use of words like "'damn' or 'hell' and the odd 'for Christ's sake' [in short stories has been deemed] . . . offensive within Newfoundland's school system, which is run on denominational lines" (Sullivan, 1989a, C3). In both instances, the ethical and educational effects of art are unquestioned; at issue is whether those effects are enlisted in the service of enculturation as it is envisaged by diverse factions, each of which has a vested interest in the implications and particular consequences of those effects.

The meta-problem—of what literature we should teach, why we should teach it, and how it should be taught—is at least as old as Plato. In the past it could be reasonably expected to be resolved, at least theoretically, by appealing to principles of poetics laid down in the various defenses of poetry in the history of Western, particularly English, literary criticism. As Walter Jackson Bate (1970) reminded us in *Criticism: The Major Texts*, "It is difficult to find, in any other literature, a parallel to the impressive group of poets in England who

have discussed their own art critically . . . Ben Jonson, Dryden, . . .
Samuel Johnson . . . Wordsworth, Coleridge . . . Shelley . . . Arnold
and Eliot" (77). The arguments of these critics have been more or less
redundant for English teachers schooled in The Great Tradition. But
these old arguments are being challenged by a new academic sensibility, one that is more theoretically self-conscious and sensitive to
conflicts generated by the physical and psychological reality of being
an educational authority figure in an age of cultural diversity.

To illustrate what I mean here, I will recount an incident that
occurred recently on the first evening of my class in Philosophy of
Literature and Literature Education. For the last few years I had been
using a film, "In the Fall" (National Film Board, 1984), based on a
short story by Canadian author Alastair MacLeod (1976), which the
NFB of Canada adapted for use in the schools. Having found it a
useful resource for focusing the central concerns of the course in
initial meetings, I prefaced the screening this time by asking the
students three questions: What do you think constitutes the educational value of this film? What do you need to know in order to
answer this question? How do you want to talk about it?

My past experience showing this film on the first night of the
course had been that it evokes strong response, both positive and
negative. Few are indifferent to its compelling narrative and the
emotional impact created by the stark images of a Cape Breton family
pushed to some hard moral decisions in their struggle for survival.
My intent had been to ground these intense reactions in the various
facets of the meta-problem by opening up what for most students
were new ways of thinking about the integral relationship among
response, the justifications for selection of curriculum materials, aes-
thetic-moral-political connections, and censorship.

The story concerns a poor family of five, parents and three sons,
the father of whom is a fisherman who must leave the children in
the sole care of the mother during the winter in order to earn a
livelihood. To supplement the family income, the mother raises
capons. Stalwart and dour, she counterbalances the romanticism of
her alcoholic husband who is deeply devoted to a sixth family
member, Scott, an aged horse, who has been with the family for the
entire living memory of the children. Scott's history with the father
was that of faithful companion, their bond formed mainly through
the horse's rescue of the drunk father one night in a blizzard. But
Scott is now sick with "the heaves"; and the mother, to remedy their
penury and Scott's encumbrance on them, resolves to sell him off for
mink feed.

The playing out of the poignant dynamics in this family drama is
reinforced by the voice-over of the narrator, the eldest son, fifteen-

years-old at the time the events took place and now grown to adult-hood. The narrative ends with Scott being carted away in a pick-up truck and the narrator's younger brother, David, in his desperate attempt to come to terms with what has happened, massacring the chickens with a hatchet. This is the conclusion of MacLeod's short story:

Within the building it is difficult to see and difficult to breathe and difficult to believe that so small a boy could wreak such havoc in so short a time. The air is thick with myriad dust particles from the disturbed floor, and bits of straw and tiny white scarlet-flecked feathers eddy and dip and swirl. The frightened capons, many of them already bloodied and mangled, attempt short and ungainly flights, often colliding with each other in mid-air. Their overfed bodies are too heavy for their weak and unused wings and they are barely able to get off the floor and flounder for a few feet before thumping down to dusty crippled landings. They are screaming with terror and their screams seem as unnatural as their flights, as if they had been terribly miscast in the most unsuitable of roles. Many of them are already lifeless and crumpled and dustied and bloodied on the floor, like sad, grey, wadded newspapers that had been used to wipe up blood. The sheen of their feathers forever gone.

In the midst of it all, David moves like a small blood-spattered dervish swinging his axe in all directions and almost unknowingly, as if he were blindfolded. Dust has settled on the dampness of his face and the tears make tiny trails through its greyness, like lonely little rivers that have really nothing to water. A single tiny feather is plastered to his forehead and he is coughing and sobbing, both at the same time. . . .

I am tremendously sorry for the capons, now so ruined and so useless, and for my mother and for all the time and work she has put into them for all of us. But I do not know what to do and I know not what to say.

As we leave the melancholy little building the wind cuts in from the ocean with renewed fury. . . .

I stop and turn my face from the wind and look back the way I have come. My parents are there, blown together behind me. They are not moving, either, only trying to hold their place. They have turned sideways to the wind and are facing and leaning into each other with their shoulders touching, like the end-timbers of a gabled roof. My father puts his arms around my mother's waist and she does not remove them as I have always seen her do. Instead she reaches up and removes the combs of coral from the heaviness of her hair. I have never seen her hair in all its length before and it stretches out now almost parallel to the earth, its shining blackness whipped by the wind and glistening like the snow that settles and melts upon it. It surrounds and engulfs my father's head and he

buries his face within its heavy darkness, and draws my mother
closer toward him. I think they will stand there for a long, long time,
leaning into each other and into the wind-whipped snow and with
the ice freezing to their cheeks. It seems that perhaps they should be
left alone so I turn and take one step and then another and move
forward a little at a time. I think I will try to find David, that perhaps
he may understand. (1976, 28–30)

On the evening of that first class, the students' reactions prompted
me to wonder if a perceptible shift in their frame of reference had
taken place. I had come to expect fairly predictable lines of inquiry:
the symmetrical organization of the plot, the social relevance of the
subject matter to adolescence, the timelessness of the theme as a
rite of passage, the deftness of the filmic treatment, especially the use
of the unaccompanied recorder music to underscore the emotional
content, and so on. These are what I would call "educated imagination" issues, that is, matters addressing the appropriateness of the
work to the curriculum, first, in terms of presuppositions about the
relationship between text and reader, and second, in terms of pedagogical presuppositions about the relationship between literary content and developmental psychology. Now I was hearing what I call
"re-educated imagination" questions, questions and comments challenging the formal, aesthetic, and ideological underpinnings of principles such as literariness, appropriateness, and the dynamics of
literary response.

   Here I will briefly sketch a few of these responses in order to
illustrate the need for different questions about what, how, and why
we teach literature. In contrast to the polarized responses I had heard
in past years—either stunned, sometimes tearful silence or palpa-
ble impatience at what was deemed blatant sentimentality—this
group surprised me as they responded with a range of positions that
seemed simultaneously to recapitulate former topics and to embrace
new ones.

   The interests of some students were focused on considerations of
literary quality, aesthetic richness, moral complexity, and the like;
but several other concerns surfaced in a manner quite different from
before. Deirdre, for example, was, like others before her, struck by the
"universality" of the piece, a quality she saw applicable to her immediate professional situation. As a teacher of English as a Second
Language in a secondary school with fifty-four "mother tongues," and
as a fervent devotee of Northrop Frye's dictum that in literature and
art the most compellingly universal is that which is most distinctively
regional (Frye, 1971), she asserted that the story was a near perfect
vehicle for introducing ESL students to Canadian literature in a way
that would engage positively their emerging identities, both individ-

ually and (multi)nationally. Chris, though, was not so persuaded. His Marxist sensibility was aroused by the uncritical acceptance, and even idealization, of the nuclear family, portrayed in the story as having "transcended" the unrelenting deprivation of their material circumstances. Margaret's feminist consciousness impelled her to notice the patrilinear trajectory of the film in its role of "constructing" the audience into particular modes of identification. Despite the final scene of recognition and synthesis, she contended, sympathies were manipulated in favor of the myth of male bonding, both between the generations and with nature (through the horse), while the mother was consigned to the role of "heavy" as the purveyor of the life force in its most pragmatic intransigence. This was, she averred, yet another example of the female as "ground," as the Aristotelian material cause of the formal cause of the heroic (male) quest for identity. By contrast, Sandra confessed that the film was so jolting for her that she would do nothing with it for two or three weeks; after which time she would perhaps initiate small group discussions and journal work, but she wasn't sure, so overcome was she at that moment to deal with the pedagogy of the thing.

The most startling remark in this initial foray into the meta-problem, however, came from Jeremy, head of an English Department for some twenty years. Visibly moved by this experience, he retorted, "I wouldn't show the film at all." To my bewildered, "Why not?" he answered, "Because it's too powerful!" He went on to explain that he saw the main problem as one of identification: students would either over-identify because the raw emotions evoked by the events in the story were too close to the feelings that arose in their ordinary experience, or they would under-identify because of the discomfiting severity and remoteness of the story's locale. Regarding the first problem, that of over-identification, Jeremy said he would not have been prepared to undertake tampering with the inchoate undergoing of students' felt life (it was all too private). As for the problem of under-identification, he would have opted for a story with a setting more familiar to the middle-class suburban student in his classes; this, in face of the fact that the very aspect of the story about which he was being cautious, the elemental conditions of rural existence in a remote corner of the vast expanse that is Canada, was, he told me later, similar to his own early years.

What do I want to make of this vignette in the Introduction to a book called *Re-Educating the Imagination*? Because of new developments in literary theory and pedagogy, teachers of English have become increasingly aware that they are no longer simply transmitters of the cultural heritage. What they should be doing instead, or in addition, is not always altogether clear to them; but they are thinking in more and more complex ways about what they are doing and why and how they are doing it. In such a state of uncertainty, I believe that the most productive model would be one that accommodates the assumptions of both the educated and re-educated imagination, of humanist, structuralist assumptions embedded in the profession, and poststructuralist ones as well. I hope this book will contribute to building such a model.

I wish, first, deliberately to blur even further that fine line between the selection and censorship of literature texts in the schools as it is, within my experience, often understood. Second, I want to point up certain inconsistencies in the premises upon which many tend to justify the educational value of literature and disclaim some of the very values propounded in our defenses when we disagree with and/or want to discredit others for taking them seriously within value systems which may be different from our own. Third, I want to discern more acutely the myriad interconnections between selection, censorship, and conceptions of reader response that might allow for refusal of the text. In what sense can we say that Chris's and Margaret's ideological commitments constitute a "stock" literary response (Frye, 1963b, 124–125)? Was Jeremy's valuation of the appropriateness of the film for use in the classroom a projection, a form of *agnosis* or resistance to knowing (Moffett, 1988), itself a kind of censorship or self-censorship? Or would it be more accurate to say that he is highly sensitive to the ambiguous nature of sympathetic identification within an educational context, a context that *de facto* makes public, thereby exposing to scrutiny of self and of others, the deeply personal psychic phenomena we call literary experience? Or could it be both?

In attempting to address these and other related questions, such as whether, and in what sense, literary experience is "real" experience, whether, and in what sense, literary response is a form of knowledge, whether, and in what sense, it is possible to have a response that integrates enjoyment and self-consciousness of the relationship between text and reader at the point of the literary encounter, I will be developing two concepts, *literary experience* and *literary literacy*. Literary experience is textual engagement in terms of the direct or participating response to literature; literary literacy is awareness of as many as possible of the conditions of that experience. I intend these two ideas to serve as a heuristic for addressing issues relating to the educational context of poetic apologetics, or the defense of literature—rationales for teaching literature, selection and censorship of the literature curriculum and student response to literature.

The power of literature to instruct through delight has been an axiom of Western culture from Plato and Horace to Frye and George Steiner. Until poststructuralism, especially feminist varieties, heightened our awareness of pedagogical matters (Hutcheon, 1989), teachers in the universities and in the schools pursued, more or less separately, their own concerns about literary education.[2] Over the past decade or so, both constituencies have shown increasing concern with how notions about intrinsic literary value are inextricably bound up with the educational context of literature and with how the material effects of literary interpretation, indeed the very category "literary," have become integral to the study of literature, as "theory" occupies ever-increasing pride of place in college and university settings, and classroom practitioners consciously appeal to the principles of practice. The function of literature has always been implicated with literature itself; but now, more than ever before, this vital connection promises to bridge the yawning gap that has traditionally characterized the disparate tempers of literary studies and English education. I hope that Re-Educating the Imagination can help bridge this gap.

## Overview of the Book

At this point it seems appropriate to say something about the general conception of the book, the content of the chapters, and the process of its composition. First, a word about my use of the term "imagination." A book entitled Re-Educating the Imagination implies belief in the existence of an imaginative faculty that can be distinguished as such; it also implies a functional use of the term "imagination." Though this book attempts neither a full definition of the imagination nor a historical overview of the evolution of its meaning, it does draw on both conceptual and functional definitions. My three main sources are Mary Warnock, Richard Kearney, and, of course, Northrop Frye. Warnock's adaptation of Sartre's definition of the existential imagination "as the faculty by means of which one is able to envision things as they are not" (1973, 113) is especially relevant to education. Though she admits of many different ways of looking at the imagination in her historical account (1976), she regards the imagination primarily as

> a power in the human mind which is at work in our everyday perception of the world, and is also at work in our thoughts about what is absent; which enables us to see the world, whether present or absent as significant, and also to present this vision to others, for them to share or reject. And this power, . . . is not only intellectual. Its impetus comes from the emotions as much as from the reason, from the heart as much as from the head. (196)

Warnock's formulation is important for my inquiry because of its emphasis on the constructive power of envisioning what is not, which has been traditionally the province of the literary, and on the education of the emotions in relating the imagination to student learning, a theme that underlies the general intention of this book.

Kearney (1988) takes a quite pragmatic, descriptive approach, employing a method that proceeds by way of "'paradigm shifts' which signal decisive mutations in the human understanding of imagination during different epochs of Western history" (17). *The Wake of Imagination* (1988) recounts a story of how the history of the concept came to be, from premodern times to contemporary postmodern culture. *Re-Educating the Imagination* adopts a similar strategy (though on a much smaller scale and with a different purpose) by looking at changing notions of the imagination as integral to the related question of poetic apologetics or the defense of poetry in the history of English literary criticism. This book moves from Plato and the "uneducated" imagination in Chapter 1, to Philip Sidney and the allegorical imagination and Shelley and the Romantic imagination in Chapter 2, to Northrop Frye and the educated imagination in Chapters 3, 4, and 5. The concept of the re-educated imagination is introduced in Chapter 6 as *the politics of engagement*, and is further developed in the later chapters by placing it more specifically within the context of other terms I associate with it: *literacy as a state of grace* in Chapter 7, *embodied criticism* in Chapter 8, *embodied pedagogy* in Chapter 9, and the interdisciplinary context of literature education in Chapter 10. But it is Frye's neo-Blakean conception of the imagination which moves me most: the idea that "the world we desire is more real than the world we passively accept" (1947, 27). The notion of the re-educated imagination is informed by what I have called *the poetics of ordinary existence*, which attempts to foreshorten the distance between what Frye sees as two worlds—of everyday life and imaginative experience.

The very word "re-educating" in the title of this book indicates that perhaps something is amiss within the ideals of the educated imagination. It would be misleading to deny this. Yet I want to stress that my conception of the re-educated imagination is not a rejection of the educated imagination, but an attempt to present it as a dilemma rather than as an answer within the tangle of the metaproblem: the place and function of literature in the curriculum, censorship, and the pedagogical context of literary response. And I do so in the desire (I hope not foolish or futile) of integrating humanist and posthumanist views of the educational value of literature.[3]

What really is the problem with the educated imagination and how is it borne out in the following pages? The re-educated imagination challenges three major principles underlying the educated imagination: the logical priority of criticism over the direct or participating literary response, the sharp distinction between the literary and the political, and the separation of the worlds of ordinary existence and imaginative experience. Throughout the book I maintain that these principles, when played out in the world of real classrooms, posit a disembodied reader who, in adhering to the tenets of the educated imagination, is conditioned ultimately to split off actual feelings from the experience of reading. In other words, I argue that the effect of the infinite regress of delayed gratification, the continual suspension of value judgments on the way to a "full literary response," in the regular course of most readers reading most of the time, contributes to the very perpetuation of dissociation of sensibility, the fissure between intellection and emotion that the educated imagination is dedicated to overcoming (Bogdan, 1990b).

The re-educated imagination is based on the following three premises: first, that literary experience is a form of real experience; second, that literary response is an embodied form of knowledge, in which the capacity for aesthetic experience is shaped by readers' situation in the world; and third, that the ethical import of literature education is associated with the transforming function of poetic power. Although I try to consider the traditional humanistic defenses of literature on their own terms, in the second half of the book I want to bring pressure upon these defenses by showing how literary engagement has clear political and social effects. In taking into account both the *effects* of direct response and the ethical importance of direct response as a condition of readers' subjectivity I add three new somewhat troublesome problems to the meta-problem, what in Chapter 6 I call the "feeling, power, and location problems." These problems arise in classrooms when teachers aware of their own positions of authority, not only confront issues of race, class, and gender, but also take seriously the experience of their students as it is socially constructed by those issues. My argument for the re-educated imagination devolves upon the implications of teaching literature within this context. Specifically, I suggest that sensitivity to the three new problems, in effect, reopens the main issue underlying Plato's banishment of the poets—if the power of the poetic can influence for good, it might do so also for ill. Though I conclude that the power of literature is a positive educational force, I make that determination after having re-examined some often taken-for-granted assumptions about what we teach and why and how we teach it.

The structure of the book is syncretic and dialectical. I introduce terms, attempt to define them, gather them up, and play them off against each other from chapter to chapter. The chapters themselves enact a dialectical struggle: the progressive/regressive movement of trying to break through oppositional concepts such as engagement and detachment, direct and critical response, the sacred and the profane, the aesthetic and the political—and of attempting to dissolve and reconfigure them. What, then, begins with an attempt to look at educating and re-educating the imagination within the meta-problem ends with the story of my own experience as a reader and, thus, within the education and re-education of my own imagination.

The movement from the educated to the re-educated imagination traces the development of my own awareness as a feminist reader and teacher, and so the book is an autobiography of my philosophies of literature and teaching. The syncretism of the book arises from my effort to contextualize my earlier work (as reflected in the first half of the book) with my later writing (set down in the latter chapters), to see it all of a piece, both parts of the book really addressing the same issues: the why, what, and how of teaching literature.

In the writing process, I found myself on what Frye (1990c) has called "the involuntary journey," where the traveler finds herself "in a quite different place" from where she began (219). The chapters on Plato, Sidney, Shelley, and Frye harken back to the days when I didn't feel the need to put mental quotation marks around many of the words that I do today: universal, god, hero, mankind, reality, truth, beauty, and goodness. These chapters do not simply glue together my previously formulated interpretations of these authors. My purpose in the first five chapters was to explore how literary critics from Plato to Frye would address the problems of justification, censorship, and response. Aware of my agenda in the second half of the book, I nevertheless tried to stand as much as possible *inside* the theories, and reserve to the second half of the book the task of subverting the arguments of the first half, thereby creating a developmental structure to the book as a whole. But I discovered that once I had completed the last five chapters, I just couldn't live with the first five. It wasn't so much their substance as the tone—the unproblematic assertion of premises and conclusions in the center of all that (male) discourse. In writing the final draft, I found myself having to make further qualifications and to flag the reader to the counter-arguments that follow in the later chapters. My agenda, then, had become more than a plan for the book; in taking on a life of its own, it had trans-plan-ted me, as a mental traveler, to an unintended, but strangely familiar place in my own thought.

This is not to say that the second part of the book is politically unvulnerable.[4] By politicizing literary engagement, I have tried to render problematic liberal conceptions of freedom of expression, democratic education, universal truth, and so on; but I recognize that

I do so from a position of privilege as a white, heterosexual, tenured academic, whose professional career, though interrupted by family responsibilities, has nonetheless been served by the economic, moral, and emotional support of a partner who is a white, male, heterosexual non-academic professional. This privilege is a bias in this book which I acknowledge even as I attempt to confront in the latter chapters my own experience of oppression and marginalization. While I have included some marginalized voices in the pages that follow, the book is in part a product of my own location, which in turn influences what I foreground and background according to my own logic of inclusion and exclusion, itself a condition of my attempt to position myself within my own writing.

## The Educated Imagination

In his description of the involuntary journey, Frye writes:

> [I]f the journey is a metaphor for life, life has to be followed to the end, but the end is the point of the journey, or at least the quality of the end is. It is conceivable, however, that a journey might have a value in itself. If so, obviously there would have to be something inside the traveller to resonate against the experience, so the theme of journeying for the sake of the experiencing of journeying would often be at the same time a journey into oneself. Such a journey implies not a progress along a straight path leading to a destination, as in Bunyan, but a meandering journey. Instead of going from point A to point B, the journey might have a moving series of point B's, a further B appearing in the distance as soon as one reaches the nearest one. (1990c, 221)

Point A, set out in Chapter 1, offers an interpretation of Plato's banishment of the poets within the framework of those critics, especially Eric Havelock (1963, 1986), who have taken seriously his questioning of the power of poetry to influence for ill as well as for good. The tradition of poetic apologetics, or the defense of poetry, though it has been dedicated to proving Plato wrong, has done so more as a vehicle for celebrating poetry than as confronting a real problem meriting a substantive rebuttal. Classical and modern commentators have tended either not to take him at his word or to dismiss the ousting of the poets as, among other things, critical naiveté, totalitarianism, personality conflict, or disapproval of the art of his time. Many do not credit Plato's insights into the double-edged force of poetry. Kearney (1988), however, notes that, with respect to the imagination, "Plato was certainly aware of the profound paradox implied in attributing the highest form of truth to [what was for him] the lowest part of the physical organism" (104).

My argument in Chapter 1, "Plato and the 'Uneducated' Imagination," does take the banishment seriously and attempts to show how it arises out of Plato's mistrust of the imagination as the most "uneducated" faculty of the soul, as well as out of his respect for it as a nonetheless powerful educator. It is this contradiction that precipitates the meta-problem—the entanglement of the justification, censorship, and response problems. Thus my discussion of the banishment is intended to set up the three questions underlying the meta-problem which provide the infra-structure for the rest of the book: what is the relationship between literature and life? (the justification problem); does literature say things, and, if so, what? (the censorship problem); and can there be an autonomous reader? (the response problem). Recurrent throughout the book are variations on the magnet metaphor from Plato's *Ion*, which signifies a continuum between author, text, and reader. The hypothesis that there is a continuum (not necessarily cause-and-effect), but also a gap, between word and world, acts as a framing device for discussion of the meta-problem in both the "educated" and "re-educated" imagination sections of the book.

Chapter 2, "Sidney and Shelley: The Allegorical and Romantic Imagination," begins with a general discussion of poetic apologetics as that area of inquiry that treats the defense of poetry within literary criticism. It then moves to a consideration of two antecedents of the educated imagination, Philip Sidney's *Apologie for Poetrie* (1595) and Percy Shelley's *Defence of Poetry* (1821). In organizing the discussion of these apologias, I had in mind three main considerations: the written attacks on poetry which provoked the respective defenses; assumptions about the nature of the imagination, including the psychological, moral, and social dynamics of literary response within which each poet was working; and, most important for the reader of *this* book, my own contention that, in penning their defenses, Sidney and Shelley necessarily invoked the meta-problem. So, part of the purpose of prefacing the chapters on Frye with a consideration of Plato's banishment of the poets and the two most famous defenses of poetry in English letters is strategic. I want to persuade readers to take seriously the meta-problem as a real problem with a history in the tradition of poetic apologetics.

Chapters 3, 4, and 5 deal with Northrop Frye's conception of the educated imagination as it addresses the meta-problem. Each of the three chapters is devoted to relating some aspect of Frye's theory to the triad: Chapter 3, the Justification Problem; Chapter 4, the Censorship Problem; Chapter 5, the Response Problem. These chapters are intended to offer an understanding of Frye within his conception of what I have called *the aesthetics of total form* (Bogdan, 1990c). Readers will notice that most of the references to Frye in these chapters are taken from his early and middle periods, in which his views on the social context of literature grow out of his anatomizing and spatializing of literary creation and response. In the latter chapters of this book, the references tend to be taken from Frye's later period, including and following *The Great Code* (1982b), where he focuses more on the temporal and the oracular. Though my critique of the educated imagination appears in the second half of the book, the analysis in these chapters does signal my reservations about the adequacy of his theory to meet the challenges of real readers reading within the classroom.

Chapter 3, "The Educated Imagination and the Justification Problem," begins with a consideration of Frye's defense of poetry under the controlling principle of the justification problem already mentioned: the relationship between literature and life. It illustrates Frye's neo-Romanticism as reflected in the ardency of his claims for the educational value of literature in ethical terms. The chapter attempts, first, to show how his often contradictory stances on specific issues, such as value judgments and the relationship between the moral and the aesthetic, are resolved within his doctrine of anagogy, that is, the broadest possible context of literature as the center of the totality of the verbal universe that "swallows" life (1963a, 33). Next follows the "application" of this theory to justifying literature as the informing discipline of the language arts curriculum. Here the operative question is, How can literature be defended as both a *language* art and a language *art*?

I should stress that, when I refer to questions of professional practice, I do not intend to make blanket assumptions about what is the case with all pedagogical situations all of the time. Teaching literature is, to be sure, as complex and diverse an activity as the context in which it is carried out. The motivating force behind this book, however, is to prompt a reconsideration of the issues I raise, which, in my experience, tend to be seen more as givens than as problems.

Central to Chapter 4, "The Educated Imagination and the Censorship Problem," is the issue of whether and what literature says. Here I advance an account of one the most prominent censorship debates in Canada within the past fifteen years: that of Peterborough County, Ontario, in which a fundamentalist religious group launched an attack on, among other books, Margaret Laurence's *The Diviners* (1974). In my analysis I argue that, so long as censorship is opposed on the grounds that literature says things which directly transmit certain kinds of values to the reader, the only foreseeable resolution of censorship disputes will be in terms of winners or losers in a values war, the chief deciding factor in any one battle being either political power or epistemological astuteness. In my view, the case of Peterborough County illustrates the censors as the better literary critics. This example is followed by an alternative frame of reference for the discussion: a consideration of the "unsayingness" of literature within Frye's conception of literature as "the stubborn structure" (1970) and of his theory of literary response as ironic detachment.

The final chapter in this trilogy, "The Educated Imagination and the Response Problem," Chapter 5, begins with a discussion of the most recent (1987) Ontario Ministry of Education guideline document for English studies, in which I compare and contrast some of the assumptions about functional literacy, media literacy, and what is referred to in the document as "The Centrality of Literature" to the curriculum (2). I then construct a taxonomy of reader responses and respondents within a developmental perspective based on Frye's ideal of the autonomous reader, which is grounded in the logical priority of the critical response over the direct, participating response. The resulting theory of literary response presupposes an oscillation between engagement and detachment and thus accepts a kind of dissociation of sensibility as a fact of reading life.

In this chapter some of the responses and respondents are actual, some simulated; but all are anonymous and more or less disembodied. My method is that of a deductive analysis of "better" and "worse" modes of response, ranging from "stock response" as automatic reflex to a "full" or "genuine" response as evidenced through literary appreciation. I conclude with the suggestion that the taxonomic structure assumes that response to literature proceeds from direct experience, but that the experience is valued in terms of knowledge about literature rather than the specificities of student readers' lives. This, I contend, posits a worldview which is hierarchically structured, one which I contest in the second half of the book.

## The Re-Educated Imagination

Chapters 6 through 10 enact the dialectical struggle proper, and can be regarded, in a sense, as the series of "points B" in the involuntary journey mentioned earlier. By surveying those points now, I will attempt to say something about the genre and informing ethos of this book. Readers might wonder where to locate it amid the array of "isms," "posts," and "ists" of current theoretical frameworks. Actually, so do I. To me, the book hovers in the interstices between structuralism, poststructuralism, humanism, posthumanism, modernism, postmodernism, and has not been cast according to any one modality. My hope, however, is that it will be regarded as a feminist work, one which contributes to the ongoing effort of breaking down monolithic conceptions of literariness, self, experience, censorship, and so on, traditionally the preserve of masculinist culture. At the same time, I hope that it will support connections between the strivings of various feminisms to make literature classes more hospitable and the world more habitable.

Readers will find scant mention of theorists such as Derrida, Lacan, Foucault, and Lyotard in these pages. This is not because I repudiate their contributions. Though I have doubtless been influenced by poststructuralist and postmodernist thought, and use feminist poststructuralist theorists to advance what in the end might very well be a kind of postmodern position, I do not regard either of these domains as "my culture." Just as I cannot live with unproblematic assumptions of universality and centrality of the "old humanism," neither can I live with the abolition of reality or the ontological bankruptcy of much poststructuralist and postmodernist thinking. Though working within a very different, more explicitly political context than I am, political theorist Wendy Brown (1991) writes that, as feminists, "we need to plot an epistemological and ontological route that slips between the transcendent subject of liberalism, the economically determined subject of Marxism, and the fully and multiply socially constructed, infinitely splitting (non)subject of postmodernism" (3). In my particular revisioning of humanism, which I take to be the central project of re-educating the imagination, I have drawn eclectically on the writings of those writers and thinkers whom I have found most helpful in working out my own dualisms in my own way and for my own purposes. I have used theorists who, though they do not necessarily dwell or originate within the humanistic ethos of my own meandering journey, can speak most directly to my general aim, which is to redraft the borders between the literary and the political while preserving the ethical primacy of readers' experience. Opening up for reconsideration Plato's hypothesis that literature might influence for ill as well as for good does presuppose some poststructuralist and postmodernist values, the main ones being doubleness and the "critical reworking" (Hutcheon, 1988, 4) of formerly unproblematized educational, literary, and aesthetic issues. But I have not self-consciously adhered to any one methodology.

One thing, though, seems clear. The hyperawareness of poststructuralism makes a return to naive realism or the "mimetic adequacy" of the correspondence between word and world (Felperin,

1985, 194) problematic. After the critique of modernism, readers think twice about the assumptions of "the solace of good [aesthetic] forms" (Lyotard, 1979/1989, 81). Yet that does not bridge the gap between analysis and experience, even if experience is redefined in textual terms. Along with Felperin, I would ask,

> Is there life after post-structuralism, and if so, what form might its institutionalization take? How may we carry on our critical and pedagogical practice under the pitiless gaze of deconstruction in particular, a doctrine that desanctifies our once sacred texts, desta-bilizes our secure hierarchies of authors and readers, classics and criticism, out of reliable relation, and demystifies our humanist vision of high cultural and moral purpose? With the cat so far out of the bag, what is our best strategy for survival? (1985, 216–217)

I agree with Lyotard about the terrorism of totalizing structures, that is, structures that unify "with an eye to power and control" in such a way as to eclipse that power (Hutcheon, 1988, xi), have threatened and silenced other players in the language game (Lyotard, 1979/1989, 63–64). Elsewhere I have commented on these issues under the rubric of *the feminization of total form* (Bogdan, 1990e). At the end of that piece, I nonetheless betrayed my desire for the beautiful, for belief in the imagination, craving for the sublime, and hunger after transcendence. And, even more heretical, I now want "to bridge the gap between the cognitive, ethical, and political discourses, thus opening the way to a unity of experience" (Lyotard, 1979/1989, 72).[5]

I also agree that it is important "to determine what sort of unity" this might be (Lyotard, 1979/1989, 72). But I would question it from the vantage point of the material effects of patriarchal aesthetics on the lives of women and indeed, from patriarchal conceptions of experience itself. And here I agree with Teresa de Lauretis (1987), who insists that there can be "no going back to the innocence of 'biology'" for our definitions of experience, especially women's experience, which, for reasons of our survival, must be predicated upon "the analytical and critical method of feminism, the *practice* of self-consciousness" of gender as it is inextricably implicated with social reality (20, emphasis original). The concept "unity," then, becomes subject to the mode and structure of its representation and now becomes a word added to the list of those enclosed by quota-tion marks.

For women, ideals of the organic whole and totalizing experience become harbingers of death because of what in the second half of this book I call women's *post-tragedic stance* (Chapters 6 and 8)—their ongoing recognition of themselves as Other within the assumptions about and the structures of male entitlement to "fulfillment."

Through the creation of a fictional persona writing to a friend, Christa Wolf (1984) asserts that "every woman in this century and in our cultur[al] sphere who has ventured into male-dominated institutions—'literature' and 'aesthetics' are such institutions—must have experienced the desire for self-destruction" (299). This notwithstanding, I would contend that there is an unmistakable ethical, even religious, demand, broadly construed, entailed by the desire for and experience of affective aesthetics, an imperative which persists despite critique upon critique of their hegemonic implications. The struggle to confront these contradictions makes, out of the latter chapters of the book, a pushing-and-pulling between "direct" literary experience and the analyzing of that experience in political and educational terms, and ultimately attempts a tentative definition of some mode of integration between them.

Chapter 6, "The Re-Educated Imagination and Literary Literacy," begins my critique proper of the educated imagination in terms of the politics of engagement. Here I subvert the taxonomy of literary responses and respondents set up in Chapter 5 and deliberately conflate the censorship and response problems by defending two groups of protesting readers: a graduate class in feminist criticism and a senior secondary class of black male and female students. My rationale for both defenses is premised on the contention that, when literary experience is taken seriously as real experience, the theoretical ground under the ideal of the autonomous reader gives way, and the hierarchy allowing for the distinction between what the taxonomy regarded as "stock" response and a "full" or "genuine" literary response is overturned.

This chapter defines literary literacy as heightened awareness of the conditions of literary response within the purview of the re-educated imagination, which attempts to politicize direct response and put it first at the same time. The theoretical task of politicizing engagement is undertaken by adding to the meta-problem the feeling, power, and location problems. The theoretical task of making direct response prior to the critical response is building theory by beginning with the respondent. In looking at *how* readers respond, Robert Probst (1988) has acknowledged the temporal and psychological priority of response to criticism: "We are simply trying to find out what the responses are. We will then be able to look more closely at the readings to discover what we can about the readers, the text, and the reading process" (11). In focusing on the fact that readers respond in one way rather than another, the re-educated imagination would make response ethically and logically prior to criticism. This stance is in contrast to the view clarified by Frye, that the critical enterprise be approached from a theoretical vantage point (be it literary

convention or the poet's imagination) and its corollary, that initial
responses are necessarily precritical. My starting point is not only
that direct response (response which is experienced as unmediated
even though the respondent knows otherwise) *happens* first but that
it provides the *necessary ground* for both the aesthetic apprehension
of literature and for the moral and political implications of its effects.
Otherwise, reading literature becomes merely a way of doing social
science. I believe it to be more. Chapter 6 also points up the rich
interdependencies between school reading and literary studies at the
university level.

Chapter 7, "The Re-Educated Imagination and Literary Experience," addresses the justification problem in the hindsight of literary
literacy redefined in political terms. In effect, this chapter asks
whether there can be literary life after literary literacy. It attempts to
remake the case for the relationship between literacy and the literary
by integrating the oral/aural and visual aspects of literacy in search of
a conception of the aesthetic as transformational experience, as a
state of grace. The chapter revisits, with the new lenses of the feeling,
power, and location problems, some of the ideas addressed in the
first part of the book, such as the Aristotelian recognition scene, stasis,
and aesthetic distance.

This chapter is the most acute in terms of the anguished dialectical struggle: the one step forward, two steps back, in questing after
the virtually impossible goal of reclaiming holistic aesthetic experience in the wake of the "isms" and in trying to claim a distinctive role
for literature education not already being fulfilled by other, "newer"
disciplines. Cultural studies and critical pedagogy, for example, also
share in the emancipatory project claimed by the traditional defenses
of poetry and of English studies (Giroux, 1988; Giroux & Simon et al.,
1989; Henley & Young, 1990; Livingstone et al., 1987). Literary experience is justified as a state of grace, as stereophonic vision, as types
of behaviors—literate, ethical, and ludic—in terms of the moving
power of poetry as a quasi-religious, transformative force. Finally,
the chapter poses the question of whether, thus conceived, literature
can be regarded as constitutive of the self in moral terms and/or
redemptive in social and political terms.

Having dealt with the meta-problem within the context of the
re-educated imagination, I continue the *agon* between the aesthetic
and political dimension of literary experience in Chapter 8 by asking
whether a return to aesthetic innocence is possible after the dawn of
political, particularly feminist, consciousness. In "The Re-Educated
Imagination and Embodied Criticism," I confront patriarchal aesthetics directly by recounting one of my own reading experiences in the
wake of the Montreal massacre of fourteen female engineering stu-

dents on December 6, 1989. This chapter brings into sharpest relief the oppositions arising from combining the two major principles of the re-educated imagination: the politicizing and the logical priority of direct response.

The convergence of the two main premises of the re-educated imagination from the angle of my own vision as a reader in this chapter provides a concrete situation for working out and working through a number of ideas fundamental to the book: embodied criticism, the poetics of ordinary existence, the continuum between word and world, reading as seduction, the alternative sublime, and the recovery of voice and hearing as the basis for the oracular in literary experience. It also affords me the opportunity to contest power imbalances among authors, texts, and readers, and dichotomies between engagement and detachment, reading and criticism, reception and creation of the text.

Teaching comes to the fore in Chapter 9, "The Re-Educated Imagination and Embodied Pedagogy." Here I try to delineate affinities between feminist and "mainstream" pedagogical practice, both of which strive to democratize education by freeing students through raising consciousness about the power of text and their own power as readers and as writers, and by creating an environment which works toward dismantling hierarchies. This chapter introduces student voices in one of my own classroom experiments, in which I was able, to some degree, to shed my role as "expert" on the content, and in which the success of my own project depended upon my students' willingness to venture something new to them—journal writing. Chapter 9 acts as a companion piece to Chapter 6 in that both draw connections between the university and school levels: Chapter 6, with respect to resistant readings; Chapter 9, with respect to pedagogical principles and methods.

This chapter also makes a case for literature education within an interdisciplinary context. Specifically, it elaborates on the relationship between literary literacy and literary experience as the ongoing dialectical process of literary reading and the self-conscious awareness of the conditions of that reading. Here the rubric is threefold: the notion of presence, that is, honoring student response as the ethical priority of human witness; the idea of the transgression—of boundaries, both generic and disciplinary; and the reading of theory, broadly defined, as a necessary component of embodied criticism.

The final chapter, "Toward an Alternative Sublime," returns to the meta-problem introduced in Chapter 1 as a defense of literature education within an interdisciplinary context. Reaching the end of my involuntary journey has brought about certain changes in the face of the three premises of the justification, censorship, and response problems. In transposing the premises of the meta-problem, I begin with the response problem, where the principle of the autonomous reader now becomes that of the embodied reader. Here I return to Northrop Frye and the "other" side of his theory: the psychological priority of direct response, which was always present in his work but taken for granted and given short shrift by both him and by commentators, in favor of the anatomy of his criticism (Hamilton, 1990). As mentioned earlier, it was toward the end of his life, after his work on the Bible, that Frye began to devote more of his energies to the relationship of literature to the oral, revelatory poetic tradition—the less vocal but omnipresent inspiration of his entire oeuvre.

Chapter 10 also reconfigures the censorship problem. Its major premise, whether and what literature says, now metamorphoses into the principle of doubleness: the double-edged power of literature becomes double vision, double-take, double focus, double perspective, and double life. In this section I attempt a critique of the hierarchy between mythology and ideology from a feminist perspective in order to put into even greater relief the urgency of the meta-problem. Here critical voices which have been heard throughout are recapitulated, and some new ones are heard on the topic of feminism and censorship.

At the end of chapter 10, the premise of the justification problem, the relationship between literature and life, becomes transfigured into that between literary experience and literary literacy, which extends the discussion from literary reading to its implications for social change through education. Here I focus on Virginia Woolf and her legacy of concern with the personal and the political, the private and the public, the literary and the educational, and their roles in changing the world. This is perhaps a grandiose agenda, as I admit repeatedly in the book. My hope is that it is not a presumptuous or redundant one.

# Endnotes

1. All page references are taken from the original edition.

2. Though the term "literary education" is less awkward than "literature education," I will be using the latter term throughout the book in order to distinguish the place and function of literature in the curriculum as a contested issue. "Literary education," as it is used here, connotes a stable meaning in the belletristic tradition.

3. For the purposes of this book, I use "modernist/modernism," "postmodernist/postmodernism," "humanist/humanism," and "posthumanist/posthumanism" in terms of the values they espouse. "Modernist" refers to aesthetic theories which are predicated upon the "ideology of artistic autonomy, individual expression, and the deliberate separation of art from mass culture and everyday life"

(Hutcheon, 1989, 15). Modernism privileges qualities such as the coherence, ambiguity, irony, and the self-containment of the artifact. "Postmodernist" is a concept with plural meanings. Whether seen as breaking away from, reacting against, or continuous with, modernism, postmodernism primarily challenges the ideological presuppositions of the modernist ideal through a duplicitous dynamic that reinforces cultural traditions even as it subverts them. (See Hutcheon, 1989, 1–29.) I use "humanist" to signify cultural and educational values with "patriarchal underpinnings . . . . In the context of humanism, the individual is unique and autonomous, yet also partakes of that general human essence, human nature" (Hutcheon, 1989, 13). Applied to education, humanism presupposes the existence of a coherent, integrated, male self which claims unrestricted access to self-expression, the unfettered right to know, and the unproblematic power of rational choice. Posthumanism challenges *a priori* notions of closed, fixed meanings and consensus. It is in subverting the illusion of public agreement through the notion of difference that postmodernism and posthumanism overlap. (See Hutcheon, 1988, 3–8.)

4. I avoid the expression "politically correct" because of the reprehensible co-opting of the term by right wing political forces as a way of blanketing over blatant racism, classism, sexism, and homophobia. (See Bernstein, 1990, 1, 4; D'Souza, 1991.)

5. This is something for which Lyotard castigates Habermas (Lyotard, 1979/1989, 72).

# Chapter One

# Plato and the "Uneducated" Imagination

Let's begin with a hypothetical test. How well "educated" is your imagination and how can you tell? One way might be to observe your critical temper as you read the daily newspapers. Do you believe that what is presented is "the truth"? Another way might be to evaluate your ability to unpack advertisements. Do you distinguish between convention and reality, between the archetypal patterns invoked by the ad-makers and how they employ convention and reality to sell something? A third way could be to gauge your response to literature. Do you read for pleasure only, as a form of escape? Do you revel in getting lost in a text, in suspending your disbelief, in immersing yourself totally in the vicarious inhabiting of other lives and other worlds through sympathetic identification, as though the characters and events were "real"; or are you also mindful of the work's structure, the author's artistry, style, and value bias? In other words, do you attend to the differences between literature and life as well as to the similarities?

If your answer to the questions above is in the affirmative, you will most likely recognize yourself as a person who opposes the censorship of literature in the schools, who believes in the moral and social value of literature, and who thinks that responding to literature creatively and critically is a valuable educational goal. The principles of poetics informing the answers to these questions and underlying the attitudes to the justification problem, the censorship problem, and the response problem, as they are outlined in the first part of this book, comprise the premises of the "educated imagination." These principles are not just academic questions of

1

interest to an intellectual elite; they are vital life skills which concern teachers, students, and a populace that has made best-sellers out of Allan Bloom's *The Closing of the American Mind* (1987) and E.D. Hirsch's *Cultural Literacy* (1987), and that refuses to let "the Rushdie affair" go away.

Plato's banishing of the poets from his Republic is the springboard for my inquiry into the educated imagination. In the first part of this book, I will sketch out some historical antecedents of the major tenets of what I take to be Northrop Frye's conception of the educated imagination by analyzing Plato's challenge to poetry as that which instructs through delight. I will also look at three "defenses of poetry" in the history of English literary criticism, through which are reflected literary and cultural values of three worldviews: Philip Sidney's *Apologie for Poetrie* (1595) and the Renaissance; Percy Bysshe Shelley's *Defence of Poetry* (1821) and Romanticism; and, finally Frye's *The Educated Imagination* (1963a) and what is generally thought of as liberal humanism. In this highly selective survey, I attempt to provide a theoretical framework for examining the meta-problem of the justification, censorship, and response problems as a way of thinking about the complex interrelationship among what, why, and how literature is taught in the schools at the senior level.

Besides indicating how any one person's educated imagination might be operating at any one time in terms of critical thinking, the reading of newspapers serves as a barometer of a general preoccupation with a host of topics about the relationship between word and world[1] that concerned Plato as well. In preparing to write this book and to teach my graduate classes in literature education, I have, over the past couple of years, found myself daily tearing out pieces from the papers on topics pertaining to the meta-problem, everything from school text censorship to the theft of Native stories by White authors, to sex, violence, and sedition in the media. Conflicts abound between the rights to read and to retain ethnic/racial identity, between the unfettered right to know and its cost in human sensibility, between censorship and pornography, between artistic expression and government control of the culture, to mention just a few of the sites of skirmish.

## Current Platonic Issues in the Relationship Between Word and World

As I thumb through my files of newspaper clippings, I realize why Plato's theories about poetry (a term I will use throughout this book in its generic sense as "literature") and its relationship to reality are so pertinent to a book addressing the educated and re-educated imagination in terms of the meta-problem outlined in my Introduction. Plato's poetics represents a system of thought that entails the enmeshment or imbrication of the justification, censorship, and response problems (the dictionary definition of "imbricated" being "lying lapped over each other in regular order, like tiles or shingles on a roof "). For him, whether to admit poets and poetry to the Republic and under what conditions was a question of poetry's social function; its social function was a logical extension of its metaphysics, of whether it could be justified in terms of what it actually *was*; and *that* was inextricably linked to its behavioral effects on respondents, effects concerning the relative state of the individual and collective imagination within the prevailing cultural ethos. In this sense Plato can be thought of as the first philosopher of literature education.

That readers in the everyday course of their lives take seriously the overlapping nature of the justification, censorship, and response problems is evident in my files filled with lead articles and letters to the editor about the erosion of the literary canon in the classroom because of pressure groups (Landsberg, 1986); about the alleged noxious effects of "subliminal messages" in rock music (Cherub, 1990); about the fine line between selection and self-censorship in children's books (Vincent, 1990). My folders thicken with each day's events.

One of the more telling instances of the sobriety with which the "average citizen" accepts the relationship between the representational and the real was the attempt in Toronto in May, 1990, to disqualify a juror in Canada's first war crimes trial for attending the film *Music Box*, after the presiding judge advised the jurors against viewing it. (The film centers on an elderly American male accused of being involved in atrocities against Jews in 1944.) Though the defense lawyer in the case pleaded for a mistrial, the judge "rejected the mistrial motion and refused to question the juror, saying he believed she was capable of distinguishing between 'a fictional movie and the facts of this trial' " (Platiel, 1990, A12).

We might say that in the above incident the judge was demonstrating his faith in the juror's educated imagination, in her ability to tell the difference between literary convention and reality, and to act accordingly, to detach the feelings induced by the filmic representation from her judgment of a similar case in "real life." Next to freedom of speech and artistic expression, faith in this faculty of the adult mind being able to separate out images from what they are thought to portray is the most commonly invoked principle held by most who oppose censorship, espouse the educational value of literature, and advocate the kind of critical acumen the media literacy people insist has now become one of the "basics."

Yet application of this principle is by no means blanket, or even consistent. Again, in the city where I live the organization Media-Watch appealed to the Toronto Transit Commission to remove from the subways a beer ad picturing a young brunette woman (Strauss, 1990, A1). It would seem that the MediaWatch representative, in contrast to the judge in the *Music Box* and the war crimes case, had no such confidence that the educated imagination of the general public would insulate individuals against the effects of what the ad intended to represent or the way it was doing so. Interestingly, neither did the transit authorities nor the beer company that ran the ad. The former agreed that it "violat[ed] new TTC guidelines prohibiting ads that are sexually exploitive" (Strauss, 1990, A1), and the beer company involved readily complied with its removal.

In my view (only one of many possible readings of this ad), it was not the image itself that was particularly offensive; in fact, this ad showed the young woman dressed in fairly conservative summer attire, and was an attempt by the brewery to avoid the sexist cliché of using bikini-clad female bodies to sell their beer. Here the pictorial connotations were far more subtle, the seductive element emanating from the demure, vulnerable look of the model juxtaposed with the title of the poster, "Canadian Wildlife—no. 9, The Rare Long-haired Fox" (one of a series) and its accompanying text:

> The fox is an attractive creature with sleek hair and lovely colouring. Her superior agility and intelligence enable her to outrun and outwit other animals, such as wolves. The fox tends to stay close to her lair during the day and can often be seen basking in the sunshine. She is usually courted by a large number of males and can be very selective when choosing a mate. (Strauss, 1990, A1)

For me, the superficial innocuousness of this ad was particularly insidious; "sleazy" would not be too strong a term for the sexism of the inferred correspondences between woman and fox as fair game. Yet there were no public complaints about this ad registered at the transit office. What are the implications here for the educated imagination and its efficacy as a tool *for* critical consciousness and freedom of expression, and *against* censorship, today? Does the absence of expressed outrage outside MediaWatch mean that the majority of subway passengers were half asleep and didn't "get it"? Does it mean that they did get it and thought it was funny, or at least clever? Does it mean that they got it all right, that they were offended by it, but were "educated" enough to the negative feelings conjured up by the ad to see it for what it is—yet another example of the commodification of sex and violence in our culture for profit—and to chalk it up to "the way things are"? If so, is MediaWatch really a kind of Orwellian dictatorship bullying government services and private enterprise in the name of protecting society? Or are the questions above misguided efforts to ground critical response in an either/or position of acceptance/rejection of a text?

What I find particularly significant about the examples above is that it is impossible to come to a logical resolution of these questions through an appeal to genre. (To try to do so would be my first impulse as an English teacher.) We cannot simply say, for instance, that both the judge and MediaWatch responded appropriately because the war crimes incident involves "literature" and the beer ad, sub-literary, "mere" rhetorical manipulation. For both the movie and the ad presume that the respondent knows the difference between representation and reality. Yet both trade on the impact of their respective messages to persuade us of a particular "truth": the film, that the heinous nature of war crimes should outweigh family loyalties (the defense lawyer in *Music Box* faces up to the moral and social responsibility not to look away when she discovers that her father is in fact guilty); the ad, that predatory sexuality is "cool" and goes with drinking a specific brand of beer. To me, the ad seems to be saying that "real" men and women—the crowd that drinks this beer—are so "enlightened" in terms of sexual equality that they can tolerate with moral and social impunity the blatant sexism of the ad, which they would read as a piece of "camp" harkening back to "the good old days" before "women's lib." In other words, "foxy ladies" are still "rare" but no longer threatened, presumably because feminism has succeeded in delivering its message that women are autonomous creatures who can "take care of themselves." (I should emphasize that this is only one of a number of possible readings.)

The newspaper examples above also make it more difficult to regard as self-evident the presumption that pictures are inherently more indoctrinatory than words, that the iconographic power of images can be more socially detrimental than verbal text, which is thought to make room for reflection because it slows down mental processes (Gold, 1990). Witness the enormous influence of empirical studies on "violence in the media" and the assumption that the very fact of simulated violence, whether it is realistic, as in R-rated movies, or highly stylized, as in children's cartoons, shapes human behavior and attitudes about the world. In the war crimes example cited here, the judge dismissed the direct "transfer value" of the film to "real life" because of what he assumed was an accompanying critical operation of aesthetic distance; whereas, in the case of "The Rare Long-haired Fox," the transit company removed an ad, the

offensiveness of which could not be gleaned without the active complicity of a fairly close, and even ironically sophisticated, reading of
the fine print. It seems, then, that the presumption of aesthetic distance is not necessarily decisive in making determinations about the
relationship between word and world. That is why I am arguing for
a conception of the re-educated imagination which stresses that
words not only have a tendency to mean but to act on their hearers
and users—negatively as well as positively. If texts read readers as
much as readers read texts, then rhetorical devices which traditionally could be counted on to insulate against verbal manipulation
have now been co-opted and, in a sense, neutralized by an ad industry that has learned these lessons as well as, or better than, students
and teachers of the educated imagination. The educated imagination
needs re-educating in part because it has been colonized by its own
sophistication.

According to one school of Platonic criticism, the hypothesis that
if the art of representation can influence for good, it can also do so for
ill was the major sore point in Plato's banishment of the poets. It is
why he admitted to his Republic hymns and panegyrics to the gods,
and why he first censored but ultimately outlawed the creations of
the poets, those well-meaning but hapless practitioners of *mimesis,*
who were determined to represent the flawed nature of the human
condition rather than its divine purpose. Plato has been regarded as
the friend and enemy of art and literature in the history of classical
and modern criticism (see Atkins, 1934; Cavarnos, 1977; Dorter,
1973; Gilbert, 1939; Hall, 1990; Nussbaum, 1990; Tate, 1928; Wimsatt
& Brooks, 1957). Both positions can be supported; for embedded in
his case against poetry is a built-in defense of it, one that has until
recently not really been credited for the insight it brings to bear on
the nature of the complex interrelationship among what we normally
think of as reality, poetic creation, and literary response.

## Plato, Poetry, and the "Uneducated" Imagination

Let's begin our consideration of Plato's case against poetry and the
imagination by speculating about his position with regard to the
newspaper articles discussed above. According to the tradition of
interpretation in Plato studies which attempts to account for his
suspicion of poetic art (Collingwood, 1925, 169–171; Havelock, 1963,
1986; Murdoch, 1977, 2; Nussbaum, 1986; Partee, 1981, 1–11), he
would have supported MediaWatch rather than the judge in the war
crimes case. Plato not only lacked confidence in the educated state of
the ordinary citizen's imagination, but also would have rejected the

imagination as a faculty of the soul in its own right. Plato's view of the imagination as the "lowest" but highly potent form of knowing, which provides the basis for my examination in this chapter of the banishment of poets from his ideal Republic and of poetry from its central place in the curriculum. It is also what accounts for Plato's ambivalence about the power of poetry to instruct through delight.

Plato's poetics is informed by his entire philosophical system: metaphysics, epistemology, ethics, psychology, and philosophy of education; but for our purposes the most important aspect of his philosophy is his epistemology. His theory of knowledge illustrates how his view of the imagination figures into his conception of what it means to live the moral life. In the parable of the Divided Line (*Rep.*, 509e–510),[1] imagination, or rather the simple act of imaging, as Plato thought of it here, occupies the bottom rung, *eikasia* or illusion (*Rep.*, 511), the least enlightened mental state of the prisoners in his "Cave metaphor" (*Rep.*, 514a–515c). Those shackled by the chains of *eikasia* could grasp only the appearance of appearances. Since Platonic epistemology is hierarchical, and since Truth, Beauty, and Goodness, that famous triumvirate comprising the end of all knowledge, dwelt unmistakably at the top, the lover of truth must climb ever upward by perceiving individual examples of beauty in the world and proceed from these to "fair forms," to "fair practices," thence to fair notions of Absolute Beauty, that is, "divine beauty," "pure and clear and unalloyed, not clogged with the pollutions of mortality and all the colors and vanities of human life—thither looking and holding converse with the true beauty . . . " (*Symposium*, Jowett, 1955, 218).

But is this not precisely where the imagination is supposed to take us? Not necessarily; for Plato, it all depends on who is doing the traveling, why, and the vehicle used to get there. The problem is that the imagination is not an autonomous faculty with its own goals and direction. If the lover of beauty were a philosopher, the imaginative impulse would be guided by reason, that aspect of the soul that is capable of distinguishing truth from falsehood. The lover of poetry, however, is typically not one engaged in the upward ascent, as is the lover of beauty. By its very nature as an artifact made and made up out of words, the poem imitates at a third remove from reality. Though it pretends to communicate truth, poetry is an unreliable, insubstantial thing, whose proper end is not the vision of Absolute Beauty through which this Truth can be revealed, but celebration of those very "pollutions of mortality," "colors," and "vanities of human life" which the Platonic philosopher as the lover of beauty would—and should—leave behind. Within this context, it would seem that both the person who requested the removal of the juror conditioned by a fictional representation of a war crimes trial and the MediaWatch spokesperson who complained about the beer ad were possessed, rightly or wrongly, of the Platonic fear that the charm of the simulacrum, the image, the unreal semblance, would foreclose prematurely on the respondent's critical judgment.

What is this fear based on? In short, on the power of the poem as a "mere" verbal construct and the enormous influence it had on human behavior. For Plato, even "ordinary" language, what we now call discursive prose, could but feebly approximate reality, could only point to the truth. But by working with it through the exacting discipline of oral inquiry, the question-and-answer dialectic of Socratic method, we can hope to get somewhat closer to the truth. Poetic language is much worse off epistemologically because it lends the illusion that it has actually arrived there.

Plato mistrusts language because of the gap between what it is supposed to do and what it actually does. For him, the job of the philosopher of language, or dialectician, in part, is to bridge the gap by the giving of names that express the essence of the thing to which those names refer. The language maker's success at imitating reality depends on the ability to generalize, to abstract from the particular to the universal. For Plato, the problem with words is that they not only have a tendency to mean but to become embodied, both as artifacts and as "hooks" in the consciousness of respondents. As way stations on the road to the Good, True, and Beautiful, they cannot completely shake off their origin in the physicality of gesture and sound. The job of the user of language is thus to counteract this thrust toward the concrete as much as possible by responding as actively as possible to the appropriateness of words. This in turn depends upon how good a philosopher the respondent is regarding knowledge of Real reality of the Forms. Though a precise correspondence between "names and the ideal of that name" (Partee, 1972, 120) is impossible, the closer the fit, the better. But the whole issue of the relationship of language to what it represents is for Plato a fairly nonrational enterprise, one that is reinforced by his lack of faith in ordinary people to generate or use words correctly. Within this conceptual framework, think, then, of how much worse off is poetry, which not only imitates the physical directly, and revels in this facticity, but also results in infusing into the soul self-conflict instead of producing in it the kind of harmony and balance it needs for contemplation of the Forms!

For Plato avoidance of self-conflict is directly related to the principle of non-contradiction with respect to the nature of truth, which can not admit of any form of falsehood. One thing seems clear from all this—the user of words is much better served by the "direct study of their correspondence to nature . . . than haggling over a particular verbal embodiment" (Partee, 1972, 124), especially a poetic embodiment, which does not just *interest* the respondent (as is the case with rhetoric), but seduces. It is the soul that deserves attention, not language. And if "words tend to make human a divine quest" (131), poetry tends to make us wallow in the worldliness of that quest instead of finding the object of it. The student of language, especially poetic language, then, must above all avoid any "violence" in the "interpretation" of words, remaining as faithful as possible to the principle of the correspondence between words and things and Real reality (Partee, 1972, 123). Poetry as its own worldview was a dangerous state of affairs in terms of Plato's hopes for intellectual freedom and moral enlightenment. His account of the dynamics of the relationship among the poem, reality, and the respondent in his dialogue, *Ion*, gives a clue to just how the enmeshment of thought, feeling, perception, and action induced by the poet through the poem can hold the respondent in thrall. Plato uses a magnet metaphor to illustrate this relationship by referring to the " 'stone of Heraclea' ":

> This stone does not simply attract the iron rings, just by themselves; it also imparts to the rings a force enabling them to do the same thing as the stone itself, that is, to attract another ring, so that sometimes a chain is formed, quite a long one, of iron rings, suspended from one another. For all of them, however, their power depends on that loadstone. Just so the Muse. She first makes men inspired, and then through these inspired ones others share in the enthusiasm, and a chain is formed, for the epic poets, all the good ones, have their excellence, not from art, but are inspired, possessed, and thus they utter all these admirable poems. (533d)

We might well ask why Plato does not see this divine madness as one of the virtues of poetry rather than as a detriment. Certainly the notion of the poet as inspired genius has underwritten humanist claims for poetry as the center of a curriculum that can impart to students the best that has been thought and said. Again, the source of Plato's objections is mainly epistemological: poets simply do not know what they are talking about, at least not in the way the philosopher, who is governed by reason, does. Divine inspiration is no guarantor of infallibility. This would not pose a serious problem if the poet could be content with being a skilled maker of poetic objects. But poets such as Homer make claims to truth that are unsubstantiated in reality; he "produce[s] without knowledge of the truth" (*Rep.*, 599a). Further, if Homer is so smart, why isn't he a better person, a great moral leader, a role model of virtue?

Poetry lovers looking for role models for human action, are, in Plato's view, dupes of those who were literally "not in their senses" (*Ion*, 534a) when they wrote poetry. Moreover, this untenable method of composition, what we might now call "the creative process," adds insult to injury; for, as the magnet/ring metaphor shows, it reproduces a kind of master/slave relationship between the poet and the respondent, a hierarchy not unlike that which many proponents of media literacy today ascribe to the inveterate TV viewer. For Plato, the poet is a puppeteer with total control, and the respondent, a captive audience whose suspension of disbelief is by its very nature unwilling, or at least involuntary. According to this view, Plato would doubtless have thought it impossible for the war crimes juror to be able to extrapolate "truth" and "reality" from the fictionalized narrative of *Music Box*. And, it is the very *power* of imaginative activity that is responsible, both for the poet's conviction that the "statements" of his poem are true, and for the respondents' inability to keep a clear head in dealing with the facts of life.[3]

## Plato, the Educational Value of Poetry, and the Meta-Problem

What *is* "the real nature" of poetry for Plato, and why does he think an antidote is necessary to what people think it is? I suggest that the answer to this question gives us a prototypical example of how the imbrication of the justification, censorship, and response problems undertaken in this book forms a meta-problem that becomes apparent once we have to deal with the educational context within which the reading and study of poetry/literature is conducted. What readers, and students, of literature *think* they are reading matters to the credence they give to what they read, the way they interpret what they have come to know (or think they have come to know), and what uses they make of that knowledge. Plato's view of the educational function of poetry is influenced not just by his philosophical essentialism or realism (certain essences or realities exist and can be known), but by his perspective on how to live the moral life in an increasingly technological society (technological in the sense that the oral culture of Athens was being supplanted by the alphabet [Havelock, 1963, 1986]).

For Plato, the question of the educational value of poetry was necessarily a meta-problem because of the complexity of the interrelationship between his conceptual frame of reference and the culture within which he lived, taught, and wrote. Classical scholar Richard McKeon (1936) tells us that art and poetry were "never dissociated in the Platonic approach from the full context of life, and . . . there [could] be no . . . purely aesthetic criticism of art" (24). Poetry, for Plato, was rhetorical because of the power of its affect, as we would say, its persuasive force that what was being represented was true and real (*Prot.*, 326a; *Phaedrus*, 245a). Because of this, it was also already in place as the core of the core curriculum or *paideia*, education *through* art (Jaeger, 1943/1969). Plato's problem was why and how it was educational; *that* it was educational, in the sense of influencing people's lives, needed no justification for educators of the time. By calling into question this justification for the educational value of poetry, Plato inquired into the quiddity of the poem— its thingness, what it really was "in itself," its ontology, the basis of the poet's knowledge. He was vitally concerned with the nature of poetic response and its effects in the world—its epistemology and psychology. In terms of today's critical language, we might say that he problematized the educational implications of imaginative verbal reality as the center of the curriculum by inquiring into how the lie of fiction makes its claim to truth and how it was responded to as such. His search for an answer led him to see poetry as a moral technology of the soul (Willinsky, 1990), which had to be cut, pasted, and ultimately thrown out per se in the interests of pursuing the virtuous life. And so, in Plato we have a paradigm case of how the censorship, justification, and response problems cannot be severed from one another. Now let's look at just how his ideas about the educational value of poetry demonstrate the interdependence of these three problems, even as we try to distinguish among them.

## The Censorship Problem

Plato scholars such as Werner Jaeger (1943/1969) and, more recently, Eric Havelock (1963, 1986), Morriss Partee (1981), and Iris Murdoch (1977) have taken seriously Plato's wariness of the epic poem as the basis of the Athenian curriculum in what was essentially an oral society. In general, scholars have tended either to whitewash the banishment by saying that Plato was only against "bad" poetry, to soften the blow of his moralistic attitude on the grounds that he was aesthetically naive, or to dissolve the paradox of his love-hate relationship with poetic art within the dialectical framework of his own dramatic rhetorical form (Atkins, 1934; Battin, 1977; Cavarnos, 1977; Hall, 1990; Nussbaum, 1986; Warry, 1962; Wimsatt & Brooks, 1957). Havelock, Partee, and Murdoch lend credence to Plato's ambivalence about the aesthetic appeal of poetic power as an educational technology acting as a means of social control. With one foot firmly planted in an oral culture, in which truth claims could be guaranteed only by the

presence and ability of speakers to defend their statements, and
another in the newly alphabetized mode of writing, which could fix
discourse so that it appeared to be autonomous, literally engraved in
stone, Plato worried about the sheer efficiency of a pedagogical tool
as powerful as that of the epic poem, whose deep structure and
multilayered meanings could perform somatic-psychic mnemonic
miracles. According to Havelock and Partee, Plato firmly grounded
his attack on poetry in his objection to it as an indoctrinatory educational force, to which philosophical reasoning was to be an antidote.

In *The Wake of Imagination*, Richard Kearney (1988) argues
that Plato's objection is not that poetry does not teach, but that it
teaches "nothing about the reality of things" (92). Poetry is, for
Plato, at a third remove from uppercase reality, unlike concrete
objects, such as a bed, which, though they are merely objects in the
world (pale imitations of their perfect, eternal, and unchanging prototype in the ideal World of Forms), are at least honest, workman-
like copies, nothing more. Poetry, on the other hand, resembles a
mirror, which purports to reflect the complete picture, the total form
of the world when, in fact, there is no such original to be reflected
(the "true" total form being the abstract World of Forms); and even if
there were such an original, poetry has no power to do what it claims
to be doing. What looks like a reflection, then, is really a projection—
of the poet's imperfect knowledge and the respondent's dreams,
wishes, and desires.

But why can't the poet imitate Reality directly? Even if poets
*were* to have perfect knowledge at the moment of divine inspiration,
even if they were to be taken over by the mystical rapture that characterizes the state of identity with the truth, they would come by this
perfect knowledge as philosophers, not as poets. The problem is the
very nature of poetry, which as we saw earlier, turns itself to and
turns on the world of ordinary existence, the "pollutions of mortality." However much poets may *want* to communicate the truth, they
cannot; for too much is lost in translation from the Heavenly Muse to
the entranced respondent (Verdenius, 1971, 262–64), with respect to
both the human imperfections inherent in the creative process and
the nature of the poem as a verbal construct, a some-thing that is
literally no-thing. It is poetry's contamination by the sensate, the
bodily, the concrete, to which Plato so vehemently objects, together
with the fact that it is not what it seems. This is especially the case
with Homeric epic narrative, where the sin of presumption (mimetic
representation purporting to tell the "truth") unites with deception
and seduction. How can the respondent possibly be able to extricate
truth from falsehood in an epic poem when the bits and pieces of
propositional and moral dicta literally embodied in it are shot

through with fictional "visibles" (*Rep.*, 509b) and threaded together by the inexorable march of a narrative that mesmerizes its hearers? Yet this "non-rational" mode of communication (non-rational understood as appealing to the emotions) was *thought* to be the best way of acquiring the cultural heritage.

*Paideia*, education through art, ran counter to Plato's educational prescription for rational thought (Havelock, 1963, 1986). In *Republic* X, with the well known example of the bent stick in the water (602d), Plato discusses the importance of getting clear the difference between illusion and reality through the measurement and evaluation of scientific method. We might say that, for Plato, the censorship problem devolves around the nature and function of poetry as the teaching, and celebration, of "bentness" rather than the dedication to "straight thinking" that he was advocating. Yet there *is* a place for "bentness" in Plato's curriculum—in the early years where poetry and music are admitted to the Republic in their censored forms. It is only the adult mind that is to be deprived of poetry altogether. That is perhaps why in the early books of the *Republic* he only censors poetry, but in Book X he banishes it altogether. According to some Plato scholars, Plato understood very well the subtle interconnectedness of mind and body; some even attribute to him a theory of the unconscious as directing "the anabolic processes of the body" that both precipitate and follow emotional states (Cavarnos, 1977, 267, 286). I believe that his notion of the interdependence of mind and body, of psychosomatic interplay (*Rep.*, 402d), accounts for his wholesale condemnation of the poets in *Republic* X. Determining just why Plato thought that poetry was educationally valid in some instances but not in others, solving the conundrum of why he censored it in Book III but completely banned it in Book X, again calls up the meta-problem and bids us view the censorship problem within the context of the justification and response problems.

## The Justification Problem

According to Havelock (1963, 1986), within the Greek curriculum, poetry was intended to enculturate young minds into the prevailing ethos—customs, morals, religion—and even function as an informational handbook, a "how to" manual for such operations as loading and unloading ships. Poetry was not written, as we have come to think of it today, "for its own sake," but as a potent means of socialization through which the cultural heritage could be implanted and transmitted. This unabashedly didactic purpose was accomplished by way of a psycho-physiological, right-brained fusion of the respondent with the text through the intermediary of a rhapsode, or poetic performer, who first memorized the poem and then incanted it with gestural expression and rhythmic accompaniment. The resulting impact was so overwhelming in its power to imprint itself on the respondent that he would actually hear voices of the gods. According to Julian Jaynes, in his controversial bestseller (1976), around 1300 B.C., the bicameral or pre-conscious mind, bereft of any conception of the "text" to separate the knowing subject from the object to be known, whenever it encountered the mental stress of having to make a moral decision, would simply summon up Ulysses or Agamemnon in a kind of auditory hallucination (67–69, 255–292) which told the respondent "non-consciously what to do" (85). Sympathetic identification with events, characters, and moral dicta was all-consuming; aesthetic distance, as we know it, was simply not available to the respondents of the time. This condition, characterizing pre-literate Hellenic culture (Havelock, 1963, 1986), persisted until Plato's day and became the framework for *paideia*.

On this view, then, a critical response to poetry, for Plato, was an oxymoron; it did not exist any more than did the notion of poetry conceived "as itself." There could be no such thing as "literature as literature"; for poetry as the embodiment of the nonrational was all-engulfing in the psychodynamics of its enactment and its utterly totalizing effects. Though he was nervous about this desultory compendium of anthropomorphized polytheistic religion, clothed in trance-inducing metre, rhyme, and narrative, as the core of the curriculum, Plato developed a justification for it within theories of early childhood and adult education. These theories constitute an implicit defense of poetry in that Plato attempted to exploit both the positive and negative effects of poetic creation and response in terms of their potential for inculcating love of virtue in the young and promoting critical thinking for those who were more intellectually and emotionally mature (Bogdan, 1983).

First, let's look at the place of poetry in early childhood education. In Books II and III of the *Republic*, the censorship problem is linked to the justification and response problems through censorship of "the entire vocabulary of terror and fear" (387c) as a way of capitalizing on the power of poetry to predispose children to a love of virtue. Plato co-opted the educational value of poetry on a basic principle of "Out of sight, out of mind," in much the same way as would-be censors of today delete offending paragraphs. So, the curriculum was carefully calculated (we might say "selected") to reinforce the virtues of temperance and courage necessary to the preservation of the common good as it was laid down by the philosopher-kings. This was done primarily through a transmission model of cultural literacy served up by the epic poem, which was, as we have seen, more or less imbibed holus bolus. According to the law of exclusion and inclusion, then, in order to move the passions in the direction of loving the Good, Plato encouraged "any words or deeds of endurance in the face of all odds attributed to famous men" (Rep., 390d), that is, stories of the gods performing good deeds but not evil ones.

Taken at face value, this action looks like rank totalitarianism (Popper, 1945/1966); yet underlying it are some of the principles of the psychology of learning still considered sound, one of which is the role-model theory of education, and its power to animate anabolic and psychic processes. In the early stages of the educational program, Plato can be seen, not as proscribing, but as celebrating the fusion of myth and reality that characterizes poetic art and its capacity for teaching emotional and moral dispositions through what he thought of as the "uneducated" imagination, at that point in their development when children would be most likely to learn best from it—that is, when their critical faculties are unprepared for the intellectual enjoyment of art. At this early stage, children are presumed either enchanted or repulsed by poetry but unable to account for their response to it. Neither should they do so, for Plato, since what is important for the young child is *implanting* the seeds of desire for the Good. In fact, Plato disallows the possibility that children can interpret myths "allegorically" rather than literally on the grounds that they cannot tell the difference between these two modes (Rep., 378e).

Plato's censorship of the curriculum, then, can be thought of both as authoritarian manipulation of youthful minds through a doctrinaire approach to poetry and as an expression of his acknowledgment that poetry operates at a preconceptual level—one of the main reasons that it is so highly endorsed by many of today's supporters of a literature-based approach to literacy. Within this context, his theory of arts education at the primary level would give free rein to the child's special gifts for melding with the world of the poem, for "gaz[ing] upward like a bird," insensible to the things below (Phaedrus, 249e). (In Chapter 9 I will argue, along with Margaret Meek [1991], that the child's imagination is in fact already highly developed before the attainment of literary skills.) We began looking at Plato's approach to the justification problem as the flip side of the censorship problem. But the only way to credit him with recommending the educational value of poetry, however contingent that recommendation may have been, is to view the justification problem within the context of the response problem; for his judging the efficacy of poetry as a teacher is conditional on turning to beneficial educational use the mindset of poetic transport. It is precisely this theory of poetic response as aesthetic rapture, however, that brings the response problem right back to the censorship problem. Plato presumes that this state, which he highly prizes for the purpose of inculcating youthful psyches with the love of virtue, actually truncates—and even precludes—rational thought. That is why he insists that poetic response must be undergirded by a theory of literary literacy as dialectic.

## The Response Problem

If, for Plato, poetry is such a good teacher at the elementary level, why is it so pernicious as a mode of higher education? One interpretation is that Plato's insights into the appeal of poetry at a pre-verbal, pre-conceptual level actually grounds his case for ousting the poets altogether. However much poetry might serve to predispose the soul to love the Good, to serve as a kind of precursor to conscious understanding, it can only be "a *rhetorical analogue* to concerned truth" (Frye, 1971/1973, 66, emphasis original); that is, it can only reinforce or countervail "real" ideas, which come about either by direct mystical union with the Forms or by the indirect route of oral questioning. Realizing the possibilities of the alphabet to free, i.e., separate, the knower from the subject to be known, Plato was impelled by the vision of an independent individual consciousness which would finally throw off the strictures of indoctrinatory teaching methods, at least for the chosen few. Thus he sought to supplant poetry and response to it with this oral questioning, rational dialectic, or philosophical reasoning (today many would call it critical thinking), as a surer method of attaining the True, Good, and Beautiful than was possible by way of a confused and confusing verbal imitation of an imitation that pretended to be relaying the truth. As an aid to this separation of knowing subject from the object to be known, Plato sanctioned writing, but not as an end in itself. "The book," then, was a piece of educational technology that offered the safety of psychic distance in that it was infinitely examinable. But would-be knowers must exercise caution about the dangers of being seduced into what Iris Murdoch (1977) calls "false resting places" (71). For Plato, "[t]hose who want to be saved," she observes wryly, "should look at the stars and talk philosophy, not write or go to the theatre" (60).

With poetic creation as the promise of truth under the guise of fiction, and poetic response, by its very nature a dreamlike state of absorption, engagement, or getting lost in the images of the respondent's own desires, poetry, then, to Plato would be more lethal still. Vitally concerned with education as a bringing to *consciousness*,

Plato insists that poetry be a dream for *awakened* minds (Frye, 1957, 111). Through the banishment he warns against addiction to reading for enjoyment, dependence on the "swept awayness" of aesthetic experience issuing forth from the magical charm of poetic utterance. Wary of poetic pleasure, which he considers seductive, he alerts readers to the risks of hankering after a state of stupefaction in which they substitute the authority of poets for the obligation to think for themselves.

It is easy to see why Plato would have thought that children cannot be held responsible for being aware of the conditions of their own aesthetic pleasure, but surely he would have trusted the adult mind with exercising critical judgement. To be consistent, instead of banishing poetry, should he not have admitted it for consumption by the adult audience by giving it the Hellenic version of an R-rating? Not necessarily. According to our argument thus far, the poetic habit of mind for Plato was, by definition, bicameral or totally right-brained (Jaynes, 1976), and, as such, it regressed the consciousness of even an adult to a state of childlike wonder, which required an "antidote in knowledge of its true nature," i.e. philosophy. The more poetic the passage, the more enslaving its effects, in Plato's view (*Rep.* 605d, cf. 387b): the potentially pernicious power of the poetic text and the fluid relationship between the poetic word as the concrete particular and the respondent's mental-emotional dispositions convinced him that any normally constituted human being of the time could not be expected to react very differently from children who cannot cope with their own reactions.

Here the operative phrase is "of the time"; and this brings us to a second connection between the banishment and literary response, one rooted in the educational function of the Homeric epic. The conditions of *paideia* (as well as Plato's own philosophical system) prevented him from being able to adopt a liberal position with respect to poetry in the curriculum. As we have already seen, poetry was regarded, and indeed prescribed, as a foolproof teaching strategy for disseminating the tribal encyclopedia of Greek culture, a guaranteed transmitter of the cultural heritage in what was still a primarily oral/aural civilization (Havelock, 1963, 1986). It *was* something to be believed in as "the truth," not just by children but the general populace. Plato approved of the educational value of the "dulled response of ignorant amazement" (Partee, 1981, 188) required for transmission of the culture inside the elementary classroom, so long as the official reading list was drawn up by those who *know* —the philosophers. Within this context, the possibly harmful effects of a misplaced mysticism could be warded off by quality control of the curriculum in ensuring the presence of positive content only, i.e., the gods and goddesses being good boys and girls. When, however, the context was adult or higher education, and the educational goal was not preparation for life but life itself, which required training for independent thought (there being no such thing as literary criticism as such then), poetic maxims had to be supplanted by philosophical attitudes and methods which could pry the mind loose from its narcissistic wants and illusions.

## Conclusion

Neil Postman has made extensive use of Havelock's ideas in *Amusing Ourselves to Death* (1985), his rationale for media literacy. It would seem that Postman assumes, first, that the bicameral habit of mind still prevails when it comes to responding to television, what can be thought of as today's counterpart to the Homeric epic poem as the tribal encyclopedia (Havelock, 1963, 1986), and, second, that the power of such a McLuhanesque living-through of the imagistic text at a mythical level is not a good thing educationally. For Postman, what education needs today is "an antidote in knowledge of [television's] real nature" in the form of reading for critical consciousness. If we substitute the media for poetry, and reading for philosophy, it might appear that not much has changed since Plato's exhortation of poetry as a dream for awakened minds. Yet, ironically, it is precisely this kind of deep, holistic realization of the poem as this lived-through mythical experience (Rosenblatt, 1978) that enjoys wider and wider currency in the philosophy of teaching literature in schools. It is one of the premises upon which I base my own defense of literature education later in this book.

Today a good part of the embattled state of the school literary text involves the collision between the presuppositions of the whole-language movement, the response model of literature education, and received wisdom about the importance of social relevance and sympathetic identification as criteria for text selection, on the one hand, and presuppositions about why we teach literature, on the other. That censorship might be closer to the "neutral" act of drawing up a syllabus is a possibility not many are comfortable admitting (Booth, 1988a). Plato's ambivalence about the dual nature of the moving power of the literary text might be a useful starting point in trying to resolve these dilemmas. It is the attempt to reopen the question of the double effect of poetry, to reconsider the hypothesis that poetry can influence for ill as much as for good, that frames this book.

Plato castigates poetry for the insubstantiality, untruthfulness, and pretensions of its statements, for intellectual unreliability, psychological oppression, for the moral danger represented by the responses induced by those statements, but mostly for the power wielded by them. Yet when we consider his measuring stick—certain knowledge, or at least the possibility of it, a form of knowledge that is literally out of this world—there is a sense in which he does offer us a defense of poetry by default. In defining poetry as thrice removed from reality, as a lack, as that which is not philosophy but rather "something else" which defies verification and generalization, he prepares the ground for the category "literature." As he reveals in the poignancy of the banishment statement, the long-standing enmity between philosophy and poetry is regrettable and should be healed if it can be:

> [I]f the mimetic and dulcet poetry can show any reason for her existence in a well-governed state, we would gladly admit her, since we ourselves are very conscious of her spell. But all the same it would be impious to betray what we believe to be the truth. . . . And we would allow her advocates who are not poets but lovers of poetry to plead her cause in prose without meter, and show that she is not only delightful but beneficial to orderly government and all the life of man. And we shall listen benevolently, for it will be clear gain for us if it can be shown that she bestows not only pleasure but benefit. (Rep., 607c,d)

As we'll consider in the ensuing chapters, included in the Platonic legacy of the definitional framework for literature is also a framework for working through its educational value under the rubric of three principles we find in the banishment: the relationship between word and world, literature and life (which I will use to examine the justification problem); whether and what literature "says" (which will frame the censorship problem); and the possibility of an autonomous reader (the main principle underlying the response problem).

Who is right, the MediaWatch objector to the beer ad or the judge in the war crimes case, why, and what are the implications for literature education? Or are they both right? In the next four chapters, we will pursue the long answer to this question by examining Sidney's, Shelley's, and Frye's "defenses of poetry" "in prose without meter," according to the three principles stated above. As we do, we will invoke the meta-problem as it looks today in terms of the virtues and limitations of the educated imagination.

# Endnotes

1. I take this phrasing from George Steiner's (1989, 55) *Real Presences*. See my Chapter 8 for a feminist reading of this book.

2. Unless otherwise stated, all references to Plato are taken from Hamilton & Cairns (1961/1980).

3. In *The Wake of Imagination* (1988), Richard Kearney summarizes five main allegations Plato makes against the imagination: ignorance of the poet, the non-didacticism of poetry, poetry's irrational mode of composition, its awesome power to corrupt, and its tendency to idolatry (91-94). These marks of the imaginative domain indicate why for Plato the imagination as a faculty is "uneducated," and why the best that can be done with it is to press it self-consciously, through education, into the service of reason, thereby making it perform its proper function as an aid to contemplating the Good, the True, and the Beautiful. Given the poet's *hubris* in pretending to knowledge, and given the deceptive nature of poetry as a mirror that seems to create the entire world at once (Cornford, 1941/1945/1975, 325-326), I would add to Kearney's list of marks against the poetic imagination that of incorrigibility. For Plato, the problem with poetry and poets was that they just didn't know their place. If they did, they would be pretty harmless, but they insist on usurping the place of reason as "top dog" in the soul (Frye, 1990d, 171). What is more, their readers and audience respond to them as though they possessed knowledge, without the benefit of rational dialectic—that is, philosophical inquiry—to give them an "antidote in a knowledge of its real nature" (Cornford, 1941/1945/1975, 324).

# Chapter Two

# Sidney and Shelley
## The Allegorical and
## Romantic Imagination

In the last chapter we saw how one interpretation of Plato's banishment of the poets invokes his theory of the imagination as that faculty of the soul that is essentially "uneducated," and how his conception of the nature and educational function of poetry is linked to this theory of the imagination. We also saw how, in dealing with the consequences for literature education of the ideas expressed through the banishment, the justification, censorship, and response problems form the triad of the meta-problem. In this chapter we look at the meta-problem as it was faced by the authors of two major defenses of poetry in the history of English literary criticism: Philip Sidney and Percy Bysshe Shelley. In taking up Plato's challenge to defend poetry "in prose without meter," each apologist encounters the meta-problem, as Plato did, but frames it by their respective conceptions of the imagination and worldviews, which colored the way they thought about the educational value of literature.

## Why a Defense of Poetry?

If valid reasons within Plato's own system of thought can be offered for his expulsion of the poets, why has responding to his charge constituted such fertile ground for critical activity throughout the history of English literary criticism? The answer comprises what critic Murray Krieger and others call "poetic apologetics," the discipline devoted to the Platonic conception of the poet as licensed liar (1966, 10). Harry Levin echoes Krieger in speaking about the special problem of literature as an art form which, because it is a fabrication out of words, is susceptible to what Plato said was a "true falsehood" (Cornford, 1941/1945/1975, 24).

> The veracity of art . . . has been called into question just as frequently as it has been confirmed. The very word *poetry* broadly construed to cover works of the imagination literally means something which is made up; while the word *fiction*, which carries similar connotations, passes as a synonym for falsehood. The compound *make-believe* is apt in linking this sense of poetic artifice with "that willing suspension of disbelief" which the poet requests from his audience. (Levin, 1958, 18, emphasis original)

As the above quotation shows, poetic apologetics embraces the many dimensions—psychological, epistemological, moral, social—of the relationship between poetry and poetic response in terms of its ontological status, that is, what it actually is or is not.

In his landmark work, *The Mirror and the Lamp* (1953), M.H. Abrams adds historical considerations to the discussion. "The need to justify the existence of poets and the reading of poetry," he states, "becomes acute in times of social strain" (326). Northrop Frye makes the same point from the opposite perspective. As "society becomes more confident about . . . values, the help of the poet in publicizing them becomes less essential" (1971/1973, 80), and presumably less contentious. Implicit in both these statements is the assumption that the habitual response to the voice of poetry is mainly allegorical; that is, readers naturally tend to relate literature to life along the lines of a Platonic truth of correspondence between the one and the other.

In the last chapter we saw how mimetic fusion of the Homeric mind with the epic poem can be seen as a paradigm case of the way in which response is directed towards poetry as a form of knowledge. Abrams suggests an alternative to this Homeric mindset: "[p]oetry has intrinsic value, but also extrinsic value, as a means to moral and social effects beyond itself. The two cannot or at least should not be separated by the critic in estimating its poetic worth" (1953, 327). The apologist for poetry tries to ascribe both kinds of value to poetry so as to preserve both its moral seriousness and its aesthetic integrity. This critical endeavor has had a long history, dating back to classical times and carried through to the Middle Ages, the Renaissance, the Enlightenment, and down to the last and present centuries.

With the resurgence of classical texts in the Renaissance, there grew up a parallel interest in poetic apologetics, especially in Italy.

According to Wimsatt and Brooks (1957), "the apologetic essay" or "defense of poesie" became one of four major genres in literary theory to derive from this revitalization of critical issues set in motion not just by Plato, but by Aristotle, Horace, Longinus, and others (155–157). Italian Renaissance critics, such as Vida, Mazzoni, Tasso, Minturno, and Castlevetro, greatly influenced the poetics of the Elizabethan thinking about what poetry was, should be, and should do. In the Renaissance, the Platonic tradition of criticism that had called up the problem of the relationship between text and respondent was enriched both by neo-Platonism and neo-Aristotelianism, which established "a transvalued Platonic theory of imitation." This theory provided the basis for answering Plato's banishment of the poets by asserting that poetry need not "be false in the factual, historical sense," and that, "even when it *is* false it has its peculiar kind of truth" (Wimsatt & Brooks, 1957, 165, emphasis added).

Though the "transvaluation" of Platonic poetics marked a radical shift in the premises for thinking about the relationship between literature and life, it did not necessarily resolve the issues for those asking the questions—which sound very much like those that plague English teachers and letter-writers to the editor today. Reader-response theory has been here for a long time:

> [T]he theorizers of the 16th century were debating (by a highly codified and crabbed convention) nothing else than the degree of correspondence which should obtain between art and reality. Is a mixed genre (let us say tragicomedy) an offence against reality? Certainly not in one sense: it is not an offense against realism or naturalism, because events in life do tend to occur mixed, the sad and the happy and the funny close together. But if we are willing to speak of such occurrences with an accent on our responses to them—if we confer on "reality" something of . . . an ideality in its easiest sense—we may arrive at a situation where . . . we have to say that to mix tears and laughter is unreal. If such mixtures . . . are to be received kindly on stage, clearly some sophistication must be at work—ideality at a special remove. On this point no very explicit theory appears to have been entertained during the period of which we speak. But about the ideality of poetry in still a third sense . . . —the sense of poetic fantasy and invention in contrast to the ordinariness of actual life—there are some more or less enlightened Aristotelian and Platonic speculations. (Wimsatt & Brooks, 1957, 163)

In his *Apologie for Poetrie,* published in 1595, Philip Sidney developed a reader-response theory that attempted to answer the charge that poetry corrupts morals. Sidney also formulated a theory of the imagination that anticipated quite modern notions of the Romantic imagination popular today.

## Sidney and the Allegorical Imagination

In order to illustrate how a defense of poetry can be thought of as a meta-problem in which the premises of the defense are integrally related to those of censorship and reader response, let's begin our investigation into Sidney's approach to the justification problem by speculating about his position with respect to the censorship problem. Where might he have stood regarding the alleged power of the effects of the verbal representations implicated in the examples that began the last chapter: the dilemmas of the juror in the war crimes trial and the beer ad poster? Whether either example actually qualifies as "poetry" or "literature" is a question on which we will reserve judgment for now. What we are primarily concerned with is how texts work on readers.

In addressing this problem, I'm going to try to stand as much as possible "inside" the literary critical and value traditions out of which Sidney was writing. As stated earlier, the influence of Aristotle as the "inventor" of the notion of text, his idea of a play as something made and made up, distinct from that which it represents (along with his notions of catharsis and aesthetic distance), was well in place as part of Renaissance consciousness. Though the ethical dimension of poetry, very much a legacy of Plato and the neo-Platonists, was still operating within the Renaissance sensibility, it had been, as we saw earlier, "transvalued," in that now the poet could be said to be imitating the Forms directly, in his capacity as poet, not necessarily as philosopher. This was reinforced—and made possible—by the changed relationship between poetic text and respondent, from that of the Hellenic oral tradition to that of a well-established print milieu: "The humanists . . . inherited from Augustine a rhetoric where the written text rather than the spoken oration had become central, and when the study of texts was as important as the production of texts" (Bergvall, 1989, 31). Thus the theory of mind and pedagogical techniques, now those of a writing culture, had stabilized the separation of subject from object, knower from known, reader from text, which Plato had instituted with the tradition of rational dialectic. Sidney, writing in the late 16th century, was thus able to presume an audience of a literate intellectual elite that could well appreciate the pleasures of poetry, fiction, and drama, now understood as "literature." These readers shared a common participation in the Christian worldview, which imposed a certain homogeneity on their ideas about the relationship between the Good, True, and Beautiful, also left over from Plato and now enjoying a comeback under Renaissance neo-Platonism.

Though the prevailing ethos did not *equate* virtue with knowledge, as it did for Plato, that virtue was to be the *end* of all knowledge was assumed in both the Renaissance philosophy of education and mode of literary interpretation. Both poet and reader were expected to share this " 'inward light' " (Bergvall, 1989, 39). What was thought of as "serious" literature was both literary and didactic; a nonutilitarian, "less pragmatic idea about the civilizing value of literature was one of the basic premises of Renaissance humanism and . . . theory of education" (Wimsatt & Brooks, 1957, 167). Because of the influence of Ramist logic on Elizabethan poetic imagery, "the didactic amounts to making it a desideratum that images be functional" (Tuve, 1968, qtd. in Connell, 1977, 40). At the same time, poets could safely presume that their works would be received within an already understood frame of reference that facilitated the making of correspondences between poetic texts and their meaning in the world according to "the allegorical habit of mind." This mindset was conducive to moral behavior as both "moral elevation" and as a method of persuasion that "might quite well assist a poet to argue cogently against accepted moral attitudes" (Tuve, 1968, qtd. in Connell, 1977, 40). In any case, a system of symbolic interpretation operated which provided the groundwork for the allegorical imagination.

In Sidney the allegorical imagination connects author to reader. Through the operation of the imagination, the poet, "disdaining" to be subject to the metaphysical abstractions of the philosopher, and "lifted up with the vigour of his own invention," creates a "golden" ideal world out of the "brazen" one of ordinary life "in making things either better than nature . . . or, quite anew, forms such as never were in nature . . . " (Sidney, 1966, 23).[1] Readers, then, would adduce its message within the context of a mutual understanding, a unified mindset, which accepted the function of poetry as a handmaiden to "truth." While Plato conceived of poetry in terms of its double moral effect (it could go either up or down—reinforce or subvert the truth), Sidney insists that, despite its "moving power," which was formidable indeed, poetry naturally inclines the soul toward the good. For Sidney and his readers, the poetic text, then, regarded as text— not as "reality" but as the verbal representation of reality—was still "a *rhetorical analogue* to concerned truth" (Frye, 1971/1973, 66, emphasis original), reinforcing emotionally and imaginatively what was already thought to be the case as it was set down by the discursive prose of the "hard" disciplines—philosophy, history, and science, those forms of knowledge which were thought to really mean what they say (Frye, 1971/1973). Within the Elizabethan world-picture and the Christian worldview, the ethical and the aesthetic were assumed by both poets and their readers/audience to be interdependent aspects of the Renaissance belief in virtue as the end of knowledge. That the aesthetic is the ethical *par excellence* "is so basic" to Sidney, observes C. S. Lewis (1954), "that he never argues it. He thought we would know" (346).

Why, then, did Sidney have to write a defense of poetry? Despite the assumptions underlying the deductive synthesis of Renaissance values described above, poetry still suffered from its detractors, as it has done in every age. Sidney's *Defence* was prompted by the allegations of Stephen Gosson, a Puritan clergyman and playwright, who dedicated his diatribe against poetry, *The School of Abuse* (1579), to Sidney. Gosson uses the same chain reaction metaphor that Plato does in the *Ion* (cited in the last chapter) by charging poetry with influencing in a single direction only—down, not up. Poetry goes directly "to piping, from piping to playing, from play to pleasure, from pleasure to sloth, from sloth to sleep, from sleep to sin, from sin to death, from death to the devil" (qtd. in Wimsatt & Brooks, 1957, 168). Sidney answers Gosson's challenge that poetry incites to moral evil with a plea for poetic art to be taken more seriously as a moral teacher equal in stature and status with other Renaissance arts— painting, music, and architecture, which were revered for their capacity to instruct through delight. For Sidney, serious literature was not taken seriously enough, it having fallen "from almost the highest estimation of learning . . . to be the laughing-stock of children" (18). We might say that Sidney was arguing for literature and the response to it to be credited for more than its entertainment value, as something other than an educational frill. In doing so, he gives us another example of the meta-problem of justification, censorship, and response in literature education.

## Poetry as a "Speaking Picture" and Reader Response

Problems having to do with the censorship of literary texts devolve in one way or another around tacit acceptance of the power of verbal art to say things that presumably act upon respondents in ways censors do not approve. This presupposes a conception of poetry as a kind of propositional statement. It is this issue of whether and what literature says that provides our way in to Sidney's version of the meta-problem. But, as we shall see, in all three defenses of poetry dealt with in the first part of this book–Sidney's, Shelley's, and Frye's—the question of literature as saying/not saying, which I have suggested defines the censorship problem, leads into the relationship between word and world, literature and life underlying the justification problem, and into the idea of the autonomous reader suggested by the response problem.

Throughout his defense, Sidney appeals repeatedly to the "moving power" of poetry: as "heart-ravishing knowledge" (21) and "the medicine of cherries" (41); it is not "an art of lies, but of true doctrine" (61)—again, Frye's "*rhetorical analogue* to ... truth" (1971/1973, 66, emphasis original). Yet Sidney is not so naive as to assume that simply asserting "delightful teaching ... [as] the end of poetry" (68) is proof of such a claim, and so sets out to demonstrate it. This was no easy task, for Sidney's fervor about the educational value of poetry did not blind him to the potentially pernicious effects of poetic power. By using the analogy of a needle and a sword, he illustrates why poetry "by reason of his sweet charming force ... can do more to hurt than any other army of words. ... Truly a needle cannot do much hurt, and as truly (with leave of ladies be it spoken) it cannot do much good: with a sword thou mayest kill thy father, and with a sword thou mayest defend thy prince and country" (55). Notice here the militaristic implications of verbal power and the shift in the genderization of poetry from the feminine in Plato to the masculine in Sidney.[2] Poetry changes its image from a seductive mistress in *Republic* X,[3] whom the educated man must, however reluctantly, renounce in light of his higher moral purpose (Cornford, 1941/1945/1975, 340). For Plato, poetry is a *pharmakon*, or poison and cure (Derrida, 1981, 70), a site of simultaneous fear and desire, which must be tamed by the authority of (male) rational discourse; for Sidney, it is an "army" that unequivocally vanquishes evil and falsehood.

How can Sidney be so certain that poetry serves only the good? In answering this question, he offers a definition of poetry as that which both says and does not say, as a kind of language that is both propositional and hypothetical. On the one hand, poetry is defined as *ut pictura poeisis*, a form of imitation, not in the Platonic sense of a representation of unreality, but in the Aristotelian sense of something made up, a "counterfeiting, or figuring forth ... a speaking picture" (25), whose educational or extrinsic value lies precisely in accomplishing its intrinsic "end, to teach and delight" (25). I would say, rather, to teach *through* delight; for it is through the very concreteness of which Plato was so wary that poetry has the capacity to increase "judicial comprehending"(32). Its impact on "the powers of the mind" is thus greater than the "wordish description" of philosophy. As Bergvall (1989) puts it: "The poet's job ... is not simply to provide a textbook in ethics ... [but] by making living characters out of dead precepts, [the poet] helps the reader imagine and judge the fore-conceits provided by the moral philosopher" (39). Poetry

presents a "perfect picture" of reality, which can "strike, pierce . . .
[and] possess the sight of the soul" (Sidney, 1966, 32). Plato would
have agreed that poetry speaks powerfully, and for these very reasons, reasons which, for him, however, were enough to condemn it
for telling lies about reality. Sidney, however, rescues poetry from
Plato's charge of distorting reality by asserting that poetry says nothing that is falsifiable:

> [O]f all writers under the sun the poet is the least liar. . . . [F]or the
> poet, he nothing affirms and therefore never lieth. For, as I take it, to
> lie is to affirm that to be true which is false. . . . The poet never
> maketh any circles about your imagination, to conjure you to
> believe for true what he writes. He citeth not authorities of other
> histories, . . . not labouring to tell you what is or is not, but what
> should be or should not be. And therefore, though he recount things
> not true, yet because he telleth them not for true, he lieth not. . . .
> (52–53)

How can Sidney have it both ways: justify poetry on the basis of
its pedagogical function as a "speaking picture" (25) and, at the same
time, disclaim that its pronouncements intend to speak the truth,
especially since, according to the above quotation, poetry invokes
the moral domain by telling us "what should or should not be"? Here
Sidney combines the Platonic and Aristotelian traditions of poetics
in conceiving of the poetic imagination as a form of making and also
a mode of knowing. The imaginative maker of "poetry strictly speaking" (26), that is, poetry which is not tied to the propagation of
this or that intellectual precept or moral maxim, but poetry in its
own right, by its very nature fuses the ethical and the aesthetic in
the notion of the possible and the conceivable; it imitates by
"borrow[ing] nothing of what is, hath been, or shall be; but rang[ing],
only reined with learned discretion, into the divine consideration of
what may be and should be" (26). And the poet does this by
"counterfeiting" or "feigning" "excellently" (27). Poetry thus teaches
through delight because it is a creation which offers the reader/
respondent a synthesis of the ethical and the aesthetic. What "should
be" (the moral ought) in poetry is indistinguishable from "what may
be": that which is most fervently wished for (the highest level of
human desire). The content of poetry is thus made morally inviolate
because the "perfect pattern" of the "golden world" is created by
poetic form. The "good," "right" (26), or imaginative poet is not so
much creating a pattern of moral content as producing a flawless
portrait constructed of "virtues, vices, *or what else*" (27, emphasis
added)—including emotions and other psychological states. So,
though poetry "nothing affirmeth" in terms of what is morally right or

wrong, it nevertheless presents the picture of truth because it offers itself as a "perfect pattern" (36), a hypothetical construct of the best conditions of existence that either poet or respondent can possibly imagine. The poem can never be morally neutral because of its moving power, but it succeeds in being morally autonomous because its subjunctive mode opens up realms of possibility for the respondent.

Sidney's conception of poetry as hypothesis could apply to the war crimes trial in the following way. His theory of reader response, which is premised on his conception of poetry as that which says and does not say, would cause him to support the position of the judge. The allegorical habit of mind did not wed Sidney or his readers to a "Monkey See-Monkey Do" literalist psychology of response because they *accepted* the degree of "ideality" of the text as at a certain remove from "reality." As well, the "ingrained habit of scrutinizing texts was a premise, not a conclusion" of the allegorical imagination (Bergvall, 1989, 41). The notion of the text as the "golden world" of poetic hypothesis affected the stance of readers. Just as the judge in the war crimes trial assumed the juror to be approaching the text of *Music Box* as one who can tell the fictional from the real, Sidney presumed his readers would not have been reading "affirmatively," but "allegorically and figuratively" (53). ("What child is there, that, coming to a play and seeing *Thebes* written in great letters upon an old door, doth believe that it is Thebes?" [53]) Even more important, Sidney insists that readers of the day would not have been going to the text "as in history, looking for truth" (53) in the first place. They would have been reading "for fiction, [and] us[ing] the narration as an imaginative ground-plot of a profitable invention" (53). That is, they would have interpreted poetry according to what is on offer in poetry—verbal art that is made up and made of the imagery and metaphor of poetic language.

Let's now look at how the psychodynamics of the allegorical imagination might play themselves out in an example of what for Sidney and his readers would have been correct reading. Sidney's highly visual poetic epistemology provides us with a foremother of the "The Rare Long-haired Fox" poster in the image of "the constant though lamenting look of Lucretia" (26). Lucretia (the Roman matron who took her own life in order to save her husband's honor after she was raped by her brother-in-law) was Sidney's paradigm example of poetry as a "speaking picture" (25), a verbal icon of marital fidelity; and he was confident that it would have been responded to as such. This expectation of moral consensus informing poetic response was made possible by a twofold process of abstraction and particularization undertaken by the poet and then reversed by the reader according to the laws of faculty psychology. The poet's allegorical imagination would typologize her as a Christ-like martyr, displaying the "outward beauty" (26) of the virtue of constancy such that it becomes an emblem or "figuring forth" (25) of a truth generally accepted by poet and reader. The poet would intuit, generalize, and typify the essence of constancy (make up "the profitable invention") and then clothe it in narrative, meter, and rhyme (construct "the imaginative ground-plot"), thus presenting a graphic illustration of some aspect of a common heritage about which readers could be presumed to be culturally literate. The reader, in turn, would start with the particular and move to the universal, deducing "the general notion" from the particular example set up by the poet (32).

Theoretically, for Sidney and his readers, the relationship of the poetic representation of Lucretia to life would have been unproblematic because of the consonance of the ethical and the aesthetic symbolic system contained by and within the Christian worldview. As a "speaking picture" (25), Lucretia would have been understood neither as a condoning of suicide nor a signifier of patriarchal hegemony, but as a concrete hypothetical, a "perfect pattern" (36) of a virtue whose ethical/aesthetic significance was assumed and agreed upon. It would have "affirmeth nothing" (52) except what the reader would have already known—that virtuous action is to be followed in all things. Any representation of vice, or a mixture of virtue and vice, would have been coded accordingly, on the presupposition that whatever evil is described should be avoided. Here, again, the ethical and the aesthetic cohere: the morally good reader is the autonomous reader who makes "right use" (55) of poetry by responding "naturally" to the symbolic import of the text and who exercises a "wit" (25) "erected" by poetic reading in order to shore up "infected will" (25) weakened by original sin and the Fall of Adam. If evil behavior should result from the reading process, it is not the fault of poetry "the thing" (60), which has done its job well, but the "abuse" (60) of poetry by a reader with an intractable conscience. In such a case the reader would suppress the moral dictates of "erected wit" and persist in following his "infected will" by refusing to make the "right use" of poetry and perversely "acting out," as we would say, instead of translating the "good things" (54) poetry teaches into morally appropriate behavior.[4] Thus the educational value of poetry resides in its capacity to inspire respondents to act as they already know they should. If it does not, the fault lies squarely with the reader, who should know better.

Similarly, though the morally good poet is to be imitating "good things" and not "unworthy objects" (54), "the right poet" (26), or "maker" (23), is one who writes good poetry as poetry. Content matters, but its moral efficacy is as much a function of imaginative appeal as it is of the ethical or religious legitimacy of the "truth" bodied forth. Though the possibility of the morally bad poet still exists (a poet can consciously set out to teach evil), chances are that these poets would most probably be the "bastard poets" or "paper-blurrers" (63). The really bad poets are cast in intellectual and aesthetic, not moral, terms: the derivative dullards, mechanistic versifiers, undisciplined geniuses, or hapless hacks—the "poet-apes" (74), who by very dint of their didactic purpose, lack the conceptual clarity ("*energia*") to put to "right use the material point of poesy" (70).

Plato would have seen the educational value of the Renaissance poem as his dream for awakened minds come true, according to the interpretation followed in Chapter 1. His precognition of poetry as the "something else" that needed to be contained by an entity more reliable than itself was possibly actualized by Sidney's conception of poetry as that verbal form of making that teaches for good but not for ill, the kind of poetical/ethical myth that Plato was looking for but never found (Edelstein, 1949). By conceiving of poetry as that which both says and does not say, within a worldview that could guarantee poetic meaning,[5] Sidney's *Defence* can be seen as a precursor of a more modern conception of the educated imagination by thinking of poetry as something other than a rhetorical analogue to truth. Resting on the moving power of the speaking picture of poetry to exalt the soul, Sidney's case for poetry exploits the power of poetry (as Plato illustrated it in the magnet image from the *Ion*) but without succumbing to its nonrational determinism (Ferguson, 1979).

## Sidney's Defense of Plato and the Meta-Problem

In its attempt to extricate poetry from charges of falsehood and immorality, Sidney's argument invokes the premises of the meta-problem. Through his aim to champion poetry as a moral force—i.e., his tackling the justification problem (establishing a moral basis for the relationship between literature and life)—he necessarily deals with the censorship problem (whether and what poetry says) and the response problem (the autonomy of the reader/respondent.) As already stated, Sidney defends poetry principally *by way of* defining poetry as that which says and does not say—the controlling premise of the censorship problem—and its effects as powerfully influencing one who responds autonomously as a dreamer with an awakened mind—the controlling premise of the response problem. His defense of poetry assumes that engagement with the text presupposes the operation of an intelligence that accepts poetry as an aesthetic construct with moral implications, not as an inducement to imitate blindly this or that representational character, action, or event. Sidney assumed reading to be "an active process of judgement, . . . a reflective re-reading rather than an impressionable first reading" (Bergvall, 1989, 40). In other words, the reader's intelligence was one that did distinguish between literary convention and reality as a matter of course. Even though "infected will" was wracked by concupiscence, readers were nevertheless predisposed by the moral/ aesthetic autonomy of poetry to act in good faith, "wit" having been "erected" by the purifying dialectic of the allegorical imagination.

The presupposition that the poet's imitations are not "life" is what specifically connects the justification and response problems to the censorship problem. Given that the poet is creating within the worldview of the allegorical imagination, in which aesthetic laws are thought to live in perfect harmony with moral ones, and given that the respondent can escape the fusion of intellect and will implied in Gosson's chain reaction from poetry to the devil, poets were thus absolved from moral responsibility except insofar as they were "feigning excellently," as makers of fictions. For Sidney, then, poets should not in any way be censored, for they could be held accountable only within their own category, as poets, "good" and "right" denoting both the ethereal and aesthetic dimensions of poets who wrote imaginative poetry or "poetry strictly speaking" (26). As such, they were to be evaluated on the poetic qualities of their creations and not for the truths or untruths of the value system out of which the "brazen" world becomes a "golden" one. So long as the poet was imitating well, moral responsibility for the effects of the text lay with the respondent, "the force of a similitude not being to prove anything to a contrary disputer, but only to explain to a willing hearer" (71).

Sidney brings this position to its extreme, though logical, conclusion by actually rescuing Plato himself from the charge of being the enemy of poetry. It is in his vindication of Plato and the "lying" Greek poets that Sidney provides the clearest answer to what he might do with the subway beer ad poster. And it is here that I find the richest invocation in the *Defence* of the meta-problem. In making his case *for* poetry, Sidney was up against the well-known Platonic case *against* it (Heninger, 1983, 158), which was an embarrassment to him (Roberts, 1966, 22). But Sidney denies the banishment, not just because he was co-opting Plato for strategic reasons, but because doing so reveals Sidney's standard for the "good" poet as precisely the pre-Romantic aesthetic theory that defines poetry in terms of the hypothetical concrete (that which says and does not say) and judges the poet in terms of the excellence of the "feigning" and not the moral content of the objects being imitated.[6]

We can then conclude that, for Sidney, moral responsibility for the effects of poetry lies with the respondent—the individual reader or the collective audience as participants in a particular worldview. In either case, Sidney's idea of imitation here is one of creation rather than reflection as the direct mirroring of reality. The "right poet" does not swallow subject matter whole but refashions it. The Greek poets who told "lies" about the gods (59–60) are not only not guilty but are doubly innocent: first, because they cannot control the imperfect intellectual or moral framework out of which they spring; second, because they remodel it into a hypothetical construct through poetic imitation. If only the "lying" Greek poets had been privy to the "light of Christ" (59), implies Sidney, their fictional lies (Plato's true falsehoods) might have been fictional truths. That these poetic lies were in fact falsehoods does not necessarily prevent the poets from teaching virtue. Similarly, if Plato had only known that Christianity would have rectified all "hurtful belief" (60), he needn't have worried about the malevolent effects of poetic imitation. Thus Sidney has effectively separated the moral function of the poet from the religious and philosophical dimensions of truth, even though, for him, they were one and the same. Regardless of whether the poet's "erected wit" has been "cleared by faith" (22) or framed by a pagan culture, the "good" poet is one whose poetry exhibits a kind of artistic integrity or poetic fullness of being, which includes both the moral and the aesthetic. The "good" poet teaches not by the sugared pill of propaganda but by the excellence of the feigning, which succeeds in producing "learning" as the "purifying of wit . . . enriching of memory, enabling of judgement, and enlarging of conceit." The educational value of literature, then, is that of education itself, whose "final end is to lead and draw us to as high a perfection as our degenerate souls, made worse by their clayey lodgings, can be capable of" (28).

We are a long way here from "The Rare Long-haired Fox." But are we really? Her similarities to Lucretia are quite chilling, both in her vulnerability and in her subjection to objectification and appropriation by patriarchy; but most of all there is a similarity in apparent unanimity of response enabled by a worldview that can enshroud awareness of the realities of violence toward women with the slick illusion of a superficial sexual equality. Little seems to have changed on that score since 1595, particularly in view of the Thomas/Hill hearings (Bray, 1991; MacKenzie, 1991). For Sidney, however, the operative question in what to do with the beer ad poster would have hinged on whether he would classify it as "poetry strictly speaking" or "philosophical poetry," the difference between them, for him, being one of literary quality. "Philosophical" poets are like "the meaner sort of painters, who counterfeit only such faces as are put before them," whereas "right" poets, "having no law but wit, bestow that in colours upon you which is fittest for the eye to see" (26). In either case, Sidney would have been hard put to remove the poster; for he would probably have estimated its offensiveness to be a condition of the culture, which gives permission for reinforcing whatever moral, social, and political ramifications might seep through this particularly odious "speaking picture." If the poster is an example of "the meaner sort" of poetry (here it would be an advertising gimmick that simply parrots clichés), then, presumably, any normally constituted rational person would already know that its purpose was to sell beer and would pay no further attention. If, however, the poster is "poetry strictly speaking," that is, creating something entirely new, as a hypothesis about reality, it would deserve our contemplation irrespective of its content. A third alternative is also possible—that the ad is poet-aping or bad poetry, which many might agree would seem an appropriate category for advertising of this sort: clever but artistically "thin." In such a case, the criterion for response would be *caveat emptor*. Let the critical response detach from engagement with the text in recognition of the "abuse" of poetry by the perpetrators and perpetuators in society who prefer an "earth-creeping mind" to one "lift[ing] itself up to look at the sky of poetry" (75).

Sidney's *Defence* invokes the meta-problem within a Ptolemaic worldview underwritten by a Christian faith in the divine ordinance of the universe. This enabled him to argue for poetry as an efficient educational agent by demonstrating that the poet creates according to rules in which the ethical and aesthetic are both aspects of the Pythagorean music of the spheres and its counterpart, "the planet-like music of poetry" (75). Within this cultural context, a literate elite would have felt little need for censorship because they had been educated by a poetics that had transvalued Plato's notion of poetry as three removes from reality to the highest and noblest ideal form, in which what may be and what should be were enshrined in the verbal construct as hypothetical concrete, a "figuring forth" (25) of the best that could be possible, imaginable, and conceivable. Response to poetry, then, for Sidney's readers was *necessarily* an educated response because the justification for the moral value of poetry was grounded in the allegorical imagination, which, with its guarantees of predictable symbolic modes of interpretation and the psychic safety of aesthetic distance, created a moral reality in poetic creation and response.

## Shelley and the Romantic Imagination

How did the poet go from being a maker of imitations in Sidney's *Defence* to one of "the unacknowledged legislators of the world" in Shelley's (1965, 80)[7], and what can that tell us about the implications of the meta-problem (the rationale for, censorship of, and response to literature) for the schools? As with Plato and Sidney, let's begin with an example from our own culture, in this case not the war crimes trial or beer ad, but a recent film that embodies just the values Shelley was extolling in his *Defence of Poetry,* written in 1821, more than two hundred years after Sidney's reply to Stephen Gosson.

Enter *Dead Poets Society* (1989), a film by Peter Weir that celebrates the Romantic imagination as it was articulated by Shelley. Here, the teacher of literature is cast as a Socratic figure, a pusher of intellectual and spiritual drugs, who inculcates in his students a brand of social nonconformity through the subversive power of a secret society that conducts rituals in reading the poetry of "the dead poets": Thoreau, Walt Whitman, and Robert Frost, men who become, in the words of the English teacher Keating (played by Robin Williams), "sources of information for excessive self-indulgent behavior." The presiding metaphor for the socially redeeming value of this clandestine, esoteric knowledge would be what Frye has referred to as

a secret, perilous and forbidden knowledge, like that of Adam in Eden, snatched from under the nose of a jealous Jupiter, and transmitted through the murmuring oracular caverns of the human poetic imagination. Such knowledge, though secretly acquired, is extremely simple in content, being the message of love that comes through hope. (1968, 106)

In his efforts to illustrate the social function of reading the dead poets, Mr. Keating gets the students to stand on a table in order to see the world differently. Reading poetry will alter their point of view, broaden their perspective, thereby making them better people, perhaps even *acknowledged* legislators of the world. Though by the end of the film Keating is sacrificed to the conservative forces of the educational establishment, he is vindicated nonetheless. Having accomplished the mission of awakening his students' poetic engagement, he leaves the school undaunted, with a heartfelt "Thank you, boys!"— ever faithful to their now mutual utopian vision of universal love and readiness to enlist their poetic imagination in the service of humankind.

Mr. Keating and his dead poets are direct descendants of the Romantic neo-Platonism of Shelley. With the advent of Romanticism, Sidney's allegorical frame of reference alters dramatically: poetry changes from the "mirror" of imitating the "content" of external reality to the "lamp" of recreating its form through the metaphorical habit of mind (Abrams, 1953, 214–250). Whereas the combatants Sidney and Gosson could at least share some common ground—the coherence of the Elizabethan world picture and Renaissance worldview—Shelley and Thomas Love Peacock differed on metaphysical, epistemological, psychological, and moral counts—at least regarding poetry. In Peacock's invective against poetry, *The Four Ages of Poetry* (1820), and in Shelley's rebuttal, *A Defence of Poetry* (1821), we see each an infidel to the other's presuppositions about how the world turns. So the ensuing battle about poetry ranges over reason versus imagination, extrinsic versus intrinsic poetic value, the analytic versus the synthetic faculties of the mind, and competing conceptions of primary and secondary human need based on differing definitions of social utility and personal pleasure.

When Peacock (1965) charges that the "poet in our times is a semi-barbarian in a civilized community," whose "march of . . . intellect is like that of a crab, backwards" (17), his rhetoric is governed by the rationalism of Descartes and the empiricism of Locke. His worldview is not Shelley's. Peacock conceives of poetry in terms of a historical, utilitarian primitivism, which evaluates it as a repository of knowledge that really "means" what it "says." According to Peacock, poetry best performed this function in the "golden age" of Homer, when poets were rightly the custodians of the culture, "not only historians but theologians, moralists and legislators" (6). Through time, however, the intellectual disciplines (those that always mean what they say) took over this hieratic office, and so poetry had to defer to "[p]ure reason and dispassionate truth" (9), unornamented with verse (Plato's prose without meter). In the Augustan period, poetry served a useful purpose because it reinforced "[g]ood sense and elegant learning, conveyed in polished and somewhat monotonous verse, . . . the perfection of the original and imitative poetry of civilized life" (10). But, Peacock feared that the separation of poetic truth (as expressed in the classic texts of versified poetry) from other kinds of truth augured ill for the moral-literary sensibility, especially as evidenced in the romantic spillings-forth of powerful feelings characterizing the then new poetry of William Wordsworth and his brothers. (See Chapters 8 and 9 for further discussion of Romanticist poetics.) Peacock didn't really *mean* that poetry was "a mental rattle" (18); he was just afraid it was becoming one.

Peacock was in a sense right in that the eighteenth century saw a subsumption of art by nature. We might say that Sidney's golden world was actually taking hold in the brazen one of real life through neo-classical poetic values most evident in the poetry of Alexander Pope and *his* brothers. Though the canon of poetic texts of past and present was argued about, it was accepted as given (Prickett, 1986). But Frye, for example, contends that a religious and political conformity, and possibly even a "repression of creative power" became "fundamental principles of art" of the period (1947, 162; see my Chapter 10 for an alternative view). In any case, whereas the allegorical imagination of Sidney's world was the world of an elite but publicly shared discourse, that of the Romantic imagination was intensely private. The idealism of the Romantic imagination, according to Kearney (1988),

> as a world unto itself, . . . may be understood largely as a reaction to historical circumstances. With nature becoming increasingly dominated by mechanistic principles of the positive sciences and society riven apart by the industrial strife and exploitation of expanding capitalism, imagination felt more and more compelled to recoil into a magical world of its own making. In this way, human subjectivity could ostensibly continue to be creative in spite of history—by negating history. (186)

Shelley's *Defence* became one of the manifestos of this intensification of the private sensibility. While Peacock was writing a defense of *poetry*, Shelley's *Defence* was more one of the poetic or metaphorical habit of mind.

In making his case for poetry, Shelley shifts the premise from "the historically to the psychologically primitive" (Frye, 1971/1973, 94) by wresting the grounds of the discussion from empiricist notions of objectivity and substituting Bishop Berkeley's philosophy of immaterialism. Berkeley attempted to repudiate Locke with a theory of knowledge that would magically alchemize sense knowledge into a condition of the mind. Co-opting from Berkeley such phrases as "All things exist as they are perceived; at least in relation to the percipient" and "The mind is its own place, and of itself can make a Heaven of Hell, a Hell of Heaven" (74), Shelley answers Peacock directly by providing scientific grounds (through a system of optics) for the claim that the world is really ruled by the poetic imagination. In other words, Shelley argues that the metaphorical language of the poetic text no longer simply reinforces or countervails truths, as it did for Plato; nor does it conduce to the good because it creates a "perfect pattern" of a "golden world," as it did for Sidney. For Shelley, poetry actually forms the basis of a new reality conceived in terms of human subjectivity. Metaphor, in its capacity to unite the human and natural worlds and to generate sympathetic identification, produces a pleasure that is both intrinsically and extrinsically moral because it propels humankind towards universal fraternity.

## The Romantic Imagination and the Meta-Problem

The above gives us a sense of how Shelley approaches the justification problem; but, as I have been arguing is the case with Plato and Sidney, he cannot make his argument without reference to the other two problems. Though censorship as such does not concern Shelley in his *Defence* (Peacock was more worried by poetry's so-called irrelevance, redundancy, and inutility than by its immorality), he indirectly addresses the censorship problem in terms of its underlying premise—whether and what poetry says—by dealing with the issue of the poet's moral intent. Resting his case solely on the nature of poetry itself as the cause of its moral value, Shelley contends that it is poetic inspiration, not a didactic aim, that is crucial to the moral effects of poetry.[8]

Germane to the meta-problem is the intimate connection between the justification and censorship problems with respect to the importance Shelley attaches to poetic form and inspiration as the essential causes of poetry, and their relationship to the poet's moral function. For him, this function actually precludes a moral aim on the part of the poet, in direct contrast to Peacock, whose Benthamite litmus test for poetic worth was the degree of authority a poet like Homer could command as the voice of the tribal encyclopedia. Shelley values Homer, too, but not for Homer's social function as a guide to life. Rather, Shelley esteems Homer's power of inducing the very identification process Plato abhors in *Republic* X, praising Homer for how "the sentiments of the auditors must have been refined and enlarged by a sympathy with such great and lovely impersonations, until from admiring they imitated, and from imitation they identified themselves with the objects of their admiration " (38). But, again, as with Sidney, this is no simplistic psychology of response. Respondents would not mindlessly imitate the vices depicted in these characters; for vices merely provide "the temporary dress . . . [of the poet's] creations" through which "the spirit of its form" would shine. In fact, worldly imperfection and moral weakness are necessary disguises "to temper th[e] planetary music for mortal ears," because the poetic "conceptions" would be ineffable, were they to be presented "in [their] naked truth and splendour" (39). Such power is inspired by the poetic impulse, not a self-consciously moral one. Proof of this is to be found in the second-string poets, whose purpose, according to Shelley, is more didactic than literary:

> Those in whom the poetical faculty, though great, is less intense, as Euripides, Lucan, Tasso, Spenser, have frequently affected a moral aim and the effect of their poetry is diminished in *exact proportion* to the degree in which they compel us to advert to this *purpose*. (1965, 41, emphasis added)

By contrast, Shelley's highest order of poets includes Dante (the modern Homer) and Milton, the supremacy of Milton's genius being due precisely to his "*bold neglect* of a moral purpose" (1965, 60, emphasis added). So poetry, for Shelley—first-rate poetry—is Sidney's "poetry strictly speaking," which is moral *sui generis*, not because of its moral content or ethical aim, or even the golden world of virtue as the end of knowledge, but because of poetic "form," which creates works, such as "Divinia Commedia and Paradise Lost" (61). Thus poetry becomes morally inviolate because it is no longer a reflecting mirror, but a transforming one, "which makes beautiful that which is distorted" (36). And it does so through the medium of metaphor, which makes poetry a better teacher than the other arts because poetry is the only one that dictates the actual material of its expression. Language, especially metaphorical language, is by its very nature more "plastic" in its capacity to represent directly "the actions and passions of our internal being" (32). Language is more immediately obedient to control by the imagination because it is the very stuff of human feeling and desire.

The issue of censorship of poetry would virtually be dissolved for Shelley because the content of poetry is not anything poetry says or does not say, but its central core, which, as metaphor, transforms the world of ordinary existence, with all its imperfections, into one informed by the perfect beatitude of self-transcendence:

> The great secret of morals is love; or a going out of our own nature, and an identification of ourselves with the beautiful. . . . A man [sic], to be greatly good, must imagine intensely and comprehensively; he must put himself in the place of another and of many others; the pains and pleasures of his species must become his own. The greatest instrument of moral good is the imagination; and poetry administers to the effect by acting upon the cause. (1965, 40)

The "effect" is personal freedom brought about by the "cause"—sympathetic identification with what is Other, made beautiful through poetry. This is what makes up poetry's moving power, that which "awakens and enlarges the mind itself by rendering the receptacle of a thousand *unapprehended* combinations of thought" (39–40, emphasis added). Whether or what poetry says pales in light of the fact that it is a veritable life force that "reproduces all that it represents" (40) in a way that makes better human beings of us all.

It is Shelley's characterization of the voice of poetry as a suprarational force unifying the ethical and aesthetic that for him connects the censorship to the justification and response problems. With respect to the censorship problem, the "whole objection . . . of the immorality of poetry rests upon a misconception of the manner in which poetry acts to produce the moral improvement of man [sic]" (1965, 39). The Peacocks, Gossons, and Platos of the world presume a disjunction between morality and pleasure; but Shelley identifies them with each other in the form of love, that going out of our nature, that putting "[one]self in the place of another and of many others" (p. 40), which is both cause and effect of human desire itself. Such pleasure for him is the very antithesis of the moralistic attitude. "Poetry ever communicates all the pleasure which men [sic] are capable of receiving: it is ever still the light of life; the source of whatever of beautiful or generous or true can have place in an evil time" (50). This is for him nothing other than the pleasure of the poetic imagination, which is inseparable from the definition of poetry itself.

The pleasure of the poetic text as a powerful moral force is just what relates Shelley's treatment of the justification problem to the response problem—again, in terms of their underlying principles— the relationship between literature and life and the autonomous reader. Literature and life become one because the poetic text is already suffused with love as a moral agent endowed with empathy-inducing properties. This exclusive moral property has the effect of dissolving any barriers to the normative value of reader response. All readers need do is engage with the text directly, emotionally, imagi-natively, and with pleasure, and the resulting response will logically and automatically become an imaginative recreation of the moral reality of human concerns, needs, and desires. Thus Shelley makes no real distinction between the direct and critical responses. In con-trast to Sidney, who presupposes a critical response, Shelley pre-sumes that the intuitive "first" response carries with it all the epistemological weight required.

Justification for poetry and response to it are interdependent aspects of the ontology of poetry as a transformational power that of itself affords the clearest moral vision which, when responded to as itself, purges egoism, the enemy of universal love. The attainment of an all-embracing humanity was, for Shelley, just as easily done as said because, for him, simply to see the good was to perform it. As with Sidney, when the vision of the Good is informed by the poetic mode, the will is co-opted by instinctual response, which has been made morally inviolate because of the chain reaction set in motion by the dual forces of poetic inspiration and imagination. In yet another borrowing from Plato's *Ion*, Shelley claims that the "sacred links of that chain . . . descending through the minds of many men is attached to those great minds, whence as from a magnet the invisible effluence is set forth, which at once connects, animates and sustains the life of all. *It is the faculty which contains within itself the seeds at once of its own and social renovation*" (1965, 50, emphasis added); and it does so because the language of metaphor, the building block of poetry, is "*arbitrarily* produced by the imagination, and has relation to thoughts alone" (32, emphasis added). That is, other arts have some kind of middle term, the artistic material, such as paint or sound, interposing itself between "the conception and the expression"; poetry alone actually produces the material of its own ontology, so to speak. Poetry, alone, is "the hieroglyph of . . . thought" (33), and thus can be "the image of life expressed in its eternal truth . . . according to the unchangeable forms of human nature" (35–36).

We can see from the above how impossible it is to separate the moral effects of poetry—the relationship between literature and life—in Shelley from the question of whether and what poetry says, and even more so from that of the moral autonomy or social responsibility of the reader. If poetic inspiration and imagination cause their own effect and effect their own cause, as the above quotation implies, and if poetry "purges from our inward sight the film of familiarity which obscures from us the wonder of our being," then poetic response "*compels* us to feel that which we perceive" and thus "creates anew the universe" (1965, 74–75, emphasis added). Shelley's conception of the autonomy of poetic response strikes us as something of an oxymoron in that the respondent is forced into a kind of moral freedom. But it is just this compression of the three premises of the meta-problem—whether and what poetry says, the relationship between literature and life, and the autonomous reader—into the unity of a rhapsodic paean to the moral power of poetry as the process and result of imaginative poetic reading that makes Shelley's *Defence* so appealing, at least to one already persuaded of the moral value of poetry, even though, as Frye reminds us, it may not "convince anyone who needs convincing" (1963a, 8).

## Conclusion

Shelley can be said to have legitimated the "something else" of which Plato was so suspicious. For Shelley, that something else becomes the Romantic idealism of a hypothetical knowledge-in-relation, whose moral power is the passion of the possibility of social change. In a passage with a remarkably contemporary ring, Shelley prophesies the cannibalistic age of environmental destruction in which we now live: "We have more moral, political, and historical wisdom than we know how to reduce into practice. . . . We want the creative faculty to imagine that which we know; we want the generous impulse to act that which we imagine; we want the poetry of life; our calculations have outrun our conception; we have eaten more than we can digest" (1965, 68–69).

Like Sidney, Shelley attends to the justification problem by safe-guarding the honor of poetry and attributing the cause of immorality to the society out of which it grows; and, also like Sidney, he does so by invoking the other two problems. Though Sidney was explicitly charged with answering the censorship problem, he was more inter-ested in the justification and response problems. Of the two poets, Sidney is the champion of the critical response in his concern that readers proceed not "affirmatively" but "figuratively." For Shelley, the response problem is less of a problem because of the way he defines poetry. The respondent cannot do other than respond appro-priately because the synthetic power of the poetic imagination affords an epiphanic apprehension of artistic forms which are themselves products of human desire of the highest order. Re-enter *Dead Poets Society*. We can now see why Mr. Keating could be so sure that his students would change the world—and why they all stood on their desks in the farewell scene. They wanted to prove to him that they had learned their lesson well, that simply reading the great dead poets had purged "from their inward sight the film of familiarity," thus allowing them to "create anew the universe." Such a wrenching from the comatose state of the quotidian had inspired them to scale new intellectual and moral heights in what Northrop Frye would later describe as transfer-ring the imaginative energy from literature to life (1963a, 55).

Whereas for Plato, poetry languished in the darkest realm of *eikasia* or phantasmagoria and for Sidney, it was an intelligent "feigning" at least equal to reason, for Shelley, it had attained the highest metaphysical status, epistemological function, and moral worth, literally going beyond intellect—for the very reason that it regresses the mind to a state of psychological primitiveness. Twentieth-century humanist notions about the educational value of literature owe their genesis, at least in terms of the intrinsic social import of poetic engagement, to Shelleyean claims for the power of poetry to echo the Pythagorean music of the spheres. Whereas Sidney's poetic universe is the golden one of the allegorical habit of mind, Shelley's is the revolutionary one of the metaphorical habit of mind. Both make edu-cation *by* the imagination an inherently and necessarily moral activ-ity. It is to Shelley's successor, Northrop Frye, and his apology for education *of* the imagination to which we turn our attention next.

# Endnotes

1. All page references to this work are taken from Van Dorsten's (1966) edition.

2. Actually, Sidney alternates the gender of poetry in the *Defence* (1966 46, 54). Poetry's feminine "charm," now that it is allied with knowledge and virtue, no longer connotes the dangers of seduction, only its pleasures.

3. For a feminist analysis of the relationship among seduction, reading, the poetic, and literary theory, see Chapters 8, 9, and 10.

4. The gender connotations of these characterizations scream out to be noticed. First, it's clear that Sidney assumes a male or "universal" reader. Second, the juxtaposition of the reader's "erected wit" and "infected will" suggests a moral war raging within the reader, a war which poetry as the "good soldier" is helping "him" to win. Third, there is the alignment between the masculine ("erected wit" and the fall of Adam), on the one hand, and the feminine ("infected will" and original sin), on the other. This would seem to genderize the conflict in terms of masculine virtue defended by poetry from the "infection" of the feminine.

5. According to Bergvall (1989), this does not imply a "fixed" meaning: "contingency rather than truth characterized [Sidney's] communications model" (24) between text and reader. This relationship was a form of dialectical interplay (35).

6. Again, Sidney resolves the censorship problem by attending to the justification problem.

Sidney insists that, in the banishment, Plato "meant not in general of poets" but

> setteth a watchword upon ... the abuse, not upon poetry. Plato found that the poets of the time filled the world with wrong opinions of the gods, making light tales of that unspotted essence, and therefore would not have the youth depraved with such opinions. ... [T]he poets did not induce such opinions, but did imitate those opinions already induced. For all the Greek stories can well testify that the very religion of the time stood upon many and many-fashioned gods, not taught so by the poets, but followed according to their manner of imitation. ... Plato ... only meant to drive out those wrong opinions of the deity (whereof now, without further law, Christianity hath taken away all hurtful belief) perchance (as he thought) nourished by the then esteemed poets. ... So as Plato, banishing the abuse not the thing, not banishing it, but giving due honour to it, shall be our patron, and not our adversary. (1966, 59–60)

What are we to make of this curious apologia? And what possible connection can it have to the offensive beer ad poster? The key lies in how Sidney was classifying the "lying" poets, and how he thought Plato saw them. I have argued that, in contrast to those critics who believe Sidney (1966) regarded these poets either as "divine" (25) or "philosophical" (26), dedicated to making poetry a rhetorical analogue to truth (Bogdan, 1986c), Sidney thought of these poets as "good," "right," or imaginative poets, the "makers" of "poetry strictly speaking"; and that so long as they were engaged in imaginative activity, they were morally blameless. They "did not induce" superstition, polytheism, or belief in ungodly behavior, they "did imitate those opinions already induced" (Sidney, 1966, 59).

The problem here, as Sidney sees it, is simply that the Greeks were infidels; they did not "possess" the truth, but it was not their "fault." Their worldview was deficient in that they had no access to "the light of Christ" (59). Such a judgment in today's terms sounds chauvinistic but seems compatible with the value framework of an Elizabethan aristocratic soldier/poet like Sidney. For our purposes, the important point here is that Sidney is arguing that the poets of Plato's time could not have been expected to shoulder the blame for reinforcing belief in a misguided religion and a faulty value system. For, if these poets were indeed "right" poets of "poetry strictly speaking," they were neither affirming nor denying anything, but rather "counterfeiting" or making imitations. Whether they in fact were doing what Sidney thought, or what Plato thought they were doing, is beside the point that Sidney is making here about what he thinks poetry—real poetry—is doing in moral terms.

7. All references to Shelley's *A Defence of Poetry* and Peacock's *The Four Ages of Poetry* are taken from J.E. Jordon's edition (1965).

8. Cf. Sidney, who was somewhat suspicious of divine frenzy: Plato "attributeth into poesy more than myself do, namely to be a very inspiring of a divine force, far above man's [sic] wit . . . " (1966, 60).

# Chapter Three

# The Educated Imagination and the Justification Problem

Since publishing *The Educated Imagination* (1963a) nearly thirty years ago, Northrop Frye continued to expand his ideas on the social context of literature and the arts until his death early in 1991. Works such as *The Stubborn Structure* (1970), *The Critical Path* (1971/ 1973), and *Spiritus Mundi* (1976b) bespeak Frye's almost evangelical fervor about literary values and their importance to the preservation of civilization. Even Frye's practical criticism—his conception of Milton's epics or Shakespeare's romances, for example—is never wholly divorced from his trenchant views about the social, moral, and educational value of literature. Taken in its entirety, his writing can be seen as one great apology for the fictive literary imagination, implicitly reaffirming humanism and its ideal of a liberal education, with the study of literature at its core.

A return to *Dead Poets Society* will help us better visualize the historical context of Frye's educated imagination and its implications for the justification problem in literature education today. What can the film show us about the relationship between Shelley's and Frye's respective pictures of the world regarding the imagination? Though Frye's archetypal criticism has fallen out of favor of late in the wake of what he calls the sectarianism[1] of contemporary literary theory, his popularity among the English-teaching profession and the general public seems to be increasing.[2] In Toronto in 1989 there was a Christmas day prime time videocast of a 90-minute Canadian Broadcasting Corporation interview called *The Great Teacher: Northrop Frye*. Can it be that, given the general acceptance of the value perspective embodied in *Dead Poets Society*, Shelley's conception of

45

poetry as the informing discipline of other types of knowledge (it being closest to the metaphorical nature of the verbal imagination) is now coming true, at least in principle? And, with Frye as media star and Robin Williams as English teacher, is "universal brotherhood" just around the corner?[3]

For Frye, the answer would have depended on whether the imagination was truly educated or a captive of "sub-literary" forms (1982a, 113). Though Frye's conception of the imagination derives directly from visionaries like Shelley and Blake, Shelley's notion of the imagination as intrinsically educating was not quite strong enough for him. Frye would have had no quarrel with Shelley theoretically, but he probably would have thought him naive for supposing that a Romantic revolutionary poetics could of itself result in social change, at least today. It is true that for both Shelley and Frye, the imagination lends the value dimension to thought. In the Shelleyan imagination, reason alone can only perceive "quantities already known," whereas the imagination "is the perception of the *value* of those quantities, both separately and as a whole" (Shelley 1965, 26, emphasis added). For Frye, all philosophical and "logical" systems of thought are merely rationalizations for the metaphors that shape what counts as truth (1988, 187). But, Frye believed that the altered social conditions of the twentieth century have weakened the actual moral power of poetic pleasure. To see the good is definitely no longer automatically to perform it. Two world wars, increasing polarization between rich and poor, the rise of positivism, and the debasing of language by mass media demand a buttressing of Shelley's conception of the imagination as inherently "pure." Thus, as was noted at the end of the last chapter, education must now be not just *by* the imagination, but *of* it.

To use the language of archetypes, Frye saw the destruction of the Romantic vision of the imagination as the surfacing of its shadow. It's not that he didn't trust poetry, but that he couldn't trust the times, which he saw were vulnerable to the "sub-literary" genres of "soap operas, movies, magazine stories, jokes, comic strips, gossip" (1982a, 113). Certainly, the arts have no corner on the imagination market in the 1990s, the forces of repression being much less visible than they were in *Dead Poets Society*, where the obviously oppressive environment of the school could be used as a foil for Promethean breakthroughs of imaginative thinking and action. In the "real" world, however, engagement with the literary text must be supplemented by detachment from it through literary criticism; that is, Mr. Keating's students would have to study the dead poets, not just read them.

The price Frye was willing to pay for this distinction between engagement (the direct or participating response to literature) and detachment (the critical response), between study and just plain reading, is the incarnation of T. S. Eliot's dissociation of sensibility as a fact of reading life, something we will look at more closely in Chapter 5. For Frye, we cannot have both the experience of literature and the full consciousness of that experience simultaneously, and he was prepared to settle for some kind of dialectic or oscillation between engagement and detachment (see Bogdan, 1990c, 129–137). He was also prepared to sacrifice the aesthetic value of intensity to that of unity or coherence, a sacrifice that is inevitable if literary criticism is logically prior to direct response. (See my Chapter 10 for a discussion of Frye and imaginative intensity.)

## Northrop Frye and The Meta-Problem

The above gives us an idea of how Frye's conception of the educated imagination invokes the meta-problem, particularly the close proximity of the justification and response problems. In Frye's thought, the issues of the autonomous reader, the relationship between literature and life, and whether and what literature says are so intertwined that it becomes necessary to begin our study of the justification problem by looking in some detail at the broadest possible context, what Frye calls the anagogic perspective, which frames Frye's approach to the relationship between literature and life. The following quotation captures well the spirit of reading the dead poets of the film:

> Anagogically, then, poetry unites total ritual, or unlimited social action, with total dream, or unlimited individual thought. Its universe is infinite and boundless hypothesis: it cannot be contained within any actual civilizations or set of moral values, for the same reason that no structure of imagery can be restricted to one allegorical interpretation. . . . The *ethos* of art is no longer a group of characters within a natural setting, but universal man [sic] who is also a divine being, or a divine being conceived in anthropomorphic terms. (1957, 120)

With its stress on the hypothetical, the imaginatively conceivable, this anagogic perspective rejects a purely aesthetic criterion for judging the social value of literature. As with Plato, Sidney, and Shelley before him, the aesthetic can never really be divorced from other value questions for Frye. Indeed, the very asking of why a defense of poetry should be required places the critics squarely in the arena of extrinsic value, which Frye equates with being in "the centre of the humanist situation" (1971/1973, 64). For Frye, as for Shelley, defending poetry has to do with vindicating it as a primary human need.

> Most devaluations of poetry . . . [since Plato] have been attached to some version of a work ethic which makes it a secondary or leisure-time activity; and when poetry has been socially accepted, it is normally accepted on the same assumption, more positively regarded. (1971/1973, 79)

This statement calls up both the censorship and response problems. Social approval of art can be a dangerous thing for art and artists, to which the recent controversy over the granting policies of The National Endowment of the Arts attests most eloquently (Leavitt, 1990). It can also be a major impediment to a holistic response to literature, for social acceptability acts to pre-empt the kind of un-mediated response Plato feared, Sidney thought redundant, Shelley championed, and Frye doubted can obtain today. Whether he speaks of a defense of poetry as combatting "the abuse and perversion of art" (1963b, 73) or as "the social anxieties which work against the poet in every age" (1971/1973, 56), Frye's basic concern is for "man's [sic] right to create his world" (1970, 52). For him a defense of poetry is essential as a reflection of the practical bent of "engaged knowledge. Adam may explore his world, but the most important thing for him to know is how to defend it" (Frye, 1965b, 57).

Frye inherits from Blake the idea that the social value of litera-ture has nothing whatever to do with the opposition of what the world calls "moral good" to "moral evil." Neither does it turn on its efficacy in teaching what the world calls "writing skills," conceived in terms of the separation of the discipline of words from the art of words. For Frye, the censors and bureaucrats who would demand accountability in these terms are, as they were for Blake, Urizen authority-figures who "cannot distinguish the release of energy from the release of chaos" (1947, 221). What has to be safeguarded is not poetry or literature thought of as morality or knowledge, but the kind of knowledge and morality of humankind to which poetic creation attests. This sense of the infinitude of verbal meaning is what the anagogic perspective is about. It is what allows art and literature to be the cause rather than the effect of civilization. Frye defends litera-ture, then, not as raw material for fostering literacy or inculcating personal and social values, but as a kind of moral and rhetorical education that is intrinsic to literacy itself.

To take on the task of justifying the educational value of poetry is to confront directly the same question that Stephen Gosson asked of Sidney; and Peacock, of Shelley, that is, "why Plato was not right, and why the poets with their outworn modes of thought and their hankering for the fabulous should still have a claim on our attention" (Frye, 1971/1973, 64–65). For Frye, simply to espouse extrinsic and intrinsic value for poetry is not enough; we must be prepared to demonstrate how the principle of social responsibility is compatible with the dialectic between textual engagement and critical detachment, how, in fact, the twin goals of instruction and delight can be accomplished without doing violence to each other. Frye sees the tension between the two as "a central dilemma of literature. If literature is didactic, it tends to injure its own integrity; if it ceases wholly to be didactic, it tends to injure its own seriousness" (1970, 169). This double-bind generates some paradoxical and often confusing assertions by Frye about the integrity of literature and the moral seriousness of its effects, which I hope to clarify in due course.

Within the ethos of the educated imagination, preserving the seriousness and integrity of literature in the classroom would be a central concern, when both literary integrity and the seriousness of literature are under attack. Attacks come from without and from within: from censors, from current utilitarian notions about knowledge, and from the crisis of humanist underpinnings of a liberal education (Cairn, 1984). With the advent of posthumanism, poststructuralism, and postcolonialism, the "disinterested" study of literature would seem to be an oxymoron. My aim in this book is to explore the possibilities for a defense of literature education in the wake of "newer" disciplines, such as cultural studies[4] and critical pedagogy, which share common cause with the emancipatory aim of the educated imagination. It is not my intent to rescue the "old" conception of humanistic education as unproblematically emancipatory for all. The second half of this book attempts a critique of the idea of a liberal education regarded as innocently normative. In this chapter, however, I am concerned to set out the justification problem within my interpretation of how certain assumptions underlying the educated imagination, as conceived by Frye, might frame the problem.

That there is a problem seems to be generally accepted. As an observer from outside the discipline of English studies has recently written, "Voices are raised all around us deploring the lamentable state of English studies and demanding progress and reform" (Meynell, 1990, 14). In any case, one common complaint might connect all the factions in the current debate about the educational value of literature: the concern that "basic literacy" is increasingly associated with a "tightening up" of both moral discipline and syntactic order. Within this framework, the pursuit of literary study as literary art is seen as an "enjoyable" but largely dispensable activity; and the teacher of English, pitifully undertrained, is assumed to be anyone who can speak the language. In a society where study of the mother tongue as literature can be equated quantifiably and qualitatively with the transmission of other kinds of skills and information, Frye would have said that art has slipped into the position of a secondary social need. Making it a primary need was one of his major projects.

With respect to literature as a primary need, Neil Postman underwent something of a conversion to the necessity of reading "serious" books in *Amusing Ourselves to Death* (1985). But he was not so inclined in *The Soft Revolution* (1961), written just two years before Frye's *The Educated Imagination*. I remember Postman and Weingartner's contention that cherished notions about the civilizing power of literature are "[b]y far the most amusing of all our superstitions" (1961, 38) considering the fact that Joseph Goebbels had a Ph.D. in Romantic Drama. Yet literary critics such as George Steiner and Richard Poirier have questioned the transfer-value of humanism and on the same premise as the authors of *The Soft Revolution*. Corroborating Steiner's observation that "[w]e now know that a man can read Goethe or Rilke in the evening—and go to his day's work at Auschwitz in the morning," Poirier disclaims any *necessary* connection between the knowledge and the moral influence of literature (1971, 82). Frye also doubted the validity of this assumption. Citing the same war criminal example as Postman and Weingartner, he asserts that thinking of the arts as having or being based on values is a form of social ego-massage. "The arts approached in that way," he contends, "can add pleasure and refinement and cultivation and even some serenity to life, but they have no power to transform it, and the notion that they have is for the birds" (1976b, 121).

Frye's conception of the transfer-value from literature to life— the major premise of the justification problem—is predicated on any society's vision of itself. This brings us back to the very issue of the kind of moral and psychological "primacy" that underwrites the educational value of poetry for both Shelley and Frye. For Frye, the arts *in themselves* have no power to ennoble humankind so long as society conceives of them as fulfilling some kind of secondary need. The notion of the social value of the arts is problematic for Frye because it raises the hoary question of value as evaluation, as something imposed rather than inherent. The intrinsic value of art has to do with its creation and existence as art, and its extrinsic value or social effect has to do with how that art is perceived or society's response to it. The former is a primary human need; the latter, contingent upon the society's attitude to that need.

Frye perceives a disjunction between art and society whenever society relegates art to the periphery of what it deems to be social necessity. Value, then, becomes an add-on or frill. The result is a view of art as a kind of elegant accomplishment or cultural embellishment based on the commodity status of the artifact. Within such a context, response to art cannot be directed to the worth of a work of art itself but becomes subject to a prefabricated value system. Art thus becomes contained by whatever vicissitudes of taste or ideology that currently prevail and is valued or evaluated accordingly; for response becomes conditioned by a relativistic yet closed value system which has been interposed between the work and the perceiver. Within that context, value can only be a condition, not an effect, of response, resulting in a narcissistic relationship of response turning in on an existing value system. Thus response, robbed of its power to influence directly or beyond the vicious circle, becomes paralyzed. That is why Frye says the arts "can add pleasure and refinement and cultivation and even some serenity to life, but they have no power to transform it" (1976b, 121). For him, the crux of the issue of the educational value of literature and the arts is to make society aware that even posing the question of what value society should place on them shows that we have already missed the point. To ask the question is to be on a different playing field. And so we come full circle to the central problem of the meta-problem—the Platonic connection among valuations of art, response to literature, and "our social context and personal commitments" (Frye, 1976b, 44).

Crucial to this problem is the necessity of resolving the ancient Platonic dilemma about how the lie of fiction can make a claim to truth—the principle of whether and what poetry says underlying the censorship problem. If the voice of poetry is to achieve its proper effect, what and how it speaks must first be clarified, and the stigma of its dubious epistemological status removed. Not surprisingly, Frye formulates one of his most direct references to this problem within its educational context:

> Ever since Plato the question has been raised: in what sense does the poet know what he [sic] is talking about? The poet seems to have some educational function without being himself necessarily an educator: he knows what he is doing, certainly what he is saying but *qua* poet can say it only in the form of his poem. (1971/1973, 70)[5]

Frye's resolution is contained within meta definition of the problem. For him, the message of poetry can only be heard within the context of its own voice, that is, the poem itself. Just as the value of art cannot be divorced from art itself, neither can its truth be separate from its form. This premise formed the basis of his conception of a "genuine," "literary" response and of literature as a primary human need. Frye advances no practical prescription for creating social conditions amenable to response. Instead, he erects a giant metacritical system with its own laws of metaphysics, epistemology, psychology, and poetics, which synthesizes extrinsic and intrinsic value, social responsibility and aesthetic detachment, and the seriousness and integrity of literature within the larger question of the place of art in human existence. It is from this revolutionary neo-Romantic, quasi-religious position—the anagogic perspective—that he becomes a kind of archetypal apologist for poetry in the liberal tradition.

Frye makes some rather extravagant and apparently contradictory claims for both the seriousness and integrity of literature. On the one hand, he is unabashedly zealous about literature's extrinsic value. Firmly planted in the humanist tradition of Milton and Arnold, who believe that social liberty depends upon intellectual freedom and the self-determination of culture, Frye views literature not only as a "means of expression" or "method of thought," (1970, 97) but "an ethical instrument, participating in the world of civilization" (1957, 349). On the other hand, he jealously guards the intrinsic value of literature. It must not be regarded as an emotional reinforcement or "rhetorical analogue" only of the world of ordinary experience or the realm of thought (Frye, 1971/1973, 66; 1957, 13; 1970, 47). But neither is it a reflection of life, a form of propositional statement, nor even communicable experience. It is simply an "order of words," (Frye, 1957, 17; 1970, 102, 1963b, 127; 1963c, 15), that is, a verbal structure embodying the totality of mythological imagery. "The archetypal view of literature shows us literature as a total form and literary experience as part of the continuum of life, in which one of the poet's functions is to visualize the goals of human work" (1957, 115). This principle is intended to justify the extrinsic, instrumental value of literature. But it is the anagogic phase of this total form, the broader perspective that allows us to pass from civilization to culture itself as "the order of words," that grants literature's intrinsic value—"where it is disinterested and liberal, and stands on its own feet" (1957, 115)—and hence discloses its human significance as a primary need. As total form, literature does not admit paraphrase. It must be protected from translatability, ensured of its fundamental ineffability. Above all, it is never to be mistaken for a canon of precepts or a set of principles to live by. Yet it "create[s] a moral reality in imaginative experience," whose direct transfer-value to the student is that of a potent social force which gives humanity "not only a means of understanding but a power to fight" (Frye, 1970, 101, 105; 1963a, 55).

The foregoing statements raise two major questions within the humanist perspective out of which he wrote, about the co-existence of poetic integrity and seriousness. First, how can Frye at the same time espouse and reject a principle of aesthetic self-containment for literature? Second, how can he affirm its moral value while denying that the arts, of themselves, can transform life? The answer to the first question furnishes us with an insight into Frye's conception of creation, which will be discussed more fully in Chapter 4 under the censorship problem; and to the second, of response, which we will expand in Chapter 5. Both hinge on his views about the superiority of literary or "imaginative experience" (1970, 101) to ordinary or "real" existence (1965a, 129; 1976a, 186). It is this distinction that provides the key to the relationship between literature and life underlying the justification problem.

## The Anagogic Worldview of the Educated Imagination: The Poetics of Total Form[6]

In *Creation and Recreation* (1980), Frye articulates his view of "the cultural envelope" (27), in which he defines art as a containment of nature that insulates against nature. Springing from a blend of ideas drawn from Plato, Christianity, Blake, and Berkeley, Frye's theory of art is based on a metaphysics that reverses conventional notions of illusion and reality, a psychology that reassigns the imagination from the bottom to the top of Plato's Divided Line, an epistemology that deems the poetic the highest form of knowledge, a poetics that views literature as a kind of Platonic Form, an ethical system that equates human value with the Good, and an educational theory that identifies literary criticism with "education for life." Within this framework the worlds of art and nature are counterposed as greater and lesser forms of Being.

For Frye, "nature" (which includes not only the physical environment but realms of existence and modes of thought devoid of the imagination) is an inferior reality inimical to humankind in a fallen universe. The hostility of the natural order stems from its "otherness," that is, from those elements in our surroundings that challenge human sensibility and defy our efforts to harness them, to encompass them within the capacity of human perception and understanding. The undomesticated is both unconscious and formless. Thus the power of nature becomes dumb and brutish; the chaotic events of everyday life are but a passing show; and scientific method or truth of correspondence as a self-propelling tool for human development is the deification of illusion.

Conversely, the "real" world is the order of human value, where human needs, desires, and aspirations are given intelligible form by the imagination as the world of art. What is normally regarded as the real world—social convention, unexamined belief, everyday life— then becomes the content only of real or ultimate reality, which, in turn, is brought into being by the containment, "swallowing," or formalization of fallen existence by the imaginative process (Frye,

1963a, 33)—anagogy in action. The dialectic of the imagination (which is "rigidly conventionalized" if "left to itself" [Frye, 1976a, 36]) makes of the creative act a morally inviolate objective process by purging the human sensibility of ego-involvement. What emerges is a giant profile of the human visage, a kind of transcendent or archetypal validation of the human personality that simultaneously describes and defines the human condition. Frye calls this phenomenon "myth," and it is for him the closest approximation to recovering the edenic paradise of prelapsarian bliss. The knowledge it emits discloses all manner of spiritual secrets, "from the height of imaginative heaven to the depth of imaginative hell" (Frye, 1963a, 44). In literature, myth is expressed as "the vertical perspective" (Frye, 1963a, 40), those myriad aspects of genre or literary structure that comprise the entire spectrum of the order of words. This is myth in its anagogic context, the level of poetic *gnosis* that can synthesize seriousness and integrity, instruction and delight, by showing human nature so concretely magnified that some aspect of self-knowledge is revealed as a kind of second sight. In the world of literary reality, all distinctions between the moral and aesthetic are obliterated. Sidney's "what should be" becomes "what may be" as "Everyman" melds with the anthropomorphic universe in a bodying forth of the collective human imagination.

Within this philosophical perspective, each reading experience becomes an occasion for enlightenment, in which the individual reader enjoys increased awareness and psychic growth, participating in the fulfillment of human desire simply by attending to the story. This identification between poetic form and function is effected through Frye's analogical use of Aristotle's concept of *anagnorisis* (Aristotle, 1965, 40, 46). It is "discovery" or "recognition" that ultimately links literature to life for Frye. Within a single work, *anagnorisis* is the technical aspect of plot that signals "completion of the design" (Frye, 1970, 164), that point "where a hidden truth about something or somebody emerges into view" (Frye, 1963b, 25); and it coincides with the discovery of identity in the hero and/or the society to which he belongs (Frye, 1965a, 78). A good example of this occurs in *Macbeth* just before the "To-morrow and to-morrow" speech, after the third of the witches' prophecies comes true, where the respondent is able to grasp the total form of the entire play at once.

Within the respondent, who has now become the (ungendered) "hero" of the reading, the "divine being in anthropomorphic terms" (Frye, 1957, 120), discovery of the theme as the linear movement of the plot, frozen into an intelligible shape, annihilates the sense of alienation that on the mythical level originates from the loss of Eden, and, on the experiential one, from the imperfection of ordinary existence (Frye, 1976a, 186; 1965a, 129). To glimpse the perfection of being, then, in terms of "the imaginative model of [human] desire" (Frye, 1965a, 117) as formal literary reality, is the recognition scene as an act of literary criticism (see also 1957, 346). The insights it confers accumulate and assimilate with the products of every other recognition scene to create a potentially infinite storehouse of consciousness. It is at this anagogic level of literature as "an order of words" that literature becomes a "moral reality" and that literary experience becomes educational.

Frye's literary worldview, then, can be seen to address the meta-problem by its very definition, what we might call *a poetics of total form*. The justification problem and its underlying principle, the relationship between literature and life, revolves around this meta-structure spread out in space, the all-enclosing cultural envelope, the order of words, which refashions the malignant natural world of nonhuman values. This controlling metaphor serves to solve the response problem in that a genuinely literary response will inevitably be shaped by myth and metaphor, thus enabling the reader, however fleetingly, to participate in the entire world of verbal experience as one who has been educated to the total form of literature (Frye, 1957, 115; 1963b, 31). This mechanism also solves the censorship problem; for the respondent, now equipped with an imagination educated to the difference between total and partial form can answer the question of whether and what literature says. As a result, advertising bromides and political double-speak can be seen for what they are—partial, sub, or perverted literary forms—and offensive or so-called "immoral" literature for what it is—embodiments of certain kinds of values that are to be judged for what they are, nonliterary bits of social mythology (1963a). It is this infrastructure that protects respondents from regressing to the condition of Julian Jaynes's (1976) bicameral mind, which flicked a switch in order to hear the voices of the gods.

Frye's anagogic perspective provides him with a tautological structure that resolves the justification problem, vindicating the goals of literary education at the same time that it invokes the meta-problem. The world of art and literature can offer the sort of knowledge and experience that should inform civilized life because it is the only "truly human" world, "truly human" precisely because the norms of the real and the true have been transposed from "ordinary existence" (1976a, 186; 1965a, 129) to "imaginative experience" (1970, 101). The extrinsic value of literature, then, derives directly from its nature as an order of words that radically changes the "brazen" world of flawed existence into the "golden" one of perfect Being.

If Frye's anagogic theory of art preserves both the integrity and seriousness of literature, if the "work of art suggests something beyond itself most obviously when it is complete in itself" (Frye, 1947, 418) why, then, does he insist that the notion of the arts transforming life is "for the birds"? How can he attach moral significance to art in one context and strip it away in another? Since for Frye the moral import of art depends on whether a given society regards it as a primary or secondary need, the answer to the social significance of art and literature in Frye rests with how a society defines art and, conversely, reality. Within a positivistic value system that regards what is other than the genuinely human as primarily real, then art can only subserve other kinds of knowledge as "a rhetorical analogue." If, on the other hand, art is regarded not as an escape from reality but a deliverance from a lower to a higher reality, then the very recognition of that fact is itself socially redemptive. As we have already seen, then, a defense of poetry will be convincing only to the converted, to those who have already pledged allegiance to the superiority of the imaginative over the purely rational, of poetic over factual knowledge.

In ascribing the burden of moral responsibility to society rather than to poetry, Frye's position here echoes Sidney's and Shelley's. Frye's prescription for making the required leap of faith in recovering art as a primary social need is to supplant the scientific epistemological model with the mythic one. Through myth and metaphor, readers resist "the descriptive use of language and the correspondence form of truth" (Frye, 1976a, 46) in favor of imaginative truth as a form of lying that is "truer" than "truth." This inversion of the premises of truth has the effect of placing the widest possible distance between art and nature; for we thus respond to myth not in terms of its life-likeness, its resemblance to ordinary existence, but in terms of its outline, shape, pattern or form, which alone distinguishes it from life and which Frye says art throws away "when it tries to imitate life" (Frye, 1970, 45–55). In Frye's hands, Aristotle's imitation of "men in action" becomes more like the imaginative projection of, say, "men in dream," with the emphasis on "the *independence* from real experience which the term 'imagination' expresses" (Aristotle, 1965, 33; Frye, 1963c, 149, emphasis added). (The implications of this gendered poetics are dealt with in the later chapters of this book.)

The basis of Frye's entire apologia for poetry, then, is his insistence on the autonomy of literary reality as the separation of the imaginatively conceivable from the tangibly real. This formal disjunction between literature and life, effected by myth and metaphor, and the conventions or structural principles of poetic creation, is logically prior to the subsequent reunion of literature with life through response to those same formal elements. Educating the imagination is seen as basic training in response, according to the metaphorical and mythic structure of literature. This critical process reveals the kind of poetic knowledge that myth and metaphor figure forth, namely, the vision of humanity at home in a world of fulfilled desire. In this way, the universe becomes not "otherness" but "here-ness"; and literature, not a variation of truth of correspondence or an artful facsimile of content, which may or may not add refinement and serenity to life, but a continuous recognition scene of the human truths and values that Frye maintains are existentially built into all art. For him, this is the recovery of art as a primary need, where delight becomes instruction; integrity, seriousness; and intrinsic, extrinsic value.

In his theoretical resolution of the three problems of the meta-problem, does Frye claim too much for the educated imagination? His defense of poetry as Plato's "dream for awakened minds" (Frye, 1957, 111) espouses art as a second-order divinity with a peculiarly narcis-sistic circularity, beginning and ending with human creativity. Are we really redeemed by the "motive for metaphor," (Frye, 1963a, 1, 11), this compulsion to transmute everything outside ourselves into purely human terms? For Frye, the answer to this question is the same as the answer to how criticism or the perception of literary forms can translate into "education for life," i.e., insofar as the act of conscious-ness, by informing the power of choice in the "real world," defines what it means to be human, and the critical temper characterizes what is called civilization. Within this context, genuine literary experience is neither purely experiential nor critical, but the ongoing assimilation of both the experience and knowledge of literature that enables the overcoming of Eliot's dissociation of sensibility, as the continuous awareness of our existence, "a spectator of [our] own life" (Frye, 1970, 43; 1957, 348; 1973, 129). Through this Janus-like thrust toward art and nature, we glimpse Frye's "third order of expe-rience," that "world of definitive experience that poetry urges us to have but which we never quite get" in the "real world." In this "third order," criticism *would* be redundant, "and the distinction between literature and life would disappear, because life itself would then be the continuous incarnation of the creative word" (Frye, 1971/1973, 170–71).

## The Educated Imagination and the Justification Problem in Language Arts Education

Can Frye's anagogic perspective, so powerfully transcendent in its illimitable vision, work in the real world of English classrooms as a valid basis for a defense of poetry? I think there would be little doubt that the world of Frye's order of words would be too rich for the blood of many of today's educational utilitarians, who have eroded the study of English literature to make way for more "useful" subjects and who rush "back" to the basics and "ahead" to standardized testing, dismissing the motive for metaphor in the learning of both writing skills and moral principles. To the extent that, as I have argued, the justification problem needs to be reopened, English teachers find themselves cast either as latter-day Platos, Gossons, Peacocks, or Poiriers, who challenge the educational value of literature, or as Sidneys, Shelleys, or Fryes, who argue for it. Both sides are addressing why Plato was or was not right. The meta-problem provides a framework for challenging and arguing for the educational value of literature by interrogating its commonsense, taken-for-granted premises. In the remainder of this chapter, I will focus on the merits and limitations of Frye's anagogic perspective in the real life context of teaching English.

How can studying the dead poets accomplish what Shelley and Frye say it does? Frye's poetics of total form, his verbal universe as an order of words, places literature squarely as the cornerstone of a liberal education by articulating a philosophy of language arts education on the basis of language as both an art and as a discipline, in which literacy and the moral imagination become two sides of a coin. It is this conjoining of the moral and the literary within Frye's order of words that would rescue literature from being the "secondary social luxury" (1976b, 121) Plato saw it as in the *Republic*.[7] Here, uncompromising beliefs both in the inward drive to know and to act in accordance with the liberated imagination and in English literature as "the best subject matter in the world" (Frye, 1988, 5) endorse literature as a primary social need which can unproblematically accomplish both senses of education—a leading out of, a self-transformation; and a leading into, the enculturation into the ethos of the upright citizen. Another way of looking at this is to examine the underlying principle of the justification problem—Frye's view of the relationship between literature and life. First, we'll see how his claims for literature as the informing discipline of the language arts addresses the relationship between the literary and literacy in terms of the reading and writing curriculum. Then we'll take a closer look at some of the implications about the study of literature as influencing the moral sensibility by awakening human consciousness.

Today the assumption that literacy entails the literary appears to bear an inverse correlation to stages in educational development. At the primary and junior school levels, "storying" is an activity endemic to basic linguistic skills. Here assumptions about narrative as a primary act of the mind need no defense (Britton, 1982, 139–45), and notions about what constitutes the literary pose little problem. Literary works of the imagination are virtually indistinguishable from Aristotle's and Sidney's definition of literature as the creating of fictions, or that which is literally made up. "Children's literature" is a term equally applicable to what children read and what they write.

As we ascend grade levels to the intermediate and senior divisions, however, reading, writing, and literature tend to become separate categories; and while the integrated approach to the language arts curriculum seeks to preserve the holistic nature of language activity, it has not succeeded in preserving the *logical* connection between linguistic and literary literacy in the minds of many educators. This logical relationship is ignored when literature as the *art* of words is regarded as distinct from literacy as the *discipline* of words. Consequently, educational bureaucracies and teachers are lulled into thinking that students can do with less literature in the curriculum. In Ontario, for example, victories in implementing progressive writing programs recognizing "process" are hard won at the price of literature; and teachers acquiesce, out of loss of faith, exhaustion, and even guilt. As one teacher observed a few years ago, directives are "telling us not only to bring writing back into the classroom, but to spend one-third of class time on it. What's being reduced is the amount of time we spend on literature. About time too, although many of us are going to miss that. Let's be honest. We enjoyed teaching literature. That's what we were trained for" (Liptrot, 1986, 56).

According to the dictates of Frye's educated imagination, once literary works of the imagination are seen as instrumental to rather than formative of students' power to articulate, language arts become inevitably rent into competing definitions of literacy as either a primary or secondary need, and thereby spawn a host of ideologies about the moral, social, and educational value of words. Language as a primary need is seen in terms of communication skills, self-development, abstract reasoning, and vocational objectives; as a secondary need, in terms of literary appreciation, moral awareness, and aesthetic refinement. Language art becomes disjunct from fine art. The interconnectedness between literary form and content that characterizes myth, legend, and fairytale in children's literature, on the one hand, and children's composition, on the other, breaks down into skirmishes among a wide array of vested literary and educational interests: bibliotherapy versus literary analysis, mechanical correctness versus imaginative creativity, the workplace versus the university, social criticism versus literary integrity, and, inevitably, process versus product. Add to this the erosion of time and space spent on literature and the challenge of the humanistic mandate of literature by proponents of other disciplines also dedicated to changing consciousness, and we see, too, the recurrence of yet another call for a defense of poetry.

Literature as a field of study, in its equal emphasis on the cognitive and affective, does seem unique in its capacity to fulfill the goals of two aspects of the curriculum that need attention: aesthetic education and critical thinking. As a *language* art, it is the only one of the fine arts to literally speak recognition scenes. But because discussions about the educational value of literature are habitually grounded in the presumed divorce between "literariness" and "communication," between verbal form and content, between linguistic manner and matter, literature gets short shrift on both counts. On the one hand, proponents of aesthetic education tend to emphasize development of music and visual arts programs, understandably, believing that literature as a language art is taken care of within its own discipline. On the other, the teaching of critical thinking tends to stress rhetorical analysis, life skills, information theory, deductive logic, and media study.

Through the practice of literary criticism, literature appears to be the only one of the fine arts in the school curriculum to enjoy systematic inquiry in a mode of intellection consonant with the educational establishment's conception of critical thinking, or at least it did in 1977 (see Ontario Ministry of Education, *Curriculum Guideline for the Senior Divisions*, 1977, 7, 10). New methodologies in the teaching of literature which downplay the critical response in favor of aesthetic engagement (Probst, 1988) privilege a kind of knowing incommensurate with what is deemed in education circles as the highest level of mental operations. This book espouses the principle of literary engagement as the logical premise for defending the language arts curriculum, as Chapters 6 to 10 will attest; and so I am doubly concerned about defending literature on a basis other than the logical priority of the critical response. Yet many proponents of education for critical consciousness would not see aesthetic engagement as contributing directly to the attainment of literacy. Frank J. D'Angelo, for example, in outlining the characteristics of a literate person, makes the following hierarchical distinction about criteria for determining definitions of literacy and nonliteracy:

> The cause-and-effect explanations of literate people tend to be scientific, that is, they are hypothetical, abstract, and objective. The cause-and-effect explanations of nonliterate people tend to be descriptive and narrative. If asked, for example, to explain a very simple phenomenon, such as why the turtle has a flat shell, nonliterate people will tell a story—an etiological tale of origins or a myth. The logical relationship of cause and effect is implicit in the imaginative story, but it is not differentiated. The nonliterate person

does not abstract these relationships in a specific, logical form. If asked to explain the phenomena involved in a sunset or sunrise, the literate person will give a scientific explanation. The nonliterate person, however, will tell a story, personifying the sun as a being who leaves his cave in the morning and returns there at night. (1982, 160)

The ethnocentricity of this view is patent, but my point here is that if the literate person is primarily one who is able to handle logical relationships in scientific terms, we are tempted to ask why Frye complains that school systems are impoverished because, alas, there are no courses in "remedial metaphor" (1970, 94).

It is just this assumption that a literary education is *per se* the heart of literacy training that is being questioned now inside and outside English studies, not just with respect to reading but also to writing. In an exchange of views between two Ontario English teachers a few years ago, John Borovilos, then president of the Ontario Council for Teachers in Education, responded to the concerns of another Ontario teacher, David Pritchard, who expressed his unabashed cynicism "about how essential a literary education is to the 'average student'" (Pritchard, 1984, 242–243). Like Sidney and Shelley, Borovilos responded to his opponent by meeting him on his own ground—the utility of literature to literacy—by quoting Robert Evans, the Vice-President of Massey Charbonneau Inc., who emphasized the need for "the highest level of language and communication skills" from the standpoint of the business community. For Evans, only "literate, able communicators will survive and prosper." Not only will those who do "not read extensively and critically" be apparently left behind on the road to consumer heaven, but they will surely become "fair game for demagogues" (Borovilos, 1985, 1–2).

In a replay of the Peacock-Shelley debate, Evans corroborates Borovilos' claim that literacy is a primary, not secondary need, but on different premises from Borovilos. In Evans' response, the issue of a *literary* education as an essential component of literacy still remains unanswered. We recall that it was precisely this desire to formulate the values of a conception of literacy characterized by abstract thought that precipitated Plato's outlawing *poetry* as the core curriculum, in favor of philosophy. I would want to ask Robert Evans what kinds of books he would prescribe in his list of "extensive and critical reading." Would he consider the literary genres of poetry, fiction and drama a first priority? Evans might argue that communication skills can be more efficiently taught through writing courses based on works closer to the career interests of students than the "classics."

Borovilos anticipates this objection by positing a necessary connection between what he terms a "thorough knowledge of and . . .

ability to perceive and manipulate English structures," on the one hand, and, say, media literacy, on the other. By a full grasp of "English structures" Borovilos could be referring to grammar, linguistics, rhetoric, literary criticism, or semiotics. But specialists in each of these fields could launch a similar defense of their field of study as more crucial to the attaining of media literacy than is the study of these structures in literature. As a devotee of the educated imagination, however, Borovilos[8] probably means that myth and metaphor, which shape conceptual thought itself, are learned primarily through literature, and that, as formal structures, they have a direct transfer-value to all modes of human communication. In other words, remedial metaphor as the identification of the nonhuman and human worlds is, in the end, the most basic of the basics. This position is a logical extension of Frye's anagogic perspective of literature as the order of words, but it is a position related more to belief and assertion than to verification.

Some researchers in literary reading, Russell Hunt, for example, contend that no empirical test can demonstrate specific consequences of reading literary or nonliterary texts on writing because reading varies so much from one case to the next. No text by itself, observes Hunt, will determine that the

> reader will actually perform any particular act, or employ any particular skill. Depth of processing and levels of engagement vary from reader to reader, and indeed, from reading to reading by the same reader. A text may invite a reader to engage himself with it in some particular active and whole-minded way, but many readers (and this is especially true of those who are also poor writers) simply don't know how to recognize, much less accept and act on, such invitations. It is vitally important to acknowledge, furthermore, that what we are dealing with here is not a problem we can solve by telling people to read more deeply, or by assigning texts which "require" that sort of reading. Reading in such ways involves a sophisticated set of attitudes toward language and of linguistic and social skills and abilities, which must be patiently nurtured and helped to develop. (1983, 7)

Hunt's skepticism about "hard" evidence on this topic is borne out in research studies themselves. For example, a quick perusal of the literature section of *Research in the Teaching of English* at any given time will disclose a host of conflicting data on the effect of reading literature on literacy. No longer are literature courses thought to result *automatically* in improved writing skills; to wit, the thriving freshman composition industry both in Canada and the United States. What is needed, according to Hunt and others, are pedagogical methods that teach students reading and writing in an integrated way such that, in Roland Barthes' terms, they learn to read in a writerly way and write in a readerly way. Reading in a writerly way is simply the kind of reading characteristic of any fluent reader who is "not looking at things, but at relations between things" (Hunt, 1983, 7). Many would concur with him that an enlightened view of the reading act not only provides a defense of the dictum, "better readers, better writers," but also defends the place of literature in the curriculum. He concludes that "the more active, creative, engaged readers are, the better writers they are likely to be. The kinds of texts that allow for, and most richly reward, that kind of reading, are, of course, literary texts" (8). This position would be endorsed by educators such as James Britton, John Dixon, and James Moffett, and the increasing number of adherents to a compositional or actualization model of reading (see Bogdan & Straw, 1990). Hunt's parenthetical "of course," though, betrays the bias of the English major; and however much I agree with him, I don't believe that bibliotherapists, cognitive psychologists, rhetoricians, or, ironically, converts to Language Across the Curriculum from other disciplines would necessarily be persuaded of the validity of his position. What is left unanswered is the relationship between writing and reading as thinking, and reading literature as thinking. Again, even when it comes to the relationship between the literary and literacy, a defense of poetry seems to be a sermon to the converted.

## The Problem with the Educated Imagination and the Justification Problem

Just as the educated imagination remains a statement of belief with respect to the literacy-literary debate, so does it remain with respect to the relationship of literature to morality. One of Frye's most famous students, Margaret Atwood, reiterated the justification problem in the educated imagination in an after-dinner speech titled "English Teachers Speech," at the 1985 conference of the Ontario Council of Teachers of English:

> When I was in high school, nobody felt compelled to think up reasons about *why* we were studying Shakespeare, Shelley, Wordsworth, Hardy, Eliot, Chaucer. . . . No apologies were needed, it seemed. It was thought that every education deserving of the name was partially an education in literature and thus in literacy; and that the imaginative world was as deserving of human scrutiny as, for instance, book-keeping; that part of the function of reading was to stretch the mind, not merely to mimic what might already be contained within it (no *Catcher in the Rye* for us, for instance).

Every one of those notions has since come under fire. You, as teachers of English are charged with holding the fort. What you are educating is the next generation of imaginations, and it is worth pointing out in this context that wars and neutron bombs do not fall out of trees, they are made by people and are products primarily of limited and/or distorted human imagination. Who knows what evil lurks in the hearts of men? [sic] The English teacher knows, or certainly ought to. (1986, 12–13, emphasis original)

Why should English teachers know better than science or history teachers "what evil lurks in the hearts of men?" Here Atwood is espousing what poets and their readers are privy to—that special cognition claimed by members of the "Dead Poets' Society" which has traditionally constituted the priestly mission of the English teaching profession, an office sanctioned by acolytes of the educated imagination and its historical antecedents recounted in these pages. For Atwood, having a literary education is not just a matter of being able to manipulate formalistic devices, but of possessing an exclusive content. The assumption that English teachers ought to know what "evil lurks" in people's hearts issues from the Romantic and neo-Platonic belief in divine inspiration: the poet "knows," embodies this knowledge in the poem as an intuitive insight, which is then presumably emitted to the reader. Frye regards this poetic knowledge, not as the privileged information of a superior human being but primarily as a form, a structure, a process of the morally inviolate operation of the imagination which produces ordered, creative thought. In the next section of this chapter we'll see how advocates and skeptics of this belief—in the morally literate sensibility informed by literature as the core of English studies—play out some of the issues captured in Atwood's passionate outpouring about literature as a primary social need.

Each year the intellectual community I call home, The Ontario Institute for Studies in Education, celebrates a renowned educator by way of a special lecture, an event held in honor of R.B.W. Jackson, founding director of the Institute. In 1989 the chosen educator was Robert Fulford, Canadian journalist, broadcaster, and editor, generally considered to be foremost among humanist commentators on literature and the arts. Fulford, an officer of the Order of Canada and recipient of a number of honorary degrees, was himself a high-school dropout who left "in academic disgrace and went to work as a copy boy on a newspaper" (Fulford, 1989, 1).

The title of Fulford's address, "Literature and Literacy: The Future of English Studies," signals his attempt to come to terms with "the central problem of education in our time ... the culture of illiteracy," which he regards as the "dominant culture" (8). Taking the audience into Ontario's historical past, Fulford calls into view the philosophy of literature education of George Paxton Young, "a nineteenth-century pioneer and visionary" (1), who was influential in infusing into "the colonies" a healthy dose of Arnoldian fervor about the power of literature to mold the moral lives of students. For Young, literature was to be the heart of the curriculum, as it was unique in its capacity for mental stimulation and character formation. Fulford delivers this paean to literature education:

> "The quickening contact with truth and beauty in studying the works of good English Authors"—that's what [Young] wanted for pupils. "Why," he asked, "should children not have their intellectual natures nourished and enriched through familiarity with exquisite thoughts and images . . . why should we not answer all their conscious and unconscious aspirations after what Matthew Arnold calls sweetness and light. . . . " (7)

Noting that the cultural ideal described above persisted throughout the last century and "a long way into our own" (8), Fulford traces the nostalgic route of the educated imagination, from Young-cum-Arnold to F.R. Leavis to Northrop Frye. Somewhere in there lies the moral literary sensibility, in the domain of the institution of English studies, lies, for Fulford and for many weaned on the delights of the trek from Beowulf to Virginia Woolf, the promise of deliverance from the scourge of illiteracy.

One of the most powerful articulations of the educated person envisioned here, to my mind, is captured in the following quotation taken from Frye's *The Educated Imagination* (1963a) itself. In emphasizing the importance of skill in educating the imagination, Frye uses the analogy of playing the piano: the *freedom* to play comes only with hard practice. Similarly,

> [n]obody is capable of free speech unless he knows how to use the language, and such knowledge is not a gift: it has to be learned and worked at. The only exceptions, and they are exceptions that prove the rule, are people who, in some crisis, show that they have a social imagination strong and mature enough to stand out against a mob. In the recent row over desegregation in New Orleans, there was one mother who gave her reasons for sending her children to an integrated school with such dignity and precision that the reporters couldn't understand how a woman who never got past grade six learned to talk like the Declaration of Independence. *Such people already have what literature tries to give.* For most of us, free speech is cultivated speech, but cultivating speech is not just a skill, like playing chess. *You can't cultivate speech, beyond a certain point, unless you have something to say, and the basis of what you have to say is your vision of society.* (64, emphasis added)

And we might add to this the suppressed premise of Frye's position: "Your vision of society is a product, at least in part, of your literary imagination." So here we have one completed cycle of Frye's educational dialectic, the ongoing, continuous interrelationship between the utopian apocalypse encapsulated in the verbal universe, the order of words, and the routine existence of daily life—Paxton Young's dream come true as the integration of the moral and literate sensibility through the study of literature. In its most fundamental form, this dialectical struggle is "between the tendency . . . merely to accept what is handed [us] . . . and the effort to choose and control [our] vision" (Frye, 1966, 143–144).

What critics of this educational ideal are worried about is the dystopian side of this struggle, one hidden from view in the humanist account, which assumes that freedom of choice is really free, that most illiterates have no social imagination (see my Chapters 9 and 10), and that literature confers this vision in an unproblematic way. Frye's critics would suggest that literature is not exempt from "conditioning" defined as adapting, conforming, adjusting, accommodating, being constructed by. Ironically, one of Robert Fulford's sources on Paxton Young is the doctoral dissertation by Professor Robert Morgan of the Ontario Institute for Studies in Education. However, the intent and thrust of Morgan's thesis is the polar opposite of lauding the Arnoldian model extolled by Young. Morgan's analysis, propelled by such thinkers as Marx and Foucault, examines the coercive effects of the educational reforms introduced by Young, effects constituting what we might call demonic detritus of the ethical imperatives of Young's moral-literary prescriptives. For Morgan, these prescriptives circumscribe the learning process as a kind of technology that delimits what is educationally possible (Robert Morgan, 1987; see also my Chapter 7).

As mentioned earlier, implicit in Atwood's position are assumptions about the source of the poet's knowledge, the nature of poetic truth, and literature itself—all issues challenged by contemporary criticism. Catherine Belsey tells of the disappearance of the author "as mysterious genius" (1980, 138). Gone apparently is the Romantic legacy of Plato's poet inspired by "divine madness" (my Chapter 1) and of Shelley's claims for poetry's innate gnostic powers (my Chapter 2). Replacing them is the poet as a "worker transforming a given raw material through the methodical employment of determinate means of production" (Macherey, 1978, 137; cf. Althusser, 1969, 167), and criticism as "the science which offers a knowledge of this mode of production" (138). That reading literary texts yields a form of gnosis presupposes that there is such a thing as literary text, and, for Belsey and other poststructuralist critics, that there is such a thing as any kind of text "as it really is." Such a notion derives for Belsey from empirical notions of the correspondence between words and the world and the perception of reading as the ferreting out of an intended meaning.

> [T]he objects of any rational investigation have no prior instance but are thought into being. The object does not pose before the interrogating eye, for thought is not the passive perception of a general disposition, as though the object should offer to share itself, like an open fruit, both displayed and concealed by a single gesture. The act of knowing is not the listening to a discourse already constituted, a mere fiction which we have simply to translate. It is rather the elaboration of a new discourse, the articulation of a silence. (Macherey, 1978, 5–6, qtd. in Belsey, 1980, 138)

Belsey insists that the reader is not a consumer but producer of meaning, not a recipient but transformer of the raw material comprising the text by means of applying to it "existing forms of knowledge," i.e., poststructuralist critical methods (139). She advocates deconstruction, feminist criticism, "post-Saussurean linguistics, Lacanian psychoanalysis and Marxist economic theory" (139), all schools of thought embodying what Frye would see as reinforcing "extra literary" values. The effect of the poststructuralist critique of the educated imagination is to render thoroughly problematic the notion of reading literature as literature. I do not believe, as did Frye, that this can be dismissed as critical "sectarianism" (see my Chapter 10), but neither do I want to devalue the emancipatory agenda of literature education.

What actually constitutes reading literature as literature—and, what is literature? The conception of literariness as a canonized list of great books or as a set of properties attributable to one text as distinct from another has, of course, been widely challenged by literary theorists and educators. What makes up the canon? For Terry Eagleton (1983) it is a slipping and sliding barometer of taste serving the power proclivities of a dominant class. (See also Eagleton, 1990.) Along with Belsey, he would reject the legitimacy of uncritical identification or engagement with words "as they really are" and disclaim the power of particular texts per se to enhance the moral lives of their readers. This would include the manifestos of the liberal/humanist ideal that find their way into virtually every official guideline for teaching literature put forward by educational bureaucracies.

Poststructuralists are not the only ones who problematize the definition of the literary canon as "the classics." For philosopher John Ellis and theorist of literature education Louise Rosenblatt, literary texts are defined by the stance adopted in reading them. The difference between their positions is Ellis's emphasis on the social aspect of reading and Rosenblatt's on the private and individual experience. For Ellis, "Literary texts are not defined as those of a certain shape or structure, but as those pieces of language used in a certain way by the community" (1974, 42). Literature is language no longer responded to

> as part of the immediate context we live in and as something to use in our normal way as a means of controlling that context; nor do we concern ourselves with the immediate context from which it emerged, and so are not taking it up to learn in our normal way something about that actual everyday context; . . . literary texts are defined as those that are used by the society in such a way that *the text is not taken as specifically relevant to the immediate context of its origin.* (43–44, emphasis added)

Ellis would agree with Frye that literature is neither self-expression nor a direct reflection of life, but he would emphasize literary language not as the structures of language of myth and metaphor so much as what a particular social group has decided to separate out from life to be read in an aesthetic mode, that is, "not specifically relevant to" life.

Louise Rosenblatt defines literature as an aesthetic attitude toward reading too, but her premises are experiential and normative whereas Ellis's are logical and descriptive. Rosenblatt would include everything in the canon so long as it was amenable to an aesthetic reading. Here aesthetic is understood not as a separate category from what would normally be thought of as "life," but rather as a kind of reading in which the object of response is the literary experience, the reader's own attention to "what is being personally lived through the reading event" (1978, 169). Unlike Ellis, who thinks of literature in terms of its distinction (though not its disjunction) from life, Eagleton and Rosenblatt regard literature as an actual form of life experience, as compared with Frye's and Susanne Langer's (1942/1982, 1953) notion of aesthetic experience as virtual experience. But Eagleton, suspicious of aesthetic absorption, views what goes by the name "literary art" as constructs of social existence, constructs that must be enlisted in the service of social criticism. For Eagleton (1983), the literary experience induced by the symbol "was the keystone of an irrationalism, a forestalling of reasoned critical inquiry, which has been rampant in literary theory ever since. It was a *unitary* thing, and to dissect it—to take it apart to see how it worked—was almost as blasphemous as seeking to analyze the Holy Trinity" (22, emphasis original). For him, then, what must be dissected is the constellation of beliefs and belief systems that prompt certain people to call certain texts literature (16).

Rosenblatt is unequivocal in her championing of the holistic literary experience:

> The lived-through event has a certain autonomy of time and circumstance. The experience can be judged independently in terms of its own dynamics, its coherence, its subtlety, its intensity, its ordering of sensation, thought, feeling, its opening up of new vistas. It can be evaluated as an aesthetic event. Yet in the life of the reader, the aesthetic experience, though distinguishable, is not separable from the ongoing life out of which he comes to the text, and to which he must return. The literary transaction, like the act of literary creation, has social origins and social effects and hence can be evaluated by other categories of criteria. (1978, 156–157)

For Rosenblatt, then, literary experience is connected to reality in that it is a psychological event "in the life of the reader," but it is logically separable from it as a phenomenon which can be bracketed out and pondered according to aesthetic and extra-literary values. Within Rosenblatt's purview, literary experience does not rule out the possibility of a subsequent critical response, and so, would seem to escape Eagleton's charge of "irrationalism." As Alan Purves puts it, literary reading for Rosenblatt is "a set of mediated experiences, which can be used to challenge the mind and its values" (1991, 210). Frye would agree, but, as we shall see more fully in Chapter 5, for him criticism must have logical, if not psychological, priority over experience. Thinking is not, for Frye, "a natural process like eating or sleeping," but "real thinking is an acquired skill" (1982a, 109). That is why the imagination has to be educated. For Rosenblatt, the experientially literary is the logically prior category, and as such assumes the status of an ontology. "What is in the head cannot be the object of censure or praise: it is, and it results from prior experience, prior reading, and prior teaching" (Purves, 1991, 211). This is the position which I shall pursue in the second half of this book under the rubric of the re-educated imagination, but it is a position also predicated on my politicized view of literary engagement (Chapter 6).

As soon as literature is defined as a kind of process or experience, we are in the realm of the meta-problem. As Plato, Sidney, Shelley, and Frye all attest—the notion of literary experience calls up the question of values, and that question goes beyond the justification problem to the response and censorship problems. What is at issue in all three problems is the nature of the imagination itself, and, more precisely, of literary experience. Rosenblatt links literary experience to rationality, not irrationality, insisting that "literature, when read as literature, is particularly adapted to providing the opportunity for fostering the ability to think rationally about values" (1985, 65). For her it is language, the stuff out of which literature is made, that implicates literature directly with human values. Reminiscent of Shelley's rationale for poetry as the informing verbal discipline (my Chapter 2), Rosenblatt insists that literature embodies values because the "very medium through which the author shapes the text—language—is grounded in the shared lives of human beings" (1985, 65). Thus it would seem that "doing literature" becomes a moral endeavor not on the basis of the moral force of its subject matter, or the secret knowledge of its authors and respondents, but because entering into literary language itself entails a working through of human experience. This conception of literature as a superior form of values education is characteristic of the many declarations of literary humanism found in official documents of Departments of Education. Their validity is contingent upon accepting their premises, i.e., that language is primarily reflexive, that literary experience is real experience, and that language embodies "the shared lives of human beings."

Like Louise Rosenblatt, John Dixon deems the moral values of literature to depend on the moral function of language itself in its capacity to further psychic growth in the reader. For Dixon, one of the fundamental tasks of language is to confer on its users "the deeper understanding of an inner life and our relationship with others" (1985, 55). In reading literary texts, this understanding springs from an empathic attitude to character and events recreated through the imagination in a way which makes literary experience a felt part of ordinary life. But what of the bracketing of that experience that must be undertaken if it is to be amenable to evaluation? What becomes of the values created in the transformation? How do readers negotiate the complex of values that seem to be both experienced and embodied in the text? Do they compare their value positions before and after the literary event? Is this movement toward self-conscious response not artificial, well nigh impossible, even counterproductive, to the very purpose of engaging in the verbal imaginative reconstruction of experience itself—a root cause of dissociation of sensibility? Can we not just "enjoy" it with moral impunity (see Gold, 1990), or would this violate the notion of the educated imagination?

These are all important questions, especially in light of the fact that Frye's concept of the educated imagination depends on assertions and admonitions about the *separation* of readers' values from those embodied in the text as much as about their interdependence (Chapter 5). It seems that the proximity between literature and life depends to a large degree upon whether we wish to justify its utility as a moral educator or protect it from censorship. On the one hand, claims for its integration with life become grounds for its efficacy as a teacher *about* life. On the other hand, the standard court of appeal in censorship debates is the insistence that readers keep "values, morals, and attitudes in texts . . . *apart* from the values, morals, and attitudes brought to the reading of a text by the reader" (Gambell, 1986, 103, emphasis added). Moreover, if we credit the findings of empirical studies on the "behavioral effects" of texts on readers, we discover that readers *do* tend to keep their values separate from what they read. Richard Beach (1979), for example, reports that stability of personality far outweighs what is ingested in literature class with respect to influencing students' values. If this is true, then what are the implications for rationalizing the place of literature in the curriculum on the basis of its ethical dimension? And how would the answer to that question connect to the censorship problem? Chapter 6 attempts to throw into question assumptions underlying notions such as "stability of personality" as contingent upon what I call "the feeling, power, and location" problems, that is, the situatedness of real readers reading.

Can English teachers really have it both ways? Can we really simultaneously affirm the dependence of literature on life and its independence from life? Can we also maintain that literature exerts a moral influence which is wholly positive? We can within the anagogic perspective, but that is a perspective which is essentially an article of faith, which is a premise, not a reason, for doing what we do. It is a premise based on identity rather than difference (see Chapter 10) and on the long-term goal of the educated imagination as it is informed by the critical response. Teachers engaging with real readers in the untidiness of real sensibilities are faced with the short-term consequences of difference—in the psychosocial development of a myriad of real students reading, students whose "knowledge in their heads" is a product of myriad beliefs and life profiles which are raced, classed, and gendered. When these beliefs and identities collide, as inevitably they must in the short run under the power of literary reading, we are thus compelled to ask why Plato was *not* right in his claim that poetry can also influence for ill, too.

Educators reject a didactic role for literature on the assumption that values reside in the reader, not the text, while nonetheless affirming an overall moral purport to the literary enterprise. We are still left wondering how, for example, Frye can proclaim that there is no such thing as a morally bad novel (1963a) at the same time that he disclaims an art-for-art's-sake aestheticism for literature, when literature is "an ethical instrument, participating in the world of civilization" (1957, 349), a potent moral force which lends humanity "not only a means of understanding but a power to fight" (1970, 105). If values *are* existentially built into literary art (Frye, 1976b, 121), how can a work of literature and its reader escape adverse affects of whatever negative values it might embody, especially if literature is to be legitimated as a primary need and not regarded as ornamental rhetoric? The impasse resulting from these anomalies in Frye's defense of poetry provides our introduction to the educated imagination and the censorship problem.

## Endnotes

1. Frye used this term in private conversation with the author.

2. Frye's aphorisms continue to pepper official curriculum guidelines across Canada; he was the honorary president of the Ontario Council of Teachers of English; and "Educating the Imagination" was the title of the 1990 NCTE conference.

3. I use quotation marks here to indicate my ironic stance to this term. See Chapters 6 through 10, which offer an explicit and implicit critique of universality conceived in male terms.

4. Cultural studies is an area of study that is as diverse as it is broad. Judging from a recent publisher's catalogue entitled "Cultural Studies," the field includes Communication (Advertising, Journalism, Video, Publishing, Media, Environment), Native studies, Women's studies, Cultural Politics, and Mind Skills. Of some ninety titles, only four pertain primarily to literature.

5. This note attests to my noticing the use of the generic "he" in various quotations throughout this book. (See also Chapter 9 for further commentary on Frye's view of this convention.)

6. I want to stress that the "reconstruction" of Frye's thought undertaken in this section is presented as an interpretive description, part of the developmental nature of the larger argument of this book as a whole. For a feminist critique of Frye's poetics of total form see Bogdan (1990b, 1990c, 1990e).

7. In *Republic II*, 373c, Plato lumps poetry in with "a multitude of things that exceed the requirements of necessity in states, as, for example, the entire class of huntsmen and . . . the manufacturers of all kinds of articles, especially those which have to do with women's adornments" (1961/1980, 619).

8. Borovilos has edited a literature text for multicultural education within a Canadian context. In workshops the author constantly reiterates that the main criterion for selection, however, was that of literary quality. See J. Borovilos (1990).

# Chapter Four

# The Educated Imagination and the Censorship Problem

## The Censorship Situation: Some Assumptions

Ever since the publication of Salman Rushdie's *Satanic Verses* (1989) and the ongoing furor that surrounds it, in both the academy and the public forum, it has become impossible to deny the complexity or the seriousness of the censorship of literature in contemporary society without risking allegations of rank racism, moral smugness, or blinkered intellectual vision. Response in North America and Great Britain to the death threat against Rushdie has taken the discussion beyond the simple matter of a morally superior us-versus-them mentality and beyond claims of freedom of expression and the right to know, traditionally the clarion calls of Western apologists for poetry (see especially Corrigan, 1989; Cudjoe[1], 1989; Miller, 1990).

"The Rushdie affair" has major implications for the school text censorship debate as it forms part of the meta-problem and its underlying principles: the relationship between literature and life, whether and what literature says, and the autonomous reader. And it does so mainly because it challenges the assumptions of liberal thought that underwrite the ethos of the educated imagination informing the way English teachers have been trained to think about what they are doing and why. In Chapter 6, I re-introduce the censorship problem under the rubric of the re-educated imagination to show how feminist literary theory can help clarify the entanglements among warring factions, not just between those who would censor and those who would defend the right to read and the right to know, but the whole thorny enmeshment of assumptions about democratic education, social tolerance, racial identity, ethnic pluralism, cultural politics, canon and curriculum, developmental theories of learning, the response model of literature education, and the educational value of literature itself—all of which are brought into play each time a censorship incident has to be adjudicated. In this chapter I begin the discussion closer to home, with an example taken from my own study of a specific censorship debacle that occurred in Peterborough County, Ontario. This case study attempts to show that the censorship problem, even as it is analyzed within the framework of the educated imagination, is not so simple as professional handbooks on how to handle existing and prospective cases sometimes suggest.

My reading of the events surrounding *The Satanic Verses* (1989) persuades me that it encapsulates just the kind of slippages among the issues of censorship, justification, and response that have prompted me to write this book. Whether authors live or die as a result of how their words have been interpreted and whether a student or parent is offended by a four-letter word in a novel represent the two extremes of testimony about the relationship between word and world, and about the power of literature to have profound effects on readers, effects which are obviously not positive for the objecting readers.

The life-and-death context of the Rushdie situation is not unique to Western culture. Writers and thinkers die for expressing their ideas and have done so in the past. Knowledge is not a neutral business, and censorship goes on all the time within what looks like a free society (Moffett, 1988).[2] But within the profession of teaching English, censorship has become a four-letter word, one effect of which has been to limit discussion about the subtlety of the relationship between words and their power to wound. The negative aspect of this power is often rationalized under the "simple" assumption that acquiring knowledge can be a painful enterprise and that undergoing this pain is a rite of passage required of all participants in the culture. Implicit in the argument of this book is the contention that a truly democratic philosophy of literature education cannot afford to resolve the censorship problem quite so easily. Also implicit in my argument is challenging the "simple" distinction between fact and fiction that grounds most anti-censorship positions. In defending his novel, for example, Salman Rushdie observes that the "case of *The Satanic Verses* may be one of the biggest category mistakes [between fact and fiction] in literary history" (1990b, 17). Yet, as Gerald Graff (1979) has argued, "As long as the referentiality of language is a part of language, there must always be room for taking the referentiality of literature seriously" (qtd. in Bleich, 1988, 23).

As an English teacher, I have been predisposed to approach the censorship problem on the basis of what my sense of professionalism and my reading of intellectual history within the discipline of English literature have taught me about the premises of the vocation of English teaching. Though I took no courses in "the defense of poetry," either as a literary genre or as a philosophical analysis of the educational value of literature, I had accepted uncritically a basic tenet of the tradition of English studies: that literature influences—and influences powerfully—and that this influence has a direct educational transfer value to life that is unconditionally beneficial. As we have already seen, this ethos has threaded itself through the history of English literature to the present day (my Chapters 1, 2, and 3) and has functioned to integrate the belief in literature as the cornerstone of liberal education within the ideals of Western democracy. Resting within the assumptions of this belief are the major premises of the educated imagination: knowledge is better than ignorance; everyone has the right to know; agnosis or resistance to knowing is undesirable (Moffett, 1988); no individual or group should impose their values on another; literature is neither good nor bad except within its own category as a work of art (Frye, 1963a, 39); the aim of literature education is to develop awareness and refine the sensibilities through the best that has been thought and said in order to produce citizens who can think for themselves. This book does not reject these values, but only interrogates their epistemological, social, and political implications for the teaching of literature. It was my own experience of working on the case study described later in this chapter that caused me to think twice about the censorship problem and its relationship to the justification and response problems.

For English teachers, department heads, and principals on the front line, in classrooms and on parents' nights, the encroachment of the censorship problem on the ability to carry out their mandate—to lead students "out of the darkness" of their social conditioning and "into the light" of the "autonomous reader" through "great works" of the literary canon—necessitated reiterations of the humanist ideal of the educated imagination and the marshalling of accessible information (arguments and procedures) for easing discomfiting scenarios that threatened to become ugly, even dangerous (See Moffett, 1988). And so, armed both with the reigning credo of the profession and with self-help books on how to neutralize present attacks and fend off future ones (see especially NCTE publications such as Burress & Jenkinson, 1982; Karolides & Burress, 1985; Shugert, 1983) educators who hitherto had only to deal with the justification problem by

writing generic defenses of their discipline in the form of the statu-
tory "Aims and Objectives" section of curricular guidelines were
now being forced to confront the censorship problem by having to
articulate to themselves and to others the principles underlying their
selection practices in the form of anti-censorship tracts, and to pen
literal defenses of individual works. Toughing out the censorship
problem invokes issues of the relationship between literature and life
and the autonomous reader, concepts we've been using to address
the justification and response problems. Now, however, we must
also attend to the literary-epistemological question of whether and
what literature says. Before addressing this in detail, let's consider
the following teacher-authored defense of a particular work.

In an editorial entitled "A Moral Drama for our Times Must Never
Be Censored," about the censorship of *The Merchant Of Venice* in
some Ontario schools, English Department head Peter Peart makes an
impassioned statement of liberal humanist beliefs about what teaching this Shakespearean play "really" says, and thus teaches:

> A genuine piece of art—and *Merchant* is certainly that—must never
> be censored. Rather it must be examined for its insight into the
> reality and complexity of the society from which it is being viewed.
>
> Yet every great writer says more than he or she intended and the
> Bard is not an exception.
>
> *The Merchant of Venice,* read in the context of 1989, is a great
> writer's ringing condemnation of the cruelty of prejudice and the
> hypocrisy of some religious adherents so rampant in Canada today.
>
> That Shylock, the play's central character, is a Jew is significant
> not so much because he is Jewish but because he is a member of a
> minority in an overwhelmingly Christian society. And he is perse-
> cuted viciously and persistently by this same Christian majority.
>
> . . . . For the Christian reader this play should result in a few
> moments of rather unpleasant introspection. The truth is that no
> Christian can live up to the standard of love established by Christ
> Himself, and that bigotry, or at least intolerance, is a fact in our
> lives. And this fact is held up to us in *Merchant* to allow us to gain
> insight into ourselves and our society.
>
> However, for a moment ignore Shylock the Jew. Replace him
> with a real person in Kingston in 1989. Replace him with a black, a
> Pakistani, an unwed mother, an old person, a gay person, indeed
> even a teenager. Each of these is subject to the intolerance of a
> society in which he or she is a minority. . . .
>
> So should we censor *The Merchant of Venice*? Heaven help us
> if the answer is yes, for to say so would be to refuse to look at
> ourselves and our society and to refuse to see the reality of our
> community.
>
> Can a youngster in grade 9 understand this? Of course. Never-
> theless, an individual child may decide (or the family may decide)

that a piece of work like *Merchant* will offend his or her sensitivities. It is then the teacher's and the board of education's responsibility to ensure that this child is exposed to an alternate academic task.

But the other side of this arrangement is of vital importance. The person who chooses not to read *Merchant* must never be allowed to impose that judgment on the other youngsters in a classroom or on a board-wide system. Our society is a pluralistic and democratic one. The will of a few must never be imposed on the others.

School board trustees and administrators are facing this problem of sensitive issues with increasing frequency. An easy resolution of a sensitive problem is to acquiesce to a vocal minority. It would be so easy and simple to remove *The Merchant of Venice*, for example, from a list of approved texts.

Yet this would be tacit, covert censorship. It would also be one of the worst lessons in intolerance, short-sightedness and political expediency that our young people could be taught. (1989, 1–2)

The example above reflects the principles underlying the rationales for individual works drafted by many school boards, English departments, and professional organizations (see Davis, 1979; Gutteridge, 1988; Karolides and Burress, 1985; Shugert, 1983). These principles, which inform the ethos of the educated imagination, can be summarized as follows:

1. Censorship in any form is intrinsically iniquitous.
2. The line between censorship and selection of texts is clear: selection is the judicious choice made by professionals (see especially Shugert, 1983, 129); censorship, political bullying by pressure groups.
3. Literary masterpieces such as *The Merchant of Venice* articulate powerful messages in a uniquely literary way.
4. Great authors say more than they intend, and what they say can be accessed through literary interpretation.
5. This message is different from and more morally uplifting than that gleaned by censors or would-be censors.
6. Literary understanding as an objective in the literature curriculum supersedes all others.
7. The skilled, sensitive teacher can/should develop this understanding in students.
8. Removing a book on the basis of parental objections is a moral and intellectual cop-out.

9. Cultural pluralism is protected by preventing a few from imposing their will on others.
10. Judaeo-Christian values are communicated by appealing to what
    the work in question is really supposed to be "teaching."
11. Covert or self-censorship is an infringement of the freedom to
    know and the right to read.
12. The power of the literary imagination influences for good but not
    for ill, mainly because of symbolic interpretation, which goes
    beyond mere literalism in a way which allows for the inter-
    changeability of characters and events across time and place in
    the communication of universal and eternal values.

In the next part of this chapter, I want to illustrate how one
English teacher chose to prevent the imposition of the right not to
read on others by making assumptions similar to the author of the
above editorial, assumptions about what literature does and does not
say, and how it "should" affect those who read it. I hope to show
that, in at least this one instance, the logical and epistemological
failure of the teacher-authored defense shows how some rationales
against censorship collide with rationales for teaching literature
and assumptions about the nature of literary response, in short,
how it connects the censorship problem to the justification and the
response problems.


## The Case of Peterborough County

In 1976 two major controversies in the school text censorship
dilemma took place in the United States and Canada: one in Kinawha
County, West Virginia, and one in Peterborough County, Ontario.
Fueled by fundamentalist objections to literary works within the
language arts curriculum, these twin landmark events denote a struggle that has, over the long term, ceased to be a series of irritating,
"harmless" brush fires, but have become a relentless conflagration
which has insinuated itself into the everyday consciousness of educational administrators, school principals, and classroom English
teachers, as an ongoing problem to be dealt with seriously. In *Storm in
the Mountains: A Case Study of Censorship, Conflict, and Consciousness*, James Moffett (1988) chronicled the devastating effects of the
decimation of his language arts curriculum, *Interaction* (1973), along
with several other leading textbooks, in the West Virginia episode. I
will use a Canadian example, which had a sequel in 1985 (see also
Bogdan, 1988b; Bogdan & Yeomans, 1986), to inquire into the kinds
of aesthetic, epistemological, and ideological concerns which I've

suggested link the censorship problem to the justification and response problems. In drawing on the Peterborough example, I am less interested in the incidents themselves, though they are fascinating to examine (see Bogdan & Yeomans, 1986, 198–203; McMurtry, 1989), or in their political ramifications, crucial though they are, than in what we might make of them in terms of the main premise of the censorship problem—whether and what literature says. This issue constitutes the "epistemo-literary" relationship between the reading and study of literature, on the one hand, and personal and social values, on the other.

Picture a bellwether community of central rural Ontario, home of Trent University, a small, prestigious institution committed to the enterprise of higher education modeled on the tutorial system of Oxford and Cambridge, boasting one of the most successful records of students admitted to graduate schools of their choice in Canada; home also of Canada's revered author the late Margaret Laurence; and of Renaissance Peterborough, a religious fundamentalist organization dedicated to eradicating "secular humanism" from the schools. Peterborough is sailing and horse country for weary Torontonians escaping on weekends; but it is also prototypical of the dispositions and predilections of small town Ontario. "As an established, small-sized city with Family Compact roots, homogeneous ethnic composition, and a balanced cross-section of socio-economic levels, Peterborough's response was found to be an accurate indicator of how that 'mythic' average non-urban Ontarian thought and behaved" (McMurtry, 1989, 22).

Painfully ironic is the chilling fact that the main target of the Peterborough dispute, which raged over a protracted period, at times hotly and openly, and at others covertly, were three novels by the very celebrated writer who lived in the midst of her censors— Laurence herself. Paradoxical, as well, is the reality that the chief architect of the censors' arguments was a professor of German literature at Trent University. In defending herself against charges of subversion and pornography, Laurence radiated a profound religious sensibility coupled with a personal conviction about the prophetic role of the poet. As she confessed in an interview (Czarnecki, 1985), "The fundamentalists could say I was possessed by an evil spirit, . . . I can't argue with that. I have a mystic sense of being given something to write. I may not be an orthodox Christian, but I believe in the Holy Spirit" (186, emphasis original). She also said, "Anyone who says I'm a pornographer doesn't know how to read" (Laurence, 1985/ 1986). Invoked here are two major epistemological issues of literature education—creativity as divine inspiration, and correct and incorrect modes of literary response—reminding us once again of Plato's banishment of the poets.

As I immersed myself in the myriad briefs, depositions, and letters of support and denunciation that poured in as a result of both the 1976 and 1985 censorship confrontations, I came away acutely aware of the deep chord Laurence's works struck in her readers.[3] Whether outrage, fear, or affirmation, the feelings evoked by Laurence's poetic language in *The Diviners* (1974) were almost primeval. Reading the primary documents of the case elicited in me empathy for all sides, with the mother who poignantly tells of her daughter's trauma in having been forced to read aloud in class four-letter words never before uttered by her; with the teacher who insists that students engaged with the work are positively reinforced through an exploration of self-awareness, self-acceptance, tolerance of others, understanding of human frailty, family responsibilities and honest relationships, love and compassion (1985); and with the citizen whose resistance to knowing was so entrenched that he asked, "[w]hen you drink a glass of milk and it's sour, you don't have to drink the whole thing to know, do you?" ("School Board Votes," 1985, 1)

Even though *The Diviners* was reinstated in the curriculum in 1976 and again in 1985, along with three other indicted novels, J.D. Salinger's *Catcher in the Rye* (1951), and Laurence's *The Stone Angel* (1964) and *A Jest of God* (1966), the reasons for their retention ultimately had less to do with the persuasiveness of the *apologias* authored by Peterborough heads of English Departments, or with any real success in making genuine conversions among the members of the Textbook Review Committee, than with political manipulation. In short, the jury was stacked in favor of the novels' supporters, at least in the 1985 instance. What was ignored in the 1985 dispute was that the trenchant fundamentalist argument written nine years earlier was left largely unanswered. A residual disquiet permeates the present practice of Peterborough English teachers, who continue to do what they do best, teaching good literature in the abiding faith that reading and studying it is a moral endeavor. In this section I want to look at the defense of *The Diviners* offered by the English department head, along with the counter-argument penned by Renaissance Peterborough, as a way of framing the epistemo-literary aspect of the censorship problem at its most vexatious.

In an article titled "Liberalism and Censorship," published in the *Journal of Canadian Studies*, Ralph Heintzman (1978) wrote:

> The bulk of recent commentary on censorship in Canada has been a crude mixture of knee-jerk reactions, unexamined premises, and the wielding of bogeys. This is as true of those who oppose censorship as of those who favour it, but it is more surprising and regrettable in the case of the former. The censorship debate has not

been characterized by the careful thought and distinctions one
would hope to find on such a sensitive and divisive issue, especially from the "intellectuals" whose special care it ought to be to
make just such distinctions. (2)

Perhaps Heintzman is being unduly harsh here if we take this term
"intellectuals" to include English teachers on the front line; after all,
courses in critical apologetics are not included in the academic or
professional training of the average English teacher. Yet, as the many
publications put out by professional organizations, school boards,
and educational bureaucracies show, today professional survival is
contingent upon writing just such a convincing "defense of poetry."
As I hope will become clear, in the Peterborough case, the weak-
nesses of the 1976 defense of *The Diviners* and the strengths of the
Renaissance Peterborough rebuttal point to the necessity of viewing
the censorship problem within the context of the meta-problem.

Running throughout the letters of support for the actual defenses
of all four novels in question are appeals to their verisimilitude, their
true-to-lifeness, and the educational importance of vicarious experience. Statements such as, "Students can relate to this novel," or
"This book helps adolescents to see life as it really is," were made as
though realism, sympathetic identification, and emotional absorption are self-evident guarantors for the moral inviolateness of literature. It was these very epistemo-literary values, however, that were
attacked by Renaissance Peterborough in their denunciation of classroom use of the novels. Both sides argued within the framework of a
theory of language which takes the above values as givens and which
takes for granted that the relationship between literature and life is
determined by the fact that literature says things symbolically, the
English head arguing that the novels symbolized one thing, thereby
influencing the reader for good; Renaissance Peterborough, that they
symbolized something else, influencing the reader for ill. Within this
perspective, who wins depends on who is the best arguer and/or
whose values have the most political clout. In this instance the teachers had more political clout but the censors were the better arguers.

The 1985 Peterborough justification for teaching *The Diviners*
(substantively unchanged from the 1976 version) was mainly a
hard-sell of the novel as a vehicle for the transmission of the Judeo-
Christian moral and religious tradition within a Platonic, representational, mimetic, or truth-of-correspondence theory of language
that recalls the banishment of the poets from the Republic. This
theory of language posits a one-on-one direct relationship between
words and things, events, ideas, or values in the world to which it
is deemed words point. Truth-of-correspondence is essentially a
belief in the transparency of words and their power to reflect or

reproduce "life as it really is." In its crudest form, referential realism shows up in the reader as interpretive literalist, who equates a literary work with "the situation and things [in the world that it is believed] gave rise to them" (Ellis, 1974, 153). That is, a literary "statement" is judged by an interpretive literalist to be profane, ungodly, or pornographic on the premise that it reveals a profane, blasphemous, or pornographic "reality" in the world. This was the main line of reasoning behind most of the objections to the novels in question.

Like Philip Sidney,[4] the English teacher apologist for *The Diviners* (1974) met his opponents on their own moral ground; but whereas Sidney articulated a theory of poetry as hypothesis in which poetry both says and does not say (it "nothing affirms and therefore never lieth" [1966, 52]), the defender of Laurence's novel remained within the conceptual framework of truth-of-correspondence. In support of the religious merit of *The Diviners*, he cast the protagonist, Morag Gunn, as a latter-day sojourner through Paradise Lost and Paradise Regained, and Christie Logan, the major male figure, as a contemporary version of John Bunyan's Muckraker. To counter the charges of "gutter" language and explicit sex, the rationale proceeded by way of an unabashedly moralistic interpretation of the novel's "message." The apologist directly paralleled Morag's giving up swearing with her moral maturation, and contextualized the sexual exploits of all the main characters in terms of retributive justice for contravening the Christian code of sexual ethics. On the view articulated here, *The Diviners* would seem to be an infallible self-help book for preservation of virtue in the young.

The problem is that it didn't wash, not only with the interpretive literalists, who would not distinguish between strings of words and the "order of words" (Frye, 1957, 17) comprising literary context, but more importantly, with the interpretively deft, who in this case played the truth-of-correspondence game with greater acumen than the apologist. By capitulating to the politics of referentiality, the defender of *The Diviners* (1974) was led straight into the censors' ballpark, with the result that the fundamentalists won the "moral," if not the actual, victory.

Despite its cloying rhetorical slickness, the brief from Renaissance Peterborough presented an argument at a more subtle level of truth-of-correspondence than that of interpretive literalism. Renaissance accepted the bid to read in literary context but extended the argument one better by extrapolating from that context what it believed to be a more legitimate allegorical interpretation than that offered by the apologist. Standing the truth-of-correspondence model of teaching values in literature on its representational head,

Renaissance Peterborough acknowledged that *The Diviners* may well reflect values, but they're not those of the Arnoldian ideal of sweetness and light claimed by the humanist literary/educational establishment. (Recall Robert Fulford's speech in the last chapter.) As stated earlier, the Renaissance paper—echoing the voices of Plato and Gosson—challenged the very literary terms of reference, such as realism, emotional engagement, and sympathetic identification (deemed self-evident justifications for teaching the novel by the opposition) as potentially indoctrinatory educational influences.

The theoretical ground of the Renaissance argument was the sociological, as well as the aesthetic, implications of reading in literary context. It is precisely the sociology—and politics—of literature that is invoked by others, as, for example, those who work for changing stereotypes about women and minorities, those who insist on a certain proportion of Canadian material, in short, all who assume that the literature curriculum shapes thinking. Whether through book-banning or revising courses of study, both the political right and left have attempted to influence curriculum, and their assumptions about the relationship between the literature curriculum and social conditioning sometimes resemble each other. Both sides repudiate aesthetic integrity at the cost of injurious stereotyping in individual works; both sides want to redress the balance of what they consider to be a lopsided picture of the world in the curriculum as a whole.

The Renaissance brief acknowledged that the "reality" of Morag Gunn comprises "much more" than someone "in need of sexual gratification at whatever cost." But it objected to the indoctrinatory influence of students' repeated exposure to female protagonists who are unremittingly drawn with "a stunted idea of their own sexuality and of their identity." If realism "offers a way of seeing, understanding and evaluating human experience vicariously perceived," Renaissance argued, then "it follows that much of the direction of such a learning process will hinge on the choice and treatment of 'reality'" (1977, 2–3). On the premise that there does exist a direct relationship between literature and life, in which literary situations are "true" representations of "reality," and that this relationship turns on the extraordinary power of literature to say things, Renaissance charged that a curriculum offering an overbalance of the realistic mode portraying the darker underside of life would seem to constitute its own form of censorship.

As an English teacher educated by the ethos of the educated imagination, my impulse would have been to regard the apologist in this case as having made a tactical error with respect to meeting the censor on his own terms and to have taken refuge in the tenets of

Frye's theory—literary genre and such expressly literary values as style, emphasis, and connotation, values which can become casualties of a truncated extrapolation of literary content from literary form. I would have wanted to quote Karlheinze Stierle on the nature of fictional representation as the "self-referential nature of a fictional text," in which "the reader [sees] its formal structures against the horizon of its content structures" (1980, 103). These structures are thought effectively to separate literature from life such that literature represents not actual but "*possible* forms of organization for experience" (103, emphasis added). The sour milk metaphor, quoted earlier, cannot hold water here (to mix the metaphor) because literary convention makes literature something other than a "*rhetorical analogue* to concerned truth" (Frye, 1971/1973, 66, emphasis original). An interpretive literalist might very well demand a textual meaning that is single and predictable, object to that meaning if it fails to conform to a preconceived value system, and, as was the case with some of the Peterborough censors, react by deleting offending passages and referring specific readers to pages judged "unprintable" when the espoused value was thought to be subverted (Textbook Review Committee, 1985). As a disciple of the educated literary imagination, however, I would have wanted to ask the censors to read the entire book and refer them to Margaret Laurence's statement that for those who "know how to read," a knowledge of literary convention helps to broaden meaning beyond a narrow truth-of-correspondence. This is what Frye calls "imaginative literalism" (1990a, 21; see my Chapter 10).

But Renaissance Peterborough already knew that and objected in spite of it. Their rationale against Laurence's novels not only challenged the exclusionist/inclusionist dichotomy often used to distinguish between criteria for censorship and "Examples of Professional Guidelines" (Shugert, 1983, 129), but expressly took into account the issue of literary convention. This excerpt from the Renaissance brief sounds less like a pro-censorship tract than a plea for a fair and balanced curriculum selection policy:

> It has been claimed that the curriculum can only work with the views of a given society, which writers have chosen to offer their readers. "If we wish other views, we must seek out other realities or other writers."[5] How are you to handle the fact that for a variety of reasons and within certain literary conventions the writers of a given period tend to select and stress some aspects of human life rather than others? To what extent should those involved in curriculum-building accept the bias of the writers or, on the other hand, apply criteria to their works by virtue of which perhaps a great many novels will be rejected? (1977, 3)

It's not my intention to downplay censorship as the political bullying of one individual or group imposing its will on others. But the issue raised in the above quotation is that the line between the censorship and justification problems becomes uncomfortably blurred when literature is conceived of only in terms of *what* things it is thought to say, not *whether* it does so. Without examining the epistemo-literary problems underlying the censorship problem, "solutions" to them look dangerously like a case of "Might makes right" in a values war.

## The Censorship Problem, the Stubborn Structure, and the Meta-Problem

Northrop Frye's anagogic perspective on literature as "the stubborn structure" (1970) provides an analytic framework for the question of whether and what literature says. According to Frye, literature is not an utterance of messages of a certain kind, not a rhetorical analogue to truth which reinforces or countervails particular values. What, then, is it? The breadth of Frye's anagogic perspective allows him to redefine Plato's imitation of content as imitation of form (1963b, 41), with the result that he synthesizes literary integrity and ethical seriousness so as to enable "literature, without moralizing, to create a moral reality in imaginative experience" (1970, 101). And he purports to do so by the sheer stubbornness of the structure of his "order of words," which refuses the "horizontal" perspective of the close proximity of literature and life required by realistic genres. Realism, for Frye, *can* be indoctrinatory if convention is not distinguished from reality; but the "vertical perspective" (1963a, 40) of myth and metaphor reinforces the *lack* of any "consistent connexion" (1963a, 39) between literature and life. Myth and metaphor work against interpretive literalism because it is these structures that lend to literature the quality of sayingness *and* un-sayingness. It is the structures of myth and metaphor that give literature its hypothetical dimension.

In *The Stubborn Structure* (1970), Frye gives us his most graphic description of what he means by the title of the book: literature is "an alien structure of the imagination, set over against [us], strange in its conventions and often in its values" (77). Here we think back to *Dead Poets Society* and Mr. Keating standing on the table. What he wanted his students to understand is the power of literature as what the Russian formalists called *ostranenie* (Hawkes, 1977, 62) or the making strange of reality to see the world anew. It is this construct that allows Frye to hold the tension between the sayingness and unsayingness of literature, thus making intelligible—and credible— such statements as this:

> There's no such thing as a morally bad novel: its moral effect depends entirely on the moral quality of its reader, and nobody can predict what that will be. And if literature isn't morally bad it isn't morally good either. . . . [There] are moral standards in literature . . . even though they have nothing to do with calling the police when we see a word in a book that's more familiar in sound than in print. (1963a, 39–41)

The basis of Frye's approach to the censorship problem as whether and what literature says is the same as his approach to the justification problem as the relationship between literature and life—the logical (not psychological) separation of literature from life. In both his theory of the imagination and in his theory of literature, the imaginatively conceivable must be kept distinct from the tangibly real. As he says in *Spiritus Mundi* (1976b),

> [W]e have to separate these two worlds in our minds, rigorously and completely, before we can address ourselves to the next question, of how to unite them again [through response]. Of course everything we do is in one aspect an attempt to unite them, but unless we distinguish them first we shall not know what we are trying to unite. (89)

So, like the judge in the war crimes trial discussed in Chapters 1 and 2, Frye insists that the educated person know the difference between convention and reality. But Renaissance Peterborough did know and still objected to *The Diviners* on the grounds that literary convention signifies a kind of subject matter so powerful in its conditioning of the reader that knowing the difference does not by itself change how readers are influenced.

Frye's theory counters this argument in an analogue of Sidney's contention that poetry cannot lie because it makes no claim to the "truth" of anything. The Word as stubborn structure, as the order of words does not, of itself, say things: "To bring anything really to life in literature, we can't be lifelike: we have to be literature-like" (1963a, 37). "There is no 'real' meaning in literature, nothing to be 'got out of it' or abstracted from the total experience" (1970, 83). Yet "the experience of literature is, like literature itself, unable to speak" (1957, 27). Above all, it is never to be mistaken for a canon of precepts or set of rules to live by.

> So however useful literature may be in improving one's imagination
> or vocabulary, it would be the wildest kind of pedantry to use it
> directly as a guide to life. (1963a, 36)

The operative word here is "directly." To interpret literature as a
one-way direct message from text to reader is to be caught within a
narrow truth-of-correspondence. What is important is the notion of
the unsayingness of literature underlying these statements and its
usefulness as a guide to the censorship problem. The theory of literature as hypothesis, the subjunctive voice of "What if?" forces us
right into the meta-problem because, in order for us to be really
helped in solving the censorship problem, it becomes necessary to
look at Frye's theory of reading.

As early as the *Anatomy of Criticism* (1957), Frye articulated its
controlling principle: in every act of reading "we find our attention
moving in two directions at once" (73), inward toward the order of
words, verbal "pattern or integrity as a verbal structure" (78), and
outward toward the world. Through the first, inward motion, the
reader gleans "centripetal" meaning, which has directly to do with
the unsayingness of literature as the stubborn structure, with its
relationship to other literature, its intertextuality. Through the second, the reader gleans outward, "centrifugal" meaning (1971/1973,
32) or that meaning which has to do with what the work seems to be
saying in terms of its correspondence with "truth" or its proximity to
actual existence. Crucial to the efficacy of the educated imagination
in dealing with the censorship problem is Frye's insistence on the
logical priority of centripetal meaning. The structure is so stubborn
because of the doctrine of anagogy (my Chapter 3), in which literature
"swallows" life and in which "the imagination won't stop until it's
swallowed everything" (Frye, 1963a, 33).

With the subsumption of life by literature as the unsayingness of
literature comes the necessity of literary criticism literally to speak
for literature and the very important by-product of its providing a
virtually absolute insulation against censorship charges. How can
literature be censured if it does not say, if, in Sidney's sense, it
"nothing affirms," if it does not "conjure" (1966, 52–53) the reader to
take the text for the "truth"? For Frye, the centrifugal principle is that
of literary content only, which must be contained and completed by
the centripetal principle of literary form, which for him is poetic
design. Though for Frye the poem is preeminently "a structure of
imagery" (1957, 136) whose "conceptual implications" can never
"serve as a full equivalent" of its mythological meaning (1963b, 32),
I detect here a certain anxiety in him about the ontological status of
the literary work as a "self-contained verbal pattern" (1957, 74), at

least in respect to how it is perceived. The reason for this is, I think, his curiously Platonic mistrust of the formal weakness of language, in comparison with other arts, which have, it seems, greater freedom from the strictures of referentiality. The "building blocks" of architecture, the "quasi-geometrical" shapes of painting, and fugal construction in music—all attest more effectively to the "elemental spirit of design" than does literary art (1971, 211; 1970, 102); all participate in an inherently more spatial, hence more visionary, epistemology. ("Great literature is what the eye can see" [1976a, 30].)

Although the poetic image can be starkly visual (Sidney's "speaking picture," 1966, 25), it is as if behind the literary, inward-looking centripetal pattern there lurks a mere string of words that continually threatens to break down into centrifugal or nonliterary meaning that says what is "true" without at the same time not saying. In contrast to this, "[p]oetry seeks the image rather than the idea, and even when it deals with ideas it tends to seek a latent basis of concrete imagery in the idea." This can become a problem for critics who deal with "philosophical novels," which "seem to be stating propositions, and yet are clearly something else than actual philosophy" (Frye, 1963b, 57). It can also be a problem for censors and would-be censors who "cannot distinguish the release of energy from the release of chaos" (1947, 221) and who believe that you don't have to drink the whole glass to know that the milk is sour. For Frye, as for Blake, the meaning of "word" is unmistakably "a single and comprehensive form" (428). But he sees literature as standing half-way between abstract and representational art, and so the reader must adopt a kind of "garrison mentality" (1971, 225, 226, 236) in face of the potential encroachment on literary integrity by truth of correspondence (1957, 78–79). Frye expresses a hypersensitivity to the epistemological vagaries of language as an art form most poignantly in *The Stubborn Structure* (1970), where he seems almost frustrated that "no art of words can ever be wholly abstract, in the way that painting and sculpture and music can be. There must always be an identifiable content . . . " (63), that content being centrifugal meaning, an indispensable part of literature, but a part only, which is not to be taken for the whole (1971/ 1973, 26, 32). Enter the centripetal force of literary convention by way of myth and metaphor, buttressed by the critical response, to guarantee a more accurate apprehension of form and content, *mythos* and *dianoia* in their ideal state of perfect co-existence (1957, 83).

It is Frye's attitude toward the dangers of centrifugal meaning as the not-literary that connects the censorship problem most intimately to the response problem. As we shall see more fully in the next chapter, his caution about literary experience and the participating response as such account for the spatialization of both literature and response to literature in his theory. "Linear time," he writes in 1949, "is not an exact enough category to catch literature" (10); and so he takes as his model for literary art other art forms, which are more readily discernible as separate from ordinary existence. The architectural motif of the stubborn structure reifies literature into a "frozen . . . simultaneous pattern" (1972, 4); the musical one hankers after a different language, more like "the sounds of violins and pianos." The Word as formal structure, then, is what saves the poet from resembling the "composer who has to make his [sic] symphony out of street noises" (1963c, 93).

Frye's flight from truth-of-correspondence spawns a view of Logos, the Word, as a giant fugue, a kind of literary counterpoint in which the logical structure of the interrelationships must be visibly spread out in space as well as experienced in time before they can really be instantiated in the reader's mind; that is, the reader only *really* reads once the sequential ordering of the images and conventions within which the narrative is perceived (1965a, 26). This subordination of time to space is echoed in Frye's conception of response (which we examine more closely in the next chapter) with the result that the direct or engaged response becomes instrumental to the "visual scholarship" of literary criticism (1965a, 22), so indispensable in Frye to the reader's perceiving literature as the centripetal organization of inward linguistic meaning. (See my Chapter 10 for another perspective on Frye's approach to centripetal meaning.)

Can the stubbornness of Frye's structure win out against the stubbornness of the Peterborough censors? In order to answer this question, it's necessary to see Frye's order of words within the context of the response problem and its application to the Peterborough case. Here the similarity between this censorship attempt and others comes together in the sour milk metaphor. As mentioned earlier, one of the strategies most often recommended by apologists for particular works, especially by advocates of the educated imagination, is to exhort objectors to read the entire book before it is condemned. But this advice is usually of little help because it presupposes a reading stance that suspends value judgments, something censors come to the text not willing to do. A plea to read the whole book is really one for literary context, which entails a commitment to the logical priority of the critical response of the educated imagination. This, in turn, is a rejection of truth-of-correspondence and belief in "direct communication" in favor of language as "indirect communication," as a constellation of verbal symbols whose meaning is multiple, indeterminate, and polyvalent, where the text is not seen as mystically expressive of certain kinds of truths or values but as Frye's stubborn structure of myth and metaphor, which both says and does not say, which, in Sidney's turn of phrase, "figure[s] forth" (1966, 25) but "nothing affirms" (52).

Yet, as Frye has already said with respect to Shelley's *Defence of Poetry*, simply to assert this belief "is not likely to convince anyone in need of convincing" (1963a, 8). Moving from the former to the latter model entails a radical transformation of consciousness unlikely to be undergone by someone who is certain that a dirty book is a dirty book is a dirty book. When this kind of change does occur, it must be prefaced by the moral predisposition[6] to resist resistance to knowing (Moffett, 1988). Examples of this sort of radical alteration of vision did occur in Peterborough. In 1976, the Chair of the first Textbook Review Committee confessed his need for study and basic guidance in reading differently, and in the 1985 debacle, a community representative stressed the importance of looking " 'at our own inhibitions before criticizing' " (quoted in Czarnecki, 1985, 190). This augurs well for at least the possibility of being educated into regarding literary works not as guides to life, but as moving, powerful hypotheses about life, as meditations rather than as poetic depictors of moral propositions, in short, as a stubborn structure, to be read and studied critically.

Besides providing a model in general for handling the censorship problem, Frye's stubborn structure also manages to avoid the pitfalls of adopting censors' premises in writing defenses of particular works. Here Shelley serves as a prototype for subverting the truth-of-correspondence values of a Thomas Love Peacock. Refuse to negotiate on the opponent's terms. Yet this position may be unrealistic. Teachers may feel they have no other choice than to argue their case on moral grounds if they are to be heard by the other side, particularly when the ethical domain is invoked in justifying literature in the curriculum to begin with. A further difficulty lies with the fact that, while the literary critical background of the best-qualified literature teachers would normally work against a narrow truth-of-correspondence between literary works and moral and social values, increasingly nonspecialists are teaching English; and neither group, specialist or nonspecialist, is helped much by the educational administration, who often want only some do's and don'ts for parents' night. A clear sense of the epistemology of literary creation and response rarely finds its way into educational documents; as a result, the professional mandate of English teachers seems to demand that they accept a simplistic version of truth-of-correspondence. Consider, for example, this directive from the 1977 *Guideline of the Ontario Ministry of Education*. Teachers are to "encourage the use of language and literature *as a means by which* the individual can explore personal and societal goals and acquire an understanding of the importance of such qualities as initiative, responsibility, respect, precision, self-discipline, judgement, and integrity in the pursuit of goals" (7, emphasis added). It's not surprising that, given the claims of the justification question, the literature curriculum is then seen in terms of its capacity for role-modeling virtue. It's also perfectly reasonable that when a novel is met with allegations of profanity, blasphemy, and pornography, its apologist should attempt to meet the moral objections by falling back on the value component thought to reside *in* the work. The Peterborough English head who wrote the 1985 defense of Laurence's *The Diviners* (1974) deliberately downplayed *literary* values and organized his rationale around the three areas of *moral* concern, "language, religion, and sex," that precipitated the outcry against its use in the schools (Buchanan, 1985).

Attempting to rebut this line of argument brings the meta-problem clearly into view; for the principles of the stubbornness of literary structure as the unsayingness of literature, the distinction between literature and life, and the notion of the autonomous reader intersect most prominently in the actual teaching of literature. And with the reader-response model in the ascendant (Probst, 1988), the actual teaching of literature favors the proximity between literature and life. If, for example, the realism of the Laurence novel were to be confronted not as a "slice of life," but as genre, as a form of literary artifice with its own built-in literary conventions and intentions, it would constitute as sure a separation from life as, say fantasy or science fiction. However, with the current emphasis on the direct, participating response, realism tends not to be taught as "a structure of imagery with conceptual implications" (Frye, 1957, 136). Often, realistic works serve simply as so much fodder for life skills within a pedagogy that elevates emotional engagement with the text (as though literary characters and events are "real" people living in the "real" world) over the study of them as confections of words that are literally "made up." (See Chapters 8 and 9 for my defense of literary engagement.) Witness the adolescent fiction industry devoted to just this endeavor. The goal of emotional identification is reinforced by the myth of the student as a genuine "primitive,"[7] that is, one who apprehends with the directness of "unmediated" experience (Frye, 1967, 95), whose "free," "open," "spontaneous," precritical response is seen to be authentic and unprescribed because it is liberated from prepackaged, teacher-imposed interpretations and uncontaminated by the study of literary structure. Frye rightly regards such a "primitive" as a metaphor only for the "pure" respondent, uncontaminated by centrifugal meaning or a knowledge (either intuitive or self-consciously learned) of the conventions underlying centripetal meaning.

We know that no reader, or reading, can be innocent in that way, and here is where the censorship and response problems fold into the justification problem. Enthusiasts of the educated imagination might argue that one of the most worrisome ramifications of the "response model" of literature education is the potential, and sometimes real, collapse of the distinction between literature and life. Some would take the position that when that distinction goes unheeded in the teaching of values and literature, we are dangerously close to believing that the literary text is a Rorschach test that will elicit all the "right" human values in its readers. I don't want to misrepresent my position here. I applaud reader response in the classroom and base my defense of literature education on the presupposition that literary experience is a form of real experience (Chapters 6 through 10). And, I'm not arguing "on the side" of the censors in the Peterborough debate. I judge their assumptions about the reading process, the educational value and function of literature, and their relationship to education in general to be misguided. But I think they're right about the potential for words to wound. Here I have deliberately tried to erode the boundaries of the very notion of "sides" to problematize these issues. So long as anti-censorship educators also think of literature and values in terms of truth-of-correspondence and centrifugal meaning only, there is no epistemo-literary solution to the sour milk metaphor. To be sure, the censorship of literature texts is a political issue which must be resolved in the political domain; however, establishing that literary texts work *on* readers indirectly in various and unpredictable ways, ways that can influence for good but also for ill, at least in terms of immediate effects, would seem to be a clarification crucial to both "sides."

## The Problem with the Educated Imagination and the Censorship Problem

Frye's conception of literature as the stubborn structure cannot wholly resolve the censorship problem because the underlying principle of the censorship problem, the issue of whether and what literature says—the logical status of literature as that which "nothing affirms" (Sidney, 1966, 52)—is compromised by the underlying principle of the justification problem, that is, the transfer value assumed to be operating from literature to life. Hopes for a smooth resolution of the censorship problem are further hindered by the legitimation of literary experience as real experience promised by reader-response theory and pedagogy, which espouses the educational value of engagement on its own terms. How can we insist, on the one hand, that an engaged response will alter lives for the better and, on the other hand, that critical detachment is necessary to ensure that students will not be co-opted by moral dicta deemed deleterious? Philosopher of education James Gribble (1983) recognizes this double bind and is willing to sacrifice engagement and *its* claims for moral improvement on the altar of detachment and *its* claims for moral neutrality. Gribble is content to risk "some form of aestheticism [through detachment] rather than to allow that a great work of literature ... could be viewed in such a way that it (or what it 'presents') could legitimately be rejected in the light of a moral code" (155).

I am not so content; neither, I think, are literature teachers and researchers who believe in literature's potential for human development; but neither was the author of the brief from Renaissance Peterborough. To assert that language does not operate as a transparent window on reality through which we look at life and to claim that verbal constructs always mediate personal experience is not to deny the emotional impact and imaginative appeal of literature. Plato was right in his claim that poetry does influence—and powerfully. That inhabiting other lives and other worlds vicariously can contribute to psychic growth, that readers knit up what is otherwise unknown through a powerful naming, conjuring, fabricating of fictional persons, places, and events, is an educational reality to be affirmed in any defense of literature. But cognitive and emotional development is inherently subversive to unexamined belief, whether it be fundamentalist or liberal-humanist; for psychic growth entails some loss of certitude in what is being grown out of. When that developmental process is fueled by the literary imagination, there are no guarantees as to what may be brought to consciousness. Minds that become activated tend to activate themselves; once the lion has been awakened, there is no putting it back to sleep. The production of independent thinkers as an educational goal can be a real threat to parents and citizens who are deeply ambivalent about the power of autonomous thought to seduce youth away from traditional moral codes. This fear has, of course, been paramount in censorship incidents but not regarded as something to be taken seriously by humanist beliefs in the inalienable right to know, to speak, and to express—all those tenets of liberal philosophies of education many of us have been conditioned to accept uncritically and to apply indiscriminately and abstractly. One of these is that the psychic pain undergone in literary experience is a necessary though "innocent" evil in the pursuit of a "disinterested" knowledge. In later chapters (6, 8, and 9) I challenge this view in terms of what I will call "the feeling, power, and location problems."

Where does all this leave us with respect to the censorship problem? The major challenge of Renaissance Peterborough, in my view, was for teachers of literature to confront the politics of engagement. This means rendering problematic Frye's stubborn structure as "the answer" to the censorship problem. The merits of the stubborn structure in addressing this problem are its contributions to the notion of literariness as polysemous or multivalent meaning. The limitation of the stubborn structure as a metaphor for literature is its denial that texts can in any way influence for ill. According to the dictates of the educated imagination, rather than a closed mirror on reality that leads the passive reader down a predetermined garden path to a set of beliefs or actions, the literary text *by virtue of its literariness* as a stubborn structure is of itself silent, but open to thousandfold interpretations. These manifold interpretations of literature accommodate the imperative for sympathetic identification so essential to psychic and spiritual growth, but they also transcend that imperative. Students do learn as they identify; that is why English educators value literature's capacity for engaging the reader in transformation. Readers do apprehend fictional worlds as if they were true and real. To deny this is to deny the experience of anyone who has been literally entranced by a book (Chapter 7). But this polysemy endemic to literary texts, by invoking the hypothetical dimension, also interrogates the very reality those texts appear to reflect. As constructed artifacts, literary texts invite the reader to make "What if?" speculations about life. Identification as a form of psychological projection is inseparable from literary knowing engendered by emotional engagement with the text, but so is withdrawal of that projection through critical detachment. That is why students need both the experience of literature as life and the aesthetic awareness that distances literature from life. The enjoyable reading of literature and the study of its craft, historicity, and ideology does give with one hand and take away with the other. But it is just this capacity of literary language to work against itself that justifies its educational significance as perhaps the best pedagogical tool we have for both individual growth and social criticism.

Yet, as stated earlier, reconceptualizing literature as open text, as hypothesis rather than as moral model, does not *itself* do away with the problem of literature as indoctrination, as the Renaissance Peterborough document (1977) shows so trenchantly. Teachers may claim that reading and studying literature confers upon the student the power of moral choice by virtue of its capacity for widening perspectives, for increasing the range of possibilities that are disclosed by literature; but there is a problem here, too. Certain kinds of literature do stake out certain conceptual and emotional territories. We cannot live what we cannot imagine. That is why, for example, feminists seek to redress the scandalous under-representation of writing about and by women in the curriculum (Chapters 6 and 8). It is not just that they want to launch an affirmative action program in social conditioning; it is that they seek to bring to consciousness "possible forms of organization for experience" (Stierle, 1980, 103) disallowed by patriarchy and the male authorial voice.

If it is admitted that certain texts tend to define certain kinds of possibilities for belief and action, then what must also be recognized is the fundamentalists' complaint that students are a captive audience in a prescribed literature curriculum where the possibilities are defined and delimited by a central authority. English teachers can profit from the censors' charge of book selection as book censorship by acknowledging that the truly educational value of engagement with the text brings with it a demand for a plurality of literary genres, themes, styles, and authors. Whether language theorists and literary critics have discredited truth-of-correspondence or not, many, if not most, readers (and writers) assume its existence when they read for the pleasure of entering a fictional world (Chapter 7). To submit to the artistic manipulation of an author is to adopt, at least for purposes of the fiction, the moral dimension out of which it is wrought (Bogdan, 1990b, 1990c, 1990e). That Morag Gunn's spiritual quest is "true," "moral," and "religious" is not determined by but is bound up with the degree to which readers can identify with liberal, Christian, largely middle-class values. Even though readers may transform their values in the reading process, the grounds of that transformation are at least in part set up by the text. Thus it would seem that the more varied the texts, the broader the base of identification, and the greater the likelihood that literary experience will eventuate in a balanced view of the world. Providing a plurality of literary texts, then, exonerates teachers from charges of subliminal ideological seduction without impeding literature's function in furthering individual growth, but it does not solve the problem of the power differential, that some groups in this "plurality" are less equal than others (Chapter 6); nor does it solve the problem of whether and how literature says things. Giving students the option to read an alternative text may solve the short-term censorship situation, but it only reinforces the censorship problem by conceding that words not only mean but act directly on readers in specific ways. Once this is admitted, we are into the meta-problem.

As we have seen, defenses of literature in the curriculum sometimes tend to downplay literature as language *art*, as the apotheosis of nonliteral, ambiguous meaning, as indirect communication in order to meet censors on their own terms. In the Peterborough censorship crisis, however, one of the novels, J.D. Salinger's *Catcher in the Rye* (1951), was defended on just this basis of its linguistic indirection. By focusing on the *language art* of the depiction of Holden Caulfield, the apologia argues, students are taught a lesson in the value of literary criticism as a life skill. English teacher E.P. McAuley writes:

> We can see . . . in our consideration of the book that language consists of far more than its literal meanings, that it is replete with social and other connotations which must be taken into account by those who would be truly proficient communicators. In this way, the book offers many excellent opportunities for investigating the extent to which meaning is determined as much by context and tone as by the content of what is communicated. Thus, students may come to understand that, in the final analysis, effective communication requires a considerable sensitivity of spirit and flexibility of mind. (1985)

The appeal to context, indirection, and nuanced interpretation in this apologia avoids the argument that literature directly inculcates values. Instead it makes claims for literature as cultivating a sensibility that entertains many possibilities before making a judgment. Censors would probably tend to see the appeal to literary context as a moral cop-out and "sensitivity of mind and flexibility of spirit" as precisely those qualities that will take their children away from them. I would want to ask whether the ability to suspend belief indefinitely in "the sayingness" of words would mean that content doesn't count, that it doesn't matter what is read. English teachers who are convinced that in "literature as literature" they have "the best subject matter in the world" (Frye, 1988, 10) for the direct communication of unmediated experience may be distressed by deflecting attention away from literary experience itself to awareness of the construction of that experience. This, they might feel, as I argue in Chapter 7, would reduce claims for the uniqueness of literature's educational power to instruct through the sheer delight of the illusion of transparency. They might also resist the thought that the literariness of a text might, can, and sometimes should be depoeticized by treating it as a "tract rather than as a poem and seek to ban it" (Purves, 1991, 216) as a *poem*.

The very idea that the imaginative vision of "literature as literature" can be refused by de-poeticizing it, by treating it as a sociological document in the way Renaissance Peterborough has done, is anathema to the ethos of the educated imagination. But the fact remains that, once we admit the double effect of literary textual power, moves to insulate against the results of that power take a number of forms, of which censorship and self-censorship are regarded as negative; and other types of critical response entailed in the self-conscious study of literature, such as historicizing, gender analysis, and deconstruction, are regarded as positive. All work to temper the psychic intensity of "pure" positive engagement. Thus the same mechanism—literary criticism—can act as a mitigating influence in the justification problem by balancing the emotions in the transfer of energy from literature to life and in the censorship problem, by assuaging the fears of those who revere the power of the literary text to say things they would rather not hear.

An apt example of the latter occurred in the 1990 petition by a black father in Plano, Texas, to have *The Adventures of Huckleberry Finn* removed from the curriculum, this despite the efforts of "the school district to hire an English professor at the University of North Texas to show teachers how to present Huck with sensitivity" ("Tom and Huck," 1990, C8). We can think of this action on the part of the educational community as an exercise in applied literary criticism within the context of attenuating strong literary experience (in this instance, offended sensibilities). Though the action was politically successful in retaining the novel on the curriculum, the sentiments expressed by David Perry, the objecting citizen, illustrate perfectly what in Chapter 6 I call "the mortification of feeling" aspect of the debate, and that is the power of literary naming to influence for ill, at least in the short-run, thus reconfirming Plato's insights about the double effect of the literary text. This is a problem that, in the Plano, Texas, case, still remains even though the ensuing "dialogue" that took place in the community was beneficial. For Perry and those like him, however, who refuse to have their feelings legislated for them, there is doubt that the "teaching with sensitivity" approach is the answer. Perry has what in Chapter 5 I will refer to as a feeling problem, a power problem, and a location problem with the sayingness of literature; here Frye's anagogic perspective of the order of words simply cannot address the ill effects of a string of certain kinds of words for some people some of the time. As Perry asserted, "When someone assumes they can teach the word 'nigger' in a way that is not offensive, I have a problem. It can't be done. . . . The word has a searing effect that just goes to the soul of a black person. By its very nature and design it is intended to be extremely offensive, take away your identity and destroy your soul." A better step toward sensitizing students, he suggested, would be for the school district to recognize February as Black History Month and conduct appropriate programs ("Tom and Huck," 1990, C8).

If the feeling, power, and location problems are taken seriously as real problems, that is, if we recognize that the conditions under which literature influences matter, for ill and for good, the above example represents a blow not only to the resolution of the censorship problem but to the justification problem as well. For what is reinforced in this incident is the limited power of literature to deal with the social inequalities of racism, sexism, and classism, which any theory of fictional representation necessarily invokes by purporting to say something about the relationship between word and world, a relationship made flesh when real readers read real texts and literary experience is validated as real experience.

Readers who were hoping for an "answer" in the censorship problem will be disappointed in these pages. Yet I cannot foresee a respite from the laborious, thorny, and unrelenting grind of rationalizing to censors and potential censors our existence as literature teachers. Nor do I have a great deal of confidence that the "solution" to teach works "critically" is wholly tenable or viable (see Chapters 6, 7, and 8). But one thing seems clear: we cannot employ a double-standard of invoking one set of arguments when English teachers' values are at stake, and another set when those who are "other" have opposing values. We cannot be satisfied with blanket assumptions about the power of literature to instruct with delight by reason of its appeal to the non- or suprarational, and then be indignant when censors claim that the very efficacy of that kind of elemental appeal can be influential in ways that they do not approve. Thinking about the censorship problem in terms of the meta-problem might work to erode the chauvinism of educational values that remain uncritiqued.

I acknowledge that the Peterborough example of the defense of Laurence's *The Diviners* (1974) can be construed as misrepresenting the various premises teachers actually use to defend what books they teach. Dependence upon truth-of-correspondence is not always the norm in writing apologias for individual works, to be sure. One need only consult the NCTE handbooks that offer rationales for a host of novels used in schools to discover that literary integrity, historical and social context, multiple readings, and ironic stance, for example, serve to confront the censorship problem for many teachers. But, as we shall see in Chapter 6, these rationales, taken together, do not solve the censorship problem because their premises beg the question of the three main principles of the meta-problem: the relationship between literature and life, whether and what literature says, and the autonomous reader.

The controlling rubric of most rationales against censorship derives from the educated imagination. In the statement below, English teachers are deemed to have the best subject matter in the world, as well as an inalienable right to teach what they love most:

> The English language arts teachers who wrote these rationales teach
> a book because the book has literary value, because students can
> understand it, because students will be led from that book to others,
> because the book's point of view bears upon democratic and Amer-
> ican values, and because the teachers love books. Now some may
> say that the teacher's love of the books constitutes a sort of preju-
> dice—an indoctrination of the teacher's values, but I say we'll be in
> a pretty putrid pickle if we condemn teachers for loving what they
> teach. (Shugert, 1983, 4)

Also, literature is thought to influence for good but not for ill, and the
reader's response is intrinsically educational:

> The best antidote I know to fictional ideas that seem distorted or
> contrary to community standards is more fiction reading, more
> experiencing of the world through other created characters' eyes
> because the balance will inevitably be found. . . .
>
> In real life, books confirm or fail to confirm the view of the
> world we already have. If they fail to confirm, they give us food for
> thought if we are inclined toward thought; they are rejected out
> of hand if we are not. I think it hardly needs to be said that in
> most instances information that doesn't fit the world a child—or
> adult—already knows is simply discarded. . . .
>
> Thought, even painful thought . . . that calls into question basic
> attitudes and values, is the very cornerstone of a democratic society.
> (Bauer, 1985, 119)

The above reflects the principles of the educated imagination. My
concern is neither to approve nor to reject them, but to reconsider
them in light of their being contingent upon espousing a worldview
that is itself blinkered by the very brilliance of the light radiating
from two thousand years of efforts to prove that Plato was not right.
To look again, by asking whether and why he may not have been
right, has been my purpose in presenting the contribution of the
Peterborough debate within the context of the meta-problem. By
Plato "being right," I don't mean that artistic creativity or the freedom
to read and to know should be curtailed by a central authority. I mean
that the personal and social context that surrounds literary reading is
not neutral, and that the bias inherent in knowledge, particularly
literary knowledge, which does shape and is shaped by the real lives
of real readers reading, is something that cannot be easily dismissed.

# Endnotes

1. See Selwyn R. Cudjoe, (1989). In a symposium, four interlocutors discussed "the Rushdie affair" from different points of view. The first speaker,

Sunil Sethi (1989), a non-Muslim Pakistani fellow at Harvard, acted as a kind of literary character witness for Rushdie, extolling Rushdie's office as hierophantic poet of Islam, who in *Midnight's Children* (1981) had awakened it into racial consciousness, and now was performing the same function by simply waking it up to its own reality. The second speaker, Ansori M. Nawawi (1989), a Muslim expatriate and Visiting Professor at Wellesley, pleaded for "common sensitivity" to the unavoidable difference of the Muslim culture from Western culture, which "cannot be privately religious and publicly secular" (10, 11). This speaker indicted Rushdie for the propositional content of the work, which he said was not critique but hate literature. The third, Larry Rosenwald (1989), a Professor of American literature specializing, interestingly enough, in the Transcendentalist poet Emerson, challenged the Western privileging of freedom of expression, but in the end rescued Rushdie on the premises of Western literary criticism. The whole debate, he averred, is a problem of undecidability, heightened by "the intertwined notions of literary indeterminacy and human fallibility" (14). For Rosenwald, the real issues are epistemological, having to do with the nature of representation, the moral responsibility of the artist, and so on. The "literariness" of the work, he asserted, prohibits categorizing it as blasphemous. "It is not that I cannot understand the outrage with which the philological conjectures are met; rather, that the outrage rests on a particular sense of certainty that I find repellent" (15). The final paper was presented by Cudjoe, an Assistant Professor of Black Studies at Wellesley, who took a political stance premised on the distinction between the sacred and the profane, a question, he says, that hopelessly separates East and West with respect to the logical and ontological status of the Word. According to Cudjoe, Rushdie knowingly conflated his dual subject positions within the sacred and the profane, using his location as a Western *literatus* to escape responsibility for inciting Muslim religious indignation that would inevitably result from any attempt to separate word from world. See D.F. Mullin (1990).

2. In a recent letter to the editor in *off our backs*, a feminist newspaper, a reader wrote to cancel her subscription. The reason was that the images and language on the cover offended her parents. The cover showed a photograph of feminist Gulf war protesters holding a sign which read, "Fighting for Peace is like fucking for virginity" (*off our backs*, xxi, 2, Feb. 1991). The reader's parents requested that she no longer receive the journal. She wrote, "On the one hand, I wish the covers . . . were less controversial so that I could receive the newsjournal without experiencing paranoia and in this case, blatant oppression. On the other hand, I am angry with myself for wanting to let the oppression work" (Minter, 1991, 26). The writer of this letter is suffering from what in Chapter 6 I'll call a "feeling, power, and location problem."

3. Since 1985 there has been relatively little activity in the Peterborough area concerning censorship. However, in opposition to the Heads of English in Waterloo County, Ontario, late in 1986 that Board of Education complied with parental concerns to shift *The Merchant of Venice* from grades 9 and 10 to grade 12 (Schmalz, 1986).

4. "Because puritan moralizing was the source of the attack on poetry which Sidney sought to counter, it is logical that, as Madeleine Doran points out, 'the poets and lovers of poetry therefore were bound to conduct their defence on the ground chosen by the attackers'" (Doran, 1964, qtd. in Connell, 1977, 40).

5. Cf. "Students should read extensively from a wide variety of literature . . . " (Ontario Ministry of Education, *English curriculum guideline: Intermediate and senior divisions, grades 7–12*, 1987, 17).

6. In illustrating this moral predisposition, Frye gives the example of what it means to change from being a bad driver to becoming a good driver (1982a, 108–109). As in the joke about how many psychiatrists it takes to change a lightbulb, you really have to want to change.

7. In writing this in 1991, I note the racist overtone of this expression, with its connotation of the exotic Other (see Chapters 8, 9, and 10).

# Chapter Five

# The Educated Imagination and the Response Problem

## The Response Problem, the Meta-Problem, and Educational Policy

In the last chapter we looked at the censorship problem as virtually unresolvable without appealing to the wider context of the meta-problem, and we ended that chapter with the observation that defenses of individual works tend to be written under the assumptions of the educated imagination and its controlling ethos—that literature influences for good but not for ill. The basis for that claim, the ideal of the autonomous reader who can readily distinguish between appearance or literary convention and reality, thus preserving the distinction between literature and life, forms the crux of the response problem. Before getting into the theory and practice comprising Northrop Frye's conception of literary experience and response, let's first look at some assumptions underlying certain recent changes in the way educators have been thinking about response to literature and its relationship to the language arts curriculum. The context for our discussion is the most recent (1987) Ontario Ministry of Education *Guideline* for English, grades 7–12, a fairly typical document.

In some respects, the epistemology of reading and studying literature in the English class now more than ever seems to be the hidden curriculum, not just of what English teachers do once they have closed their classroom doors behind them, but of their ability to defend what they do. The crisis of faith in the educated imagination, whether it is reflected in the changing canon (which seems to be going in two directions at once—shrinking because of overt and covert censorship, and expanding because of affirmative action curriculum)—or the displacement of literature by composition and media studies is part of what I have been calling the meta-problem. That is, any one of the axioms informing the meta-problem (the relationship between literature and life, whether and what literature says, and the autonomous reader), though they can be examined as discrete principles, interlock as interdependent aspects of the why, what, and how of literature education.

As an illustration of this, let me recount an episode that occurred in June of 1988, when, along with several others, I was invited to a "think tank" day at the Ontario Ministry of Education on "Controversial[1] Issues in the Language Arts Curriculum." Each of us was asked to address these three topics:

1. The overarching purposes and values of studying literature in school;

2. Examples of controversial issues that might arise in the course of such study;

3. The identification of strategies/processes that schools and school boards could implement to formulate local policies for addressing such issues.

Instead of attempting to answer the above questions directly, I suggested that whatever answers that might be offered were rendered problematic by the necessity of looking twice at some of the assumptions underwriting "the response model," at least as it is understood by a government bureaucracy trying to keep pace with developments in the theory and practice of literature education.

The Ontario English *Guideline*, mentioned earlier, professes an integrated language arts curriculum, in which the activities of speaking, listening, reading, writing, and viewing reinforce each other to produce the articulate and integrated citizen:

> Students must understand that reading, writing, listening, speaking, viewing, and dramatizing are not subjects in the curriculum, but processes that they use in combination to explore and to extend their abilities to think, to learn, and to communicate. They must understand that processes share prominence in the curriculum with the products of interaction and learning and that the skill and expertise they acquire in carrying out these processes largely determine their success in virtually all school subjects. Thus, in the ideal English or language arts program, students have daily practice in both expressing ideas and interpreting the expressions of others.
>
> Students may read and then discuss their reactions with other students and the teacher. They may write in personal terms about

what they read, hear, or view. They may view a movie based on a
novel or short story and compare the two media. They may even
make their own television documentaries, modelled on samples
viewed in class or at home. Activities such as these, in which
students experience curriculum integration, help students to
mature as learners and to acquire personal tastes in both print and
non-print media. (1987, 23)

The *Guideline* (1987) contains some assumptions about the goals of
*literary* reading, as compared with the goals of other aspects of
English studies, which are useful in addressing the response problem. Engagement with the text as Shelley's direct, suprarational
response to poetry seems now to be the beacon of reading literature
in the schools, as it was for Mr. Keating's students in *Dead Poets
Society*. Literature is neither a body of knowledge to be regurgitated
on examinations, nor a stubborn structure to be dissected, but a powerful means of furthering psychic growth and communicating values.
A rhetorical analysis of Ontario *Guideline* statements about the educational value of *literature* as distinct from that of the media, for
example, discloses a certain polarization between the vocabulary of
engagement and that of detachment. Both the sections on literature
and media literacy include the goals of enjoyment, understanding,
and appreciation; but statements on media literacy stand alone in
stressing evaluation and the processes of production. As requisites of
being "visually literate" (19),

> students need to understand what the media convey, how they
> convey it, and the effects of the media and their messages on peo-
> ple's lives. (3)

And,

> media literacy requires basic knowledge of the *language* of
> vision. . . . colour, shape, composition, line, light, texture, pattern,
> framing, movement, and juxtaposition constitute a *grammar* for
> understanding and discussing the relative merits of media images.
> (19, emphasis added)

Here, the educational establishment discloses no anxiety about
the potential alienating effects of distancing students from their personal responses to "media literature," if we can use that term. It seems
that, when it comes to images, critical detachment poses no threat to
individual enjoyment or psychic growth. What is stressed is the
importance of making students "conscious of their viewing habits"
and "acquiring skills and knowledge that will assist them in managing their own lives in . . . 'the information age' " (19). In short,
the philosophy of response to media aims at instilling a healthy

scepticism about the illusion of direct communication underlying these images. Students of media studies are to learn to become circumspect about visual images as a transparent medium of self-evident truths or universal values presumed to be transmitted in unmediated form from creator to audience. They are to learn, presumably, that the "message sent" should not necessarily be the "message received." The *Guideline*, however, contains no comparable statement on "literary literacy."

This emphasis on critical detachment and the cognitive domain in media literacy is echoed in the section on "Reading," where students are to be *instructed* in the ways of "functional" comprehension: they must be shown how to navigate their way toward meaning (1987, 17). Similarly, the section on language study stresses the importance of rhetorical sophistication as a life skill. "English usage is, in part, a matter of recognizing and conforming to the expectations in our society that different forms of language are appropriate in different contexts" (20). Clearly, then, the educational values here are those of critical consciousness—distance, analysis, detachment.

When it comes to reading literature, however, it is as though Shelley has never died. Making one's way through selected texts, it seems, is intrinsically educational, as it was in *Dead Poets Society*. Replacing the language of critical consciousness in the Ontario *Guideline* is a manifesto of literary engagement, a communication model writ large, one which, if mapped on to the "right" texts, purports to produce a citizenry with the "right" values—nationalism, pluralism, and humanism. Literary literacy, we find, is quite different from media literacy or functional literacy. It's not something consciously taught *for* within the context of its own conventions and grammar, but is, rather, a quasi-automatic by-product of personal response to literary works of art, which have "the power to shape thought and understanding" (1987, 2). This "power" is presumably empowering to students in a beneficial way simply through their engaging with these texts.

The power to shape thought and understanding believed to be entailed in media other than literature, however, is not regarded as intrinsically benign; media studies, for example, have been created as a way of defending against a force that can *undermine* critical consciousness. In the section of the *Guideline* titled "The Centrality of Literature," a passage comprising only 160 words, the word "power" or its cognates is used four times, as though the power of literature is not at all problematic. We read that if students "learn to appreciate the beauty and the power of the written word, they are likely to become lifelong readers," that "Canadian literature is especially powerful," and that the "vicarious experience literature offers is a subtle and powerful force in building the character of a nation and its people" (1987, 2). When it comes to literature, however, textual power is its own justification.

The foregoing suggests that the ideal of the engaged reader is now enshrined in educational policy, and that humanist literary values have become mainstream. Some, perhaps most, would say, "At long last!" Isn't this what every apologist for poetry from Philip Sidney to Northrop Frye has been waiting for? Yes, and no. On the one hand, reading for enjoyment, for the furthering of psychic growth, long neglected by the dogmas of New Critical textualism, has been legitimated as requisite to developing the appreciation and love of literature. Sidney, Shelley, and Frye would have no quarrel with that. On the other hand, the theory of mimetic representation which undergirds what we have come to think of as engagement with the text has been challenged by Shelley and Frye, and by Sidney in his postulate of the fictionalized world as a hypothesis ("the poet, he nothing affirms, and therefore never lieth" [1966, 52])—and, as we recall, by the religious fundamentalists in the Peterborough County censorship case (Chapters 2 and 4). Yet the "fact" of the representational nature of literature is accepted uncritically in the Ministry *Guideline*, a remarkably progressive document in other areas of the language arts. In what appears to be an all-out effort to accommodate the political demands of nationalism and pluralism within the traditional liberal-humanist mandate of literature education—to integrate enculturation with self-transformation—the Ontario document encapsulates the humanist credo that the power of literature can influence for good but not for ill, with which we began this book and this chapter. Is there any way out of this circularity?

The Ontario Ministry position on literary response is vulnerable to attack from the political left and right. Parents, politicians, and educational bureaucrats are beginning to confront the meta-problem themselves by asking what literature is for and why we should study it. They seem to know what they like and are prepared to fight for its inclusion or exclusion in the curriculum, if we can judge by the complaints from parents that flood the Ministry daily about offerings in the literature curriculum, complaints that range from objections to stories by Robert Munsch for teaching kindergarten children disrespect for authority to objections to Mordechai Richler's *The Apprenticeship of Duddy Kravitz* (1959) for teaching anti-semitism (Richler, 1990).

An engagement model of literature education is open to allegations of indoctrination, irrelevance, or redundancy posed by those who would interrogate the effects of the power of literature as "innocently" empowering to the student. As we've said already, it is precisely because literature as engagement *is* so powerful that it is transformative and subversive to the *status quo*. English teachers have always known this and have been happy about it. It is what prompts Frye to call literature "the best subject matter in the world" (1988, 10). Parents know it, and some are not happy about it. When engagement comes first, the literature class can be somewhat like a time-bomb for those who see this literary power as too liberating, on the one hand, or indoctrinatory, on the other.

The place of literature in the curriculum has traditionally been justified precisely on the presupposition of its transformative power. But, as we saw in the case of Peterborough County, change begets change. When parents object to unforeseen consequences of transformation, educators can become hoisted on their own humanist petard and the double-edge of the power of poetry becomes Sidney's sword that "mayst kill thy father," instead of that which "mayst defend thy prince and country" (1966, 55).

I'm suggesting that the Ontario *Guideline* aims to insure that the literary sword defends the country instead of slaying the father by appropriating the transformative effects of personal engagement to political purposes, and that it does so through what is essentially a transmission model of literary response. This transmission model reinforces the assumption that literature is a reflection of life with which students identify through personal response to certain truths it conveys, with the expected outcome that readers will emerge from the literary encounter as better people. (Recall the Robert Fulford address in Chapter 3.) But, in the *Guideline* statement, this transformative function devolves on a curiously mechanistic psychology of response and a monolithic conception of the literary work as an artifact that represents a moral guide to life. (We saw this theory co-opted by Renaissance Peterborough in Chapter 4.) While it is true that the *Guideline* advises that these pictures of the world must be manifold, rich, and complex (as befits a pluralistic society), it regards literature as foundational—not necessarily to world citizenship but primarily to Canadian culture because of literature's power to "say." "Literature is an inspiring record of what men and women have enjoyed or endured, have done, and have dreamed of doing" (1987, 2). Students should both be exposed to this record (they must "see men and women in a variety of roles, exhibiting a wide range of human behaviour, abilities, and emotions" [2]) and be open to the vicarious experience literature affords as "a subtle powerful force in building the character of a nation and its people.... The creation and dissemination of Canadian literature can lead to increased understanding among our many peoples by establishing a deeper appreciation of one another's experiences" (2). The tone and sentiment of this statement reflects the "universal" ideal of Shelley's empathic imagination (Chapter 2), at the same time that it is designed to transmit the cultural value of pluralism.

The Ontario *Guideline* couches the act of reading literature in the rhetoric of engagement, cultural identity, and the psychologizing of aesthetic experience. In the section titled "Reading," the focus of developing "functional readers" is cognitive. By contrast, *literary* reading is grounded in a form of affect, upon which critical skills are to be developed as a way of equipping students to participate in the culture, what in my Chapter 7 is called "literacy as a state of grace":

> Students . . . should read extensively from a wide variety of litera-
> ture. They should read for understanding and enjoyment, and for
> development of personal tastes. . . . and should begin to develop
> skills of literary criticism (still based on personal response) that
> they can use to come to a deeper appreciation of their literary
> heritage.
>
> Skills in text analysis should develop naturally from the chal-
> lenge of trying to understand literature and to share that under-
> standing with others. . . . It is in this sense that analysis of literature
> is part of the English or language arts curriculum in the Intermedi-
> ate and Senior Divisions. (1987, 17)

What, we may respond, can be wrong with such a statement? Isn't this the embodiment of Louise Rosenblatt's (1978) definition of aesthetic reading, in which students are to live through the experience of literature, coupled with Northrop Frye's ideal of the educated imagination? Again, yes and no. It is certainly Rosenblattian in its emphasis on aesthetic experience as instrumental to individual psychic growth, a concept articulated earlier in the *Guideline* through a self-expressive theory of art. Here we find that "[a]rtistic expression involves the clarification and restructuring of personal perception and experience," and that by personal response and the sharing of "thoughts, ideas, and feelings . . . students clarify and restructure their own experiences with, and perception of, artistic endeavour and, in the process, develop unique personal responses to the arts" (6).

The Ontario *Guideline* makes the determination that, psychologically and pedagogically, analysis or detachment should *follow* engagement ("the skills of literary criticism . . . [should be] based on personal response"). I would argue that this foregrounding of direct response and the emphasis on shared vicarious experience through literature signifies a position in which direct response is logically prior to the critical response. As stated earlier, this is a position I espouse in my theory of the re-educated imagination, which attempts to put response first and politicize it at the same time. My point here, however, is that Frye's conception of the educated imagination espouses the logical priority of the critical response; that is, the purpose of response is to serve interpretation which, as it becomes more refined and subtle, feeds back into the next encounter with the text. The main difference between Frye's assumptions and those of the *Guideline* statement is, perhaps, that Frye is less sanguine than the Ontario Ministry of Education about the educational value of aesthetic experience per se. Though Frye has often been quoted in Ontario Ministry of Education English guideline statements over the years to support its liberal-humanist-pluralist mandate, what is not normally acknowledged are his affinities with critical pedagogy theorists, who share with him suspicion of the aesthetic as an end in itself because of its threat to heightened conscious awareness. In the next section of this chapter we'll have a closer look at both the theory and practice of this logical priority of the critical response underwriting the education of the literary imagination. I think that such an exercise is important as a way of illustrating the complexity of the response problem in a pluralistic society. Within the ethos of the educated imagination, literary criticism functions as a conceptual "container" for conflicts generated by engaged responses. But the logical priority of direct response, as it is espoused by "the response model" and the *Guideline* statement, together with the politicization of response, which is described in Chapter 6, make the response problem thorny indeed. Resolving this problem, I believe, requires an understanding of Frye's theory of reader response.

## Literary Response and Frye's Stubborn Structure

Though for Frye literature is a form of secular scripture, in reading it the exegetical or critical function supersedes the liturgical, engaged, or participatory one; literature, then, must be understood as well as undergone.[2] What we might call Frye's "scholarship of the eye," the visual and spatial lucidity of critical consciousness (1965a, 22), is in his view lowered and debased by a fully engaged response (1963c, 123). If art must be "a dream for *awakened* minds" (Frye, 1957, 111, emphasis added), this consciousness must not be risked for "the gambling machine of an ideal [literary] experience" (1971/1973, 29). Consciousness can exact the cost of the attenuation of sheer intensity in literary experience. The engaged reader, untidy and unpredictable, is amenable to, indeed embraces, the admixture of personal experience with the literary object unleashed by the recursive processing of text. For Frye, the engaged reader meanders; the "real" reader, on the other hand, "knows that he [sic] is entering into a coherent structure of experience, and the criticism which studies literature through its organizing patterns of convention, genre and archetype enables him to see what that structure is" (1971/1973, 29). It is this structure, the stubborn one of the order of words, which both says and does not say, upon which Frye's theory of reader response is constructed and which ultimately guides the reader to a state of autonomy as a critical thinker.

As we saw in Chapter 3, this reader-response theory presumes a certain measure of dissociation of sensibility as a fact of reading life, one that cannot be avoided once the critical response takes logical precedence over the participating one. In other words, to be engaged in experience and to be fully conscious of the act of experiencing at the same time is a psychological impossibility. (Overcoming dissociation of sensibility is one of the aims of the re-educated imagination.) Undulating beneath the scattered definitions (throughout Frye's works) of several kinds of response is the observation that the reader habitually oscillates between engagement with the text and detachment from it. Frye insists that, while readers hope for the integration of sensibility that comes from the fusion of intellect and emotion typified by the union of subject and object, they should not *expect* the full Longinian response of *ecstasis*, "the true sublime . . . proud exaltation and . . . sense of vaunting joy" that makes us feel "as though we had ourselves produced" what we have read (Longinus, 1965, 107). Further, to *evaluate* individual works on the basis of their capacity to produce this joy is to submit to "the gambling machine" altogether. In Frye's view, *actual* experience of literary response is more than likely to result in some sort of imbalance of sensibility through a perceptual missing of the mark, one that is precipitated, ironically enough, by aesthetic engagement itself. That is, the very absorption produced by the participating response can tend to work against a full literary response because of the inexorable propulsion of words toward centrifugal or nonliterary meaning. It is thus the role of detachment, by way of literary criticism and aesthetic distance, to function as a kind of corrective vision, ensuring that response is grounded in centripetal or symbolic meaning.

Frye's writings are replete with the supremacy of the critical over the engaged response (see especially Denham, 1978, 189). If "[g]reat literature is indeed what the eye can *see*," as Frye asserts it is in *The Secular Scripture* (1976a, 30, emphasis added), then the critical response is what can successfully contain the wandering images of desire (1976a, 30), the visual clarity of critical consciousness being in fact weakened by a fully engaged response (1963c, 123). In art as a dream for *awakened* minds, where consciousness is all, this consciousness is spatial, not temporal (1957, 111). Therefore the "vaunting joy" (Longinus 1965, 107) of Longinian transport must be subordinated to the visual element of the Aristotelian recognition scene (Aristotle, 1965, 46). Textual engagement is a time-bound state, one easily contaminated by the accidents of human temperament (1963c, 131–32, 145; 1957, 66–67, 326), which can obscure perception of the stubborn structure. For Frye, the fully engaged reader, therefore, is both half-awake and half-asleep. Though Frye's whole aim has been to integrate sensibility through the "possession" of literature, he trusts knowledge rather than experience in achieving it (1963c, 144–145). What we are left with, then, is a kind of schizophrenia of response, at least in logical terms, a severing of the respondent's personality into the critic and the "ordinary" reader who from time to time examines the pointer readings of actual experience (1963c, 123). This split consciousness is wholly consistent with Frye's position on the justification problem and the relationship between literature and life, in which the imagination is that faculty which must be kept *independent* of real experience (my Chapter 3). Part of my purpose in writing this book is to make a case for reversing the logical priority of the critical response—on ontological and ethical grounds as well as psychological and pedagogical ones.

Spatialization of response in Frye is "a monument to a failure of experience" in a fallen world (1971/1973, 27). This view is premised on his reservations about notions such as beauty and pleasure, which rooted as they are in the vagaries of psychologism, and, by extension, centrifugal meaning, can lead to the *uncontrollable* wandering of desire. Here Frye reminds us of the relationship of the response problem to the justification problem in that attainment of autonomy in the literary reader, defined as one who is not unduly influenced by literary experience, depends upon the uncompromising hiving off of literature from life that so characterizes his mythological literary universe. Genuine literary experience, for Frye, is not that of ordinary experience but rather is the synthesis of the aesthetic, the social, and the moral. The " 'aesthetic' attitude," when persisted in, for Frye, "loses its connection with literature as an art and becomes socially or morally anxious" (1970, 82; see also 1957, 347–350; 1963b, 47, 219; 1965b, 97–98, 137; 1971/1973, 169; 1972, 14). Also, beauty's vulnerability to the uncontrollable wandering of desire is primarily sexual and brings "works of art into *direct* competition with girls in bathing suits" (1963c, 138, emphasis original).[3]

Actual readers, then, not only meander, but seek a pleasure dome; and so literary experience is better defined within the realm of the virtual. *Aesthetic* pleasure is normally "of a more muted and disseminated kind," as compared with the joy of the "unattained experience," to which any actual experience inevitably points (Frye 1971/

1973, 28). Directness of apprehension entails the innocence of a prelapsarian universe; mortals must be satisfied with an analogue *only* of that directness in the form of a mechanism for consciousness, specifically, the "structures of reason and imagination" (1971/1973, 31), which guide us, like the lover in Plato's *Symposium*, to a state of absolute identity with Truth, Beauty, and Goodness. For Frye, it is the "third order of experience," that hypothetical world that would make literary criticism redundant, which he describes in the conclusion of virtually every book predating *The Great Code* (1982b; see 1971/1973, 170–171). In the world of linear time, however, individual literary experience must submit to the buffering influence of detachment on engagement. As I said in the last chapter, it is the psychodynamics of cooling out the fevered intensity of "pure" engagement that holds the promise of resolving the censorship problem for both English teachers and would-be censors. The critical enterprise tends to short-circuit the actual effects of words on the world such that word magic can be controlled by those who praise it and those who fear it. In the next section of this chapter we look at how Frye's preference for the critical response can provide a kind of dialectic for interpretive strategies with the possibility of re-integrating sensibility.

## The Educated Imagination and the Autonomous Reader: A Taxonomy of Reader Responses and Respondents[4]

### *Total Form as Stasis*

Let's begin with the movie version of *Educating Rita* (1983), which serves as a graphic example of Longinian *ecstasis*, the model of literary experience that Frye's reader-response theory does *not* espouse (Frye, 1963c, 132). In that film an alcoholic English professor (played by Michael Caine) purports to teach his student Rita, a hairdresser (played by Julie Walters), the techniques of literary criticism. Rita, eager for both literary experience and literary knowledge, comes to her teacher as Frye's "primitive" (1967, 95), one ignorant/innocent of the knowledge of literary convention. During her first forays into literary experience, Rita undergoes a transformation of consciousness, experiencing the full brunt of Longinian *ecstasis*, which for my purposes, I'll call *stasis*. But, lacking the necessary skills, grammar, and vocabulary of criticism, Rita is unable to articulate her experience. In the process of educating Rita to literature, the

English professor chisels her *tabula rasa* squeals of "Wow!" and "Fantastic!" into polished emanations of "lit. crit.," turning his Galatea into a Frankenstein, at least in his view.

Rita's professor longs for a state of imaginative identity with the poetic object typified by the fusion of intellect and emotion in the response of a "genuine primitive." But, within Frye's formulation, Rita can only be a metaphor for the ideal literary experience, which hardly ever occurs. As a *real* student of literature, Rita is as vulnerable as the rest of us to dissociation of sensibility. The very verbalizing of any response to literature, after all, of itself lessens the intensity of the actual experience, and in a sense it is through criticism that we mourn the loss of that intensity. Fredric Jameson reminds us of the "painful 'decentering' of the consciousness" (1981, 283) entailed in literary response. Jameson is wary of the dangers in "nostalgia for the absolute" (Steiner, 1974, 69) when he asserts that "the approach to the Real is at best fitful, the retreat from it into this or that form of intellectual comfort perpetual" (Jameson, 1981, 284).

Rita's state of imaginative identity with the poetic object is what I refer to as "stasis." Stasis can be described as the simultaneous perception and experience of the "total form" of a literary work (Frye, 1957, 115; 1963b, 31), however fleeting that glimpse might be. (Chapters 7 and 8.) Rita's stasis is a phenomenon which literature teachers often aim at but rarely succeed in triggering. Stasis can be thought of as the apotheosis of engagement with the text, its most prominent characteristic being the virtual disappearance of the self-conscious critical faculty. Whatever its cognitive value, stasis resides in the instinctual and instantaneous apprehension of—and union with—the art object in terms of its imaginative and emotional impact. When it does occur, stasis usually takes place unexpectedly and outside the classroom. An intensely personal and private experience perhaps best expressed by silence, it is usually marked by a recession of cognitive faculties and a near paralysis of linguistic powers that succeeds in transcending dissociation of sensibility inasmuch as this kind of response is holistic, though acritical. (For an extended discussion of this see Bogdan [1990b] in Bogdan & Straw [1990], 119–123.)

The kinds of texts which elicit stasis on a first reading are those in which *mythos* (plot) and *dianoia* (theme) are so inextricably intertwined that the reader grasps the work holistically and instantaneously as a "frozen . . . simultaneous pattern" (Frye, 1972, 4). Short stories such as de Maupassant's "The Necklace" have the kind of clear outline that enables the reader to experience a kind of Aristotelian *anagnorisis*, or recognition scene (Aristotle, 1965, 40), fairly readily in a single participating response. Stasis tends to be most intense when the discovery of the "truth" of the situation by the reader coincides with that of the protagonist, and it is usually accompanied by ironic reversal, as in "The Necklace" and other stories modeled on the perfect symmetry of design that we find in *Oedipus Rex* (Aristotle, 1965, 46; Frye, 1963b, 25).

The clearer the outline of a literary work to the respondent, the more likely it is to precipitate stasis; the reason is the importance for literary experience of recognition or discovery as a true shock, itself contingent upon a certain aesthetic distance. That is, while there should be sufficient verisimilitude for the reader to "identify" with the characters, place, and situation (we must, after all, *care* about what happens), there must also be a real sense of separation from the world of routine experience to enable the work to be perceived as an aesthetic artifact, Frye's "alien structure of the imagination" (1970, 77). This point cannot be overstressed in understanding Frye's reader-response theory. For him, to weaken the reader's capacity for *anagnorisis* by underplaying the distinction between literature and life augurs ill in the reading of fiction, for the joy of learning occurs when we compare the imagined construct with the natural reality of "life" (Aristotle, 1965, 35). Within Frye's verbal universe, joy of learning becomes aesthetic pleasure when readers become aware of the differences between literature and life as well as of their similarities. More accurately, readerly pleasure is generated as a consequence of similarity through difference, the difference made by the imposition of literary form on the raw material of life.

Curricular implications of the above would suggest that efforts to select literary works on the basis of their ready appeal to students' "real life" interests, problems, and experience might be misguided. The social relevance of subject matter and a powerful literary response can make strange bedmates, for the sense of difference from life that is primarily responsible for intensity of impact is mitigated by "a subcritical operation based on plausibility or likelihood" (Frye, 1965a, 10) beginning very early in the reading of realistic works. A case in point is John Updike's "A&P" (1962), a story abut a nineteen-year-old grocery clerk who quits his job in protest when three teenage female customers, clad "in bathing suits," are asked by the manager to leave the store.

Stasis is an uncommon literary response in "A&P." In fact, students not only don't respond as Rita did to *Macbeth*, they tend to dislike the story.[5] One of the reasons they do so, I believe, is the close proximity of the story's action and dialogue to that of the average adolescent's "real" experience. Student readers tend either to over-identify with or to be immediately alienated by the snippets of conversation, attitude, and sensibility of the narrator; consequently they perceive the story as unfinished, as "partial form," which we'll discuss shortly. But, as we have seen, stasis depends upon perception of a work as "total form" (Frye, 1957, 115; 1963b, 31), which the realism of "A&P" works against. On the one hand, less experienced readers would become frustrated by the surface incompleteness of the story, simply because, as a story, its formal outline is obscured by the impulse to look for the kind of obvious coincidence of *mythos* and *dianoia* in works like "The Necklace." In "A&P" formal outline is secondary to verisimilitude and identification; and the reader, more apt to be what Douglas Vipond and Russell Hunt (1984) call "story-driven" or "information-driven" rather than "point-driven," often misses the point on a first reading.[6] On the other hand, more seasoned readers will more readily take the point (Sammy's passage from the world of innocence to experience); yet the very critical equipment brought to bear on this discovery can attenuate the element of shock in the act of recognition. That is, the story will be seen as a "structure of the imagination" but one not "alien" to people's everyday lives. As a result, the lightning flash of the recognition scene is less likely to occur. This is not to say that the story fails, but simply to question stasis as a measure of literary value. If the occurrence of stasis decreases in direct proportion to the resemblance of literature to life, and if the realistic mode continues to attract students and teachers of literature, it appears that a model other than the flash of lightning upon which to base our criteria for the selection, evaluation, and teaching of literary texts needs to be developed (see Bogdan, 1990c, 129–133).

## Partial Form, Partial Response

As the apotheosis of engagement with a literary work, stasis represents the intuitive grasp of total form in a kind of acritical reading within a state of consciousness that is half-awake and half-asleep at the same time. Despite its unpredictability and ambiguity in critical and methodological terms, stasis is a psychological state to be prized and luxuriated in—because of the very intensity and sense of the fulfillment of desire that literary criticism defends against—even if it is not directly to be sought after in the classroom. I have already suggested that a neophyte like Rita of the film would perhaps be more open to stasis than seasoned aficionados of the classics, whose knowledge of literary convention can mitigate the impact of a direct response. But respondents who lack expertise at making fine discriminations between literature and life are also more vulnerable to response as partial form, that is, to stock and kinetic responses. While stasis fuses subject with object, invoking the reader's active co-creation of the text, stock and kinetic responses are passive forms of automatic reflex, reinforcing what is already known rather than paving the way for what might be known—stock response with respect to the content of the work, kinetic response with respect to its form.

Within Frye's reader-response theory, stock response operates less as an authentic reaction to a text than as a projection of the reader's moral and ideological "anxieties," which, as we said in Chapter 4, would truncate progression to a full appreciation of total form. In addition, stock response values a work on the basis of the reader's projection onto the content as though one could extract what something says from the way in which it is said. Left to its own teleology, stock response, harmless enough in readers who like *Lord of the Flies* (Golding 1954/1959) because they would like to live alone on a desert island, could end up in a book-burning mob scene. As we recall from the last chapter, stock response "hankers after some form of censorship" because it favors belief rather than understanding (Frye, 1963c, 128).

In general, stock response springs from the inability or refusal to suspend disbelief, from an unwillingness to delay the kind of aesthetic gratification that comes only with the expenditure of effort to perceive total literary form. Within Frye's conceptual framework, it is a knee-jerk reaction in terms of "I like/dislike it" based on value judgments about the truth or falsity of literary statements as though they applied to "real life" and "real people." It is responding to an "aliterary," decontextualized string of words—like the Peterborough censor who cited the sour milk metaphor in Chapter 4—as opposed to Frye's "order of words" (1957, 17; 1970, 102; 1963c, 15, emphasis added). It is response circumscribed by the readily discernible, which Vladimir Nabokov says is appropriate to minor authors (1980, 2) but inappropriate to reader response.

What does stock response look like in the reading of particular texts? As suggested earlier, it is usually grounded in either a deficiency or excess of sympathetic identification. In "A&P," it would be accepting the story as Frye's *"rhetorical analogue* to . . . truth" (1971/ 1973, 66, emphasis original), according to whether Sammy, the narrator, reconfirms or countervails readers' preconceptions about events and attitudes as they remind them of their own experience or reinforce their ideological predilections. Consider, for example, the opening paragraph of the story:

> In walks these three girls in nothing but bathing suits. I'm in the third checkout slot, with my back to the door, so I don't see them until they're over by the bread. The one that caught my eye first was

the one in the plaid green two-piece. She was a chunky kid, with a good tan and a sweet broad soft-looking can with those two crescents of white just under it, where the sun never seems to hit, at the top of the back of her legs. I stood there with my hand on a box of HiHo crackers trying to remember if I rang it up or not. I ring it up again and the customer starts giving me hell. She's one of those cash-register-watchers, a witch about fifty with rouge on her cheekbones and no eyebrows, and I know it made her day to trip me up. She'd been watching cash registers for fifty years and probably never seen a mistake before. (Updike, 1962, 187)

On the one hand, "positive stock responders,"[7] if they are or have been grocery clerks say they can easily "relate to" Sammy's unabashed people-watching; as a result, they tend to delight in his caricatures of his customers and his contempt for the conformity of his dull community. On the other hand, "negative stock responders" take an instant dislike to Sammy, identifying with the objects of his sexism and ridicule—the three girls in bathing suits and the "witch about fifty with rouge on her cheekbones and no eyebrows." Many readers reject the story on the basis of what they consider to be trivial or politically reprehensible content, as though Sammy were the boy next door rather than the author's fictive invention. Often, feminist readers will not read beyond this first paragraph (see Chapter 6). Some can easily become bored because they regard the story as outdated, the details of contemporary life having changed markedly from the 1950s, when "A&P" was written. (Recall from my Introduction Jeremy's reasons for not using "In the Fall," MacLeod, 1976; NFB, 1984).

Whereas stock responders relate literature to life exclusively in terms of their current experience and values, kinetic responders simply want literature to "work" for them on a superficial aesthetic level, as entertainment only. In terms of kinesis, to say that a James Bond thriller induces physiological changes in me is not necessarily to validate it as a literary work of the imagination. If that thriller is a movie, my visceral state probably has more to do with my response to Roger Moore than with the artistry, real or alleged, of the creator of 007. With respect to "A&P," the kinetic responder views its dialogue and characterization as a kind of TV sitcom "imitation of life," deriving pleasure mainly from an uncritical acceptance of Sammy's "comical" sexist and insulting observations. These responses often take the form of remarks such as, "Updike is so true-to-life, isn't he?" and "Aren't 19-year-old boys exactly like that?" (These responses, and those I use subsequently, are not my simulations but actual responses gleaned from the annals of my own college and graduate classes.)

While positive and negative stock responses spring from a faulty sense of sympathetic identification, positive and negative kinetic responses have to do with a limited conception of aesthetic or literary artistry. Negative kinetic responders tend to complain about "A&P"'s supposed formal deficiencies, such as a weak plot ("Nothing really happens; it's kind of stupid"); choppiness ("The story is mindboggling. It jumps from one thing to another a lot"); superfluousness ("There are lots of unnecessary descriptions"); and an "unsatisfying ending" ("[T]he story leaves you out on a limb, and you don't know what happens to the guy that quits, and you don't really find out the girl's reaction to the scene afterwards.").[8] A critical rereading of "A&P" will, in fact, disclose how Updike has meticulously prepared the reader for the final action.

Two rather more subtle forms of kinetic response involve the reader's own complicity in blocking emotional response; these responders would fall into two main categories, the "predictor" and the "ideologue." The predictor's literary knowledge is so self-conscious that it impedes a "full" response by interposing guessing games between the respondent and the text. It is as though a surfeit of reading a particular literary mode or genre prompts the reader to jump the gun on the author. Remarks such as, "Not another Updike ending!" or "All these modern rites of passage stories are ironic!" reveal the somewhat jaded predictor. Here the problem is not that response is insufficiently grounded in the text, but that the text remains a static body of words because the reader's feelings are not open to imaginative engagement. With the stock responder, ordinary experience gets in the way of literary experience; with the predictor, literary knowledge militates against literary experience.

Like the stock responder and the predictor, the ideologue forecloses on a full literary response because of an entrenched mind-set; but here, the barrier against the aesthetic mechanism is constructed by "extra-literary" knowledge or belief systems. A pertinent example of negative response to "A&P" within this category would be feminist objections to Sammy's sexism. More sophisticated than both the stock responder or the predictor, the ideologue avoids both the intellectual capriciousness of the former and emotional anemia of the latter because his/her response is more likely to be informed by both literary knowledge and a conscious act of the will rather than literary naiveté or automatic reflex. (This point will be challenged and explored fully in Chapter 6. Again, this taxonomy is set within the assumptions of Frye's reader-response theory; cf. Applebee [1978]; Thomson [1989].)

The ideologue's major "impediment" to literary response is a kind of circular argument: the awareness that Sammy's moment

of illumination is contingent upon and exploits the uncritical acceptance of sexism as a historical and sociological datum is an informed
response, but one that works against the ideologue's aesthetic pleasure (see Chapter 6). Such comments as, "How typically male!
Sammy's maturation comes at a very high price—the traditional
rescue-operation of Cinderella by Prince Charming!" reflect a high
degree of critical working through of the story; but ultimately it is a
process which, rather than pushing back the limits to response,
circumscribes it by way of an *a priori* centering of the consciousness within what Frye calls "a closed mythology" (1967, 116–117).
Here the aim of the educated imagination would be to show the
reader how the story can be regarded as a "structure of imagery
with conceptual implications" (Frye, 1963b, 32) rather than a sociological document delimited by the conditions of time and place of
author or reader.

## Total Form as Dialectic

Frye's conception of total form as dialectic is the alternative to having to choose between stasis and partial form. If the ultimate objective of literary response, within this taxonomy, is the apprehension
of total form as a "frozen . . . simultaneous pattern" (Frye, 1972, 4),
the reader seems caught between the holistic, but preverbal, intuitive
nature of stasis, on the one hand, and the languaged, but fragmented
or imbalanced nature of stock or kinetic response, on the other.
Instead of the reader longing for stasis and trusting to the gambling
machine of an ideal experience, literary response as dialectic actual-
izes the total form of a literary work through the alternation between
engagement, or the participating response, and detachment, or the
critical response. Literary response as dialectic legitimates and capi-
talizes on the responses of partial form by building on whatever
emotional and intellectual raw material presents itself at a precritical
level, and in such a way that response can be deepened, refined, and
enriched through aesthetic distance, but it does so by delaying gratification. Literary dialectic transcends the impulse to limit response,
viewing the literary work neither as an object to be dissected, nor an
analogue of personal experience, ideas, or values, but as a separate
reality, an "alien structure of the imagination" (Frye, 1970, 77), a
verbal universe whose self-containment logically precedes its referential function. Through exploration of the poem as a construct of
otherness, as much as a reflection of experience, wants, and desires,
the reader comes to recognize the "self" as part of the larger patterns
of the "human condition." Thus transformation of consciousness and
transformation of literary knowledge are interdependent—what Frye

calls "the myth of deliverance" (1983, 1–2), in which readers gain the altered consciousness symbolized by Mr. Keating's standing on the table in *Dead Poets Society*.

## Teaching Total Form as Dialectic

In the remaining pages of this chapter, I will outline briefly the kinds of literary responses to "A&P" that represent movement from a precritical level to what would typify Frye's ideal of the autonomous reader. Here I present a taxonomy in which the reader approximates stasis at a conscious level rather than the intuitive one. Frye's dialectical reader encounters four stages syncretically: precritical, critical, postcritical, and autonomous, whereas in stasis, the reader passes through these stages simultaneously, much like Plato's mystical lover of Beauty in the *Symposium*. In any case, the aim of total form as dialectic is for the reader to come as close as possible to a "full" literary response within the lexicon and assumptions of the educated imagination.

The precritical response is an essential component of response-development because it registers the immediate impact of a literary work on students. In her landmark essay in 1960, Margaret J. Early stressed the importance of precritical response, which she called "unconscious enjoyment . . . the beginning of literary appreciation; it cannot be bypassed" (35). But, Early argued, teachers need to guide students to the higher level of "[c]onscious delight" (38) through "self-conscious appreciation" (37). Early's developmental rubric embraces Frye's goal of the autonomous reader and the integration of sensibility. Movement from the precritical to the critical response in "A&P" can, of course, take place in a number of ways, the simplest being the ability to interpret Sammy as a fictional personage rather than as a young man whose behavior we approve of or not. In each of the responses below, the readers remain at the precritical stage, committing what Frye calls "the centrifugal fallacy" (1971/1973, 32); that is, they strive to see the point in moral or social terms, not literary ones.

- I think that the story is not incomplete or pointless. I feel that the point was that bathing suits are not allowed in stores.
- I liked the story because it shows that there can be something to smile about even in a bad situation.
- I think that maybe Updike was trying to show us the foolishness that young men and women go through trying to impress each other.

- The inner meaning, that I grasped, was the fact that Sammy's job meant nothing to him and how this relates to how others feel about their jobs as well.

- I enjoyed the story and thought it was great for the young generation. Some of us are too headstrong at times and need to be put in our place by other people sometimes. (Hunt & Vipond)

At this stage of response, informal discussion and/or journal writing would figure prominently.[9] Here students can explore their reasons for liking or disliking the story and considering it a successful or unsuccessful work of fiction. Both topics can serve as useful means of moving students from the immediate expression of a first emotional reaction to giving reasons for that reaction. The progression from articulating impact to analyzing its causes can generally be thought of as the beginning of the critical response, but in a sense it is more appropriate to the precritical stage because, within this taxonomy, acceptance or rejection of a text based on readers' own personal experiences, predispositions, and ideology rather than on "the actual text" would be classified as either stock or kinetic response.[10]

The precritical response leaves off and the critical response begins when a class is ready to supplant the exchanging of initial musings about the story with the more precise measuring of their responses against a closer look at the text. Here the welter of "real" experience would ideally be transmuted into literary experience as students undertake their foray into the literary world with a view to the differences from, rather than the similarities to, the world of ordinary life. Within the educated imagination, this would be regarded as beginning to achieve aesthetic distance, as detachment from the direct experience of reading, which is here not being denied, but simply looked at with greater attention to the literary perspective within which the story has been constructed.

The task of the teacher, presumably, would be to build on the precritical response by formulating "bridges" between it and the subsequent stages of response. Here the assumption is that students should proceed from their early responses, springing from the particularities of their own empirical reality, to a response more firmly grounded in the text. Inquiring into whether the narrator is a sympathetic or unsympathetic character, for example, or why he quits his job encourages readers to deal with character and plot, not just as "slices of life," analogues of "ordinary experience," but as tools of the writer's craft. In having to judge whether Sammy is "sympathetic," students move from their intuitions about him "as a person" to examining him as the author's invention, as the product of a deliberate creative act with specific literary implications. Whether readers *like* the narrator becomes less important than the way Updike has characterized him. As the reading becomes more "critical," presumably the stance of applauding or decrying Sammy's social prejudices gives way to viewing them as prerequisites for the kind of moral decision he makes later on. Reflecting on why he quits his job prompts students to account for the relationship between character and plot. Some, for example, will regard Sammy as having made a genuinely heroic gesture; others will think that he is merely grandstanding for the female audience. Again, within the developmental structure of the dialectic, which is designed to focus attention more on the text and away from the reader as the stages "progress," response "should" now be rooted in the narrative itself, and final value judgments about the probability, sincerity, or prudence of the act, postponed to a later stage. (I use quotation marks here to indicate my awareness that what I'm describing is a construct. See Chapters 6, 8, and 9 for alternative ways of conceptualizing the relationship between direct and critical response.)

The "bridge" questions are also designed to make it easier to proceed with more formalistic aspects of the critical response, which examine the story as a part of "the order of words" (Frye, 1957, 17), a kind of literary artifact, including continued investigation into the author's technique. With "A&P," one way to preserve the continuity between these first two stages would be to keep building on Sammy's final action of saying "I quit" by inquiring into the author's anticipation of the ending. From there, other formalistic concerns, such as the portrayal of setting, the handling of verisimilitude, and the crafting of style, would follow. The pedagogical ethos of total form as dialectic is to encourage engagement with the story through rereadings and informal class dramatizations, to which "A&P" lends itself well. This is intended to ensure that the interpretation remains fresh and yet is "true" to the text. Here the objective is the alternation between participation in literary experience and distance from it, a continuous modification and refinement of response that is to culminate in aesthetic pleasure, emotion, and intellection fusing in the perception of literary structure. This is the point where, ideally, readers would experience the "shock of recognition" as a real catharsis, an act of the imagination that universalizes the recollected happenings of lived events within the ordered reality of literature as the stubborn structure. I use the word "ideally" advisably, in the awareness that the foregoing typological framework is highly abstracted. Below, however, I contextualize some responses of readers who actually fit into this grid.

# Some Real Readers Reading

Within the perspective of Frye's reader-response theory, the respondent described below moved from the critical to the postcritical stage, where the literary melds with the moral to produce an altered social vision. One first-year female college student's initial response was, "I know Sammy is sexist, but that's the way guys are; at least he moves, he acts, he does something different, knowing there might be negative consequences for himself." Within this taxonomy, we might say that this reader subordinated her belief to her suspension of disbelief. In short, she "transcended" the impulse to remain at the level of ideology. In Frye's lexicon, she moved from a "closed" to an "open mythology" by "going beyond" "stock response" for "literary purposes," in order to accept Sammy first on Updike's terms and to inquire into the elements of craft that make the story work at an archetypal level. In other words, she "correctly distinguished" between literature and life. (Later she reflected that the Prince Charming archetype, which embodies the rite of passage in this story, shows that males are as much victims of social rituals as females.)[11]

Another example of the critical and postcritical levels within this taxonomy is typified in the response of the graduate student who perceived Updike's foreshadowing of Sammy's heroic gesture in his description of the "clean bare plane of the top of her chest down from the shoulder bones like a dented sheet of metal tilted in the light" (Updike, 1962, 188). Here the narrator uses a classical image of beauty to describe Queenie, the principal object of Sammy's attention, in marked contrast to his flippant stereotype of girls in general ("[D]o you really think it's a mind in there or just a little buzz like a bee in a glass jar?" [188]). This same respondent linked Sammy's quitting his job to Emersonian philosophy in a critical response that proceeded to the postcritical relating of literature to life by comparing the Emersonian context of "A&P" with the Calvinist ethos of Sinclair Ross's "The Painted Door" (1971) as a way of articulating differences between American and Canadian culture (see Sutherland, 1971, 60–87).

The autonomous response is intended to represent that aspect of literary dialectic which most closely approximates the holistic nature of stasis. Frye held that most readers, whether steeped in literature or groping their way through it, lack either the innocence or discipline for stasis and must be content with one or other forms of dissociation of sensibility, as they work their way through the oscillation between engagement and detachment. In a specifically educational sense, the autonomous response is more valuable than stasis because, though it probably will not result in the "ideal experience," it eliminates the "gambling machine" by bringing to consciousness the "frozen" pattern of total form. Fusing thought, emotion, sensitivity to literary nuance and scrupulous attention to the way in which the literary dimension adjudicates the aesthetic, moral, and social elements in the story, the autonomous response (again ideally) unleashes the psychic energy that opens up the possibilities for other responses. It begins on the far side of the knowledge that sign and meaning can never completely coincide (de Man, 1983, 17) and ends with an expansion of insight and a heightened sensibility to art and to life.

What might the autonomous response look like in "A&P"? Perhaps it can most profitably be viewed within the recurrent issue of the story's sexist overtones. The account of the response that follows is the actual classroom response of a feminist student, who "goes beyond" her "negative stock response" to invoking the innocence/experience archetype, while still painfully aware of the patriarchal structure that allows the archetype to flourish. More interested in the creation of new archetypes that would signal the passing from innocence to experience by females in ways very different from Updike's, she nevertheless resists foreclosing on a "literary" response because of her ideological predilections. To have performed a gender analysis on this story that would have ignored its "literary" qualities, would, within the parameters of this taxonomy, have made the ideological motivations of the interpretation their own endpoint. (See Chapter 6 for a reversal of this position.)

The "autonomous" reader described below used her literary critical expertise to address the issue of sexism but with quite a different outcome than would have been the case had she "allowed" her response to be circumscribed by acceptance or refusal of the text on political grounds alone. (Again, see Chapter 6 for how this same reader responded differently to this same story within a different social and pedagogical context.) Here, she noted that the story's sexism devolves upon fine discriminations of voice, upon how the author modulates Sammy's tone and attitude to create an ironical stance, not only between Sammy and the reader, and Sammy and Updike, but between Sammy and himself. This respondent saw Sammy looking down at himself telling the story. This "literary" perspective, which enables reader and author to be mutual participants in "an alien structure of the imagination" (Frye, 1970, 77), works toward the realization that literary texts restructure thought itself by violating expectations of routine existence. Seeing Sammy as the storyteller, as highly self-conscious of his place in the narrative as narrator, militates against this story being interpreted in terms of a closed mythology. As some readers aver (Chapter 7), the critical reading of "A&P" can open up the possibility of a new open mythology in gender relations. As the next chapter shows, I will challenge the view of literary response as one which cannot be so easily separated out from its political overtones. But I think it essential to the coherence of my overall argument to get as full a picture as possible here of response within the taxonomy of the educated imagination. Recounted below is the interpretive response of the reader I've been describing.

> As the story progresses, the voices resonating from the narrator become more complex with Sammy's increasing self-awareness. At the beginning, Sammy's voice as narrator is uni-dimensional: he is telling the story as himself, more or less "straight." As he becomes more involved in the situation, we can almost overhear Updike's voice in his: " 'We *are* decent,' Queenie says suddenly, her lower lip pushing, getting sore now that she remembers her place, a place from which the crowd that runs the A&P must look pretty crummy. Fancy Herring Snacks flashed in her very blue eyes." (Updike, 1962, 191)
>
> In the final movement of the story, Sammy's ironic distance on himself gradually increases, beginning with his self-designation as the girls' "unsuspected hero." At the end, the modality of the "sexism" is that of tragic-irony. "I look around for my girls, but they're gone of course. There wasn't anybody but some young married screaming with her children about some candy they didn't get by the door of a powder-blue Falcon station wagon. Looking back in the big windows, over the bags of peat moss and aluminum lawn furniture stacked on the pavement, I could see Lengel in my place in the slot, checking the sheep through. His face was dark gray and his back stiff, as if he'd just had an injection of iron, and my stomach kind of fell as I felt how hard the world was going to be to me hereafter" (Updike, 1962, 192). Sammy knows they were never "his girls" at all, and the sting of his sexist caricature of the "young married," seems muted in the wake of his rite of passage.

The preceding is an example of a response that has not just been simulated for the purpose of this chapter. It was an actual interpretation, one which we might even characterize as an example of the dialogic imagination (Bakhtin, 1981). Of course, no response, nor respondent, bypasses social conditioning. The autonomous response, in the sense in which I use it, however, springs from a recognition of ideological biases and values built into the reading subject and the textual object. It is a response in pursuit of the dialectic of total form on the presupposition that the reader plays out the text literarily, that is, "freely" and "independently," as an open and hypothetical construct. The autonomous respondent accepts that the text exists in its "whites" and its gaps as much as in the words on the page, and that the response to the text may reside in the silence of stasis or in the reader's proffered meaning of the word as co-created. Gifted by some measure of simultaneity between engagement and detachment, the autonomous responder is probably not swept away by Plato's "divine madness," (trans)fixed in a state of rapt wonderment, ever gazing upward like a bird, insensible to the world of everyday reality (Plato, 1973, 56). Like Rita of the film, she would be drawn toward engagement and the desire for whole experience, while at the same time educated to detachment and the unavoidable truth that meaning is plural. Literature as dialectic, then, would provide a training ground for the imagination as a basic educational skill.

The above is a deductive analysis of the educated imagination in terms of Frye's theory of reader response. Though I agree in part with its mandate (the part that conceives of response to literature as something other than indoctrination, on the one hand, or "critical thinking," on the other), as I hope to show in the rest of this book, the problem with the response problem and the educated imagination is basically the same as with the educated imagination and the justification and censorship problems: the "solution" is apolitical, or at least claims to be, and ultimately posits a view of the reader as disembodied subject measuring pointer readings. Frye's insistence on the *logical* priority of the critical response over the direct response, in the end, results in the *psychological* priority of criticism and interpretation over personal response. This can actually *produce* a kind of dissociation of sensibility in the reader, which can work against the kind of integration of response Frye actually valued and against claims made ultimately for justifying the moral and spiritual value of literature as a form of real experience. I believe, and will argue in the rest of this book, that transformation of consciousness can be brought about as much through the direct, even "uncritical," response as it can through the study of literature (see Chapters 8 and 9).

Encouraging students to distinguish between literature and life does weaken the charge that literature is indoctrinatory, and discriminating between convention and reality does not *have* to result in a dissociation between cognition and emotion. As Frye says in *The Great Code* (1982b), reading is not a passive "reception but the unfolding of a long and complex dialectical process" (226). And, as early as *A Natural Perspective* (1965a), he writes that the "whole notion that there is one right response which apprehends the whole play rightly is an illusion: correct response is always stock response, and is possible only when some kind of mental or physical reflex is appealed to" (51).

On the other hand, "getting beyond" stock response to literary experience (which is for Frye a unique kind of experience) is hampered by the gap between engagement and detachment. While readers must not "mutilate their literary experience in favor of a literary theory" (Frye, 1963c, 141), students must respond to the poem, and nothing but the poem:

> The object of literary experience must be placed directly in front of the student, and he [sic] should be urged to respond to it and accept no substitutes as the end of his understanding. Yet it does not matter a tinker's curse what a student thinks and feels about literature until he can think and feel, which is not until he passes the stage of stock response. (Frye, 1970, 83)

Striking here is the curious juxtapositioning of stock response as automatic reflex, on the one hand, and literary object, on the other, and the curious compartmentalizing of psychic states it represents. It would seem, then, that literary response as the power of possibility is limited by not taking seriously enough what readers already know at "the stage of stock response." They may not know literature but they do know their own experience, which, I will argue, is not just reflex action (Chapters 6, 8, and 9), even though it might look like it from the vantage point of the educated imagination. The attempt to confront the "whites" and gaps of readers' experience, both in literature and in life, gaps left by the assumptions of "the best subject matter in the world" (Frye, 1988, 5) as its own worldview, is what constitutes the premises of my conception of the re-educated imagination. These premises are, first, that the direct response is logically as well as psychologically prior to the critical response; and second, that engagement with the text based on direct response as a logical priority carries with it a politics that cannot be evaded under the appellation "nonliterary." In the next chapter I hope to show that once the political conditions of literature as its own worldview are challenged, the meta-problem of the why, what, and how of teaching literature becomes an even greater problem by adding the who, where, and "who says?" questions, which I'll call the "feeling, power, and location problems."

# Endnotes

1. This word was ultimately changed to "Sensitive".

2. Cf. James Moffett (1990), "But literature exists not only to be understood but to be undergone" (302).

3. Even the most gender-oblivious reader would be stopped by the sexual connotations of this reference. Frye might have meant here that beauty contests which commodify "girls in bathing suits" are the demonic form of the ethical function of the aesthetic. The re-educated imagination works to break down fixed associations with polarized categories, including masculine/ feminine. But pointing them out is part of this process. Here I cannot fail to notice the alignment of female bodies in the world of ordinary existence with the uncontrollable wandering of desire, which poetry as imaginative experience would contain. Compare this to Sidney's treatment of the soldiering quality of the poetic function (Chapter 2). Later chapters (8 and 9) give special attention to literary reading as a gendered activity, and in Chapters 9 and 10, I argue that Frye still sees the gender implications of literary conventions as unproblematic. Note also the coincidence of the "girls in bathing suits" quotation with the prominence of this image in John Updike's "A&P" [1962]; see Chapters 5 and 6.

4. The remainder of this chapter is a reworking of a taxonomy of reader responses and respondents based on the conceptual framework of the previous section. Given the re-visioning of pedagogical theory undertaken in this book (Chapter 9), I found that including the taxonomy was much more problematic than I'd initially expected. I believe, however, that that is all the more reason for detailing here how the pedagogical context of literary response within the hypothetical construct of the stubborn structure might be typologized. (See Bogdan, 1985b, 1986a, 1986d, 1987c, 1990c.)

5. Douglas Vipond and Russell Hunt carried on a separate study with Updike's "A&P," and found that, as a rule, college students dislike the story. We had no knowledge of our mutual research interest in this story (see also Beach, 1990), even though our work was done virtually simultaneously. Some of my references to Hunt and Vipond's research are to their unpublished paper, "The Reader, the text, the Situation: Blocks and Affordances in Literary Reading" (1984), which was later incorporated into an article, "Point-Driven Understanding: Pragmatic and Cognitive Dimensions of Literary Reading," (Vipond & Hunt, 1984).

6. Vipond and Hunt make the observation that in order to be point-driven in literary reading, it is necessary that the text be perceived as an "artifact," and that students who read "A&P" tend not to be point-driven. This would support my contention that realism militates against seeing literature as separate from life, a perception so necessary to apprehending *mythos* as *dianoia*. (See Vipond and Hunt, 1984.)

7. I agree with Vipond and Hunt that "types or modes of reading . . . are not characteristics of *readers*, . . . or . . . even of whole *readings*," but of goals and attitudes during the reading process (emphasis original). I use the term "responders" simply as a way of concretizing and personalizing types of response. (Vipond and Hunt, 1984.)

8. While these examples are Vipond's and Hunt's, the categorizations are mine (Hunt & Vipond, 1984).

9. See Chapter 9 for a re-conceptualization of the pedagogical function of reader-response journals.

10. In later chapters I undertake a deconstruction of the false dichotomy between precritical and critical responses (Chapter 8) and of the logical, epistemological, and pedagogical status of stock response (Chapters 6, 8, and 9). However, in this chapter I am concerned to demonstrate the logic of the developmental nature of literary response as dialectic when the critical response is logically prior to the direct response, as is the case with the educated imagination.

11. I see this kind of statement as part of the myth of equal sexual categories, which I discuss in Chapter 10.

# Chapter Six

# The Re-Educated Imagination and Literary Literacy

## The Educated Imagination and Literary Literacy

In the last chapter, I suggested that there are a number of problems with the educated imagination as a remedy for the response problem. It would seem that Frye's ethical aim for literature education as the unification of humanity through imaginative vision is fraught with certain anomalies. These contradictions are unavoidable in a perspective as broad as Frye's; and, as we saw earlier, they do get resolved within the hypothetical dimension of his third order of experience, "in which everything is potentially identical with everything else" (1957, 124). But Frye's theoretical framework subordinates the actuality of real readers reading, and the teachers who teach them, to the infinite regress of delayed gratification. He doubtless acknowledged the *fact* of the reader, and endorsed the concept of reading as a creative activity (Hamilton, 1990, 196–199). But these realities assume the status, within his purview, of already-in-place taken-for-granteds, his main interest being to show how the journey of the reader as mental traveler through the order of words is a survival kit for living in the world. Here I believe he is right, and successful, in demonstrating the importance of the imagination as a hypothetical construct, as far as it goes (and it does go far). But what we have been laboring at in the previous five chapters is the complex messiness of the meta-problem, which, when it is lived out in the classroom, foregrounds the urgency and immediacy of material conditions, the flesh-and-blood, of literary experience.

The main problem with the educated imagination in resolving the meta-problem is that the theory is predicated upon identity as similarity. This hypothetical state of identity obfuscates and impedes a conception of an embodied reader who is necessarily grounded in differences among actual readers. The consideration of difference—difference in response, in feeling, in power, where any one reader happens to be, geographically, psychically, or culturally, within the purview of the educated imagination—gets subsumed under the developmental assumption that wider and wider reading and more and more informed responses will inexorably propel the respondent into the third order of experience, where every other voice resonates as part of our own. This goal is laudable, as I have said; but in the process of achieving it, we must deal with the fallibility of human beings whose sensibilities and worldviews collide, especially within the hierarchical political authority structure of the educational system, which privileges some kinds of knowledge over others. That is the purpose of posing the meta-problem as a problem rather than as the circularity of claiming premises which logically or politically cannot be refused within the community of English education. The problem with coping with a theory such as Frye's (and others which turn on the presupposition that literature influences for good and not for ill) is that, whether you accept or reject his premises, there seems to be no arguing with him.

To say this is not to denigrate his contribution to the discussion of the problem. Take, for example, his remarks about the mandate of the teacher of literature in his introduction to *The Great Code* (1982b). In explaining why he wants to see literature separated out from the realm of belief, Frye gets at the very heart of why many teachers who believe in the educational value of literature as a subversive activity do so: it is because of its function in disrupting the tendency of stock response to preserve the status quo—of individuals and of society. Frye accepts that stock response constitutes "the anxieties of the reader that make the primary response to what is being said" (1982b, xx). And, as we saw in the last chapter, stock response is caught within the polarity of "I like it/don't like it"; it is stuck in the rut of belief/disbelief, acceptance/rejection, in which the tenacity of cleaving to what we know or think we know circumscribes interpretation. Here the job of the literature teacher is thus to dislodge the reader from that level of response, to move students, à la Mr. Keating, to the "higher ground" of a literary response, as we saw was the case in the final example of the response to "A&P" in the last chapter. It is only when we get beyond stock response, argues Frye, that literature study can truly become a social science capable of divesting readers of their mythological conditioning:

> Why are belief and disbelief, as ordinarily understood, so often and so intensely anxious and insecure? The immediate answer is that they are closely connected with the powers of repression. . . . [which are] the teacher's first point of attack. What we usually think of as acceptance or rejection of belief does not in either case involve any disturbance in our mental processes. It seems to me that trying to think within the categories of myth, metaphor, and typology—all of them exceedingly "primitive" categories from most points of view—does involve a good deal of such disturbance. The result, however, I hope and have reason to think, is an increased lucidity, an instinct for cutting through a jungle of rationalizing verbiage to the cleared area of insight. (1982b, xx)

This cameo reveals Frye's approach to the meta-problem: reading literature becomes a moral endeavor because educating response unseats knee-jerk reactions to the "non-literary" power of words, with the result that the "natural" impulse of humankind, which is self-censorship, pushes and pulls readers to new levels of awareness. Here Frye's existentialism comes into play. People really want imprisonment, not freedom, and so "man [sic] is constantly building anxiety-structures, like geodesic domes, around his social and religious institutions" (1982b, 232). The problem here, though, is that *voluntary* flight from freedom is not the whole of the problem. People sometimes have to construct self-protective mechanisms because the conditions of their lives visit upon them anxiety structures which they themselves have nothing to do with creating. We are, all of us, situated—some more comfortably than others. This is the metaphysical gap in the ethos of the educated imagination. Myth and metaphor may indeed be the categories that upset equilibrium, but readers do not just "think" within these categories; they live them, that is, if we really accept the experiential validity of literary knowing. This is where the notion of difference makes the difference. It is all very well to say that Frye endorses creativity in readers' responses, as A. C. Hamilton reminds us in *Northrop Frye: Anatomy of His Criticism* (1990, 196–199), but what teachers of literature do not have the luxury of ignoring is that, on their way to anagogical oneness, things *happen* to people when they read, some of them negative. Perhaps Heraclitus is right that the way up is the same as the way down, and that "if one succeeds in either, one gets both" (Frye, 1970, 270); but teachers—and students—of literature have to deal with what happens to students in the darkness of the descent as well as in the light of the ascent. Doing so effectively and justly entails complicating the meta-problem even further. In the rest of this chapter, I hope to show

how the way down is not necessarily the way up, at least not in the short run, that the educational value of a literary response can be hurtful and exclusionary, and why the educated imagination needs to be re-educated to include in the meta-problem the feeling problem, the power problem, and the location problem, and to define literary literacy as the awareness of "situated knowledges" (Haraway, 1988) in the real lives of real readers reading.

A. C. Hamilton's book on Frye helps us deduce what would count as a definition of literary literacy within the purview of the educated imagination: the ability to deploy the experience and knowledge of literature as a dialectical tool in ferreting out "what appears to be said from what is really said, or the historical content from the imaginative structure" (1990, 201). Another way of thinking of literary literacy in Frye's terms would be to acknowledge that the reader must always see mythology, or the telling of stories, as superior to ideology, or how those stories might be interpreted by any one person or community of readers at any one time. For Frye, literary literacy would also mean that the reader sees "literature in its history . . . 'descending into experience,' so that Frye's criticism, in showing that descent as the humanizing of myth, becomes a kind of incarnational poetics" (Hamilton, 1990, 208). This descent, by which I think is meant the actual experience of literature as the word made flesh (what we might call just plain reading), is followed by criticism or the ascending action of "a human *consciousness* surrounding experience" (Frye, 1980, 47, emphasis added). The ascending and descending action becomes part of the dialectic of engagement and detachment, belief and vision: engagement and belief being those aspects of psychic life that want either to accept or reject, detachment and vision being those aspects of consciousness that strive toward a new perspective within the order of words.

This distinction between reading and criticism is the bedrock of Frye's search for "an active, imaginative, and therefore creative response from the reader rather than any rational agreement or disagreement" (Hamilton, 1990, 209). And it is presumably this creativity that undoes the damage of repressive forces. What Frye, however, would not see as part of literary literacy is any possibility of refusing the vision of the imaginative literary structure because of what a reader might be made to *feel* during any one act of reading. For Frye, the power of the imagination is *sui generis*, one of its kind, and sooner or later the reader *will* begin the ascent back to myth, during which s/he will eventually come to consciousness, come to understand what has been undergone. Sooner or later, there will be the realization that it has been a learning experience, as we say, and that all will be well. If all is not well, that must mean that the appropriate

level of consciousness, either of psychic life or of the stubborn structure of the literary universe, has not yet been arrived at, the deficiency of partial form reigning over the total form (Frye, 1957,
115; 1963b, 31) of the order of words. On this view, what is needed
to right the imbalance is knowledge *about* literature, literary criticism, and more direct experience of "literature as literature." As
Hamilton, I think rightly, has ascertained, any other theory of reader
response which does not so distinguish between reading and criticism, especially those theories derived from much contemporary
criticism, such as phenomenology and reception theory, within
Frye's theory, "has not been shaped out of an inductive survey of
English literature but depends upon a reader's *ignorance* of most of
it" (1990, 221, emphasis added). In other words, a reader-response
theory based on what readers bring to the text becomes, for him,
again, a "monument to a failure of experience" (Frye, 1971/1973, 27).

Within Frye's perspective, then, the meta-problem can only ever
be a pseudo-problem. For him, there should be no problem because
one can always appeal to the court of the ascending action of critical
response that comes after the descending action of participatory
reading. The reader will always be referred to the level of myth, the
third order of experience, where there is no conflict of interest,
wounding of feeling, or inequity of power operating with respect to
the act of reading as a lived activity. The important thing in this
theory of reading is constantly to be resisting closure (Hamilton,
1990, 206), at least closure on the reader's own view of the truth as
definitive, and to be forever referring and deferring meaning, within
the critical dialectic, to the "mythical level of meaning, which com-
prehends all meaning, . . . succeeded by the anagogic level, which, as
vision, is beyond meaning" (206)—the world of hypothesis.

> Reading a literary work within the history of literature both as a
> sequence of displaced myths and analogies of revelation, under-
> standing its meanings in their sequence as they make it the centre of
> the literary universe, seeing its place within the circle of *mythoi*,
> and recognizing its place within a specific genre in relation to all
> other works in their genres: these are the stages by which criticism
> produces an active but disciplined, informed but imaginative, and
> therefore creative response to literature. (Hamilton, 1990, 197)

This is the journey of the reader as mental traveler, as hero of the
*mythos,* which Frye defines in its undisplaced context as the story of
a god[1] (1963b, 127). I suggest that a smaller scale version of this stage
development approach to literary meaning took place in the deferred
response of the feminist student reader of "A&P," which I described
in Chapter 5, a student who, at least within that reading context,

could be judged to possess, within the purview of the educated imagination, a high degree of literary literacy.

Now, however, I am going to tell another story of that reader reading the same text. One of the things that happens when real readers read, not just study, literature is that those very realities of intensity of feeling, power imbalances, and differences in worldview that constitute who and where readers are, especially in classrooms of a pluralistic society, those very elements that teachers use to argue for the educational value of literature can in one context fragment a reading community in direct proportion to their efficacy in unifying it in another context. Let's now look at my own experience teaching Updike's "A&P" in another context, one in which the "ideological agenda" (in Frye's terms) pre-empted that of the order of words. In this case, feeling, power, and the location of the students who were reading became such a "problem" that it re-educated the imagination of their teacher.

## The Re-Educated Imagination and Literary Literacy

The year following the account of the student responses I detailed in the last chapter, I undertook to teach for the first time a course in women's literature and feminist criticism, which was also the first of its kind in the post-secondary institution where I work. This is a graduate school of education where the majority of the students are women, many part-time, who are committed to taking responsibility for their own learning. As an instructor in literature education, I had been become increasingly concerned with the fate of the educated imagination, given the impact on curriculum of the challenge posed by contemporary literary theory to English studies as an institution, especially to the belief in literature and the literary response as the cornerstone of a liberal education (Batsleer et al, 1985; Eagleton, 1983; Widdowson, 1982). As we saw in Chapter 4, this challenge has problematized the humanist argument against censorship. My work on the Peterborough County censorship case had seriously eroded my trust in appeals to such notions as organic unity and aesthetic distance, which subsume other values under aesthetic ones, in resolving censorship disputes. Growing awareness of the historically and socially constructed nature of the canon and of hegemonies hidden behind the veil of covert political interest had made me aware that the issue of curriculum choice based on artistic criteria was more vulnerable to attack than had been the case in the past. In other words, the meta-problem, as well as the feeling, power, and location problems, had begun to gestate for me. The issue of whose interests are being served by the teaching of a particular work, and under what conditions, had become more legitimate questions to be asking when distinguishing between selection and censorship both within the academy and the larger educational community.

My focus in this chapter is shaped by inquiring into what happens when ideology forms part of the educational enterprise, not as a species of partial form, but as an explicitly asserted bid to change the world through participation in the order of words. What I hope will come clear is how what appeared to be a case of censorship as a repressive force can be understood rather as a performative utterance about the selection of materials to be studied within an acknowledged bias. This case study brings into relief the points of contradiction at which the goal of empowering the reader, claimed by liberal humanist apologies for the educational value of literature, such as Frye's, conflicts with assumptions about the pedagogical means to effect such empowerment—if those assumptions cleave blindly and rigidly to faith in a view of the educated imagination which obstinately blinks at (and even viciously effaces) the problem posed by the unproblematic acceptance that the power of literature is not a problem, particularly in face of the real feelings and actual locations of students who inhabit English classrooms. In this study, I will expand the notion of censorship beyond its narrow connotation as the burning or banning of literature texts and even beyond the boundaries of the meta-problem. In fact, my intent is to conflate the censorship issue deliberately with that of the selection issue in order to underline the complex interrelationship between the meta-problem as we have understood it thus far—the censorship problem (which books are read), the response problem (how they are studied), and the justification problem itself (why teach literature at all)—and the feeling, power, and location problems.

## The Poetics of Pluralism

Frye's theory of the educated imagination has its counterpart, with respect to the censorship problem, in James Moffett's *Storm in the Mountains: A Case Study of Censorship, Conflict, and Consciousness* (1988). Frye and Moffett come together in the response problem through a *poetics of pluralism*. Moffett analyzes the school text censorship problem with the sophistication of a textual exegete who genuinely appreciates censors' objections. (Taking censors seriously, not just politically, but epistemologically, is something for which language arts educators are not especially renowned.) Moffett's major contribution to the debate is his conception of *agnosis* as "the blocking of consciousness" (236) or resistance to knowing, "powerful prior mind-sets" (172) that distort interpretations of a literary work because of preconceptions so strong that they "override almost any amount of contrary information given in the text" (171). Moffett recognizes that agnosis is universal and relative (everyone is afflicted with it to some degree). That human beings often opt for states of unknowing, consciously or not, is a phenomenon Moffett, like Frye, rightly envisions literature education to be working against; i.e., its prime educational function is surely to break down resistance to knowing. In "Ways of Teaching Literature" (1990), Moffett asserts that literature is there not just to be understood but to be undergone (302). The notion of undergoing literature calls to mind the latin verb, *patio, patere*, I suffer. It is thus through this "suffering" of the literary experience as such, through literature's imaginative, emotional appeal, as well as its intellectual import, that the reader becomes liberated from psychological and social conditioning. Though Frye stresses the understanding of literature rather than the undergoing of it, he and Moffett both see stock response as the chief obstacle to creative response and to the attainment of consciousness; and I believe that they are right, all things being equal. But to assume that they *are* equal would be to beg the question of the feeling, power, and location problems, which are the very sites of subjectivity, inequity, and difference that this book attempts to flesh out.

In order to see how the poetics of pluralism can pose a dilemma for the above three problems, we must first ask how the poetics of pluralism works with respect to what is taught. If we know as we identify, Moffett (1988) argues, then educators should gradually widen the circle of identification through an increasing array of literary genres, authors, and subject matters, so that readers come to accept greater kinds of difference in an ever-expanding consciousness-raising. Within this purview, literature becomes a form of moral communication based not on role-modeling virtue from literature to life but on developing an appreciation of moral ambiguity through textual complexity, which eventuates in a moral vision encompassing multiple viewpoints and centers of value. Ideally, students would come to recognize in every voice one that resonates as part of themselves.

Literary experience, then, should produce in the reader what Henry James calls "the right '*quality* of bewilderment,' intense and striving" (qtd. in Nussbaum, 1985, 528). For Moffett (1988), reading literature causes readers to expand and question what they know or think they know, pushing back "the defense perimeters of the mind" that place "parameters . . . on knowledge and understanding"

(187). Agnosis, then, is on a collision course with what in the history of Western civilization has come to be known as the open mind, the very life-blood of philosophy of education. "[L]et's suppose that everyone resists *some* knowledge. Some things we don't want to know," Moffett continues. But for him "[s]uch negative capability would seem to cut life off at its very roots" (182, emphasis original).

As with *Dead Poets Society,* it is difficult to fault such a view of reading, either pedagogically or politically. Isn't every teacher of literature dedicated to the democratic ideal of fostering tolerance through helping students to respect the identities of others? Whether criticism is distinguished from reading, as in Frye, or incorporated more implicitly into it, as in Moffett, the aim of a literary education would seem to be wider inclusiveness. But what happens when a theory of reading is based on the radical critique of the very conditions of such inclusiveness in terms of race, class, or gender? What happens when, say, feminist criticism *begins* with the premise that the canon is androcentric, or male-dominated? In theory, the aim would not be very different from that of the poetics of pluralism; both pluralism and feminism want a better world, perhaps even Frye's third order of experience, where "isms" of every description, including literary criticism, would be redundant. But in practice, as we'll see shortly, the kind of attention paid by feminist criticism to the feeling, power, and location problems can *look like* adherence to censorship, self-censorship, and stock response.

On the face of it, the twenty-year history of feminist literary criticism would corroborate the poetics of pluralism. Each of feminist criticism's three "waves"—reinterpretation, excavation, and theorization—seem to be the apotheosis of resistance to resistance to knowing. Feminist critics do not censor; like Adrienne Rich (1979) and Annette Kolodny (1985b), they re-read and re-vision. They do not deny what is there; like Showalter (1977), Gilbert and Gubar (1977), they foreground what has been eclipsed. In the absence of a critical tradition of their own, like Toril Moi (1985) and Chris Weedon (1987), they appropriate male theorists to their project. And like Teresa de Lauretis (1986), they interrogate their own ideology for racism and classism.

Applied to feminist criticism, the poetics of pluralism has succeeded in "add[ing] the variable of gender to a well-established tradition of [intellectual] inquiry" (Treichler, 1986, 89). In this sense, feminist criticism is compatible with the poetics of pluralism. Yet, feminist criticism bears at least a dual relationship to the poetics of pluralism. Inasmuch as feminist criticism has come into its own as a respected mode of (inter)disciplinary study, it makes an equal contribution, so to speak, to the existing storehouse of interpretive strategies. But feminist criticism also challenges the poetics of pluralism by calling into question the very premise of a philosophy of reading that seems to accommodate a universal "we" (see Hamilton on Frye's use of the "royal 'we,'" 1990, 205) or a unified reading subject. (See Weedon, 1987, for a poststructuralist critique of the latter.) This is not to say that feminist criticism cannot or does not practise the willing suspension of disbelief, or that it does not invoke polysemy, multiple perspectives, and so on. (See especially Kolodny 1985a.)

As reader-response criticism, though, feminist criticism, wary as it is of hiving off imaginative recreation of the text from the specificities of readers' lives, regards literary experience as a form of real experience.[2] That is, feminist criticism approaches literary reading from what I would call a post-tragedic stance. Feminist readers know before they come to a text what Oedipus had to discover—the tautology that awareness of the human condition consists in the recognition that this is the way things are. Being the questing "hero" of one's reading means, ultimately, to lose one's innocence; but the feminist—and minority—readers of the canon have long since lost theirs. It is as though the feminist reader qua feminist reader has already undergone "in life" what the "mainstream" reader comes to literature to find out—that the reader has been betrayed by her gods, that language both says and does not say. I am not referring here to individual cases of particular readers. Nor am I claiming that only women experience the tragedy of life (or conversely that women readers do not derive values from literary reading other than the tragic). Rather, I want to stress that the feminist reader is already a critic by virtue of her feminist consciousness such that agnosis is a well-nigh impossible state for her. Her gnostic vision is conferred as an *a priori* fact of her reading life, if we can think of such a categorical possibility. She is a *connata*, one who knows already, one who has been forced into literary literacy, if you will, if literary literacy is defined as that which facilitates perception of the distinction between appearance and reality. But the feminist reader has also already been educated to the kind of "social imagination" which Frye says *literature* gives (1963a). By dint of her heightened somatic knowledge, her bodily awareness of androcentric reality, the feminist reader has been educated in ways similar to the woman who didn't go past grade six but who "talks like the Declaration of Independence" (Frye, 1963a, 64). As Sandra Lee Bartky reminds us, "feminists suffer . . . a double ontological shock: first, the realization that what is really happening is quite different from what appears to be happening; and second, the frequent inability to tell what is really happening at all" (1979, 256). Divided consciousness thus becomes a precondition for feminist reading, and that fact so radically alters the relationship between language and reality that mainstream/malestream issues of conceptualizations of censorship and the notion of agnosis as a negative quality become de facto problematic.

Like any other discipline, feminist criticism has a developmental history. Now that it has come of age as a legitimate mode of reading, it might be useful to reflect on how in its maturation process the negative capability of Moffett's agnosis can operate, not as a death-wish, but as a life-force in the evolution of consciousness. When identity is fragile, sometimes maintaining it by "maintaining an enemy" (1988, 217), a condition Moffett regards as "a malady" (193), may be necessary for self-preservation. I offer the narrative below as one example of feminist criticism and some female readers reading, one that might also invoke the feeling, power, and location problems of other marginalized identities, individual and collective, which are in(deed) affected by the claim that reading literature effects change through its affect, and not always positively, at least not in the "descent" into experience.

## The Poetics of Need

### The Feeling Problem

The winter of 1986 saw the first offering of Course 1462, Women, Literature and Education at the Ontario Institute for Studies in Education. Here a group of highly combustible, critically aware graduate students repudiated the poetics of pluralism and its consorts, the willing suspension of disbelief and literary context, in favor of what Lawrence Lipking (1983/1984) calls "a poetics of need" (102). They did so by refusing to analyze, delay gratification, accept bewilderment, defer moral judgment, engage aesthetic complexity, embrace a broad perspective, or negotiate multiple points of view. In short, they insisted on taking literature personally and politically rather than mythically and anagogically.

About half-way through the course I decided to use Updike's "A&P" as a way of examining how the aesthetic mechanism intersects with female stereotyping. Instead of dispassionately considering nuances of tone, mood, voice, irony, ambiguity, verisimilitude, and the like (see Bogdan, 1986a, 1987c), all elements of Frye's "full" literary response (Chapter 5), they committed what within the educated imagination would be critical heresy—by ignoring the distinction between author and narrator, foreshortening aesthetic distance, and appearing arbitrarily to dismiss the work in what I could only describe as a stock response to its sexist overtones. Here I am thinking of stock response specifically within the connection Frye makes between it and the censorship problem, that is, reaction by way of automatic reflex to the content of a work. Stock response judges a work according to the kind of moral and social anxiety Moffett has in mind with his notion of agnosis. This kind of anxiety cannot accept the educated imagination's main defense against censorship: the dictum "that works of literature can only be good or bad in their own categories, and that no subject-matter or vocabulary is inherently bad" (Frye, 1963c, 128).

The very same student who in my mainstream course the previous year had produced the "deferred" response described in the last chapter, in which she had traced the protagonist's development through the shifting subtleties of his sexist observations and who had even written a paper cautioning against "mere content analysis" as a criterion for censoring any piece of literature, charged that within that class and our *feminist* inquiry, the literary response I was hoping for was in fact a stock response. Moreover, she challenged the very existence of the story in our course, asserting that over a span of thirteen brief two-hour meetings the class could not afford to learn how yet again sexism gets rationalized within a masculinist poetics. When queried about what, then, should be done with such a piece, the student, whose name is Judy, replied—and several of her colleagues concurred—"I am not a censor, but burn the damned thing!"

At this point, it might be appropriate to fill in some of the background leading to the situation described above. I had chosen this story for this class for a number of reasons. As I said in the last chapter, I had been using it in my course in the philosophy of literature and literature education, as well as in conference workshops, to investigate the relationship between moral and aesthetic values in literary response. Invariably, reaction to the story had raised the issue of the tensions between form, content, authorial intention, artistic craft, and literary quality, on the one hand, and the ideologies of feminism and Emersonian individualism, on the other. In the recent past, I had noticed that the classes had been more or less divided in terms of their valuation of the story's "impact" along gender lines—the men being moved by the young protagonist's journey from innocence to experience, the women being irritated and sometimes angered by the concatenation of sexist images the reader is forced to undergo along the way. I felt that an introductory feminist criticism class probably afforded the optimum opportunity for exploring these issues. What I did not realize, of course, was just how powerfully experiential the confrontation of the personal and the ideological in reader response could be.

Within the poetics of pluralism the mainstream reader of this passage, in pursuit of a literary interpretation of the story as a whole, would be prepared to transcend his/her instinctive reactions to these images, wrenched out of context, as we say. She or he would skill-fully follow out the narrative complexities and stylistic niceties of the central character's movement from innocence to experience, pre-sumably emerging from the reading with a greater awareness of the human condition, recognizing, as Maxine Greene (1986) has put it, "Ah, this is just how things are, and I didn't know it!" (240).

As was shown by Judy's "literary" response in the mainstream course (Chapter 5), the poetics of pluralism could accommodate a feminist perspective in that Frye's literary response might well lead to an increased understanding of gender relations. There Judy was the "ideal reader," in Frye's and Moffett's terms, propelling herself (or being propelled) "beyond" her negative stock response to a more refined set of moral discernments through attention to the story's literary richness. We might say that she was, perhaps then, imbued with "the right 'quality' of bewilderment," nevertheless resisting the temptation to negative closure of her response in this story. She was not just the ideal reader, but the "good reader," in both aesthetic and moral terms, her moral/literary sensibility displaying the right stuff of literary literacy in her demonstrated ability to respect the con-straints of literary convention.

Having done this in the other course, why didn't Judy, or her sisters, do it in this one? Because, as I hope to make clear, they had a feeling problem, a power problem, and a location problem. What they *did* do—reject the exercise in the poetics of pluralism—would have been easy to dismiss as "strident," "anti-intellectual" "ravings" of a marginalized group. I will argue, rather, that their response was an act of literary criticism with an invisible history dating from Aristotle's sister, the apocryphal Arimneste, the mother of feminist criticism (Lipking, 1983/1984), who was unabashed about taking lit-erature personally and politically. Within Arimneste's poetics, the call to "Burn it!" is less an act of censorship than a hyperbolic sword of discrimination carving out for women a literature of their own, responses of their own, and knowledge of their own, including the right to refuse to engage what they are already too painfully aware of. Judy and her sisters were simply renouncing—even "for educational purposes"—a story such as "A&P" in a women's literature course, where psychic nourishment was an educational value precluding reinforcement of a self-alienation already imposed on them by the literary/educational establishment. For them, liberation from condi-tioning meant throwing off the oppression of having been schooled to identify against themselves (Fetterley, 1978). There was neither the time nor the stomach for revisiting the old wounds. They were unwilling to deny their post-tragedic insight into the relationship of life to literature, to compromise their newly found safety of a feminist literature class, or to risk the double indemnity of undergoing what they already understood all too well—that they were most emphatically not the heroes of their reading of the story of this particular god.

Now, writing this is very difficult for me, as it would be for most academics committed to the spirit of free inquiry, particularly in English studies, where the expansive power of inhabiting other lives and other worlds through sympathetic identification has been so paramount. What educator would knowingly vilify the poetics of pluralism or regard agnosis positively? How can one quarrel with such deep-browed humanism that simultaneously recognizes the limitations of human consciousness and envisions the overcoming of them? I endorse the poetics of pluralism as a form of literary literacy, as the life-enhancing *outcome* of literary education, and I celebrate the merits of literature as a means of achieving that goal. Mind expansion is hard to argue with. Who in education would consciously espouse blinkered perception as an educational objective without being called a bigot? It is precisely literature as *ostranenie* (Hawkes, 1977, 62), as "an *alien* structure of the imagination, set over against [us], strange in its conventions and often in its values" (Frye, 1970, 77), that makes it especially valuable as a destabilizing mechanism in divesting the reader of entrenched habits of mind, habits which, Frye rightly asserts, though they may be unconscious, are themselves "linguistically structured" (1982a, 101). But how does simply asserting this help us solve the feeling, power, and location problems?

## The Power Problem

The poetics of pluralism is predicated upon a conception of literariness as the interplay among processes of identification so crucial to the kind of suffering-through that affords correspondences between self and other, thus "calling something into existence that was not there before" (Plato, *Symposium*, 205b). But sometimes the actuality of time, place, student body, and educational context—in this case the "need" of a feminist criticism class to preserve their identity—precludes magnanimity as a first priority. Sometimes student readers have no "excess" of spirit to give. The poetics of pluralism is contingent upon a certitude of identity that comes with being in power rather than out of power, individually and/or collectively. When readers are not in power, as is often the case for students in a feminist criticism class, or, indeed, in a mainstream English classroom populated by minority students, the first priority may be consolidation of identity, an objective that puts psychic safety and/or comfort ahead of the decentering brought about by further instances of *ostranenie*.

In their desperation to proclaim the expressly political mandate of feminist criticism, bodily, Judy and her sisters recall Virginia Woolf in *Three Guineas* (1938/1966), who, when asked to contribute to a building fund for a women's college, wrote:

> No guinea of earned money should go to rebuilding the college on the old plan; just as certainly none could be spent upon building a college upon a new plan; therefore the guinea should be earmarked "Rags. Petrol. Matches." And this note should be attached to it. "Take this guinea and with it burn the college to the ground. Set fire to the old hypocrisies. Let the light of the burning building scare the nightingales and incarnadine the willows. And let the daughters of educated men dance round the fire and heap armful upon armful of dead leaves upon the flames. And let their mothers lean from the upper windows and cry, 'Let it blaze! Let it blaze! For we have done with this "education"!' "(35–36)

Here, as in the response to "A&P," militance is no impairment to intelligence, as Moffett sees it (1988, 162), but epistemological revolution. I think that Frye would have been hard put to see the "negative" aspect of this revolution, this poetics of refusal, as part of the "honest struggle" of the dialectical process (Frye, 1970, 89). Rather, he would have regarded it as a part of a "closed mythology" that turns on belief or dissent rather than as the "open mythology" (Frye, 1967, 116–117) of the ongoing "struggle to unify and relate" (Frye, 1970, 89) literature to literature. Constance Penley (citing Shoshana Felman, 1982), however, conceives of the feminist epistemological revolution as directly related to the learning process itself, as the productive nature of miscognition, "a means of access to 'information hitherto *unlearnable*' " (qtd. in Penley, 1986, 134).

For Arimneste, Woolf, Penley, Felman, and Judy and her sisters, feminist criticism is not just another literary "approach." To quote Judith Fetterley, "At its best feminist criticism is a political act whose aim is not simply to interpret the world but to change it by changing the consciousness of those who read and their relation to what they read" (1978, viii). This means changing what, how, and why they read by invoking the meta-problem and the three problems—feeling, power, and location—added in this chapter. On the face of it, such a mandate would not encourage the refusal to read. Feminist criticism shares with the poetics of pluralism a commitment to accepting difference, and could be served by pluralism in the best of critical and political worlds, that is, one in which aesthetic pleasure

wouldn't depend upon a forced "immasculation" of the female reading subject (Fetterley, 1978; Schweickart, 1986). This psychic bifur-
cation, brought about through unconscious identification with the
male values coded by linguistic structures, one of which is misogyny, reinforces the divided consciousness, the post-tragedic stance,
which the feminist reader already brings to the reading experience.
Such a reader would agree with Frye that criticism is a leading
"*through*—not *away from*—the immediate experience of reading a
literary work" (Hamilton, 1990, 204, emphasis original) but would
ask how that experience might influence for ill, at least in the short
run, in theorizing the ethical aim of literature education. Rethinking
that aim in moral and political terms is the mandate of the re-
educated imagination. (Not since Plato has reading for pleasure been
so much thought of as an activity for consenting adults.)

Feminist criticism holds no monopoly on the desire to change
the regulatory nature of reading literary texts. But feminist theories of
reading reconceptualize literature as moral communication by questioning the grounds of literary importance in terms of a gendered and
divided consciousness. Under the gaze of a woman reading with the
passion of her subjectivity, a subjectivity formed by self-conscious
awareness of her post-tragedic quality of bewilderment, literary taxonomies topple, aesthetic categories dissolve, and "strong writers
turn pale" (Lipking, 1983/1984, 103). A poetics of need would build
a literary theory by taking literature personally and politically, and
through it embrace a tolerance of difference akin to the poetics of
pluralism in that the goals of both are the goals of literature as moral
communication, again, not as a role model for behavior, but as a
scrupulous "self-consciousness—of reading, speaking, and listening
to one another" (de Lauretis, 1986, 8), or, as Felman (1982) has put it,
as a "self-subversive self-reflection" (qtd. in Penley, 1986, 140). But
whereas the self-reflection of pluralism conceives of difference in
terms of equality, that of a poetics of need does so in terms of an
oppression which is entrenched and often invisible.

Yet such a poetics, still in the writing, is not systematic. Women
readers participate in a host of diverse practices that write the story
of their bewilderment. In so doing they act both as *connatae* and
*(in)connatae*. As *connatae* they continue to unearth lost authors,
deliberately misread found ones, and steal the language through
puns and neologisms. As *(in)connatae*, those bewildered by unantici-
pated painful discrepancies between appearance and patriarchal
reality, sometimes they just say "No" as a kind of civil disobedi-
ence. The immolation of John Updike by Judy and her sisters was
not resistance to knowing, not an inability to see alternatives, but
rather the conscious suppression of them for their own good. This

might be construed by a poetics of pluralism as at least a case of self-censorship. However, I would defend their cry to "Burn it!" as a self-empowering choice to enact a poetics of need.

The conceptual framework of feminist criticism is engaged and emergent; there is no literary theory "that builds from the ground up on women's own experience of literature, on women's own ways of thinking" except through "masculine modes" (Lipking, 1983/1984, 87). And, the road to self-subversive self-reflection is arduous enough without the accumulation of depression and despair (Ruthven, 1984, 87) that can come from studying male-authored texts in "images of women" criticism, though this kind of study is relevant to most courses in women's literature. Theoretically, of course, there is no reason why research into sexual stereotyping in literature should not enrich understanding of aesthetic mechanisms, literary conventions, the history of taste, and feminism itself. But feminist criticism is an instrument of "counterhegemony" (Gramsci, 1971). Through it, women, especially at the graduate level, live out their self-transformations. Within this context, it is difficult to simply "academise material which many women feel cannot be handled 'objectively' because it touches too raw a nerve" (Ruthven, 1984, 71–72). The "polysemous bliss" (Lipking, 1983/1984, 97) promised by the poetics of pluralism can be threatening to women who fear their theorizing can only be reactive to the law of the father. One way of "giving the lie to daddy" (87), then, is to refuse to theorize, a refusal that "could in itself be to create a theory" (Meese, 1986, 144).

Hence the call to "Burn it!" To brand this action an instance of censorship would be to detain Judy and her sisters in the double bind of the educated woman, articulated so eloquently by Jane Roland Martin in her critique of R.S. Peters. According to Martin, in order for a woman to be educated along the lines of Peters' rationalist model, innocent as it is of the qualities of affect, she would have to undergo a double immasculation similar to some female readers of "A&P." For both Martin's educated woman and Judy and her sisters, "To be unalienated they must remain uneducated" (1981, 104). We can change the ideal of the educated person by supplanting Peters' model with Martin's. The remedy, however, for feminist readers/critics is less sanguine, as Martin herself acknowledges; for, in order to engage the logical structure of their oppression, they must submit to the androcentric order of symbolic thought and language itself (100–101). Ways of crossing this double-cross (Meese, 1986) tend to be radical. I submit that Judy and her sisters staged their defiance of the poetics of pluralism through the minds and voices of their own readerly bodies—the site of their literal and metaphorical appropriation (Meese, 1986, 120) as the "ground," the material cause, so to speak, of the *mythos* of the male hero's individuation process.

## The Location Problem

In making inferences about the significance of Judy and her sisters to the relationship between feminist criticism/pedagogy and the selection/censorship problem, it's important to understand the actual context in which this story was so vehemently rejected by these students. I've recounted the surrounding circumstances in detail elsewhere (Bogdan, 1987a, 1990a, 1990d); but here it will suffice to sketch out the constellation of some of the forces that predisposed these students to act as they did. This was a course that was being offered for the very first time. While women's literature and feminist critical strategies had been used in other disciplines, this was the first forum at OISE for focusing on the literary as such within a feminist purview. I was, at the time, a part-time instructor, new to feminism, and strongly identified with the students, some of whom were personal friends, whose counsel I'd sought in drawing up the syllabus and whose advice I continued to solicit as the course progressed. These were women (and one man) whom I regarded as equals in every way.[3] From the beginning, the question of whether to read male authors at all had been a political one on which we had disagreed. I believed that it was historically, aesthetically, and peda- gogically correct to include male-authored literature primarily as a way of raising consciousness about "images of women" and theories of representation; conversely, the students felt that time and psychic space were too precious for such ruminations, however critically enlightening they might prove to be.

The pedagogical dynamics of the first-half of the course had foregrounded issues of pedagogical style and authority for the stu- dents. They had been feeling dislocated for a number of reasons. In the first place, three guest lecturers had overwhelmed them with the "performance" mode of teaching. As well, I had to be absent from the class just when the students' confidence in themselves and in the collegiality of the course needed reinforcement. Bereft and recalci- trant on the evening of my return (the occasion of this account), they simply occupied the space when given the chance. Intending to pre- sent the taxonomy of responses and respondents I'd developed on "A&P" from Frye's theory (Chapter 5), I played a taped reading of the story (rendered by a male in this first-person narrative) to provide some "common ground" from which to discuss the orchestration of possible interpretations. In order to avoid a wholly direct instruc- tional mode of pedagogy, I encouraged the class to respond freely after the tape, thereafter to "fill in the gaps" according to the tenets of the taxonomy.

In terms of what transpired, there was doubtless a much wider range of response than I remember now or was aware of then; but my theoretical taxonomy recounted in Chapter 5 was certainly rendered futile and irrelevant. Through it, I'd hoped to demonstrate just how the dialectical working through of the sexist biases in the story, by way of inducing the "right 'quality' of bewilderment," could ultimately neutralize the story's offensiveness. In face of the call to "Burn the damned thing!" I lost any hope of moving my students from engagement to detachment in a single evening. In fact, since then I have realized that the very polarization of these two states masks a false dichotomy in modes of literary response, a dichotomy that trivializes the intuitive and privileges the ratiocinative, which denigrates readers' tacit knowledge in favor of critics' "objectivity" (Chapters 8 and 9). While there is always somewhere to go in criticism, one can only be where one is. Though I did not understand why or how, I felt that something other than censorship, self-censorship, or critical naiveté was going on in that class on that evening, and that not only was it something that had to be recognized, but that it was something I needed to honor.[4] Perhaps the right quality of bewilderment was beginning to induce post-tragedic consciousness of a different conception of literary literacy.

## Pluralism, Need, and the Problem with the Meta-Problem

When the re-educated imagination adds the feeling, power, and location problems to the meta-problem, the underlying premises of the justification, censorship, and response problems begin to shift. Take the relationship between literature and life. Instead of literature "descending into experience" (Hamilton, 1990, 208), we now have, with the infusion of life into literature, the emphasis on psychic and imaginative energy flowing in the opposite direction. What might that mean for the justification problem? From Philip Sidney to Northrop Frye, defenses of poetry have assumed the salutary educational effects of imaginatively inhabiting other worlds and other lives through sympathetic identification. Indeed, I would hazard that every school guideline for literature on this continent is replete with claims for the power of literature to educate by vicarious experience. But there is rarely an acknowledgement within the academy that literature has imaginative limits, that it sets up the intellectual and emotional territory framing moral choice, or that identification cuts both ways, that it can be alienating as well as uplifting. If, as educators, we continue to enlist the educational value of literature on the basis of its capacity for culturing the emotions through sympathetic identification, we will have to look at dis-identification and the "descent" into real feeling as a logical and psychological priority in handling classroom response, and that is likely to produce problems.

This point leads directly to the premise of the censorship problem —whether and what literature says. It can be argued that protection from discomfiting emotional experiences in reading literature is no grounds for exclusion, that through discussion of the issues confronted in strong works, students erode their resistance to knowing, thereby becoming initiates of the poetics of pluralism by broadening their spheres of identification and sharpening their critical faculties. This is what I take Frye to mean when he speaks of transferring the imaginative energy from literature to life (1963a, 55). I agree with this and have already expressed my reservations about engagement with the text as a transparent window on reality (Chapter 4). I believe, too, that students should examine the evidence, not throw it out. But that simply begs the question of the shaping power of identification and the practical problem of text selection. Reading literature from the standpoint of "life," being a real reader with real feelings in a real time and place foregrounds the fact that, notwithstanding its hypothetical nature as part of Frye's order of words, literature does say things. If this is so, and if literature *is* to be undergone as well as understood, and if psychic nourishment, socialization, and taking responsibility for one's own learning are held up in literature education as values equal to those of critical judgment and aesthetic appreciation (and they are), then the poetics of need must at times displace the poetics of pluralism. As K. K. Ruthven asks rightly, "[W]hat can you do with a text once you have exposed it? . . . Whether acknowledged or not, censorship is inevitable in the compiling of a feminist syllabus, especially if one of the criteria for selection is that the work should instil a positive sense of feminine identity" (1984, 73). Within the context of identity-building (which I stress is not the *only* reason literature is on the curriculum but it is one of them, at least at the school level), reading in terms of that and what literature says can do damage. To acknowledge both sides of the identity issue, as the case of Judy and her sisters has purported to do, is to challenge the premises not only of the justification and censorship problems—the relationship between literature and life and whether and what literature says—but of the response problem—the autonomous reader.

How can a pedagogical theory preserve the notion of the autonomous reader in the hindsight that literary experience is real experience and that literature says things? The action of Judy and her sisters underlines the delicate balance between the power of literary naming, the self-determination of the reader, and the problematic nature of autonomy based on traditional developmental notions of response. In theorizing the complexity of the relationship between censorship and response, the operative word is not "choice" but "agency," which can sometimes be exercised by the refusal to read. Sometimes agency and autonomy presuppose first closing down alternatives, using negative capability as a way of calling things out of existence for a while in order to make way for new growth (Plato, *Symposium*, 205b).

The call to "Burn it!" raises the question of the developmental assumptions underlying the poetics of need. Does a poetics of need, defined by the imperatives of identity and identification, turn on a conception of lack? Does need merge into pluralism once it becomes "positive" rather than "negative"? I'm not sure about the usefulness of such questions because the answer presupposes a simplistic view of the issues of feeling, power, and location. I hesitate to view feminist criticism in terms of "evolution" or "progression," for valuations of greater or less "maturity" or "sophistication" reinforce stereotypes about "shrillness" and "ax-grinding" by those who locate themselves comfortably, but mistakenly, outside the problem. I say "erroneously" because all intellectual inquiry is politically interested and all knowledge is partial however much the act of knowing, when it happens, seems universal and is experienced holistically (See Chapters 7, 8, and 9).[5] These are important lessons taught by a poetics of need.

The developmental assumptions of the poetics of need also point up rich correspondences between feminist criticism and a Freirean pedagogy of the oppressed, particularly with respect to classroom implications of the elevation of identification *over* reason (Scahill, 1989, 96, emphasis added) in the acquisition of literacy skills generally. Perhaps the psychological/epistemological question of whether Judy and her sisters were suffering from agnosis is less important than the moral/political one of whether they should have been made to suffer "A&P" at all. Surely the operative phrase is, again, *patio, patere*, what can and should be literally tolerated by students in any given educational situation, and who decides. A poetics of need recognizes the developmental value education places on building individual, social, and political identity through identification. So does every literature curriculum guideline; and that developmental mandate complicates the meta-problem far more than is comfortable for most educators, pointing up how the justification, censorship, and response problems can never leave each other alone, and how an adequate definition of literary literacy must now deal with the feeling, power, and location problems as the politics of the engaged reader.

Whether it is feminist, nationalist, pluralist, or consumerist, the bias inscribed in every literature curriculum makes it problematic to speak of the educational value of literature as self-evident, intrinsic, ideologically neutral, or morally inviolate in unqualified terms. As Michael Ryan writes:

> The practice of knowing is itself already a form of bias, because it entails selecting and excluding, more often than not, according to historically determined institutional norms of what *should* be studied and known. . . . Education . . . enables knowledge, and education, . . . necessarily produces bias. (Ryan, 1982, 142, emphasis original)

Rarely is that bias made as incarnate as with Judy and her sisters, but their exclusion of "A&P," I think, is co-dependent on teachers' inclusion of the widest possible range of authors, genres, and subject matters in the literature curriculum. If this co-dependence is acknowledged, then the poetics of need might in fact become inseparable from the poetics of pluralism. In one respect it already has, in the form of feminist criticism as a kind of "polyvocality" (see Martindale, 1987) that celebrates rather than dreads, evades, or merely tolerates difference.

## (Dis)Identification, Response Development, and the Pedagogy of Need

In my many discussions with Judy and her sisters about the implications for learning in that initial course offering, I have come to wonder about the educational value of dis-identification. Neither Judy nor I, for instance, are conscious of having had a learning experience equal in emotional intensity to that recounted in this paper, not just in terms of what we were forced to undergo on that fateful February evening, but in terms of the tough re-examination of our beliefs it has precipitated for our lives since. For example, I have since dismantled and reassembled my taxonomy in the light of feminist, Marxist, and deconstructionist literary theory (see Bogdan, 1990b, 1990c, 1990e). Undisplaced extremity can be a powerful condition of learning; making strange may be more educationally profitable than making nice. One thing, though, is certain: throughout all that pain, no one ever seemed to stop thinking. Alienation, then, can be transformative. In this sense the educational value of literature *is* intrinsic, self-evident, and morally inviolate. Plato had one thing right—literature influences, and influences powerfully. That this influence is not empirically measurable in terms necessarily persuasive to all is to my mind a blessing; for if it were, the subversive role of literature traditionally claimed by its apologists would be seen (and suppressed) for what it is—a vehicle for transformation as well as enculturation—and the literature curriculum consequently sanitized into a parody of itself. This is, of course, precisely what is happening now throughout the Western world, where the raising of consciousness seems to have become ironically counter-productive: either incurring the ire of those who know, or the fear of those who prefer not to know. Increasingly, it has become difficult to speak, to take a position without offense to what is "Other." Yet, as has been acknowledged, the very mortification of feeling induced in the case of Judy and her sisters proved to be personally cathartic and educationally gratifying in the long view.

The above constitutes a state of contradiction I will not attempt to resolve, especially when, as has already been noted, the importance of individual, social, and political identity in learning to read and write is now taken for granted. But problematizing the problem is better than thinking it a simple matter. Educational values themselves (as they are often conceived by progressive, liberal, educational bodies), even when those values include such objectives as eroding sexist and racist stereotypes, call forth the paradox of education's dual aim to enculturate and to transform simultaneously. This paradox is nowhere more apparent than in the task of justifying and implementing the literature curriculum, which purports both to lead students *out* of themselves and whatever security the culture has succeeded in providing, on the one hand, and *into* an awareness of how that security is controlled and manipulated by language itself, on the other.

In a culture as diverse as that of multi-cultural Toronto, for example, where in a single school there can be represented sixty-two nations and fifty-four first languages, one student's imaginative heaven is bound to clash with another's imaginative hell. How to maximize this reality, not defend against it, is one of today's major challenges to literature education. In order to meet this challenge, those who draft official guidelines for the teaching of literature need a consistent philosophy of literary literacy based on a sober appreciation of the meta-problem as augmented by the feeling, power, and location problems. But even a theory of literary literacy cannot solve the problem of what is to be read, by whom, and under whose aegis. The options for such decisions range from the adoption of a single literary text for seventh grade (as is now the case in one Canadian province) to abolition of the literature curriculum altogether in favor of class libraries (Moffett, 1988). Given the premises of this chapter, a narrower range of identification would be more consonant with the poetics of need; and a wider one, with the poetics of pluralism. The literature curriculum needs to accommodate both so that literary literacy signifies the feeling of coming to know the truth about oneself and/or the world and getting distance on that feeling.

I don't expect that even attaining such a goal could be a panacea in resolving the meta-problem. But awareness of the political context of the engaged reader is a logically and psychologically prior question in respecting readers' individual, collective, and imaginative identities. That is the motivating force behind the project of the re-educated imagination in raising the feeling, power, and location problems. If literary literacy is to be truly emancipatory, it must acknowledge patterns of dominance and control of the culture and provide for recognition of those patterns as part of its educational mandate. Within those patterns of dominance, the overarching question becomes that of agency, the transformational effects of induced alienation notwithstanding. It is too easy to cloak these realities under the arrogance of a humanist/pluralist hieratic mantle that assumes that the category "literature" confers upon its readers the right to say anything about, or impute anything to, anybody at any time without regard to the conditions of feeling, power, and location framing that saying or imputing. True transformation occurs only when learners transform "the structures by which they are formed" (Reither, 1989, 7). Sometimes this will involve the critical reading of existing texts; sometimes it will involve calling a text out of existence for a while to make way for new growth. If the poetics of need, then, is to be "equal" to the poetics of pluralism, the literature curriculum would adopt an affirmative action policy, giving pride of place to identities now marginalized (Zita, 1988) and "depoeticiz[ing]" some literary texts (Purves, 1991, 216). At the same time, it would have to guard against the kind of chauvinism that would result in making the plays of Shakespeare museum pieces accessible only to an elite fortunate enough to be privy to the cultural legacy of a poetics of pluralism. This is a dilemma teachers of literature face, in the knowledge that their decisions and premises for those decisions make them unwilling bedmates with the religious fundamentalists in Peterborough County, who were within a different context and perhaps with a different agenda also worried about the feeling, power, and location problems.

Logically, censorship defined as political coercion, as the imposition of one individual's or group's values on others through impeding the acquisition of knowledge, is a separate question from that of text selection raised by the poetics of need. This is also the case in practice. Most educators do recognize the difference between restricting access to materials and being sensitive to the cultural climate of the school, as well as to the importance of psychological readiness for some literary works. Yet, given the educational authority vested in a curriculum, the logic of classification as the dance of inclusion and exclusion in choosing what is to be taught challenges the presuppositions of the very notion of appropriateness, development, (dis)identification, and the educational value itself of literature. So do feminist challenges to aesthetic distance, formalist conceptions of literary evidence, and the uncritical acceptance of dominance and of humanism.

To render these notions problematic is, of course, a first step only in resolving the meta-problem, which, within the first five chapters of this book has been understood primarily in epistemological terms. In the "real world," teachers and administrators must make logical arguments in defense of particular books, write rationales for the teaching of literature itself in the face of other competing aspects of the language arts curriculum, and deal with the political consequences of their everyday decisions, which are taken up more concretely as formerly disenfranchised minorities become aware that what and how students read affects their literacy and figures in shaping their values and forming their identity. This dialectical activity forms the backdrop of the re-educated imagination. I conclude this chapter, not by offering strategies, advice, or principles for how to proceed, but rather by using the case of Judy and her sisters as a heuristic for further contradictions about the relationship between censorship/selection, identification/identity, and the poetics of need/pluralism.

But haven't we had enough "problems"? Surely some things are clear. For one thing, English teachers do not bully students and parents; they provide alternative texts for those whose sensibilities, identities, and empowerment are at risk in the descending action of real readers reading. When they do, when the "alternative text" approach is adopted, it's as a "remedy" for individual students who "have a need" to take refuge in agnosis. Yet it's still the canon, the central text, that normalizes what is read and studied. If an alternative text is legislated by teachers, especially if it replaces one about which parents or students complain, then teachers can be accused of censorship. In the final section of this chapter I will present another Toronto example of the politics of the engaged reader, in which one English department of one school practiced what in my view was both the poetics of pluralism and the poetics of need; others would say it was censorship and self-censorship along the lines of the rationalization offered by Renaissance Peterborough against Laurence's *The Diviners* (1974; see my Chapter 4). In the case below, the teachers came to the decision *not* to teach critically what was there, but to call something else into existence for a while. And they did so because of their sensitivity to the three new problems introduced in this chapter.

## The Meta-Problem Expanded: Feeling, Power, and Location

Three years ago the English department of a Toronto secondary school with a large population of black students complied with a request from a black student movement to remove from the curriculum William Golding's *Lord of the Flies* because some students were offended by a single line which referred to blacks pejoratively. The passage occurs near the end of the novel where Piggy asks the boys, "Which is better—to be a pack of niggers like you are, or to be sensible like Ralph is?" (1954/1959, 221). How could those members of the polarized English faculty who voted against the book have come to such a decision when their training in literary context and their commitment to literary values would normally have militated against judging the work racist? To answer this question, let's first return to the why of the meta-problem, enculturation and transformation, and its underlying premise, the relationship between literature and life in the hindsight of acknowledging the feeling, power, and location problems.

Enculturation and transformation are directly related to certain givens of the literature curriculum: sympathetic identification, vicarious experience, and social relevance. On the one hand, literature is supposed to lead into and out of the individual "self" by way of a positive engagement with the text; on the other, it is supposed to result in that "self" accommodating and assimilating the values of the society in which its future citizens are to dwell. It is not difficult to see how these two aims of leading in and leading out are diametrically opposed in the case of *Lord of the Flies* (Golding 1954/1959). The black students being enculturated into an ethos of liberal humanism, which prizes racial tolerance and celebrates the multicultural fabric of Canadian national identity, were being asked to identify against themselves (Fetterley, 1978). The argument that the Golding novel is a "classic" whose expulsion threatens cultural literacy conflicts with other criteria simultaneously operating in selecting curriculum, for example, ease of positive identification, a principle upon which the adolescent fiction industry, supported by schools, thrives. To honor positive identification in one context and dismiss it when it becomes inconvenient to espouse it, to invoke the ideals of cultural heritage and literary context for one group of students and not another, especially when the "inconvenient" group is a minority in a culture whose diversity is otherwise touted as a mark of national identity, but whose consciousness is already mired in Bartky's "double ontological shock" (1979, 256)—of knowing that things are not what they seem and that the situation is not likely to improve—is at best anomalous and at worst racist. Within this context enculturation and transformation seem not just incongruent but counterfeit.

Logically and ethically, educators cannot embrace an affirmative action curriculum policy that seeks to engender attitudinal change and then suddenly cry "Censorship!" when that policy is interpreted (by those whom it purports to liberate) as the right not to read books that reinforce for those oppressed by them the very psychic anguish the affirmative action seeks to erode. Failing to address the feeling, power, and location problems results in a curriculum policy which can all too easily apply with apparent impunity the double-standard of accepting the criterion of positive identification in the case of young adult fiction (a category whose questionable "literariness" is tolerated because of its motivational benefits) but of rejecting it in the case of a group objecting to the real life oppressive effects of a work whose "literariness" is accepted. That the first instance constitutes the adding of material, and the second the subtracting of it, does not alter the unacknowledged bias in the decision; nor does it erase the power differential between the assumed rights of the dominant to transmit their culture, and the "obligation" of the marginalized to accept it in a society that boasts equality for all.

As mentioned earlier, there is also the danger of trading off strong literature for "sub-literary" pap such that no student's interest would likely be engaged by it anyway and of perpetuating, in the name of sensitivity to the feelings of women and minorities, the very chauvinism a fair curriculum policy would attempt to eliminate. The pluralist solution of striking a balance among various literary pictures of the world, in attempting to give equal weight to all points of view, simply undercuts the intent of affirmative action and again begs the question of the reflectionist theory of literature (Sidney's "speaking picture" [1966, 25]) challenged by much recent literary theory and critiques of English studies as a historical and political institution (Moi, 1985; Robert Morgan, 1990; Weedon, 1987; Widdowson, 1982). Further, though the humanism of an ever-widening pluralist canon is appealing theoretically, the logic of inclusion and exclusion makes it impossible to teach everything, and it's simply naive to suppose that there should be no conflict over the various pictures of the world the literature is supposed to be "figuring forth," in Sidney's sense (1966, 25). If the students in the *Lord of the Flies* (Golding, 1954/1959) instance had asked for the addition of a book sympathetic to blacks rather than for the removal of Golding's novel, the issue might have escaped the censorship label, but it wouldn't have avoided the reality of the feeling, power, and location problems. The English department, in this instance, knew they couldn't have it both ways: to take seriously literature's transformational function in empowering students to be responsible for their own learning and to deny those students' agency. In short, they knew they could no longer blink at the principle of the double effect of the text: its influence for ill as well as for good. Here the students were well aware of the liberal humanist agenda of the literature curriculum and could understand the educational project of reading the book "critically"; but their feeling, power, and location problems outweighed "educational purposes." From where they stood, as for Judy and her sisters, and as for David Perry from Plano, Texas, who resisted knowing *Huck Finn* (my Chapter 4), they just couldn't stomach it!

Was the English department in the above example practicing censorship by abrogating responsibility for transmitting the cultural heritage or was it practicing what it preached in terms of its mandate to foster respect for the dignity of minorities and to nurture their emergent individual and collective identities? I believe that in the short term they were doing both, by attending to the poetics of pluralism *within* the poetics of the need—by recognizing the feeling, power, and location problems. What they did *not* do was erase the lived experience of the students in front of them under the cloak of an abstraction. This took courage, especially in face of the enormous sway of liberal beliefs about the unfettered right to know regardless of its cost in human suffering, or of the opprobrium borne by those who risk challenging the blanket application of the principle of the intrinsic and inviolate nature of knowledge, particularly literary knowledge. Again, this is hard to write. Let me state here that I'm not advocating the capitulation of the entire Western tradition of arts and letters to pressure groups. What I am saying is that if all knowledge is biased (Ryan, 1982), and if education is implicated in that bias, and further, if educational policy continues to enshrine the power of literary knowledge in advancing the cause of what Frye calls "concerned truth" (1979/1973, 66), then the tension between the espousal of that concern and the freedom to pursue it must be held before it can ever be resolved, if indeed it can be resolved at all. Holding the

tension means attending to the exigencies of the asymmetrical relationship between the dominant and the marginalized, between those
who would know, the "heroes" of the intellectual quest, and those
who provide the "ground" for that quest. Ideally, of course, these two
roles would ultimately be exchanged, wherein every voice eventually resonates as part of one's own. But that time has not yet come.
And so, those in control can afford to relinquish some control, giving
pride of place in the curriculum to what is "Other," to new stories
and to different voices.

Golding's *Lord of the Flies* (1954/1959) has not disappeared from
Toronto high schools; it has merely taken a well earned rest from
center stage for a time. But there's no mistaking that at least in this
one school, the novel is a casualty (it remains to be seen whether
temporary or permanent) of the logic of inclusion and exclusion.
Moffett's (1988) recommendation is that the only way to eliminate
the either/or choice of such a logic is to abolish the educational
authority of any literature curriculum by doing away with a syllabus
altogether in favor of class libraries; thus students can counterbalance the power of bureaucratic authority, learn the power of
choice, and be granted agency by exercising it. This solution may or
may not be practicable. Meanwhile, the key players in the Toronto
controversy have reached a prototypically Canadian compromise
solution. For two years now, *Lord of the Flies* (1954/1959) has been
officially reinstated in the literature curriculum. Though withdrawn
from the secondary school in question, the indicted book continues
to be compulsory reading in eight Toronto schools; but the conflict
has resulted in a number of positive strategies. The school board has
recommended, first, that "teachers should be allowed to decide
whether or not to use the book"; second, that a rationale for the
withdrawal of the book in the instance described above be circulated
to all schools; third, that the Board "ask its committee on bias in the
curriculum to determine how the book could be suitably used";
fourth, that teachers be trained "in the selection and use of novels";
and finally, that money be provided "for replacing biased books"
("School Board Rejects," 1988, A4). The political implementation of
literary literacy has, then, already begun; it is hoped that a theory of
literary literacy will help make the practice of it logically consistent,
epistemologically sound, and socially equitable. As for The Great
Tradition, Shelley can surely rest content that no longer are poets the
unacknowledged legislators of the world.

We began this chapter with a review of a conception of literary
literacy under the auspices of the educated imagination. That definition embraced literature as the stubborn structure of myth and
metaphor, which as a *structure* in itself is dumb and needs literary

criticism to speak for it. There, literary literacy encompasses the dialectical road of engagement and detachment. When traveled by the reader as mental pilgrim in Frye's vast mythological universe, the road of literary literacy leads to the transcendent vision of seeing everything as potentially identical with everything else (1957, 124). Within this purview, the main task is to be sure to know the difference between appearance and reality, ordinary existence and imaginative experience, partial and total form, stock and a "full" literary response. Here, boundaries and distinctions are clearly drawn along the lines of literature and life, the literary and the sub-literary, imaginative insight and social conditioning, canon, curriculum, and censorship, on the presupposition that the why, what, and how of teaching literature work together to produce citizens who think for themselves.

In this chapter I have tried to blur these boundaries and then redraw them along the lines of the feeling, power, and location problems in terms of taking seriously the proposition that the literary use of words has real effects in the world (for ill as well as for good), that the material conditions determining which students read what in schools are different for each student, and that this makes a difference to the influence of literature in the marking of difference—something the educated imagination has eclipsed. Re-educating the imagination means partly recasting the definition of literary literacy from something that has to do with reading and studying literature in the abstract to that which is accountable for the concrete consequences of students as embodied learners. Re-educating the imagination also means repositioning literary experience from something that is a given to something whose logical priority to criticism takes on the status of an ethical demand. In the next chapter we'll explore whether, in the hindsight of politicizing the definition of literary literacy, there is a sense in which literature can still be justified as the best subject matter in the world.

## Endnotes

1. In *Words with Power: Being a Second Study of the Bible and Literature* (1990e), Frye changed this definition to read "a story (*mythos*), usually about the acts of gods" (27).

2. The issue of experience itself in feminist literary criticism is highly contested. What feminist literary critics do agree on, however, is that abstractions, such as taxonomic structure described in Chapter 5, are indicative of androcentric modes of thinking. I have discussed this point more fully in Bogdan, 1990b, 1990e, and 1990g.

3. For a discussion of the importance of dismantling the power of pedagogical privilege, see Bleich, 1988.

4. In a recent class discussion, one of my students suggested that it was my previous reading in feminist theory along with my experience in a feminist community (minimal though they were at the time) that were the major factors in my decision to "let" Judy and her sisters occupy the space that was opened up. In other words, my emergent, though not yet self-consciously formulated, sense of the feeling, power, and location problems was tacit but necessary preparatory work in order for this event to have been made possible. She also made the observation that, in the account of Judy's response within the taxonomic structure of Chapter 5, Judy had remained nameless, and that it was only within the actualized context of this chapter that I named her. My thanks to Christabelle Sethna for these observations.

5. As one who does not locate himself outside the problem, David Bleich states that, within the feminist movement, "militancy is the unrelenting exercise of free speech and the continual announcement of the changes that are being sought. . . . the feminist movement is trying to enact what men have said they wished to enact but have never really succeeded in doing: transforming fights and wars and 'militant' action into purely social and verbal forms of conflict resolution" (1988, 27).

## Chapter Seven

# The Re-Educated Imagination and Literary Experience

### Is There Literary Life After Literary Literacy?

In the last chapter I offered a conception of literary literacy that took seriously literary experience as real experience. In fact, I suggested that literary experience needs to be taken so seriously that the meta-problem, in which justification, censorship, and response are inter-twined, has to be made more complex by adding to it the feeling, power, and location problems. In short, the educated imagination has to be re-educated to include the politics of the engaged reader. The last chapter also indicated that poets have become acknowl-edged legislators of the world in that readers are attesting more and more to the powerful influence of literature in their lives. Does this mean that the justification problem has been resolved? Yes and no. Yes, because recognizing the feeling, power, and location problems reconfirms the poetic as a shaping force in the real lives of real readers. No, because, in dealing with this force, teachers are faced with poetry's actual and potential influence for ill, especially within an educational setting. As we saw in the last chapter, a poetics of need might dictate refusal of a text by reason of political commitment and the right to reject certain psychic undergoings wrought by liter-ary experience in terms of the feeling, power, and location problems. Just saying no *can* signify a kind of literary understanding.

Though the strategies of critical circumspection used to extricate readers from the ill effects of literary experience may solve problems immediately related to censorship and response, they throw open to question the normative value of literature as *experience* in the hind-sight of the politicizing of literary literacy undertaken in the last chapter. What I want to explore in this chapter is whether and how, given our redefinition of literary literacy in political terms, literary experience as engagement or involvement can be intrinsically con-nected to literacy as a poetics of need in expressly aesthetic and ethical terms. A conception of literary literacy as awareness of the *conditions* of literary experience seems more appropriate to the idea of literacy than does literary experience, if what we mean by literacy is conscious control of participation in the culture. Proponents of critical pedagogy and cultural studies might argue that this kind of control can be attained through a conception of literacy that is "aliterary," in which the disengaged *study* of textuality, intertextual-ity, or discourse, can, and should, take place quite independently of literary experience in its aesthetic sense.

As we saw in Chapter 5, it can be argued (as Frye himself arg-ues) that, in fact, literary experience as such actually impedes self-conscious awareness of how the constructedness of texts works on readers (Frye, 1963c, 123). It would seem, then, that showing literary experience to be a precondition for literate behavior would satisfac-torily resolve the justification problem. On the other hand, if literary experience is really just ancillary to literacy, a "rhetorical analogue" to "truth" (Frye, 1957, 13; 1970, 47; 1971/1973, 66), perhaps, then, the fervor of educators' belief in the educational value of literary experience as such is misplaced. Just how pervasive this sense of the normative power of literary experience is throughout the profession, as it informs practice, is illustrated below.

Recently I conducted a workshop on three approaches to gender in teaching Updike's "A&P" (1962) as a response to K.K. Ruthven's question, "What can you do with a text once you have exposed it?" (1984, 73). These "approaches" focus on critical analysis. They are pedagogical applications of three poststructuralist literary theories: the Anglo-American school of feminist reader-response theory, the psychoanalytic framework of Julia Kristeva, and the implications of Michel Foucault's theory for popular culture. The educators who formed the audience of that workshop were less interested in what to *do* with the story than in whether to teach it or not. People seemed to be divided into three camps: those who would "teach it critically" in the mode of critical pedagogy or cultural studies; those who would not use the story at all because they thought the feeling, power, and location problems were unresolvable in classrooms at present (their argument being that if literary experience is a form of real experience, the experience of "A&P" is one feminist readers don't especi-ally need right now); and those—mainly men—who felt that *their* experience of "A&P" was precisely what they and their students needed today. One participant confessed that it was the rereading and rethinking of the story within the context of the meta-problem that made him realize just how this story, which he had been using for years, really can affect the lives of women for ill. He would have used it as a point of departure for discussing how prototypical Sammy's sexist attitude is in contemporary culture. Another member, a woman, felt that the story was valuable in raising consciousness about the centrality of the rescue fantasy to Western thought and about its real costs in the lives of both sexes.

The workshop described above can be thought of as an exercise in literary literacy addressed to resolving the censorship problem in "A&P." As such, I think it would be successful so long as one subscribes to the principles of good will and openness—to the belief that "getting it out on the table" will make everything all right in the end. But this points up a number of additional problems which are raised by thinking that the censorship problem can be "solved" through pedagogical strategies based on literary criticism or sociological analysis. Such "solutions" are most often studies in detachment that bypass the meta-problem by treating the work in question as a textual document, in which the critical response is given priority over direct response. Teaching controversial works "critically," however, through a "pedagogy of detachment," can reproduce the very dissociation of sensibility, the split between thought and feeling, direct experience and conscious awareness of that experience, from which Frye has said all along we cannot escape. One workshop member, for example, insisted that his students would be corraled into parroting "right" answers modeled by the teacher's knowledge of literary symbolism or by the ideology of moral idealism. Another felt that his pedagogical agenda of delayed judgment would conflict sharply with some students, whose identification with the girls *and* Sammy as the younger generation *against* the older one would be so strong that they "wouldn't move past it." So the response problem still remains unresolved.

With respect to the justification problem, neither teaching the story nor not teaching it really comes to terms with the problematic nature of the moving power of poetry, in Sidney's and Shelley's sense. The dialectical strategies of the workshop (see Bogdan, Millen, & Pitt, 1992) would certainly reconfirm Frye's assertion that literary criticism is a form of social science, but what do they say about the importance of literature as an identifiable category or legitimate school subject? Why should we teach *literature* in the schools if the emotional power of literary experience, which seems to mark the uniqueness of literature as a school subject, needs to be continually defended *against* via literary literacy? Is response to literature merely a language game (Bleich, 1988)? A fundamental and "purely" literary critical objective, of course, would be to use the story to teach the distinction between character and narrator as a means of deepening the appreciation of the literary quality of "A&P." But that simply begs the question of the poetics of refusal made by Judy and her sisters in Chapter 6. As the negative effects of the sexist images of the story are experienced by some real readers reading, this distinction between the conventional and the real is a difference that seems to make no difference. And even if it *does* make a difference, it is as though literary criticism has become the means by which teachers have agreed to become philosophers who "chant over" to themselves a "countercharm" to the spell of poetry (*Rep.* 608a). In any case, what seems to be reinforced in this discussion is Frye's claim that "the emotional response" is one readers should "distrust" (1963c, 59).

The question seems to be, then, How can we distinguish literature from other disciplines which also develop critical thinking, and how can we legitimate literary experience as a unique way of being in the world—and in the school—without being trapped in the meta-problem? How can literary experience per se be something other than a necessary evil, a false resting place, (Murdoch 1977, 71), on the way to a kind of dialectical rationality? How can the answer to that question repair the split between the two Janus-like goals of literature education: enculturation and self-transformation? And, if our argument thus far has successfully challenged the assumption that literature influences only for good, what can be said about literature as literature? In the end, why was Plato not right? The meta-problem, as complicated by the feeling, power, and location problems, attests to *how* literary texts work on readers; but it also speaks to the fact that they *do*. If the feeling, power, and location problems are acknowledged as real problems, in attempting to formulate a rationale for the necessity of literature to the English studies curriculum, it seems crucial to look at the implications for literacy of literary/aesthetic experience itself.

What I now want to reconsider is the phenomenon of the Aha! response, the recognition of someone in an aesthetic attitude of feeling that they have come to know the truth about themselves and/or the world, so characteristic of the totalizing state associated with utter absorption in a work of literature—what in Chapter 5 we called stasis. This kind of experience, along with the desire for it, continues to recur even after the conditions which are thought to produce it have been scrutinized through the feeling, power, and location problems. The case studies in this book are examples of literature and aesthetic experience as powerful influences—for ill and for good. My intention in this chapter is to tease out just how these influences might be justified in terms of literacy. In doing so, the aim of this chapter is fourfold: first, to attempt to rescue the notions of stasis and aesthetic distance in the hindsight of a poetics of refusal, which makes direct response logically prior to the critical response and which politicizes literary engagement at the same time; second, to make a claim for literature as a unique, non-indoctrinatory form of raising consciousness; third, to consider whether literary experience as experience might be constitutive of a moral sensibility; and fourth, to consider whether literary experience can of itself bring about social change.

## Transformation and Enculturation: The Sacred and the Profane of Literary Experience

My notion of literary experience as aesthetic experience, while it may include literary appreciation, in the sense of understanding the author's craft and/or being sensitive to the qualities of textual complexity, ambiguity, and the like, stresses that aspect of aesthetic experience shared by other kinds of experience, such as mystical/ religious experience and learning experience, i.e., its transformative power, the very power that is assumed and celebrated in the excerpt from the Ontario *Guideline* (1987, 2) cited in Chapter 3—the collapse of ego boundaries, a sense of oneness with "what is." Heidegger's notion of "the unconcealedness of beings" (1971, 98) as that quality of interiority, of holding oneself open, is characteristic of what I want to claim is the spiritual quality of such experience. I would argue that it is this spiritual quality that is essential to the formation of human subjectivity. (Here art, which Terry Eagleton reminds us "began in the broadest possible way as a concept covering the whole of our bodily, sensuous life" [qtd. in Souchard, 1990, 165] would be a paradigm case of the aesthetic.)

In literary experience, this sacred quality can manifest itself as that feeling of coming to know the truth about oneself and/or the world, a state of imaginative identity with the poem, characterized by the Aha! response to poetic or universal truth, in Aristotle's sense (1965, 43–44): ". . . this is just how things are, and I didn't know it!" (Greene, 1986, 240). It is this very sense of the transparency of poetic truth that marks the appeal of transformative experience itself. It is what Plato saw as the apotheosis of all knowledge— mystical contemplation—which language, for him, could point to but never really convey nor exhaust, and what Frye sees as that which is "represented by what Milton calls the perfect diapason of a tonic chord, painting by Giotto's O, literature by the syllable *Aum*" (1965a, 31).

But, as we saw in Chapter 1, the problem with poetry, for Plato, was that this feeling of transparent truth is so compelling in its *poetic* formulation, which presumes to say "the truth," and say it powerfully, when it has no business making truth claims, that there is no recourse but to submit to it. Poetry thus becomes a moral technology of the soul which renders its devotees prey to the forces of domination and control, and resisters to those forces subject either to charges of censorship and self-censorship (as was played out in the case studies of the last chapter) or to the mediating—and emotionally attentuating—influence of literary criticism.

In view of Plato's wariness of respondents mistaking rhetorical verbal strategies for eternal verities (the phenomenon that makes poetry influence for ill not just for good), he can be thought of not only as the first philosopher of literature education, but as the first theorist of cultural imperialism. By adding the feeling, power, and location problems to the meta-problem in the previous chapter, I've stressed the importance of guarding against cultural imperialism by considering the material effects of the assumption that literature says things and says them powerfully. This sayability can be thought of as the "profane" aspect of poetry's influence, profane in the sense of making reference to things in the world. But, as we saw in Chapter 3, literary language is also "unsayable." This would constitute its sacred dimension. In this chapter I am exploring how literary/ aesthetic experience as direct response to the sayingness and unsayingness of literary language, so mistrusted by Plato because of its power to influence through the illusion of transparency, can be regarded as essential to attaining literacy. In other words, I'm looking at how literature education might be necessary to literacy because of the sacred, spiritual dimension of literary experience revealed by just this notion of transparency, not as naiveté, but as a mark of the ineffability of literary art. In doing so, it becomes necessary to examine direct response in individual reading acts and within the twin political goals of literature education, self-transformation and enculturation. Here the idea of stasis becomes useful to our inquiry.

## Stasis as Transparency

As stated in Chapter 5, stasis can be thought of as what takes place when readers respond directly to literature enveloped by a totalizing desire for transparency. Transparency, of course, has been much maligned in contemporary literary theory mainly because it tends to conflate the distinction between "discourse and disposition, a language and a mentality" (Robert Morgan, 1990, 207). For decon-structionists especially, transparency is suspect because it reinforces the myth that speech supersedes writing. To privilege writing over speech is to repudiate transparency; but repudiating it does not stamp out desire for it, which is the desire for the congruence between sign and meaning, symbolized by a flash of lightning (Godzich, 1983, xx) as a moment of perfect presence in the Aha! response. In Chapter 5, I suggested that stasis functions mostly as a metaphor for the literary event in which the reader experiences the work as a total form (Frye, 1957, 115; 1963b, 31). There *is* such a thing as stasis, however, though it happens rarely; and the possibility of experiencing it, I think, informs the belief in the conception of literary power we saw articulated in the 1987 Ontario Ministry *Guideline* statement (1987, 2; my Chapter 3). The importance of stasis to the relationship between literary experience and literary literacy is that it epitomizes the irresistibility of the aesthetic and thus provides a way to examine its interworkings with literary literacy as I have defined it in terms of awareness of the "real life" consequences of engagement with the text.

The "literary literate" who takes seriously literary experience but who also recognizes the politics of the engaged reader in terms of the feeling, power, and location problems knows, of course, that the irresistibility of the Aha! response is constructed, that it is brought about by cannily plotted tensions between the worlds of text and reader. Yet, paradoxically, attempts to interrogate these relationships would seem to be inappropriate, undesirable, and even counter-productive to attaining the state itself, which is, as we saw, intuitive, "acritical," and, to some extent, preverbal. Stasis always "takes us" by surprise. Part of its power is that it signifies a state of effortlessness and rest: stasis signals the resolution of three human imperatives— the search for truth, the fulfillment of desire, and the impulse to action (Bogdan, 1990b). Stasis can be thought of as a compressed communication-interpretive model of reading, in which everything is pre-designed to enable the lightning "power" of the text to work on readers. The price for such literary experience, though, if respon-dents are to escape cultural imperialism, is the loss of stasis through literary literacy defined as consciousness of the conditions of the sayingness, in personal, aesthetic, material, and political terms, of literary verbal power.

## Harmony as the Auditory Ideal

Why might the attainment of stasis be a precondition for cultural imperialism? As I argued in Chapter 3, stasis is a holistic apprehen-sion of the "total form" of a literary object. Transformative in the sense of identifying the "self" with the "other," it thus precipitates movement from one level of consciousness to another. But stasis has limitations as a conception of literacy because of its lack of self-consciousness. Its cognitive component is hidden from view. As literary experience, stasis is what Walter Ong (1988) calls an "auditory ideal" (42), one that moves toward the preconscious consolidation of individual identity. This oral musical aura of literary experience, what Ong claims is its "interiority," is, for Ong, necessary for the evolution of human consciousness. Its centripetal process works to unify, ultimately resulting in the "conservative holism" of a "homeostatic present" (Ong, 1988, 43). That is to say, the *feeling* of poetic truth stabilizes the respondent in a movement that works toward a state of equilibrium. Musically speaking, the presiding metaphor for such a centering would be harmony, "a putting together" (Ong, 1988, 42).

Literary literacy, on the other hand, involves a visual distancing from the text necessarily disallowed in the swept-awayness of stasis. In the definition of literary literacy sketched out in the last chapter, we accepted literary experience as real experience. But, as teachers, we also accepted responsibility for dealing with its real effects in the school world of student readers; and this, as we saw, demanded taking into account the feeling, power, and location problems in a highly self-conscious way. For educators to hold to a notion of stasis as a legitimate condition of literary experience, in the hindsight of having politicized textual engagement, would be to ask the respondent both to conquer and surrender to the text, not only to overcome the dissociation of sensibility of engagement and detachment in any one reading act at the psychic level, but to be accountable for the gap between self-transformation and enculturation at the social, political, and cultural levels. This would seem to be not only unfair but impossible without a theory of literary experience as a literate behavior (Heath, 1983, 1990) to cope with these dichotomies. So now we must ask whether, and in what way, this "harmony" is conducive or counter-productive to literacy—in personal, moral, social, cultural, and political terms.

Just how yawning the gap between spiritual self-transformation and political enculturation is in terms of our discussion of aesthetic/literary experience can be traced in two recent texts by Canadian art critic/aesthetician Asheleigh Moorhouse (1989) and theorist/historian of English studies Robert Morgan (1990). In exploring their ideas, I find the notion of stasis useful because, as the apotheosis of aesthetic experience, it conveys well the relationship of the sacred to the process of self-transformation, on the one hand, and, on the other, of the profane to the process of enculturation. Within the context of the sacred, stasis is literally sacrosanct, untouchable; within the profane, it is vulnerable to state control under the rubric of "the educational value of literature" regarded as a benign, ideologically neutral taken-for-granted. From different vantage points, Moorhouse and Morgan focus on the importance of looking beyond transparency and stasis to renegotiating the relationship between text and respondent, Moorhouse from the "sacred" perspective of redefining "I" and the "Other" in the phenomenology of "reading" works of visual art; Morgan, from that of the "profane" locating of English studies as a discipline with a political history. Both presuppose literary-aesthetic experience as a given of re-educating the imagination: Moorhouse, as a necessary ingredient to embodying the reading subject; Morgan, to regarding that subject as part of a socially organized dialectical process.

## Self and Other in Literary Experience

Useful to us here are the ways in which Moorhouse and Morgan illuminate the conserving action of Ong's homeostatic present, the "voice" of direct aesthetic response, in both the sacred dimension of self-transformation and the profane domain of enculturation. Both turn on Barthes' "jouissance of being" (qtd. in Moorhouse, 1989, 24) as the elevation of the pleasure principle in responding to texts, whether they are those of the visual arts, as in Moorhouse, or of English literature, as in Morgan. Using Lacanian psychoanalytic theory, Moorhouse outlines at the level of ontology the imperative for the respondent to establish a sense of equilibrium and coherence through the aesthetic pleasure of direct response to the art object. This imperative is inextricably bound up with the sense of ineffability resulting from the jouissance of being as the desire for the Other (1989, 24–25). Applied to literary experience regarded as Ong's auditory ideal, then, this need for direct response is crucial to self-transformation, which cannot take place without this sense of "the restoration of homeostasis" in the respondent (Moorhouse, 1989, 25).

By contrast, Robert Morgan moves outward, centrifugally, from aesthetic experience to reflecting on its implications for cultural imperialism. In "The 'Englishness' of English Teaching" (1990), an exhaustive trek through the history of English studies in the Canadian province of Ontario, Morgan advances a scathing critique of "English" as a self-conscious project of colonizing the souls, and bodies, of that province's young, in the service of WASP racial supremacy. He documents repeatedly how belief in the "intrinsic" value of the literary "classics" in English to the "timeless truths" of the human condition through a "disinterested aesthetic" is conflated with and co-opted by a relentless political machine bent on the "mapping of social identities" (215). These identities were formed and nurtured precisely under the assumption that literary experience operates on just the kind of homeostatic present Moorhouse and Ong deem necessary to psychic equilibrium and spiritual awareness—the relationship between self and Other. Morgan argues, however, that in the archives of Ontario's language arts educational documents, this Other invokes a suppressed construction, which functioned as a benchmark against which the white, middle-class, and English norm—an "Identity *against* alien Otherness" (204, emphasis added)—made its case for "the belief that 'English language and literature', . . . reflects the immutable truths of the human condition" (200). The sacred Other, then, becomes the profane Other. In this chapter—and the next—we're concerned with determining whether and how such Otherness, when placed within the context of its relationship to literacy, can be spiritually defensible and socially redeemable.

## Literary Experience as Stereophonic Vision

*Defining Literature and Aesthetic Experience*

I realize, of course, that I have been using the "L" word again, something which those of us who used to use it without quotation marks are now rather loathe to do. So let me say here that I don't consider what is called literature to be fixed, in terms of canon or curriculum, and I don't think of literature or literariness as primarily a set of properties that are inherent in a text, despite my temptation to enumerate such descriptors as structural depth, textural complexity, lexical ambiguity, intertextual richness, metaphorical force, or musical recursiveness in my list of epithets for admission to the literary elect. Though I accept that literature is a contested and contestable term, that it is complicitous in inscribing and reproducing ideology, and is thus accountable in educational terms, at this point I still would define it in terms that would distinguish it logically from the nonliterary. (See Chapter 10 for a modification of this view.)

John Ellis (1974) uses the analogy of a weed to define the literary: you can't come to an answer by a listing of attributes. A weed may have the same characteristics as a flower, tree, or bush; it does not exist by virtue of its "authorial intention" but by its function. It comes into being only when a community which recognizes it as such decides to make it a weed (37–41). So too with literature. A text becomes literary when a reader or readers assign to it the category "literary," that is, when an interpretive community decides to call it a work of literature and to use it in a literary way or not; in short, when one reads aesthetically (Rosenblatt, 1978) or poetizes a text (Purves, 1991, 216). As we saw in Chapter 3, Ellis defines literary use as distinct from the ordinary use of language in that literary use is that in which *"the text is not taken as specifically relevant to the immediate context of its origin"* (1974, 44, emphasis original). The immediate context of origin might be the personal expression of sorrow in the face of, say, an untimely death of a family member; the *literary* context, an elegiac use of language that would arouse interest among those who would not necessarily feel sympathy personally in the actual situation (44). Yet when literary experience is regarded as real experience, interest and/or sorrow will be enmeshed in aesthetic or literary response according to the specific circumstances, needs, and desires of readers, according to how they are situated in terms of the feeling, power, and location problems. David Bleich also defines literature as a use, but with an emphasis on the social aspect of "a culture's uses of language. Even in nonliterate societies, a literary event (a performance, for example) is a pause in everyday life marked by a gathering of people with the common purpose of experiencing the event" (1988, 114). We'll return to the social context of the definition of literature in Chapters 9 and 10, but next I want to consider literary experience specifically in terms of individual aesthetic response.

Ellis thinks of aesthetic response in literature as the immediate conscious awareness of all that makes an impact on "our minds, consciously or unconsciously, in works of literature" (1974, 243). This definition is useful in showing the differences between literary experience and other forms of psychic and intellectual activity in that it privileges immediacy and intensity, those aspects of literary experience that distinguish it from the operations of literary criticism and literary appreciation, which require a certain distance from the text in order to understand its significance, detect its structure, marvel at its craft, and so on. Though these forms of awareness may be present in literary experience, they are not logically prior to it, at least not within the conceptual framework of the re-educated imagination, which seeks to legitimate textual engagement as the primary principle for justifying literature in the schools.

The comparative state of detachment from the text demanded by self-conscious literary appreciation can be thought of as alphabetizing of literary experience. According to Paul Ricoeur (1976), the experience itself has to be shored up "by relating it to the ontological priority of discourse," the "fleeting character of the literary event" (1976, 9) being epistemologically weak. Literary experience *qua* literary experience bespeaks the aural/oral aspect of the Homeric mind, which, in obeying voices of the gods, was possessed of an imagination that today some would think of as "uneducated" (Cf. Meek, 1991, also my Chapter 9). Reminiscent of the acoustical verbal power of the oracular, literary experience (in the sense that we have been using it) is marked by the immediacy, intensity, simultaneity, and interiority of pure utterance. Literary experience can be thought of as a state of transparency of meaning that is rendered opaque by literary literacy. As Ong's "auditory ideal" (1988, 42), literary experience exists in time; literary literacy, on the other hand, espouses a visual ideal spread out in space, "laid out before [our] eyes, as in a modern printed atlas, a vast surface or assemblage of surfaces (vision presents surfaces) ready to 'be' 'explored'" (43), rather like Frye's "stubborn structure" (my Chapter 4).

This auditory ideal, according to Ong, invokes the desire for presence through its musical voice. In contrast to the visual, which dissects, hearing unifies: "When I hear, however, I gather sound simultaneously from every direction at once: I am at the center of my auditory world, which envelops me, establishing me at a kind of core of sensation and existence. This centering effect of sound is what high-fidelity sound reproduction exploits with intense sophistication. You can immerse yourself in hearing, in sound. There is no way to immerse yourself similarly in sight" (1988 42). I hope to show that literary experience as stereophonic vision is, in fact, a way of immersing respondents in sight.[1]

Ong juxtaposes this oral/aural ideal of the homeostatic present with the visual ideal of a writing culture, which he assumes to be liberated from what he calls the agonistic struggles of an oral culture. "When all verbal communication must be by direct word of mouth, involved in the give-and-take dynamics of sound, interpersonal relations are kept high—both attractions, and even more, antagonisms" (Ong, 1988, 37–38).[2] By contrast, writing cultures, which free the knower from the known, provide a kind of safety net of attraction (37), in which the author can, so to speak, hide behind the written text. For Ong, then, literacy becomes a defense against the sonic boom of orality and is regarded as an "advance" over oral cultures. David Bleich (1988) is severely critical of Ong's radical distinction between literacy and orality, indicting Ong's theory of literacy as a highly conservative, elitist social ideology "that represents the motives and purposes of establishmentarian support of literacy programs" (316). For Bleich, Ong's conception of the literatus is that of the male, white privilege of Arnoldian excellence (1988, 329).

The above has crucial implications for the justification of literary experience undertaken in this chapter and in remaining chapters.

Implicit in both Bleich's critique of Ong and in my own attempt at a "defense of poetry" is a concern to return the definition of literature to its oral roots (Bleich, 1988, 114–115). This entails upsetting hierarchies and blurring distinctions not only between literacy and orality, but between literature and life, imaginative experience and ordinary existence (my Chapter 8). Throughout this book, I am arguing that all such polarizations be broken down in order to democratize literature education. Brian Street's (1988) critique of Ong's artificial distinction between orality and literacy underscores the need for reconceptualizing literacy in order to eliminate categories of literate "haves" and illiterate "have-nots." According to Street, an emancipatory definition of literacy requires thinking about literacy in theoretical terms more as a "mix" between orality and literacy, as well as inquiry into "more specific relationships between literacy events and *practices* on the one hand and oral conventions on the other" (5, emphasis added). Like Heath (1990) and Bleich (1988), Street emphasizes the social context of literate behaviors (see also Stuckey, 1991; Street, 1984; my Chapters 9 and 10). My specific focus in this chapter, however, is to reclaim the oracular element in literary experience as a mark of the sacred process of consolidating a sense of individual identity. To this end I find Ong's conception of a "homeostatic present" (1988, 43) useful in signifying a sense of spiritual consciousness, which carries with it the visual quality of literacy when this experience is construed as a *literary* experience.

But even if I were to be successful in justifying literary experience as a literate behavior according to what I've outlined above, how do I do so within the context of arguing for literature in the curriculum? Legitimating this centripetal or conserving motion as an individual psychic process or spiritual force is a separate issue from justifying it as a school activity, especially in light of the importance of making students "culturally literate," that is, of developing their critical capacity for cultural forms and cultural products. This latter goal is, of course, a praiseworthy one; but, as we have seen, it is more the province of literary literacy and the pedagogy of detachment. On the face of it, the aural/oral aura of literary experience simply begs the question of literary literacy as a conscious event or an event of consciousness. In trying to answer whether literary experience as such can close the gap between transformation and enculturation, we are thrown back on the Platonic paradox of how the lie of fiction can make a claim to truth. What Plato rightly saw was that poetic truth is not propositional truth but "something else." Attempting to argue for the educational value, at least institutionally, of this something else may very well be a futile endeavor. As Philippa Foot (1972) has said about the logic of moral judgments, "when people are prepared to fight so hard for certain ends—'for example, for liberty and justice',—this may depend 'on the fact that these are the kinds of ends that arouse devotion' " (qtd. in Olsen, 1978, 223). Her observations on moral imperatives might also apply to literature. It may well be that a defense of poetry can only be a sermon to the converted, as our impasse at resolving the meta-problem seems to have shown, but that defending it is a religious act.

## Literary Experience as a Feeling Behavior

In his bestseller, *Read for Your Life* (1990), English professor Joseph Gold attempts to convert the unconverted by making a case for bibliotherapy—literary experience as a survival skill, which, according to him, should be incorporated into all school subjects, not kept as the preserve of English studies. Like Sidney and Shelley, Gold (an inveterate reader from his childhood and certified psychological counselor) bases his defense of poetry on the unqualified belief that literature influences for good and not for ill because of its moving power, its capacity to elicit and deal with the reader's psychic reality, past and present, in consciously working through, and thus altering, the way we look at the world.

Gold's main premise is that literature says things and says them in ways which subvert repressive forces. For Gold, fear of feeling is the controlling mechanism of the English-teaching business. In contrast to Frye, who sees the educational value of literature in terms of its distinction from life, Gold champions literature's *direct* connection with life, and the imagination as that faculty enabling readers to realize more tangibly those intense affinities. Here Frye would agree with Gold in holding to a notion of literary experience as the realm of the sacred. But Gold insists that literature has been desacralized to the degree to which it has been professionalized. In order to "practice what they were taught to do [teach literary criticism in terms of a correct response], English teachers need an audience pretending that they don't feel anything when they teach fiction or poetry" (1990, 20). Gold's prescription for reading as a life skill exhorts readers and would-be readers to give themselves permission to regard literary experience as real experience, one of the tenets of the re-educated imagination. His psychologized view of reading assumes that, in literary reading, readers dialogue with themselves in ways which can only influence for good.[3] But the theory of literary literacy described in Chapter 6 has shown that, particularly in school settings, this assumption devalues the thorny nature of the feeling, power, and location problems. In Chapter 9 we'll return to this question when we consider the pedagogy of literature, but for the remainder of this chapter I want to reflect on how the implications for the justification problem of literary experience as both immersion in sound *and* in sight can qualify literary experience as a literate behavior.

## Literary Experience as a State of Grace

Sylvia Scribner (1988) conceives of the literary in terms of literacy as a state of grace. Here the power of literacy is seen to transcend the politics of the engaged reader. The literate person's life derives "its meaning and significance from intellectual, aesthetic, and spiritual participation in the accumulated creations and knowledge of humankind, made available through the written word" (77). Scribner offers this statement as a "metaphorical" assertion (77); that is, literacy as a state of grace acts as a representation of the actual participatory character of being-in-the-world, of which literary experience is a part. Her concept is similar to Ong's notion of literacy as a musical voice and Gold's as a survival skill. This is the liturgical or sacred aspect of literacy that leads inward toward the realization of a "homeostatic present" (Ong, 1988, 43). In order to call this consolidating movement of literacy as a state of grace emancipatory, though, it would be necessary to show that its profane manifestation, its worldly visage, would result in active participation in the culture, not manipulation by it. In exploring this further, let's return to stasis and Aristotle's conception of the recognition scene as Frye's "frozen . . . simultaneous pattern" (Frye, 1972, 4; see my Chapter 5).

In the Aristotelian conception of tragedy, the experience of stasis through the apprehension of total form (Frye, 1957; 1963b, 31) brings with it the sense of the inevitability of the events: there is conferred on the respondent the knowledge that, given this situation and these characters, everything that had to happen did happen. And so, despite the array of dead bodies on the stage at the end of the play, the audience is supposed to emerge in a state of emotional serenity. The transparency of the literary experience involved here is produced through the co-conspiracy between the dramatist and the respondent by what Aristotle called "thought" (1965, 39, 41), the entire complex of values uniting them. Thus, even though the literary work is literally "made up," is a *poeisis*, a "making" through the word, in order for it to achieve its proper effect in bringing about poetic truth defined as the sense of universality with respect to "the way things are," readers must share in certain moral, social, and political assumptions *before* this form of literary experience can be undergone. Thus, literary form becomes a kind of content. Respondents must suspend their disbelief that the literary work is not life (pretend that it *is* life); they must also suspend belief in any ideology that may run counter to that embodied in the work upon which the aesthetic mechanism of the tragedy turns (pretend that it is *not* life), at least for purposes of the literary/aesthetic experience. Paradoxically, then, the state of imaginative identity incarnated by the recognition scene demands the tacit complicity of the respondent in a whole host of hypotheses about the way things are in order for him or her to participate in this feeling of inevitability about the way things are. It is, as philosophers say, a tautology.

## The Recognition Scene, Hegemony, and Ethical Freedom

The main recognition scene in *Macbeth*, mentioned in Chapter 3, for example, occurs when the third of the witches' prophecies is fulfilled, thus bringing in its wake the simultaneous realization on the part of both protagonist and respondent of the multi-layered horror that has been disclosed. The literary experience of this scene can precipitate stasis only if the respondent were to share in certain assumptions about the nature of evil, about the collective symbolic meaning of king-killing in Renaissance England, about the psychology of human ambition and remorse, and so on, not to mention notions of the feminine underlying the characterization of Lady Macbeth. These assumptions inform the laws of probability and necessity (Aristotle, 1965, 45) governing plot and character upon which the tragic action devolves. One reason why the aesthetic could be regarded as hegemonic would be that it renders invisible the conditions of the way it works on the respondent. It was precisely on this basis that Judy and her sisters and the students who rejected the Golding novel refused to make themselves vulnerable to textual power. It is also why Robert Morgan (1990) alleges English studies serve to reinscribe existing power relations (see also Bogdan, 1990c).

But there is a sense in which literary experience as recognition can defend literature against these charges. The ethical demand of literary experience lies in the source of its appeal—its irresistibility—a quality that really stems from the desire for the Other within our own experience. Perhaps this recognition is a mere projection of the reader onto the text, as Plato insisted it was. But it is not just that; if it were, it would be characterized by sympathetic identification alone, in which the respondent says, "There but for the grace of God go I!" The deliberate plotting of tragic action itself, its artificiality, its constructedness, its very Otherness "as an *alien* structure of the imagination" (Frye, 1970, 77) moves the respondent from identification to recognition, from engagement to detachment, simply by the force of its own laws—laws which, when obeyed, construct the respondent into a feeling state about poetic truth defined as the way things are.

This feeling state brought about by the recognition scene epitomizes a heightened and lowered consciousness at the same time—heightened, because of the irresistibility of the sense of coming to know the truth; lowered, because awareness of the conditions of that feeling is conferred only in hindsight, i.e., after the play is over. Emotion wrought by tragic action, then, appears to be a highly contradictory form of subliminal seduction, demanding, as it does, complicity as *active* participation of the respondent. (See Chapter 8 for a gender analysis of this relationship.) The recognition scene entails a certain preverbal, quasi-mystical mindset on the part of the respondent. This stance is at the same time a *willing* submission, for purposes of the story, to whatever worldview provides the ground of the plotting and characterization as well as the structure for how respondents construe "the way things are." But isn't this captivity by the tragic genre, in which the reader succumbs to "the 'fate of beauty' " (Bogdan, 1990e; Robinson, 1987) a kind of aesthetic hegemony? Perhaps. Yet, as we'll see shortly, the very fact that the attitude of aesthetic contemplation *forces* itself on the respondent is what saves the aesthetic from being hegemonic.

In *Oedipus Rex* and other tragedies constructed on the model of virtual, absolute symmetry, the recognition scene cannot be escaped from: we cannot look away, cannot over-distance without denying its human significance (that would be to descend into a kind of nihilism); neither can we directly confront it, cannot under-distance without denying its constructedness (that would be to fall into dogmatism [Boullart, 1988]). We must identify because of the true-to-lifeness, but cannot identify totally because the dramatic structure as a contrivance becomes so apparent. Here the respondent is inside and outside the dramatic event at the same time, the very power of the aesthetic force alchemizing lowered consciousness into the giftedness of second sight (see also Miall, in press). The auditory ideal now becomes a visual one, too, in that it is the very attending to the laws of the aesthetic construction, it is hearing the speaking picture as a picture, in both Ong's and Sidney's sense, that reveals its iconicity, its opacity, to the respondent, enabling *and* forcing the respondent, literally, to understand the transparency of the experience as it is being undergone. It is literary experience as stereophonic vision.

## Literary Experience as a Literate Behavior

In Ellis's definition, literariness is the usefulness of the aesthetic as use*less*ness; it is that which the literary community finds useful because of its having been taken out of the context of its origin. It can be argued that this use, aesthetic contemplation, is normative because of its gratuitousness and its inescapability, both of which are bound up with the notion of literary engagement. It is this aspect of literary engagement as aesthetic experience that it shares with religious experience, the indescribable sense of the "Wholly Other," the "mysterium tremendum et fascinosum," to use Rodolph Otto's terms in *The Idea of the Holy* ([1950/1968], qtd. in Jacobsen, 1976, 3]). If aesthetic/literary experience is defined in terms of how the respondent is affected by the feeling of coming to know the truth about oneself and/or the world in terms of an intuitive seeing and hearing, what is there about the nature of that visual hearing or aural seeing that might be inherent in the notion of literary experience as a literate behavior?

Aesthetic engagement in general, as typified by the Aha! response, is like the recognition scene in a tragedy in that it is at once completely irresistible and totally inaccessible, an analogue of self and Other. The tragedy must be experienced on the respondent's terms so there can be engagement as identification. It must be experienced on its own terms so there can be detachment as recognition. In her monumental study of Greek philosophy and poetry, Martha Nussbaum (1986) imputes both a truth value and ethical imperative to the processes of identification and recognition in Greek tragedy. That respondents have to *care* about the characters in order for identification to take place "imposes conditions on the ways in which [the characters] can be good. . . . [T]hey must be good in a representative and not an idiosyncratic way" (386). That is why tragic heroes come to their demise through *hamartia*: they can be neither godly nor reprehensible, but only imperfect; otherwise "the sense of similarity that is crucial to tragic response will not develop" (387). Thus respondents will see their humanness because of what is represented *and* because of the imperative to look arising out of the emotions of pity and fear. To look and not to look—both are unspeakable, but we persist anyway in seeing feelingly through tragic response.

What and how do we see? According to Nussbaum, we recognize the objectification of someone like ourselves who is trying to be good and fails to achieve happiness. Another way of describing it would be as the empathic realization of human limitations. This gap between human striving and human fulfillment, endemic to tragedy, confers a particular view of the way things are: it shows "us something of the importance about the human good" (1986, 388). In aesthetic/literary experience, we have no choice but to be thrown back on ourselves in the face of the uncontrollable. Under the conditions of tragic emotion, engagement with the text means being shocked into awareness of self as Other, Other as self, in a state of unremitting contingency through pity and fear.

But what does it mean to justify literary experience as a literate behavior on the basis of shock therapy? There's nothing intrinsic to shock itself that furthers the definition of literacy as the sense of the text separate from either its author or reader, is there? In fact, the opposite would seem to be the case. All such distinctions between text and reader, convention and reality, are more likely than not to be "swept away" in the auditory ideal of aesthetic experience. It is stereophonic *vision* that is crucial to literacy. Surely what is at issue is taking control of the text, of appropriating it to cultural participation and transformation. This, as we have already noted in this chapter, can be accomplished without the intervention of literary/aesthetic experience as such. Why isn't literary literacy as the political awareness of the engaged reader, in providing a discursive field upon which to exercise literacy skills, a sufficient condition for literacy? What might count as an argument in favor of the educational value of literary experience as literacy as a state of grace, as being-in-the-world by virtue of sheer involvement, absorption, trance, or stasis? I will argue that it is in fact the antithesis of literary literacy as awareness of the conditions of response, that it is the very loss of control afforded by surrendering to as unmediated a response as is possible that lends this sacred dimension to literacy.

## Literary Experience as an Ethical Behavior

Here Nussbaum's analysis of the normative value of the tragic response is helpful. For her, pity and fear are not emotional add-ons, nor are they guaranteed outcomes of the play even if the play is perfectly crafted. They are themselves contingent on the aesthetic stance of the respondent as one who enters into the drama predisposed to taking seriously the cognitive and moral value of emotional involvement, and, by implication, of human vulnerability or openness to the unknown. Here the literary imagination is as much a condition of the text as a product of it. Experiencing tragic emotion demands divesting ourselves of single mindedness self-mastery (what we could call "mind over matter") before the fact of the aesthetic event (what we could call "the willing suspension of disbelief"). Nussbaum's view of Aristotelian Greek tragic theory shows that this aesthetic attitude is not limited to the "purposes of enjoying the play." The aesthetic attitude is, rather, a way of being-in-the-world which is intrinsic to the tragedic habit of mind itself. Catharsis is defined not as "moral purification or medical purgation" (1986, 388), but as "psychological, epistemological, and cognitive" clarification "produced by the influence of pity and fear" (390). Nussbaum's articulation of catharsis as clarification is worth reproducing fully. In Aristotle's view, according to Nussbaum, tragedy contributes to human self-understanding precisely through its exploration of the pitiable and the fearful. The way it carries out this exploratory task is by moving us to respond with these very emotions. For these emotional responses are themselves pieces of recognition or acknowledgement of the worldly conditions upon our aspirations to goodness. . . . We can ascribe to Aristotle a *more generous view* of the ways in which we come to know ourselves. . . . Just as, inside the *Antigone*, Creon's learning came by way of the grief he felt for his son's death, so, as we watch a tragic character, it is frequently not thought but the emotional response itself that leads us to understand what our values are. Emotions can sometimes mislead and distort judgment; Aristotle is aware of this. But they can also, as was true in Creon's case, give us access to a truer and deeper level of ourselves, to values and commitments that have been concealed beneath defensive ambition or rationalization. (1986, 390, emphasis added)

The moral function of literature, then, clarifies values by destabilizing ordinary experience—the making strange of reality, the *ostranenie* (Hawkes, 1977, 62) so prized by *Dead Poets Society*. Gold (1990) gives a telling analogue of the above argument in his apologia for Cynthia Ozick's "The Shawl" (1980), in which the particularity of the story's literariness works to redress the impersonality of abstract knowledge about the Holocaust. "For many readers, this story shatters their intellectual and rational reserve, shakes their self-protective idea that the hideous experience of others can be generalized into statistics" (Gold, 1990, 286).

But why should *schools* be the providers of opportunities for exercising the interiority of verbal centering through literary experience, especially when (as we saw in the last chapter) individual instances of that kind of knowing can wreak psychic havoc in persons and engender moral outrage in the collective of a pluralist society? It is a certain myopia about just this point that has raised suspicions about the unqualified claim of humanistic education that literature influences, but only for good. Nussbaum and Aristotle acknowledge the risk in making emotional response logically prior to detached intellection but believe it is a risk worth taking in moral terms. Indeed, the foreknowledge of possible failure in the wake of possible loss, for Nussbaum, marks the ethical superiority of the Aristotelian worldview over the Platonic: it is nothing less than the worldview of "love and openness" in the present rather than "the safe and the eternal" (Nussbaum, 1986, 420) of delayed gratification.

The lesson, then, in the sayingness of tragic action and in direct response to it is that human vulnerability is a higher moral good than human self-sufficiency; and it is a good which can best be taught by engaging in the activity itself as an invitation to risk. Ultimately, reader respondents must decide whether they "want an art of thought, and also of writing, that engenders, and embodies, fixity and stability, or an art that encourages our souls to remain plantlike and fragile, places of glancing light and flowing water." In sum, "the Aristotelian argument, which continues and refines the insights of tragedy, reminds us that we do not achieve purity or simplicity without a loss in richness and fullness of life—a loss, it is claimed, in intrinsic value" (Nussbaum, 1986, 421). This "plantlike flexibility" in the face of the contingency of being human, according to Nussbaum, provides "the best sort of stability for a human life" because it "insists on fidelity to standing commitments, both individual and social, as the basis for true flexible perception" (421).

Should the nurturance of such an attitude be part of an educational system? Perhaps it is simply a matter of devotion. If you think that there's a gap between living according to your best lights and "managing to live out a fully good life" (Nussbaum, 1986, 382), then the ethical demand of recognizing it might dictate including literature in the curriculum. If, on the other hand, "you think that there is no such gap or that it is trivial," you will adjudge tragedy, or, literary experience itself, to be "either false or trivial; and you will not want to give it a place of honor in a scheme of public instruction" (382).

## Literary Experience as Misrecognition

Yet I think it's more than simply a matter of devotion. Nussbaum (by way of Aristotle) argues for thinking our way feelingly. Gold (1990) asserts that reading literarily causes readers to "*think our way to feeling, however fast the reading seems*" (258, emphasis original). My claim for the educational value of literary experience as stereophonic vision—for literary experience as a form of literacy—would be based on the argument that the oracular in a postliterate society, unlike that of Homeric Greece, is not only immersion in sound but immersion in sight, that literary reading defined as the aesthetic *use* of language provides the visual container for literary experience, which allows literary knowing to retain its transparency with cognitive impunity. What makes literary experience a literate behavior is that engagement is a language act *before the fact*; that is, direct response is a response to a *metaphorical* utterance, one that enables readers to hear the text as Sidney's "speaking picture" (1966, 25), but in the foreknowledge that in *metaphorical* utterance sign and meaning can never really coincide.

The recognition scene, then, is recognition not of a consonance but of a dissonance between sign and meaning; literary recognition is really a *misrecognition*; "'all understanding is at the same time a not-understanding'"(Humboldt, qtd. in Prickett, 1986). Even to aspire to live a languaged life is already a lesson in tragic consciousness. Language, then, goes beyond communication (Bogdan & Straw, 1990). The "truth" of poetic truth is thus seen as *poetic*, as Plato's "something else," if readers come to their reading conscious of the literary as a language *use*. That is what is taken for granted in literary reading, what the very designation "fiction" discloses. Indeed, literary reading is the only form of reading which is "free from the fallacy of unmediated expression" (de Man, 1983, 17). It is this very suspension of disbelief in the constructed nature of the fiction (pretending that the fiction is *real*) that guarantees the suspension of belief in poetic truth as propositional truth. Reading literarily entails its own critique precisely because the literary text *is* a construction contemplated for its own sake within the aesthetic stance, out of the immediate context of its origin, as Ellis would say. Literal meaning self-destructs into figurative meaning because that is the only way it is possible to save the wholeness of the utterance as metaphorical (Ricoeur, 1976, 50). It is the only way to remain in the state of engagement as rapt wonderment. As Frye (1990b) has asserted, the poem is a radically "*oral* production, an utterance" (110, emphasis original)[4]; and as such, a creation in time; the function of literature is now to restore to poetry its original magical power by "transfer[ring] it from an action on nature to an action on the reader or hearer" (Frye, 1982b, 25). Does poetry, then, read the reader? If so, how can literary experience per se be a literate behavior?

As we've already seen, the interiority of literary experience as a form of literacy in its own right proceeds from the *awareness* of the dislocation between sign and meaning even as the reader reads in the "wishful assertion of the opposite" (de Man, 1983, 17), as the *willing* suspension of disbelief. In contemporary culture this literary centering of the auditory ideal is already a splitting of consciousness, which has the effect of possession and dispossession of the self, most evident in the aesthetic stance of the recognition scene as a misrecognition. Literature, then, both says and does not say; and it cannot close the metaphysical gap between what we have and what we want. But it is better to know it than not to know it. Knowing it allows the text which is offered and accepted for literary use, for aesthetic contemplation, by the very designation as a literary use, then, to act as the ground upon which control is wrested, lost, regained, and voluntarily relinquished, in an ongoing formative and transformative centering and decentering. This dual textual movement and dual stance of the reader allow readers to engage language at the level of affirmation and hypothesis both, to ask, "*What if* this is the way things are?" even as they seem *sure* that "This *must* be the way things are!" Whatever new insights may be gleaned from immersion in these new sound-in-sights work ever to center and decenter as indistinguishable aspects of a single literacy process (Straw & Bogdan, 1990).

How does the above differ from the conception of literary literacy espoused by the educated imagination, in which the operative principle is distinguishing between convention and reality, as in the examples of the beer ad and the war crimes trial (Chapters 1 and 2)? We're not supposed to go to the text, as Sidney says, "looking for truth." We go to the text knowing that it is not life but literary language as a use, as a paradigm case of the mismatch between sign and meaning. My argument for literary experience as a literate behavior rests on the reader recognizing a misrecognition between sign and meaning, on verbal indirection rather than direct communication. But my emphasis on engagement rather than on the psychic distance between word and world takes seriously the educational value, and indeed, the educational right, of students to engage in an engaged response—with its joys and perils—as a legitimate form of looking for a certain kind of truth, the truth of their own experience, as something to be worked with, but also as something to be possessed. Again, it is the inward sacred quality of literary/aesthetic experience—immediacy, irresistibility, and interiority—rather than the sophistication of an informed "profane" response upon which my defense of poetry would ultimately rise or fall. I should stress that interiority, immediacy, and critical awareness are not mutually exclusive as aims, but they tend to be, within Frye's formulation, as actual states. Thus far in this book, we have seen them either as states of uncritical acceptance or of critical refusal. To bring them together as the creative critical would be to integrate the sacred with the profane, as I hope to do in later chapters.

Nussbaum's reading of Aristotle would seem to confirm literary engagement in tragedy as testimony to the rational and moral value of the emotional life. In generalizing from tragic emotion to literary/ aesthetic experience itself, I have tried to make a case for the logical priority of direct response over the critical response as testimony to a worldview premised on acceptance of the contingency of human striving and what it can and cannot presume as its own reward, what Nussbaum (1986) in the very title of her book calls "the fragility of goodness." Honoring this fragility signals an attitude to the world that embraces human vulnerability as a moral good, a vulnerability reflected and produced by literary misrecognition. But when does psychic vulnerability as a moral good lead to immoral harm? As was shown in the case of Judy, her sisters, and their brothers, this vulnerability to "a loss of spirit" (Sethna, 1990), even if it is a textual or symbolic loss, is risky, given what we know about the feeling, power, and location problems, which are acute in direct proportion to students' marginality within the social construction of "the way things are." Their susceptability to psychic wounding as real emotional damage thus throws open to question what any one respondent would construe as a "representative" or "idiosyncratic good" (Nussbaum, 1986, 386).

## Literary Experience as a Ludic Behavior

Cognitive psychologist Victor Nell provides a counterbalance to Nussbaum's concept of vulnerability in literary reading. In *Lost in a Book: The Psychology of Reading for Pleasure* (1988), Nell corroborates empirically philosophical and literary critical perspectives on the logical priority of engagement by measuring and analyzing the physiological and psychic states of "ludic reading," or reading for pleasure. Nell is interested in the widespread practice among sophisticated readers who continue to be entranced by what they consider to be "trash," readers who "are intrigued by the pleasure they derive from material they know to be culturally worthless" (xiii). His contribution to the phenomenology of reading ranges over the social and historical influence of taste, reader-response theory, and aesthetics. Important for our purposes is his success in demonstrating that reading for pleasure is a profound cognitive activity resulting in the transformation of consciousness, *irrespective of the content of what is read*. Again, the major factor is the mental and emotional disposition of the reader. In detailing the nuances of states of engagement, from tranquility to involvement to absorption to entrancement to excitement, Nell provides a number of insights into ludic reading. Acknowledging (along with Frye) that "pure" engagement is both heightened *and* lowered consciousness (Nell, 1988, 227), he nonetheless indicts the long tradition behind the pejorative attitude to ludic reading as a symptom of a puritanical work ethic (241). It seems that engaged readers are neither vulnerable nor fragile. Quite the opposite. Nell confirms the autonomy of the ludic reader as inhabiting "a marvellously safe place" (226) because readers habitually *choose* whether they want to increase consciousness or escape from it and have good reasons for doing both (226–230). Ludic readers, then, are masters of their own destinies: readers whose egos are normally constituted do not lose their identity but are able "to control their reading to avoid emotionally overwhelming experiences" (264).

Nell's study is good and bad news for the re-educated imagination. On the one hand, it reconfirms the logical priority of the engaged response by acknowledging entertainment word-hunger as an "existential problem" that can be seen within a psychological context as a reflection of "separation anxiety"; but it can also be seen within a philosophical context as a "variant of ontological anxiety" (1988, 64). Within the perspective of the re-educated imagination, we might describe this susceptibility to word magic as desire for the Other. In Nell's conception of ludic reading, it is the engagement itself which creates the Other, less as "a new and discrete alternate state of consciousness" than as an "attention construct" brought about by getting lost in a book (264). The assumption of literary experience as a construct of the reading "self" is good news for the re-educated imagination because it validates engagement as a sufficient condition for literacy as a state of grace in that the reader enveloped in aesthetic pleasure participates in the culture with a certain degree of autonomy, what Nell calls "reading sovereignty" (247). This allows for the kind of stabilizing and destabilizing action we saw earlier in our description of the reader both asserting and hypothesizing through engagement as a literate behavior in a dialectical process that functions as a kind of rehearsal for life (244–245).

Nell's profile of the self-sufficient reader assumes what he calls a "regnant ego" (1988, 225), that is, one in control of the imagery that appears, both bidden and unbidden, through reading. This readerly stance would seem to reinforce the case for literary experience as values clarification. At the same time, it would seem to weaken the possibility that literary reading, conceived in terms of engagement, can influence for ill as well as for good. Nell's sovereign reader can certainly take care of herself. But this readerly self-sufficiency would also seem to erode the ethical argument in favor of the truth-value of engagement put forward by generalizing from Nussbaum's interpretation of Greek tragedy, i.e., that, as a predisposition to the world, vulnerability is of a higher moral order than self-sufficiency. How can literary/aesthetic experience, seen here as engagement, be defended on the grounds of safety and risk at the same time? In the next chapter I'll deal with these problems by recounting one of my own reading experiences undergone within what Nell would call a regressed reading consciousness (228–229)—what Plato would have seen as the "natural" condition of receptivity to poetic response. But first let's see where we are with regard to literary experience as literacy in light of the politics of the engaged reader.

## Literary Experience and
## Literary Literacy as Cultural Critique

In this chapter I've been trying to show how an analysis of literary experience from a number of vantage points can further a conception of the re-educated imagination by justifying the logical priority of direct response. If literary engagement can indeed qualify as a literate behavior, if engagement alone can be regarded as a sufficient condition for literacy as a state of grace in terms of enabling active participation in the culture, can it be a sufficient condition for evaluating that culture? Even if Nell is correct about the psychic sovereignty of the engaged reader, how might the assumption of a regnant reading ego (1988, 225) contribute to a theory of cultural exchange within the context of the re-educated imagination, which takes seriously literary experience as real experience at the same time that it accepts that feeling, power, and location in literary reading are problems, not unproblematic givens?

Barbara Herrnstein Smith (1988) is one of the literary theorists who insists that communication is never "transferred." She argues that aesthetic experience is a kind of solipsism, that value judgments coalesce in proportion to the degree of homogeneity of interests, desires, and backgrounds among people (93). If we live in an increasingly diverse society, in which literary literacy makes me aware that my imaginative meat can be your imaginative poison, how, then, can my imagination be re-educated through literary experience to living with my neighbor in a way that goes beyond the tepid virtue of social tolerance? In other words, would my conception of literary experience as a literate behavior be sufficient for me to live in solidarity with my neighbor as alien Other? I think not. I think that what is required would be a dialectic between literary experience— the centering and decentering process of literary engagement—and literary literacy—awareness of the contingency—of time, place, privilege, feeling, power, location, of that process, for both myself and the Other.

If, for example, I or someone from my interpretive community were to read stories outside the scope of our "thought" (in Aristotle's sense), outside the stable domain of the conditions that define our experience and judgment, stories written, by, say, nonprofessional writers from a different culture, stories whose literary quality, within my interpretive community, is an open question, those stories can generate for me a literary/aesthetic experience only if my subjectivity is attuned to hearing their voices. And I can hear those voices more clearly if I've already been dispossessed of my blindness to my privilege and to their marginalization. The degree to which I can move from outside their stories to inside them, the degree to which my literary literacy as political awareness can become my literary experience as sacred self-transformation, in any one instance, would depend partly on my previous literary experiences and partly on how hard I've worked at improving my literary literacy. This improvement would demand that I go beyond literacy as a state of grace to become conscious of the contingency of my literary experience as it has been shaped by my social, cultural, and professional conditioning.

Literary experience, after all, does depend upon the qualities of a reading "self," which is produced through interaction with social processes. Even Nell's notion of the sovereign reader is qualified by his recognition that for ludic readers "book-selection preferences are culturally determined" (1988, 260). As the conscious awareness of the conditions of literary experience, literary literacy by itself can't confer aesthetic experience. It can't *argue* a reader into feeling this or that about what it values, especially its aesthetic values. This propensity to agnosis or resistance to knowing in ludic reading is borne out by Nell and his fellow empiricists who tell us that when subject matter is unfamiliar, ludic readers habitually take refuge in propositional mental operations rather than create "imaginal" ones (220) because constructing images is more stressful than relying on our tacit knowledge. (That's why stock response, in Frye's sense [Chapter 5], is a kind of automatic reflex.) Imaginative activity becomes "work," then, when readers are confronted with the alien Other; and readers are more likely to remain where they are than to move somewhere else, they're less likely to meet the Other on its own terms, when both the conventions and the value assumptions upon which the conventions devolve are strange, as when we encounter literature of another culture, or, when we're feeling psychic pain wrought by literary experience, as in the examples of Chapter 5.

Aesthetic reading, as living through the experience of the text, then, entails a system of noticing and "un-noticing" (Robin Morgan, 1989, 60) which has a great deal to do with the anabolic processes of pleasure and pain (my Chapter 1). But if we are serious about accepting literary experience as genuine experience, these processes are directly related to how any individual reader has been situated with respect to the feeling, power, and location problems. When my identity is comparatively free from threat, my reading ego can be more expansive, and I can embrace the unknown with a minimum of psychic risk, living-through aesthetically with an equal chance of being influenced for good. If, however, I have just been sexually accosted in the subway station, the radiant regency of my reading ego in a story replete with sexist images might well be "regressed" from an attitude of aesthetically living-through the story to one of fight or flight. Nell observes that "high-anxiety individuals are unable to read for pleasure" (1988, 229; see also Booth, 1988a, 69). I would modify this to say that ludic reading would be difficult or impossible for anyone in a state of high anxiety at any one time, and that the nature of the quality of that reading would depend in part upon the context of what is read and of the feeling, power, and location problems of the reader. As Nell notes further, readers can be pushed to "generate [the] images" necessary to aesthetic reading only when it is pleasurable to do so, and seeking that pleasure depends upon fulfilling their need to know. Readers create images, that is, they read aesthetically when trying to figure things out propositionally doesn't work for them (Nell, 1988, 220). It would follow, therefore, that going with what we know propositionally is a strategy readers would employ as a first recourse when they feel threatened. Living through the aesthetic event, then, is more like work than like play when the reader is either too close for comfort in her text or in alien territory.

This same tendency to fight or flight of a "regressed" reading ego, which is less in control than a "regnant" one (Nell, 1988, 225), might also be likely to occur in trying to live through aesthetically the literature of another culture. In the former case, the bridges between the fictive and the real are all too real; in the latter case, there are too few bridges between the familiar and the strange. It would seem, then, that in such an instance Rosenblatt's (1978) aesthetic reading as the lived-through experience of the text would collapse into efferent reading somewhat involuntarily. That is, when I am already destabilized by my life circumstances, I would more readily domesticate a "strange" text into the categories with which I am already familiar than I would be moved to create the new ones required to "live the text through" aesthetically. Myth and metaphor, ways of connecting the familiar to the strange, of building a bridge between the known and unknown, of making work more like play, afford the ludic reader a way of knowing what cannot be understood in any other way. This understanding can produce an epistemological shift, a change in perspective issuing from the making of implied comparisons between the strange and the familiar that brings about the joy of learning which Aristotle called aesthetic pleasure (1965, 35; Miall, in press).

The empirical connection between the psychological and the aesthetic explored by Nell is paralleled by the philosophical analyses of the fictive and the real in the work of Kendall Walton. Both authors are helpful in thinking about the overlapping principles of the meta-problem: the relationship between literature and life, whether and what literature says, and the autonomous reader. In *Mimesis as Make-Believe: On the Foundations of the Representational Arts* (1990), Walton concedes that, even when a reader is operating within what Nell calls a "regnant ego" (1988, 225), actual feelings are so intimately involved with fictional ones even though the reader is acutely aware of those feelings as objects of the imagination, that, within fictional experience, the actual and the fictive are interdependent. Walton asks questions about what we have been calling literary experience which have ethical and ontological implications, questions such as "What is to be gained from fictionally caring?" (1990, 271) What *is* the nature of literary experience that makes it seem "so natural, so nearly obligatory," such as to impel readers to think it is real when they *know* that it is "only" imagined (241)? And why does this experience have such power over us? (272). He also takes great pains to discriminate between the fictive and the actual in texts and in feeling states, and between what he calls "appreciation" and "participation" in the respondent, regarding these readerly stances as Frye's single "complex dialectical process" (Frye, 1982b, 226), not as dissociation of sensibility. "Appreciation and criticism, participation and observation are not very separate. One can hardly do either without doing the other, and virtually simultaneously. In order to appreciate the work one must notice what makes it fictional; one must be sensitive to the fictional world. . . . " Participatory appreciation "and criticism are intimately intertwined, and so are the activities of pretending to describe the real world and actually describing a fictional one" (Walton, 1990, 391).

Walton's fine discriminations between literary experience and real experience in the end reinforce their mutual complicity. We can distinguish all we wish between the fictional and the real, as Walton indeed does.[5] But these fictional truths are generated in part by actual states of mind; and actual states of mind are generated in part by one's literary literacy. The overlap between the actual and the fictional and between literary literacy and literary experience has to do with how the fictional truth is construed and with what it is in one's personal history and cultural conditioning that can make the "[t]ears coursing down the cheeks of a viewer of *Ivan the Terrible* . . . also the tears of genuine grief" (1990, 253).

We might say that the ways in which literary experience becomes real experience, how fictional truths are generated, and how actual feelings and fictional feelings coincide and converge depend upon how one apprehends the fictional world, unconsciously and according to how one has been taught, upon who one is, where and when the reading is undergone, and the kind of agency one enjoys. In other words, whether a reader feels fictionally or actually and in what way depends a great deal on what readers think they're doing when they read, and that ultimately depends on the three principles of the meta-problem—the relationship between literature and life, whether and what literature says, and the comparative autonomy, sovereignty, or vulnerability of a particular reader in any reading situation.

## Conclusion

What, then, can we conclude about literary experience as a literate behavior? First, it simultaneously revels in and resists the impulse to remain in the state of Ong's Homeric auditory ideal. Literary experience creates what we might call a heterodynamic present: in attaining a state of equilibrium through its stabilizing, conserving action and simultaneously unseating it through its turning toward the Other. It is this wrenching from the comfort zone of the previously known in the very act of coming to know that can be claimed as the necessary connection of literary experience to literacy, the predisposition to, if not the actuality of, accepting what is Other on its own terms. Literary experience can be said to be its own worldview in that, as we saw earlier, the recognition scene of aesthetic pleasure is always a recognition of misrecognition that the word is different from the world, that text is not "reality." That is why Nell (1988) can conclude that the ludic reader can choose either to embrace consciousness or hold it at bay.

But can literary experience bring consciousness to genuflection? By itself, can it *change* the self? Yes, if readers are openly receptive to the kind of shock therapy that literature "as an *alien* structure of the imagination" (Frye, 1970, 77) can work on readers. No, if their sovereign self-sufficiency insulates them against thinking feelingly and feeling thinkingly in a way that prevents the altered consciousness of the reading self from transferring and translating itself into an altered worldview. In other words, the sacred realm of *self*-transformation, of literacy as a state of grace, where self and Other are contained within Nell's "attention construct" (1988, 264), must be brought by literary literacy as awareness of the conditions of that experience, into the profane domain of enculturation into the ethical demand of being-in-the-world with the Other.

Literary reading, however, cannot of itself change the world. The metaphorical habit of imagining, even when it is constructive and transformative of the self, needs to be helped along in the project of social change by literary literacy, which can make the strange more familiar through changing the ground of what readers *want* to know. Then the reading self can be propelled beyond a recycled "attention

construct" into a truly "new and discrete alternate state of consciousness" (Nell, 1988, 264) by predisposing the reader to aesthetic experience such that the literary/aesthetic lightning (Godzich, 1983, xx)
flashes under conditions *different* from in the past. Literary literacy
interacts with literary experience, then, in charting new ground for
literary/aesthetic experience, in reconfiguring what earlier we've
been referring to as Aristotle's "thought," that whole constellation of
assumptions shared by reader and writer through the construction of
a transformed social vision. This predisposition to bridging the gap
between self and Other can, I think, fortify the fragility of goodness
by transmuting the literary imagination into the moral imagination
through the good will of a "more generous view of the ways in which
we come to know ourselves" (Nussbaum, 1986, 390). Literary experience needs literary literacy so that the literary/aesthetic recognition
scene isn't just a misrecognition of the discrepancy between sign and
meaning, but also a misrecognition of the way things "really" are—
what we desire is not what we've got. If it is to be re-educated, the
imagination must take on the burden of finding out what we want by
working, through literary literacy, to predispose itself to listen better
to the voices and stories of the Other.

   In this chapter we've examined the possibilities for literary experience as a literate behavior in the hindsight of literary literacy,
defined in Chapter 6 as awareness of the politics of engagement. In
attempting to credit engagement itself, that is, the direct, participating response to literature, with ethical value in its own right, a value
related to but distinct from either the literary or moral "worth" of the
content or the cogency of any critical reflection that may accompany
such response, we concluded with a number of speculations. If we
think of the process of identification and recognition as a kind of
stereophonic vision that enables readers to think feelingly and feel
thinkingly in a single process, we can justify literary engagement,
conceived as being lost in a book, to use Nell's (1988) phrase, on
educational grounds, as bibliotherapy (Gold, 1990) or as values clarification (Nussbaum, 1986).

   On the face of it, this doesn't seem to be much of an accomplishment. Yet the task of re-educating the imagination is a monumental
one when we consider its major challenge: to bring together literary
literacy as awareness of the many ramifications of politicized engagement, especially within the social context of a classroom, and literary
experience as the logical priority of direct response—literacy as a
state of grace. At stake is nothing less than closing the metaphysical,
epistemological, psychological, and pedagogical gap between critical
analysis and literary experience. This chapter has focused on a discussion of literary reading as stereophonic vision, as a literate and

ethical behavior, a state of grace, in which the processes of identification and recognition invoke what I want to call the sacred dimension
of direct response. It has also concentrated on vulnerability and
sovereignty as two ethical-psychological stances to be considered in
the reading "self," respectively: Martha Nussbaum's (1986) conception of the moral nature of the tragic attitude as that of sensitivity
to and acceptance of the fragility of goodness and Victor Nell's (1988)
buoyant optimism about the psychic security afforded by a regnant ego occupying the center of that reading self. These contradictory states are not binary opposites of adequacy/deficiency or
health/disease, but co-existing stances of noticing/unnoticing and
remembering/forgetting, under the assumption that literary experience is a form of real experience. Here, the willing suspension of
disbelief, a turning of the cheek outward to the vicissitudes of luck
and chance (Nussbaum, 1986) enables readers to move simultaneously outward and inward, protected by the knowledge that
descent into the unconscious is a conscious choice, and that in a
post-Gutenberg society, we know the distinction between convention and reality.

Yet, as we've already seen, it's not that simple. In the very determination to make that journey of finding oneself more truly through
the temporary loss of identity, readers seek to blur and redraw those
boundaries, and they do so for good and for ill. When juxtaposed
with the axioms of the re-educated imagination—i.e., that literary
reading affects and is affected by the specificities of our feeling,
power, and location, which in turn are constantly changing, this
fluidity of boundaries between self and the world, ordinary existence
and imaginative experience, consciousness and repression of consciousness, identity and loss of identity—makes the reading experience fraught with the potential for the kind of destabilizing that
student readers may neither expect nor welcome, depending on
where they might be in terms of feeling, power, and location, especially in a classroom. By continuing, nevertheless, to press for this
kind of engaged reading, teachers of literature are burdened with an
awesome responsibility; and here is where the pedagogical context,
in providing a safe psychic and social environment, becomes crucial.

The assumption of a regnant ego that can always "handle" what
it passes its eyes over, then, is more problematic than it would at first
appear, psychologically and morally. In Nell's (1988) ludic reading
and Gold's (1990) "reading for your life," in particular, the relationship between literature and life, both of which might be thought of in
terms of reading-for-identity or literacy as a state of grace, prized
within one context, in another, can get too close to home, as witnessed in the cases of Judy and her sisters and the students in the

Golding novel recounted in Chapter 6. Whereas the educated imagination, premised on a work ethic of self-discipline and maturity, takes for granted the reader's desire and capacity to distance psychically, the re-educated imagination makes both the desirability of and capacity for such distancing contingent on the feeling, power, and location problems. These protesting readers not only throw open to question aesthetic distance and agnosis (Moffett, 1988) as unproblematic concepts, but they suggest that the conditions under which distance, proximity, yielding, or resisting knowing are invoked are directly related to how readers are situated within the three problems posed by the re-educated imagination, and to how the dialectic affects their "sovereignty" and/or "vulnerability" as readers.

What I want to stress here, however, is that the spiritual dimension of literary experience, "the highest *intensity* of consciousness" (Frye, 1990e, 128, emphasis added), which all the apologists for poetry we've been discussing assume goes beyond consciousness, might well depend upon obliterating the illusion of aesthetic distance. What Plato calls "the honeyed muse" (Jowett, 1892, 322); Sidney, the moving power of poetry; Shelley, the suprarational quality of poetry; Frye, the oracular; Ong, the auditory ideal of the homeostatic present; and Nussbaum, the fragility of goodness, might be better addressed in terms of a dialectic between sovereignty and vulnerability, between seeing and hearing and not seeing and not hearing premised on "pure" engagement. It is this sense of surrender to the text that is implied in my conception of stasis, and to which I turn, yet again, in Chapter 8.

After the attainment, or at least the awareness, of literary literacy in political terms, can there ever be a return to aesthetic innocence? As we saw in the previous chapter, literary literacy entails a heterodynamic present, that is, a reading consciousness that has been irrevocably ruptured by the awareness of difference. And, we have also seen that the "bentness" of the world, which, according to Plato, characterizes what poetry celebrates (my Chapter 1), is indeed a fact. Literary experience has already delivered one ontological shock— that the Aristotelian recognition scene is really a misrecognition scene of the fragility of goodness. Literary literacy adds a second, epistemological shock to "bentness"—"splitness"—the mismatch between sign and signified, text and reality, as well as a third, political shock—the fractured reading subject in the post-tragedic stance of knowing she has been betrayed by her gods, not just textually but materially, before she even opens the book. This is a painful space.

If consciousness is inseparable from decentering, from remembering what we cannot afford to forget, and if literary experience is inseparable from centering in a way that cannot support psychically what we've remembered, what might be the consequences in the world of words, psychically and politically, of a deep forgetting to alphabetize oneself? What might happen if a resistant reader tries to approach the literary text naked, as Frye's "genuine primitive" (1967, 95), in search of consolidation of identity within a safer space than that of a fragmented identity? What happens to such a reader who puts herself at risk unwittingly, who thinks she is at home when in fact she is in danger? In the hindsight of literary literacy and in defiance of aesthetic distance, what might be at stake for such a reader who gets lost in a book, who just plain reads for her life? Next I tell a "true story" of one of my own reading experiences as a way of illustrating the relationship of literary experience to literary literacy, or the lack of it, not in a piece of fiction, drama, or poetry, but in the reading of aesthetic theory, in which the intention was, at least unconsciously, to go home again, to inhabit the old places as a literary *il*literate.

# Endnotes

1. David Bleich (1988) uses the term "cognitive stereoscopy" to signify the naming function and "the ability to distinguish onself from others and from everything else, and the characteristic human (species-specific) self-awareness" (87; see 87–90, 95–98).

2. See Chapters 9 and 10 for a discussion of the importance of foregrounding "interpersonal relations" in literature education.

3. Coincidentally, Gold also uses, as one of his examples, the (Canadian) National Film Board film (1984) and story "In the Fall" by Alistair MacLeod (1976; see Gold, 1990, 256–258), which I discuss in my Introduction.

4. "This utterance is not a direct address to the reader; it is broadcast, like a radio program, and is separate from both reader and poet" (Frye, 1990b, 110).

5. "I have emphasized the separation between our actual mental lives and the mental lives we lead in the worlds of our games of make-believe. We do not actually grieve for Anna Karenina . . . when it is fictional that we do" (252); and "fictional truths" are constructs generated by the "the appreciator's participating in a game in which the artist's work is a prop" (Walton, 1990, 228–29).

# Chapter Eight

# The Re-Educated Imagination
And Embodied Criticism

## The Re-Educated Imagination and the Power of Horror

In March of 1990 I was a participant in the Embattled Books Conference at the University of Calgary, in which I asked the rather grandiose question: On the brink of the next millennium, what can count as a defense of poetry? That paper was written in a psychic space shrouded by the Montreal massacre of fourteen female engineering students who were gunned down in their classrooms for being what they were—female students in a male-dominated professional school. They were also killed because of what their murderer thought they were—feminists. In this chapter I will re-enact parts of that paper in order to explore the implications for the re-educated imagination of direct response within the context of a feeling, power, and location problem that was particularly acute for me as a reader.

With the advent of Montreal, Canadian consciousness had irrevocably changed: grief over our slain daughters seemed to confer upon most citizens a sense of interdependence, an ethical demand that had set us apart. Fear of the feminine/feminist had become part of the fabric of Canadian culture, a fact of our anthropological history. In suffering this archetypal affliction, we could now in fact say the word "we" within at least one definable context; we had been shown, through no choice of our own, what Julia Kristeva (1982) calls the "powers of horror." In a quite literal sense, we had been "revealed to" at the same time that we had been made to undergo individual and collective anguish that was all but unnameable—the unspeakably nauseating vision of defilement at the core of being,

195

extremity in the face of abomination. For those who were willing to look, this misrecognition scene plunged us past the border between desire and its prohibition ("City of tears" 1989, A13).

Because of their immediacy and their proximity, the events in Montreal had added new layers of inhumanity and complexity to the power of horror, politically and personally. National reaction was plagued by a paradoxical agnosis. Private and public discussion became polarized as to cause: was Marc Lepine's serial killing a "random act" of a "psychopath" (Sweet, 1989), or was it fuelled by a continuum between word and world that gave license to violence against women in the dailiness of ordinary existence (Picard & Lalonde, 1990)? Within the public perception, attention was deflected away from societal sanction to issues of gun control and campus security (Cleroux & McInnes, 1989; Harper, 1989; Taylor, 1989). In mourning and sore afraid, academic women were asked to argue as we wept. The task of making linkages between misogyny in word and world felt like fighting for our lives. It *was* fighting for our lives. For me personally, as the mother of a daughter enrolled in a school of architecture, so closely related to the "nontraditional profession" which those young women sought to enter, reality had become surreal.

The power of horror is predicated on the thwarted desire of ordinary existence. Thwarted desire as a condition of ordinary existence represents misrecognition, not just as a metaphor for literary meaning as indirection, but as the triple ontological shock of bentness, splitness, and the post-tragedic stance. Because of their gender in a culture plagued by denial of its own terror of the feminine, in its multifarious forms, this shock is a condition of women's ordinary existence. The power of horror induces a consciousness without excess, stripped of the luxury of voluntary suspension of belief in the *literary* recognition scene. It constitutes the post-tragedic consciousness of Cassandra, who lives, not just reads, with disbelief: what Teresa de Lauretis (1987) calls "*recognition of misrecognition*" (124, emphasis original), Simone Weil (1952a) calls "affliction" (72–76), Kristeva (1982) calls "abjection," and Christa Wolf (1984) calls nameless terror, "the naked, bare fear within which a woman is alone, limbs trembling and sleepless, and which no one believes she feels" (304). It is a monument, not "to the failure of experience" (Frye, 1971/1973, 27), but to the ethical demand entailed by experience, to the power of the *tremendum* (Boullart, 1988; Jacobsen, 1976) to incite to moral outrage and, it is hoped, moral action.

In literary response, the power of horror is "undisplaced" reaction to "the way things are" and not being able to escape from either the reaction or the situation precipitating it. (Of course I have to put quotation marks around these phrases to show that I know that there is no such thing as experience unmediated by language.) But media accounts of the Montreal massacre were texts which read me in a way that left virtually no room for resistance. The power of horror disempowers a regnant ego in control of "emotionally overwhelming experiences" (Nell, 1988, 264), even in reading the day's news.

I noticed that the British Columbia Court of Appeal had upheld a ruling that gave a suspended sentence to a man found guilty of sexual abuse of a three-year-old girl, on the grounds that she was "sexually aggressive" and had already a history of sexual abuse (" 'Aggressive' tot ruling" 1990, A24). This, I saw, was the way things really are: the same country that declares a day of national mourning over the Montreal slaughter also hands down a legal judgment deeming a baby fair sexual prey. The stomach turned as I simultaneously denied and accepted, wanting to wash it away, in both senses of saying it could not be so and of believing that it could be put right. Perhaps Plato *was* right, after all. For Montreal had borne witness to the continuum between word and world, which, on the one hand, creates a path of social and cultural permission for violence against women and, on the other, "manufactures consent" (Herman & Chomsky, 1988) to normalizing violence in the daily lives of women (Randall, 1989).

Complicity between the power of horror and the continuum of world and word has direct consequences for the re-educated imagination, which would take seriously the claims of poetry as a form of *felt* life by giving direct response psychological *and* logical priority over the imperative to "read critically," in the knowledge that direct response is neither natural nor innocent but a necessary condition of affirming ordinary existence. The power of horror can turn a critical reader into an escapist who seeks the dulling, not the heightening, of consciousness. "For an individual whose inner life is governed by fearfulness, anxiety, guilt, or other negatively toned affective states, empty periods during which fantasy can develop will be especially threatening" (Nell, 1988, 228). As we saw in Chapter 7, the line between convention and reality is blurred in direct proportion to the proximity of events in the "real" world to their textual representation and to the "sovereignty" or "vulnerability" of the reader to how that reader is constituted by the feeling, power, and location problems.

As a result of this realization, however, I wonder more than ever whether poetry is threatened by the power of its own influence, which cuts both ways, positively and negatively; and I am impelled to think twice about the suspension of disbelief as a consenting activity. Even when my ego is more or less regnant, I cannot say that

I have never been depressed by "a well wrought piece of literature" simply because I can recognize its facticity as something someone has made and made up (Moffett, 1988, 184). Like Judy and her sisters, it is not that I don't *know* the difference between signifier and signified, it's that I resist the way the categories apply to me. This may not be a very "literary" way of going about things. Yet isn't this reconnection of literature and life part of what we are seeking in the oracular quality of literacy as a state of grace?

When responded to as "unmediated" experience (in quotation marks because we know there is no such thing, but out of quotation marks because in literary reading we want to forget that we know), verbal art coalesces word and world such that we can never really transcend that which literary texts as "lived-through experience" (Rosenblatt, 1978, 27) visits upon us. Mnemonic and numinous conspire literally to imprint us, a phenomenon literary theory seems to endorse with one hand and subvert with the other. How can the stakes of the sayingness and unsayingness be so high and so low at the same time? And, in the evolution of consciousness, is there only mind control over the language game?

If a defense of poetry is to rest on whether and in what way we can speak of the aesthetic integrity and moral seriousness of literary experience as the sonic power of the word, as stereophonic vision, as the Numinous, as the *tremendum* (Jacobsen, 1976, 3), then such an apologia would have to take into account the moral and aesthetic implications of language, not just as the power of possibility, but as the passion of presence. In the hindsight of poststructuralism, I realize, of course, that any such claim must take into account polyvalent meaning, the fragmented subject, historicity, and the difference of difference, all of which deepen the recognition of misrecognition—of the triple ontological shock that not only are things not what they seem, but that they are not all right, and that they will probably not be put right, at least not by literature as "the myth of deliverance" (Frye, 1983). How can the re-educated imagination escape the strictures of its own self-awareness? And how can the spiritual vision of poetry redeem, or, at least, heal, a verbal universe now rent by partialities, fragmentations, and dissonances?

Since the advent of the educated imagination, the world has turned again. Pluralism is not enough; freedom of speech masks dread of the Other; and good will aligned with false consciousness is a condition of bad faith (Narayan, 1988). The educated imagination turns on the identifiability of everything with everything else (Frye, 1957) in the verbal diapason (Frye, 1965a, 31) of the order of words; the re-educated imagination mistrusts the magnanimity of such rationality, refusing to forget what we now know about the difference made by difference to the double-edged power of the Word. The re-educated imagination addresses the same questions as the educated imagination but seeks to redress the imbalances created by the logical priority of criticism as a corrective lens to the "excesses" of art. The re-educated imagination would encounter the poem in respect of its necessity, immediacy, interiority, irreducibility, incommensurability, gratuitousness, and the "incalculability of life" (Alter, 1989, 76) *but in light of our lost innocence and our lost faith.* If the crisis of modernism and of postmodernism is also that of literature, art, and education—the problematic power of communication itself—freedom of expression and self-censorship seem doomed to live as demon lovers, the dialogic as mutuality or reciprocity contaminated by knowledge of the unbridgeable gap between intention and effect (Rushdie, 1990b) and of irremedial inequities among speakers.

In her critique of critical pedagogy, "Why Doesn't This Feel Empowering?" Elizabeth Ellsworth (1989) insists that until universalist notions of the Other are broken down, we must admit that not only can we not know another's experience, but our very effort to speak to and reach out to the Other is contaminated by our own power over the Other. This is Logos as the power of horror. It is what impels Ellsworth (1989) to call for "a pedagogy of the unknowable" (318) to temper inflated educational ideals of the Enlightenment, which still presume that "free," "open," and "rational" dialogue *of themselves* can effect social and cultural transformation. Her uncomfortable assertion that "no one affinity group could ever 'know' the experiences and knowledges of other affinity groups . . . not their own" (318–319) prompts a reconsideration of presuppositions about the nature and purpose of education in terms of the unknowability of the Other. In calling for "alternative ground rules for communication" based on recognizing the strengths of difference, Ellsworth wants a "social and educational interdependency" (319), and she is right to point to the limitations of language in achieving this goal. Identity must be a starting point, not the endpoint (cf. Frye, 1965a, 78; 1990e, 248).

When it comes to identity, talk is not enough. In order to shoulder the stress on language imposed by not being able to forget about difference, we need, says Ellsworth, personal trust, political commitment, a predisposition to recreating the Other as our liberator, and, curiously enough, the aesthetic, which she lists as one of Reason's "others," along with "women, people of color," and "nature" (305). If the educated imagination eclipsed difference as a primary moral need, much contemporary critical theory fails to deal directly with ethical imperatives (McCarthy, 1989/1990, 241). What place can there be for the educational value of poetry within a conception of reality that is linguistically structured, where the best that can be thought and said are forms of "partial" knowledge (Haraway, 1988)? Though Ellsworth's focus is somewhere else, she invokes the literary through the voice of African-American Barbara Christian (1987): "For me," confesses Christian, "literature is a way of knowing that I am not hallucinating, that whatever I feel/know *is*" (qtd. in Ellsworth, 1989, 302).

Christian's affirmation endorses the project of the re-educated imagination, which would turn the impossibility of direct communication into the ardency of direct communion. A pedagogy of the unknowable could combine Ellsworth's heightened self-consciousness of naming oppressions, entrenched and invisible, with direct response to literature while acknowledging that the very inexorability of the aesthetic event and its unspeakable covenant of truth, though evanescent, is the lie of fiction as a primary datum of ordinary existence. Might this mean that ultimately the re-educated imagination must reject views of civilization predicated on harmonious resolutions (Greene, 1990b), on the reinscription of the Pythagorean music of the spheres?[1] If so, would that not be to deny poetry rather than to defend it? What follows is my reading of a book on aesthetic theory which I hoped would satisfy my spiritual hunger in the wake of poststructuralism[2]—against the backdrop of the Montreal massacre—the reading that formed the central core of the Calgary Embattled Books Conference paper (Bogdan, 1990f).

## Literary Response as Embodied Reading: On First Looking Into Steiner's "Presences"

In George Steiner's *Real Presences* (1989), the author offers a phenomenology of aesthetic reception within the language of unabashed commonsense but in the wake of the "new knowledges" of poststructuralism. Steiner asks, "How can personal sensibility go upstream, to the living springs of 'first being'? Does such an image of the primal have any legitimacy?" (40). His answer is metaphysical and ethical (134, 145), premised on Heidegger's condition of art objects as inherently free and necessary—they exist in face of not having to be (152).

Steiner's book is one I'd been seeking for a long time. While other critics have addressed the fate of the aesthetic in the age of "isms" and "posts," their accounts have tended either to reinforce the deconstructive denial of presence—to anaesthetize the aesthetic (Felski, 1989)—or to return to a New Critical rhetorical analysis (Alter, 1989). But Steiner validates the respondent's attachment to experience in light of revisionist theories of the text. Like its predecessors in poetic apologetics, his statement is more a benediction than a vindication (1989, 199). Less concerned with refuting his opponents than showing that their claims are not enough, that however successfully readers have been disabused of naive notions of the stable, unchanging self, divine inspiration of the poet, transparency of language, innocence of pleasure, and all the rest, Steiner points to the anemia of contemporary theory in speaking, except by default, to the ineffability of the something else in art. The Numinous, the *tremendum*, the *fascinans* (Jacobsen, 1976; Boullart, 1988), that unbidden aspect of aesthetic experience, makes us resort to a dead language for its expression.

For Steiner, the collective conscious and unconscious both suffer from inhibition. This avoidance of the primary, in his view, constitutes the current crisis of psychology and of feeling, what the educated imagination would address but what its critical system cannot cope with. In order for the core of Frye's mythological universe not to give way, the ontological center must be the order of words, not of experience. The containment of desire, this holding back from Being, limits the moral/literary project of the educated imagination to the social values of tolerance and pluralism. Though Steiner does not refer to the educated imagination itself, he calls into question, as I also am trying to do in this book, the abstract resolution of the "ironies and liberalities" of humanism, which, though "attractive," ultimately reflect the very "reduced condition of the poetic and of the act of creation in our culture" (Steiner, 1989, 200) that such a resolution would redress. Within the purview of the re-educated imagination, this missing of the aesthetic mark is insufficient both to the political and textual realities of difference, on the one hand, and, on the other, to the "seismic tenor of [the aesthetic event]" and its aftershocks "unfold[ing] patiently out of immediacy" (Steiner, 1989, 186, 187). Here Steiner corroborates Plato's premise about the double-edged effects of textual power. Awareness, analysis, and control turn pale in face of the *fascinans* or the *tremendum*, which, like love, "does not argue its necessities" (Steiner, 1989, 185).

I read *Real Presences* with greater hunger than vigilance, with the attunement of aesthetic engagement and the psychic centering of looking for reconfirmation of what I had already felt to be true to my own thought and experience. Disheartened by the casuistry of the language game, I sought permission to regain my center, and *Real Presences* quickly became ballast to that center. Here was a compelling encomium on the aesthetic that recapitulated my own besieged beliefs. Through reading Steiner I recognized what I'd already felt but had repressed under the "post" revolution—that it isn't plenitude but the unendingness of discourse that's heretical (45)!

Steiner turns the misrecognition scene of the failure of words to mean, the incongruity between sign and meaning, into a moral/aesthetic virtue by declaring the metaphysical gap between word and world a consecrated place (175). Using music as the supreme example of the poetic, he enunciated for me ineluctable re-cognitions of early memories of undifferentiated experience, from when I was six or seven and couldn't tell the difference between Chopin and Liszt. His description of the aesthetic as the reception of unbidden totality reinforced the fervency of my musical listening, poetic reading, literary theorizing. There, in the gospel according to St. George, I found respite from relentless attempts to unveil the concealedness of Being. On first looking into Steiner's *Presences*, I heard old music with new delight, unearthed yellowed piano pieces, and re-opened Rilke, silent in the presentment of his "cry to the 'Angels', to those who break him open at the beginning of the *Duino Elegies*" (qtd. from Steiner, 1989, 211). I thought of how it feels to listen to the Mendelssohn *Octet*, where the sheer teleology of it all is so compelling that any attempt at analysis would seem almost sacrilegious, or at least boorish. Reading *Real Presences* allowed me to reclaim my birthright as one whose own "nostalgia for the absolute" (Steiner, 1974) had compelled her to look past the social construction of desire to the ineffable oughtness of naked want.

By taking Plato seriously, Steiner scales the heights and depths of aesthetic experience, confronting the "demonic" issues in textual power (144, 145)—censorship and pornography. In a polemic redolent of, yet again, the magnet image in the *Ion*, he recalls Plato's stance on engagement as the double-edged sword:

> Censors, book-burners, pornographers bear corrupt but unmistakable witness to the ambiguous mastery of texts over life. The effects are those of a chain reaction, much as high-energy physics recounts them. The verbal suggestion, the image or tonal associations released by aesthetic forms, in turn, generate further sequences of analogous . . . formulation within us. Dormant wants are given a habitation and a name. The script of imitative possibility unfolds. A radical verity underlies, underwrites Sade's crazed prolixity. Written out, sexuality, the phantasms of exploitation and enslavement which continue to shadow our fragile schooling in humanity are unpunctuated. There can be no full stop to them. . . . The power of consciousness of the pornographic and the sadistic, of the literature and graphics of hatred, is the exact and symmetrical parody of the power over consciousness of the discourse of love. (Steiner, 1989, 193)

Steiner's reconfirmation of the dual effect—in *malo* and in *bono*—of aesthetic experience addresses Ellsworth's (1989) problematizing of the Other in critical pedagogy. Situating the Other in the ontological space of art, as Steiner does—in the freedom, the gratuitousness, and the necessity of there being such a thing—embraces the awe-ful mystery of Otherness on its own terms, auguring both joy and terror as the moral dimension of art. I think of Simone Weil's notion of benefaction as "a humiliation still greater than pain, a still more intimate and undeniable proof of dependence" (1952a, 60). Ellsworth, Steiner, and Weil offer trust in the Other, in the foreknowledge that It might be betrayed by the visitant turned recalcitrant, "despotic or venomous" (Steiner, 1989, 156). But, writes Steiner, we proceed anyway, as though reciprocal transformation *were* possible, "the 'otherness' which enters into us mak[ing] us other" until "[b]oth sides of our skin are, as it were, made new" (188).

I found nothing to complain of in this defense of poetry, this neo-neo-Aristotelian *mimesis*—art as a "counter-creation" to reality (203). Steiner's analysis of contemporary "isms" of critical theory, his weighing and measuring the contributions and limitations of Marxist, psychoanalytic, and deconstructionist criticism (116ff., 174) in addressing problematic issues of the text, had furnished him with a conception of presence consonant with the post-tragic misrecognition scene: the possibility of absence as the very condition of Being (155).

Positioned in stasis throughout my entire reading, I was literally swept away by the oracular power of this aesthetic—until I came to page 207, where Steiner confronts feminist criticism. Acknowledging male bias in his agonistic model of aesthetic creation (1989, 206), he takes up the poetics of gender as it pertains to his fundamental questions about the relationship of word to world. I am embarrassed to say that his self-confessed genderization of poetic creation and response had not even occurred to me until George himself brought it up, so all-consuming was my return to presence, this despite my own feminist analysis of total form (Bogdan, 1990e, 192–94). In keeping to what is "primary," Steiner diagnoses what he perceives to be the obvious absence of "any major woman writer" from the "drama" of art. Could the problem be, asks he, in duly (politically) correct rhetorical form, that "the biological capacity for procreation, for engendering formed life which is cardinal to woman [is] in some way, at some level absolutely primordial to woman's being, so creative, so fulfilling, as to subvert, as to render comparatively pallid, the begetting of fictive personae which is the matter of drama and of so much representative art?" (207)

Now, it is very difficult for one who is not a writer herself to register the melding of shock and disbelief at this yet another down-from-the-pedestal case of biological determinism. I am not referring here to the disappointment of discovering the clay feet of a cultural mentor whose shoddy scholarship would blanket over all the work done in the social history of women's literature, education, creativity, and sexual aesthetics (Ecker, 1985; Fausto-Sterling, 1985; Gilbert & Gubar, 1977, 1979; Greer, 1981; Mahowald, 1983; Oakley, 1981; Sang, 1981; Spender, 1984). Nor do I mean my anger at his constructed stupidity about the conflictual nature of motherhood itself, which imposed on at least one major writer, Charlotte Perkins Gilman, the excruciating decision to voluntarily give up her daughter at the age of six in order to be able to be who she was (see Berkin, 1979; Hobbs, 1987). I speak of a cathexis of negativity so repugnant that wrench and retch became simulacra of my being, my body the emblem of its defilement; my trust, of its betrayal; my bliss, of its desecration.

This man invited me to his house and then asked why I had come. Worse yet, he ruptured the trajectory of my remembered past, usurping the joy of my imaginative life. In order for me to have owned my primary experience of reading that book, I would have had to regard it as little more than a seduction and betrayal. My misrecognition of the "truth" of Steiner's account was not just my assent to a theory, but a condition of my somatic consciousness, a fact of my felt life, a confession of my aesthetic faith—where now there was only denial and erasure. Worse even yet, knowing that his house was the birthplace of my inner life, he barred my entry except on his terms: exclusion became expulsion as he muscled me out on page 207. Then, on page 208, having dispensed with "the woman question" in a single paragraph, he gets on with the important stuff—counter-creation—and its unruffled premise "that the great artificers, . . . and they *are* essentially men, have made no secret of their wrestling." I presume that he continued to use the word "we" in the remaining pages, but I wouldn't know, since I never could finish the book.

Now—was this agnosis, resistance to knowing, emotional immaturity, a "hysterical overreaction" perhaps, at least an acute case of critical fundamentalism? After all, it's not "life," is it? It's not even literature. It's only a metaphor for a theory. This plundering of psychic space; this Heidegerrian thrownness, which is also a thrown-awayness; this mark of dispensibility in the greater scheme of things; this abjection by avoidance of the feminine; this sacrilege in the name of do-gooding was not helped much by invoking competing "paradigms" or by saying that I had learned something. It was not enough to know that it had been an interesting exercise in the re-educated imagination. I am now and will be forever marked by both the splendor and the ignominy of that book, *and I wished that I had never read it!*

I could not rationalize that experience under notions of partial truth, decentered subject, deferred referent, multiple selves, polysemous meaning, beautiful paradox, or living contradiction. My way of being in the world had been irreparably altered by my realization that an aesthetic theory which promised me an equal share had put me in place as Other, now made knowable and nameable. But, I said to myself, hasn't feminist theory taught me this law of the father already? Yes, but "to know a thing is not to realize it" (Frye, 1976b, 13), and literary reading realizes things in readers. For me, realizing what George had said meant that I could never again hear Mendelssohn's *Octet* without thinking that somehow what I thought was me is not really me. What is me is not the *connatus* (Boullart, 1988), the (universal) one who would know; but the gendered subject, the *connata*, who already knows that reception of the art object will henceforward ever be for her informed by her construction as exiled Other, caught between choosing to accept or refuse what is handed her.

Like David Perry and *Huckleberry Finn* (my Chapters 4 and 6), I couldn't stomach it. And it didn't matter that I wouldn't let George do it: that I could refute him with my "sources"; that I could dismiss him as just another colonizer and get on with my work; that I could say I was interpellated (Althusser, 1971) as Cassandra to his Apollo (Wolf, 1984); that I could separate myself out from "the men" and fashion my own "model"; that I should have said to myself "*Caveat emptor*"—that's what I get for thinking I could still read as a unified subject; that I could commit theory about *his* gender relationship to the text, his terror of the feminine causing him to "put on" the feminine as his generic respondent to poetry. I could have vowed that if I couldn't go back to my innocence, I would go back to my suspension of belief. I could have chided myself for having stopped at a false resting place instead of playing the language game. I could have rejected the history of Western thought—or accepted the frangibility of what is and kept the faith. The problem was, though, in not being able to shut out consciousness of my oppression, I was dispossessed of an agency I could not disclaim, my imagination an inextricable part of my identity. In knowing both that I could not look away from what I knew, and that I could not *not* know, instead of feeling my skin anew, as George could his, mine was the feeling of "the horror within" as though my "skin, [my] fragile container, no longer guaranteed the integrity of [my] 'own and clean self'" (Kristeva, 1982, 53).

## The Poetics of Ordinary Existence:
## Toward an Ontology of Literary Subjectivity

It is at this outer limit of primal repression that Julia Kristeva offers her defense of poetry: the abject as that point of collapse between inner and outer, at the blurred borders of the ego, slain in name of someone else's reality. For me, abjection provides the ground for a new apologetics: the poetics of ordinary existence, which would supplant the transcendence of imaginative vision with the ontology of subjectivity. As Kristeva (1982) insists, "[If] one imagines (and imagine one must ... ) the experience of *want* itself as logically preliminary to being and object—to the being of the object—then one understands that abjection, and even more so the abjection of self, is its only signified. Its signifier, then, is none but literature" (5). This state of forcibly forfeited existence is not to be escaped from in literature but welcomed as a condition of both its creation and response. That is where the order of words gives way to the order of Love—Logos to Eros—as the incarnated "religion of full experiencing," "a way into life, not a way out of it" (Falck, 1989, 170).

In a letter to his lover, Rilke asks, Is the poetic faculty the *gnosis* of the artist alone "*or is it the gift of those who are full of yearning?*" (1989, 115, emphasis original). This human yearning as the ground of a poetics of ordinary existence returns us to the impotence of logic in the reason for art. My abjection at the hands of Steiner is not something that could be reasoned away, for what he was tampering with was the state of my soul. At this primary level, language cannot supply a middle term: its dialogic function atrophies and there is only faith or despair, stupefaction or abjection. These, I submit, are religious states which truly *are* unspeakable in the realm of sacred unsayingness, as "form[s] of attention" (Kermode, 1985) that logically precede language, infusing ethics and aesthetics. What can be said about such things? That the goodness of such imperatives remains too fragile for language: they are simply "the kinds of ends that arouse devotion" (Foot, 1972, qtd. in Olsen, 1978, 223).

How might this relate to abjection as the basis for a defense of literature, the poetics of ordinary existence, Montreal, and the power of horror? Canadian women are now *connatae*, a chorus of yearners, not for the harmonic convergence of universal brotherhood, but for some recognition that their difference is life-threatening and for some change in the way things are. The abjection of that realization is now out there, in our country, public, as an effect of "the 'power' of communication," to be dealt with or not, but impossible to turn away from. It is also out there as the relationship between word and world as the enmeshment of ideology and language in condoning of violence against women. Montreal has opened up a space for linking other instances of difference, oppression, and emancipation through the Word, instances of paranoia and terrorism resulting from denying that the symbolic social order is a "sacrificial contract," in which a scapegoated *"counter-society"* becomes the necessary stabilizer of the privileged (Kristeva, 1986b, 200, 202, emphasis original).

This relationship bears directly on *Real Presences* (1989). Steiner's adherence to art as a "counter-creation," with its normative assumptions about the poet as artificer and poetic effect as unproblematic transcendence, is an act of violence turning on his blissful oblivion to the reality that women and other Others "are forced to experience this sacrificial contract against their will" (Kristeva, 1986b, 200). In what now seems prophetic to the Montreal bloodbath, Kristeva writes: "[women] are attempting a revolt which they see as a resurrection but which society as a whole understands as murder. This attempt can lead us to a . . . sometimes more deadly violence" (200). At stake, then, is not just pluralism, but the principle of sociality itself (208).

Whether intended or not, what Steiner did in *Real Presences* was a crime against the Other. Perhaps I should have read better, but he should have thought harder, seen further, and felt more. In his drive for inner coherence of his own worldview, in his pursuit of a homeostatic present, he exercised the intelligence "fore-backwardly," as Sidney would have said; instead of having "exercise[d] to know," he "exercise[d] as having known" (1966, 64). I would go further and charge Steiner with a refusal to embrace the Other. His was a wilful blindness, a failure of love, a lack of devotion, a repudiation of his own recognition that "the knives of saying [and not saying] cut deepest" (Steiner, 1989, 58). In *Real Presences* the aesthetic fantasy of totality, unity, and narcissistic completeness trades on the idealization of the female procreative function and indeed of Woman "imagined as harmonious, without prohibitions, free and fulfilling" (Kristeva, 1986b, 202).[3] And, my recognition of my misrecognition, my realization of my own complicity in this conspiracy against myself, though unwitting and unavoidable, just deepens my abjection.

Steiner's theory of counter-creation is not just neo-neo-Aristotelian but neo-neo-Romantic in positing art as a "motherless fathering" (M. Ross, 1988, 48), and "real" aesthetic experience as the masculine self-possession of "feeling one's skin anew." George *had* to obliterate real mothers by canonizing them: real mothers imperil the totalizing power of word over world; ideal mothers ground the reading subject as *connatus*, assuage dread of absence, stave off mortality (Benjamin, 1988). What might this mean for *Dead Poets Society* (Chapters

2, 3, 5, 6, 7) and the educated imagination as paternalistic constructs? In suppressing difference, they both disembody the reader in search of the dream, enlisting the eternal feminine, the exotic Other, to escape the limitations of corporeality.

What might this mean for this book? As has been the case throughout the history of criticism, that a defense of poetry is only ever as good as the social conditions that support it. Steiner's *Real Presences* and Kristeva's *Powers of Horror* both are supported by the conditions of ordinary existence as the abject, made visible and tangible by the sacrificial contract of the symbolic order—*Real Presences* from the position of privilege, *Powers of Horror* from that of Other. These conditions would change the premises of literary transformation from pluralism and social tolerance to an ontology of subjectivity through re-educating the imagination to honor the singularity, complexity, and heterogeneity of the Other—*in face of knowing that the Other cannot ever really be known*. In musical terms, we hear the modulation from the verbal diapason (Frye, 1965a, 31), the astral music of the spheres, to the diminished/augmented modality of difference.

If the educated imagination positions the reader within the interpretive process of the verbal universe, the re-educated imagination makes the material reality of the reader's subjectivity a primary condition of incarnating the Word. But, so long as the "fundamental act of criticism is a disinterested response . . . in which all one's beliefs, engagements, commitments, prejudices, stampedings of pity and terror, are ordered to be quiet" (Frye, 1963c, 140), sense knowledge, which is of *embodied* readers, cannot do its crucial work in the ethics of art. Since the Renaissance we have known that knowledge undistilled " 'through the senses can produce none but destructive truth'" (da Vinci, qtd. in Wolf, 1984, 268). Renewed awareness of this principle, disaffection with the fetishizing of language, has prompted some critics to turn to the aesthetic for nonlinguistic relief from industrial theories of endless verbal makings (Shusterman, 1989, 620–621).

Literary experience and ordinary existence are of the same ontological order—Eros, not Logos. Yet language is what we have. I make no grand claims for the re-educated imagination to redress the failures of what has gone before. And I am not so sure that we have failed all that much, at least not in the schools, many of which recognize the verbal power of horror. Here is where the pragmatics of an educational theory can counterbalance the abstractions of literary theory. Teachers of the inner city know the interactions and incarnations of textual embattlement, and deal with it through the "aesthetic practices" (Kristeva, 1986b, 210) of reading and writing (Fine, 1989). We are, despite our sexism, racism, classism, and violence, breaking through, with literature texts celebrating difference (Borovilos, 1990; French, 1990), with pedagogical theory that attempts "to alter perceptions and dispositions . . . on the basis of identification rather than reason" (Scahill, 1989, 96), and with pedagogical practice committed to the literary enterprise of culturing feeling states as inviolate and inviolable primary data in the *transfer of energy from life to literature*.[4]

I realize that the above has only begged the question of what to teach, why what we teach should be "literature," and what literature is. For that, I can only appeal again to re-educating the imagination by encouraging shared interiority and by examining the grounds of that interiority, without consigning any part of the process to the twilight zone of the "sub-literary" or the "stock response" of readers' "moral and social anxieties" (Frye, 1965a, 35, 51, 130–131). But I can also appeal to my conviction that those "literary" qualities (referred to in my Chapter 7), qualities of structural depth, textural complexity, lexical ambiguity, intertextual richness, metaphorical force, deemed properties of some texts rather than others, are forms of attention that help avert the gaze toward the Other.

Can commitment to the interiority of full experiencing—of seeing, hearing, listening, to attending to the Other's reality through literature, turn poetry as a false resting place into a redisposition toward the Other that will produce genuine attitudinal change, a true "epistemological shift" (de Lauretis, 1987, 10), in individuals and the culture, too? As we saw in the last chapter, if a defense of poetry is only as good as the social conditions that permit it, essential to those conditions must be the desire to see things differently. Wolfgang Iser reminds us that "we can only make someone else's thought into an absorbing theme for ourselves, provided the virtual background of our own personality can adapt to it" (qtd. in Kolodny, 1985b, 55). Both the sacred and the profane of literary reading, the *tremendum*, on the one hand, and the political recognition of difference, on the other, prepare this virtual background for possible new awakenings—among men who don't just shake their heads over violence against women, but are willing to take personal responsibility for the perpetuation of it (Boyd, 1991; Campion-Smith, 1989; Graham, 1990). They might also awaken Western *literati* to noticing our own obsession with literariness, censorship, and freedom of expression as absolutes that can swamp self-recognition of a racism in which "underlying metaphors of difference are intended to organize a discourse . . . meant to depict [the Other] as being beyond the veil of reason, civility, and decency" (Cudjoe, 1989, 18).

The power of the poetic *is* the "double" (Kristeva, 1986c, 40) with which we began: liberating and tyrannical. It is the excess of reason, the "something else," the desire for and fear of the Other, the abyss between the sacred and profane that the sayingness of the Word can approximate but not catch. In the dual process of reconfirming and sundering the certitude of the previously known, the literary constitutes the relationship between word and world as that radical uncertainty between spiritual and material life and death. In the sight of its saying, in the urgency of its want, in the hearingness of its music and the seeingness of its silence, it can visit here, summon there. Whether the plangency of its appeal can be justified as a premise for educational practice is in the end not a question for philosophy, but a moral and political matter of appealing to our devotion.

## Coda

I thought yesterday that I had finished this paper, but today I'm back to thinking about Steiner's *Real Presences* (1989). I know that my insistence on plenitude has detained me in the binary opposition of victim/executioner. I need something that can speak to self-acceptance of my subjectivity at the same time that it breaks through the solipsism of totalizing structures. If I know that the poetic is a double, why have I been so attached to the truth of my inner speech? Why, after all I had been through, did I give George so much power, committing the sin of abrogating to writers the responsibility of thinking for me? I make no apology for my desiring presence in the hindsight of difference. The way things are demands that I accept myself as a gendered reading subject, and for me that means nothing less than continually having to reaffirm my existence in face of being positioned as the infinitely fungible Other. But somehow that doesn't seem to be enough; neither is having analyzed the conditions under which I was constructed that way; nor is realizing that "the potentialities of *victim/executioner*" in each of us "characterize *each* identity, *each* person, *each* sex" (Kristeva, 1986b, 210, emphasis added).

I've just been reading student papers, and I glance at an article, "Watching the Watchwords," which was slipped in with one of the reader-response journals. The author of this piece, Canadian writer/critic Erin Mouré (1989), offers a remedy for readers like me, readers who are silenced by the negative power of writing, "persons who become affected . . . , who are bound to feel observed, pinned down, categorized, misjudged, or worse still, betrayed, always kept at a distance" (qtd. from Christa Wolf's novel, *Accident/A Day's News*, 1989). According to Mouré, readers should think about voice not just "as the articulation of the self, but as link or thread with those others whom we inhabit, who inhabit us, who caress us with their voices and bodies, and the weather in which they come to us" (3).

Why don't I want to hear those words that now seem old to me, words about "the *seams* of the construction," "the *movement* of the linkages or the threads," words that sound like those I used against Steiner, words about the centered glory of the individualistic imagination as "the dominance of the *voice-that-speaks* over that which it observes" (1989, 3, emphasis original)? It's that the modulation to the diminished chord of the split reading self is still unresolved. It isn't enough either. It's that even though, in the very process of reading and deconstructing George, you were producing the fluidity of your own subjectivity, love doesn't argue its necessities. It's that I can't give up the centripetal movement of the aesthetic, this psychic centering in my reading of *Real Presences*, however precarious, however vulnerable to betrayal, as testimony to the sacred quality of lived experience, the continuous acceptance of the gratuitousness of existence.

Something in this piece, though, does resonate afresh—the notion of interdependence, the theme of this paper, which has been forced underground somewhere between the middle and the end. In speaking my rage against Steiner, I silenced those Other voices that form part of my own. Might that be enough—being, living, writing, speaking the "watchwords that failed," to open a space for the un-imaginable to enter? Mouré recapitulates the sub-text of my paper in a way that literally brings it home to me. Writing is, after all, what my students do—with apprehension, trust, resistance, courage, exuberance—in the art, the aesthetic practice of self-disclosure. It is also what I have done by confessing my abjection in a theory of *co*-creation, not *counter*-creation—an aesthetic practice of non-artificing as self-performative utterance. But surely this isn't "women's work" alone, as recent developments in the "common cause" between philosophy, criticism, pedagogy, and "the long-marginal discipline of 'creative writing'" (Arcilla, 1990, 39) have shown. My students' poetics of ordinary existence enact in me their gift of my "self," trying to link reading and writing as the aesthetics of full experiencing and the poetics of making ourselves anew. Perhaps this will make "the thought of death, bearable" (Kristeva, 1986a, 185). I play the Mendelssohn *Octet*. It's still there, and we're still here. Then "let us again listen to . . . the music, all the music" so that one day "the goddesses" will be redundant (Kristeva, 1986a, 185), swallowed up in the "*infinitesimal chasm of hope*" (Mouré, 1989, 4, emphasis original).

## Reading the Seduction

So ends the text of the "Embattled Books" paper. Now, a full year later, I want to reread it by reflecting on my response to Steiner and its implications for a conception of embodied criticism as the logical priority of direct response within a poetics of ordinary existence.

My writing about my reading of *Real Presences* (which was in effect a re-reading) catapulted me out of the text and into my reading self through an ontology of literary subjectivity. This may not seem like much of an achievement, given that reader-response theory has been around for a long time. Yet, if what has come about has in fact been "a genuine epistemological shift" (de Lauretis, 1987, 10), a true "experiential realization" (Woodman, 1985, 157–158) in perceiving "the way things are," then what is involved is not just a refocusing from vision to voice, but an alteration of the very conditions of desire from the realm of "imaginative experience" (Frye, 1970, 101) to that of "ordinary existence" (Frye, 1965a, 129; 1976a, 186). How is such a notion useful to the re-educated imagination?

In view of the meta-problem and how it is compounded by the feeling, power, and location problems, I realize that the "Embattled Books" paper was constituted in part by Nell's (1989) notion of the regressed reading ego (225, 227–230) brought about by the Montreal massacre. In other words, my whole position with respect to feeling, power, and location had been changed by the events of Montreal such that I could no longer main- or sustain the critical distance that would have allowed me to contextualize Steiner's theory within the lesson about the patriarchal bias of Western culture taught me by literary literacy. The violence of appropriation and expendability, of being Othered, of being dreaded in direct proportion to being desired, was just too real.

This realization does not change my argument or conclusions in that paper, but rather brings into even greater relief the importance of the three "re-educated imagination" problems—feeling, power, and location—to the three principles of the "educated imagination": the relationship between literature and life, whether and what literature says, and the autonomous reader. Because of my vulnerability in that reading situation, the inextricable relationship of the where, when, and who of teaching literature as the politics of place, time, and agency of engagement, to the why, what, and how of teaching literature had become part of my felt life. As a result, my reading sovereignty had been compromised. Steiner, though, *had* taught me something: the continuum between word and world connects Plato's contention that poetry can influence for ill with the normalization of violence against women. The discourse of hatred can be nothing other than the symmetrical parody of the discourse on love (Steiner, 1989, 193) so long as the psychopathy of misogyny is a condition of ordinary existence.

I do not believe, however, that the advantage of hindsight has necessarily moved me from a "naive" to a more "sophisticated" response. In face of the feeling, power, and location problems, this binary is as falsely dichotomous as that of the regnant and regressed reading egos, which Nell (1988) asserts are ambiguous "permeable" categories that can "temporarily or permanently turn into each other" (228). In any reading act, then, different kinds of knowledges come into play and recede according to different purposes and circumstances. Though my initial reading of Steiner was "precritical" or "acritical" with respect to my literary literacy as feminist consciousness (I should have seen that agonistic model coming from the start), it proceeded from a complex system of assumptions and experiences about art, reading, music, literature, and a host of other cultural and personal phenomena which worked to reveal and conceal a whole constellation of values and identifications, themselves turning on a series of affirmations and denials, accommodations and resistances that make up the history of my reading life.

Within the context of the Montreal massacre, my "regressed" reading ego enabled me to see some things and limited me from seeing others through a different schemata of noticings and un-noticings than would have been the case within a different nexus of feeling, power, and location. I was hanging on to my aesthetic theory for dear life, even as it was articulated for me by someone very little interested in female centering. It is this dual motion of what is seen and heard and what is not seen and not heard that constitutes the dialectic of literary experience and literary literacy of the re-educated imagination. This is not to say that knowledge *about* literature is irrelevant. But, as Barbara Herrnstein Smith (1988) has argued, "response development" (set forth in my Chapter 5) has less to do with the truth-value of the literary work or the aesthetic judgment of the respondent than with how the person who is thought to have "moved from darkness into light" (84) has learned to manipulate the various discourse categories of specific kinds of appreciations (83).

As an aesthetic practice of self-disclosure, the Coda recapitulated the theme of interdependence connecting the Montreal massacre to my final gesture outward from my "self" to my students. But it was doing something else—enacting my recognition that my writing of that paper was itself the misrecognition scene of my reading of Steiner's book. The Coda expressed a resistance to my own resistant reading/writing of that misrecognition scene: it was with real reluctance that I resigned myself to Mouré's "solution" as reading and writing against the grain of the individualistic imagination. In lashing out at Steiner, in pushing back the very boundaries I refused to be contained by, I was resisting the conditions of my own liberation because of what I stood to lose in the process. It seemed as though my very insistence on an ontological argument committed me to repeating the dance of seduction and betrayal with a demon lover, where recognition can *only* be of misrecognition in a universe already shaken by so many ontological shocks. So, in one sense, forcing things to the "primary" doomed me to reproducing a host of binary opposites in addition to victim/executioner: self/Other, plenitude/lack, fulfillment/frustration, rigidity/fluidity, augmented/diminished, excess/lack, centripetal/centrifugal, love/hate, reading/writing, poetry/philosophy, life/death, acceptance/rejection, desire/dread, seduced/seducer.

Yet the reading as a whole subverted those binaries through a poetics of ordinary existence. Here I aligned myself with Judy, her sisters and brothers in their refusals of the text. Whereas they rejected the text, I accepted it—all too well. We were, all of us, trying desperately to center ourselves in the face of extremity. I now believe that what I thought at the time was a naive reading was in fact a primary act of the re-educated imagination, as was theirs. My reading was anything but critically detached; rather, it was a reading-for-my-life that was critical for my survival. Because of the circumstances of that reading, of my being dis-abled—emotionally, psychically, culturally, and politically—by the Montreal massacre, my reading "self" was encumbered with a grave feeling, power, and location problem. As a result, that reading blurred even further the oppositional categories of participant/observer, vulnerability/sovereignty, sacred/profane, and regressed/regnant reading ego described in the last chapter. By responding directly, by trying to remain embodied, to keep in sight both my politics and my aesthetics, it seemed at the time that I had lost both. But perhaps I had kept both.

Abjection as a psychic state can be seen as the demonic form of stasis, as the hellish inversion of fusing with the Other turned despot—a location, feeling, and power of horror. As such, it is the apotheosis of Nussbaum's fragility of goodness (1986), in which the vulnerability of the abject as a predisposition both to the world and to the text makes it susceptible to captivation by a rescue fantasy. Seduction/betrayal is a highly charged sexual dynamic between two agents of unequal power. Abjection, seduction, and betrayal describe well the Gordian knot of repressions, denials, desires, affirmations, and aspirations of a female academic like myself, having come late to political awareness, whose upbringing and education have been a curious admixture of privilege and marginalization within the context of a whole array of factors ranging from an intense early musical education to growing up female, Catholic, and second-generation Italian in a WASP neighborhood of a country with an emerging and ambiguous identity of its own (Frye, 1971, 126).

This is not a confession, but an aesthetic practice of self-disclosure, as one possible solution to the response problem: an ontology of literary subjectivity that explores the myriad influences bearing on our willingness to understand our undergoing of literary experience—reading our own embodied readings as embodied criticism. As Margaret Meek (1990) reminds us, "Literary criticism, as a way of passing the time or earning one's living, is the constant consideration of difference and why we react as we do to what we see, hear, and read, and why we mind about it" (2). Part of this work is to honor a temporary forgetting as a condition of knowing. What I have been calling the sacred, literary experience, is what we tend to forget in our conscious mind but what foregrounds itself in the aesthetic attitude of consolidating identity in the homeostatic present: literacy as a state of grace. What I've been calling the profane, literary literacy, is what we consciously remember, about literature and other things, that explicitly guides our literary reading. The dialectic between the two is always contingent and forever fluid. This is why there is neither a "correct" response, definitive interpretation of a work nor final definition of the self.

The informing principle of my direct response to Steiner's text was not what I *didn't* know about feminist literary criticism or aesthetic theory, but how what I knew but couldn't accept figured into what *happened* in that reading in a complex way, given what I needed from it in terms of my feeling, power, and location problems. It was my construction of the text in constructing my self. Within Rosenblatt's (1978) frame of reference, we might say that my aesthetic reading, my lived-through experience of that text, was both a cause and an effect of my efferent reading, i.e., the very condition of reading for my life, a life that was literally threatened by the odious reality of the patriarchal continuum between world and word played out in the Montreal massacre. Though that does not excuse what George did, it does mean that I need to look again at what *I* did, if we listen to the apologists for poetry, from Sidney to Kristeva, who have argued that readers must take responsibility for the moral effects of literary experience.

Now, I see that there was a four-part structure in my response to Steiner. First, the blissful centering/forgetting of thinking that I could go home again, and all the personal and cultural connections that allowed me to do it—almost. Second, the nauseated rupture of realizing what George had done and of my painful complicity in that undoing, which implicated me in the text. Third, the articulation of my rage at Steiner and my attempt, after my initial paralysis, to commit theory in coming to grips with what he had done. Finally, the Coda itself, which worked to alleviate the pain of realizing I wasn't willing to pay the political and emotional price of going home again, while at the same time inflicting its own pain of the reduced expectations of "mere" reading and writing. In the final section of this chapter, with the help of some of those "other voices" forming part of my own, I try to recapitulate that structure by creating another one in which I reflect on my response and on some assumptions—personal and theoretical—underlying that response.

## Embodied Criticism: The Scale of Seduction

*Reflection: Feeling Feeling—The Music of*
*the Spheres (Tonic Major)*

Why was a tenet of my aesthetic faith implicated so abjectly in that Steiner text? Mainly because my initial reading of *Real Presences* had reclaimed for me the oracular in literary consciousness. One of the most poignant testimonies to the loss of the oracular in literary consciousness comes from Margaret Meek (1990), who confesses that her "adolescent passion for Burns' love songs (which has not changed much) had to be modified in essays about 'poetic diction,' and so [she] learned to sing them in order to express what [she] thought they really *meant*" (4, emphasis original). My reading of Steiner had bridged the gap between singing and stating. And it had done so with the bliss of going home to the consolation of the world of aesthetic Being which was the mark of *my* difference: the difference that was both refuge and empowerment, a way out of the ethnic and religious stereotype of the grocer's daughter into the groves of academe; the difference that recompensed early ill health with a rich fantasy life; the difference that separated me from my peers and drew me to my life partner; the difference that linked the Palestrina of cathedral liturgies to the dead poets of Romanticism 200. And it was the difference that led me to theory. As Jane Miller (1990) observes, what besides the magical charms of the aesthetic can sweep a woman up into complicity with a theory, the very breadth of whose explanatory power excludes her (121–122)?

You have only to go to Pythagoras to see the force of the connection, the mathematical certainty of the I AM THAT AM radiating as the music of the spheres, the Great Chain of Being, microcosm as macrocosm. And you can go there solely by way of your own patterned logic of noticing and un-noticing just as you can orbit the dizzying galaxies of Frye's order of words. Except that now you know that it's *not* your pattern; nor is the journey on your terms. How *can* it be, with the unconscious structured according to the law of the father? You've been abjected from the very first incarnation of the Word.

While "abjection" is an apt trope for the grounds of a poetics of ordinary existence, "seduction" suits better a *reading* theory of ordinary existence, which requires an active participant. As total victim, Kristeva's abject negates. Out of control, of what is happening to her and of feelings that have been induced, she is protected by her innocence. Miller's seducee, on the other hand, refusing negation, is "responsible." A scarlet woman, she complies. As the commonplace goes, she must "want it." Miller uses seduction metaphorically to understand "sexual relations as an absolutely central term for any understanding of how power is experienced in societies based on inequality" (1990, 23). She wants to know about "women's willingness to be led and spoken for by men, [about] the attraction for women of theories from which women and feminist analysis are absent" (25). So do I. Ultimately, these understandings interconnect as the relation between word and world, as the asymmetrical symbiosis between masculine and feminine, and between women and men, whose lives are materially, psychically, and spiritually implicated with each other on male terms.

As a female scholar fascinated by the structure of ideas and the power of the aesthetic, I let George speak for me; and it was my consent that made reading a seduction and a betrayal rather than a rape. Yet, as Miller (1990) argues, the issue of complicity is not so simple. It, too, must be problematized, made ambiguous. Once the complicity of "women as simply undifferentiated members of the human race . . . is taken for granted, their needs are bound to be ignored" (26). So also are the needs of those women and other Others pinned and pinned down by the feeling, power, and location problems, needs which all too easily remain undifferentiated by the "we" of the order of words, by any monolithic conception of white, liberal feminism, and by an aesthetic addicted to harmony (Greene, 1990b). The way out is not through resistance alone, which simply consolidates the strengths of the seducer, be it the text or the linguistic power game. Cancelling out the seduction through separation, denial and distance, as I did with Steiner, is to invite apellations of misnaming, misinterpreting, and overreaction (Miller, 1990, 27). Rather, we should become *students* of seduction, exploring the conscious and unconscious conditions of acquiescing to oppression (20). In reading, what it comes down to is understanding our undergoing, looking at our own history to see how what has been a dispossession can become an empowerment. In her book, Miller describes her own history. The key to *my* vulnerability is the music of the spheres and the desire for transcendence. And even after all this, I still want it.

## Locating Location: Rupture and the God Trick (Minor Second)

One thing is fairly clear: the state of my literary literacy as conscious political awareness was well hidden in that first reading of Steiner, until, of course, I came to page 207, where I recognized his "bad attitude":[5] his flexing without re-flexing, his speech from the throne, that "higher" ground of moral, political, and aesthetic superiority. Had my reading ego been more regnant, I would have known from the beginning that I had a location problem with George. I could have *chosen* displacement instead of waiting to be shattered. I could have read *Real Presences* from what I already know is the post-tragedic stance of all those ontological shocks. I could have begun by seeing from below, put *myself* in place as exotic Other. But doing that is a skilled, not a "natural" activity. As Donna Haraway (1988) puts it:

> To see from below is neither easily learned nor unproblematic, even if "we" "naturally" inhabit the great underground terrain of sub-jugated knowledges. *The positionings of the subjugated are not exempt from critical re-examination, decoding, deconstruction, interpretation. . . . The standpoints of the subjugated are not "innocent" positions.* On the contrary, they are preferred because in principle they. . . . are knowledgeable of modes of denial through repression, forgetting, and disappearing acts—ways of being nowhere while claiming to see comprehensively. The subjugated have a decent chance to be on to the god trick and all its dazzling— and, therefore blinding—illuminations. (584, emphasis added)

By "the god trick" Haraway means the illusion that scientific or ethi-cal objectivity is achieved through the totalizing vision of abstraction which refuses to locate itself anywhere and is thus able to remain unaccountable. But rather than repudiating vision, she reclaims it by embodying it. Insight becomes the ability and the will to name the impossible space we inhabit, not a sense of transcendence as "a theory of innocent powers to represent the world" (579). Rejecting the god trick, the chimera of omniscience, then, would be to repudi-ate stasis ("Fusion is a bad strategy of positioning" [585]) in favor of the "embodied nature of all vision," which must learn to converse with "the world as coding trickster" (596). To see from below is to cancel out the possibility of being seduced by the god trick; it is to be grounded in partial perspective, objectivity of "situated knowledges" (590).

Embodied vision shares common cause with literary literacy. Both stress location as an essential condition of knowing, not as a generality but as the tangibly real that makes "claims on people's lives" (Haraway, 1988, 589). The "only way to find a larger vision is to be somewhere in particular" (590). Haraway's conception of "situated knowledges" brings together science and the poetic in the image of the trickster-as-Coyote drawn from the native American mythology of the American South-west (593). The trickster, of course, is also the shadow archetype of the *puer aeternus* (Von Franz, 1981), the divine child, who also makes claims on people's lives in the infinite playing out of the creative imagination. Living in a world run by such a figure is full of ironies, surprises, and ontological shocks, some more serious than others. For Haraway, stability becomes redefined as "a reinvented coyote discourse obligated to its sources in many kinds of heterogenous accounts of the world" (1988, 594). In my reading of Steiner, that wasn't enough. My situated knowledge was precisely what I was fleeing from, and I ran right into a trickster, who promised what he could not deliver—a transcendence of "innocent powers to represent the world" (579).

Haraway's conception of situated knowledges sits well with literary literacy in stressing the political nature, the non-innocent, one might say "profane," cast of all human conversation. But, as a theory of science, what would it think of literary experience as a state of grace? For Haraway, the literary is the world as coyote, "a figure of the always problematic, always potent tie between meaning and bodies" (1988, 596). But literary experience, as we've been defining it, *is* a god trick. It desires rest without falseness somewhere in infinity, at least for awhile. Literary experience, as the horizon of infinity, refuses "limited happiness" (579) as the best to expect. But it is a god trick in the hind*sight* of the powers of horror. Transgressing the boundaries of the possible and profane, it would enter the sacred as the conceivable and the inconceivable, the imaginable and the unimaginable. Unlike Haraway, who rejects subjugation as "grounds for an ontology" (586), (her feet are firmly planted), I would claim the abject as at least a starting point for an ontology of literary subjectivity, the literary as stereo*phonic* vision,[6] precisely because of its promise to teach "how to see [and to hear] faithfully from another's point of view" (583). Maybe Steiner wants that too; but his passion needs a victim.

### (Dis)Empowering Power: Appassionata
### Furiosa (Diminished Mediant)

My theoretical raging at Steiner grew directly out of the powers of
horror that link the Montreal massacre, unproblematic entitlement to
knowledge, the feminization of the aesthetic experience, and what
George did through uncritical acceptance of the feminine as just the
kind of exotic Other that Steiner would (p)reserve for motherhood,
and others, like Jean Baudrillard (1990), would enshrine as aesthetic temptress. In *The Demon Lover: On the Sexuality of Terrorism*
(1989), Robin Morgan indicts the entire system of metaphysics, epistemology, aesthetics, and social life predicated on the rationality of
abstraction, emotional distance, and compartmentalization, which
have wrested vision from the material reality of life. Here, the mad-
nesses of Western civilization are laid bare as the accoutrements of an
archetypal tragic hero and his mission to resist the goddess who
continually threatens him with *life* (80). The only way for Morgan to
be able to "go sane" (289) is to theorize her own version of chain
linkages in the theology of disconnection, in which "fucking" and
"killing" are celebrated as twin ideals (171) of a collective *ethos*
obsessed with the sovereignty of single-mindedness. This in turn
devolves upon the vicious "un-noticing" (60) of the Other[7] so vital to
the dialectic of our reigning "thanatotic sensibility" (115). It is this
(pre)occupation with transmuting something into something else,
taking matter and putting it to a "better use" which underlies the
violence of that continuum between the psychotic fantasies of the
Montreal killer and the counter-creation of an aesthetic theory. It
also underlies the analytic tradition of Western culture, in which the
"eye fucks the world" (Haraway, 1988, 581), a world conceived as
"mere resource . . . mother/matter/mutter" (596).

Instead Morgan (1989) formulates an aesthetics of ordinary existence, which makes "lovely things" and makes "things lovely"
(110–11). Heroes, numinosity, all the trappings of the obsession
with "tragic beauty" (110) give way to "the grace of comedic self-
creation" (330). For her, Eliot's dissociation of sensibility as a "fact" of
life would be an obscenity all too readily taken as given in a society
enthralled with death. To replace this with "connectivity" (53) is to
give up democratization of violence and normalization of terrorism, which turn on a collective consciousness in love with the
"abnegation of the self as the highest good" (85).

Morgan's theory supports the connections I tried to make in the
Steiner reading between the horror of Montreal and the centrality of
the poet as counter-creator originating from Romanticist poetics. As
transcendent visionary, as motherless father (M. Ross, 1988, 48), the

inspired genius stands over and above "mother" nature, which he colonizes, appropriates, and transmogrifies, eternalizing her into a mantra for his spiritual sovereignty. This want of vulnerability, this presumption of the right to dis-incarnate the object, idealized as feminine, undergirds the single-mindedness of all systems of noticing and un-noticing that make Othering and "going home" partners in crime: from misogynistic murders to killing-made-easy by idealizations of home and hearth (Theweleit, 1987); from the patriot's blind fidelity to the ascetic's flight from life (Von Franz, 1981); from the artist's imaginative freedom to the homeostatic present of readers hell-bent on identity.

## Reconstruction: Reclaiming Power
## (Perfect Sub-Dominant)

This will to control, is, of course, not innately masculine but constructed through the continuum of word and world that ignores at its peril the destructive forces of visions presuming to speak for the Other (M. Ross, 1988, 49), ignoring the possibility that feeling, power, and location might be problems, not just givens. "Why," asks Robin Morgan, "must passion demand a victim?" (1989, 120, emphasis original). A victimless passion would require an epistemology that doesn't cannibalize its object and a poetics that can close the gap between singing and stating: a listening in the present, like "a young doe in the forest," and "the delicate virtues of ambivalence—hesitation and patience" (Robin Morgan, 1989, 342, 85–86). Morgan's ontology of literary subjectivity alchemizes abjection into a "politics of Eros" (326), a celebration of difference, and the "ecstatic perspective" (331) of reconstructing the self through reading books that slay the demon lover, replacing the supremacy of vision with other "forms of perception, including remembering, imagining, intuiting, hallucinating, dreaming, and empathizing" (328). In doing so, she enunciates a defense of poetry based on her literary experience of Toni Morrison's (1987) Beloved, through which, she maintains, the female reader can unlearn misplaced fealties and relearn "to deserve herself" by locating "ecstasy not as a 'standing outside of' the self but as a standing, for the first time, inside the self." Only then can we adopt the perspective of the Other: by imagining through literature what we deserve "from others," we can begin "to imagine what others deserve" (1989, 330, emphasis original).

Morgan's defense of poetry builds on the abject by professing the experience of oppression as a metaphysical reality. As such, it is a

normatively female, woman-centered, and oppositional consciousness, teetering on the gender essentialism it critiques. But Morgan
resists a facile hierarchy of a fixed feminine identity by invoking the
indeterminacy of field theory, which defies a priori models of any
kind. Her resistance to seduction, like Miller's, involves the study
of it. Morgan is unabashed about situating herself in a concept of
home—the home of political solidarity among women, a solidarity of
interdependence as a consolation for the loss of transcendence. To
start over, to embark on the long process of reconstructing identity,
which is, of course, always in the making, had to begin for me in
oppositional consciousness; but I couldn't afford to remain there.
Out of my anguished literary experience grew an awareness that I
had to *do* something about it. That awareness forced me, with the
help of my students' papers then and a few of those "other" voices
here now, to transmute aesthetic experience from "moral outrage"
(1989, 132) and an agency of "assertion and will" (Rose, qtd. in de
Lauretis, 1990, 125) into the aesthetic practice of working with texts.
It also meant re-vising the meaning of seduction from "the alternatives of being either hysterical or perverse, . . . [to] . . . another sense
of the word *seducere* where the prefix "se" is at once reflexive and
diacritical—leading back to a self which is already a marker of difference" (Evans, 1989, 83–84).

### Relocating Identity (Imperfect Dominant)

Teresa de Lauretis (1990) holds another view of going home. Hers
is a theory of leaving a home that is all but inhabitable. Rather
than stay anywhere, the "eccentric subject" (131) displaces herself (116). She refuses a fixed identity either in abjection, its obverse,
or anything else. For de Lauretis, women win power by exchanging
safety for risk—physical, emotional, linguistic, epistemological, conceptual—through a "discourse from which speaking and thinking
are at best tentative, uncertain, unguaranteed" (138). This refusal to
be mired in oppositional consciousness deconstucts and recon-
structs the "one-way relation of oppressor to oppressed, colonizer to
colonized subject" (131). De Lauretis pursues consciousness by
beginning with the recognition of misrecognition, acknowledging
location, turning inward, and through self-displacement, questioning possible complicity with "assumptions and conditions taken for
granted" (138). Applied to reading theory, this would be to foreground the grain, with one eye always peeled on the seams of the
construction, "linkages" and "threads" (Mouré 1989, 3).
    Even though I'm still betrayed by patriarchal aesthetics, I'm no
surer now than I was in the Coda that changing location is for me.

Can an eccentric subject close the gap between stating and singing? Leaving George meant exchanging the music of the spheres for the self-renewal of my emergent identity, unstable, fluid, multiple, marked/wracked/blessed by the ambivalence of that space between the desire for bliss and the acceptance of "limited happiness" (Haraway, 1988, 579). Moving from "raw" experience to the textual practice of reading and writing in my Coda was not something I welcomed, though I granted its "educational" value for my student Others. Giving up the primary meant embracing language, and that mixing of the personal with the conceptual was for me, as de Lauretis warned that it would be, "the cause and/or the result of pain, risk, and a real stake with a high price" (1990, 138). My persistance with the "primary," my replaying the Mendelssohn *Octet*, showed my reluctance to live within the imperfect interval of a transfiguration so shaky and alien. Major and tonic felt familiar and safe. Being eccentric was definitely not being at home.

But I have to get on with it. My movement from Steiner to Kristeva was an oscillation between desire for father and mother. While attached to both textual parents (Gallop, 1982), I was working out difference through either/or. To reach both/and required the double vision of the post-tragedic stance without the nausea of going cross-eyed (Weigel, 1985). De Lauretis' theory of self-displacement is helpful here. An unabashedly "discursive position" (1990, 139), it costs—in the pain of "remapping of boundaries between bodies and discourses, identities and communities" (138) and in the sacrifice of aesthetic experience as we've been defining it. An empathic theory of literary reading (Bousson, 1989) might mitigate this pain by reading against a theory of the Other conceived as identifiable, representable. But where would such a theory, not already marked by the law of the Father, come from? Perhaps from some notion of the unconscious "as excess" (de Lauretis, 1990, 126), as something other than what is presently allowed under unproblematic presuppositions about the "power of choice." It must come from a notion of resistance in the unconscious that would enable agency, an agency of crossing and crossing over boundaries of every description.

## Voicing Voice (Augmented Sub-Mediant)

But why should we care? Why do "reading models" matter anyhow? Because once we accept the feeling, power, and location problems, once literary experience is accepted as a form of real experience, once literary form is seen as a kind of content that is gendered, and once we espouse a theory of literary reading that preserves both forgetting as the "sacred" dimension of the aesthetic and remembering as the "profane" dimension of the discursive, then the relationship between literature and life begins to look less and less like the reader reading the text in terms of the "simple" ability to distinguish between the conventional and the "real," and more and more like a continuum between word and world, in which the power to read the reader remains formidable even when it is mediated by philosophical and/or rhetorical critique. If Plato *was* right about the double-edged power of poetry on the emotions, goodness might be more fragile than we think.

As a kind of content, literary form structures literary experience, and indirectly cultures the emotions. De Lauretis (1990) is right that the importance of resistance in the unconscious cannot be over-stressed (1990, 126). If such resistance is implicated in repressions and forgettings, and further, if a deep forgetting is to be valued as intrinsic to the sphere of the sacred in notions like literacy as a state of grace and if a conspiracy of "un-noticing" (Robin Morgan, 1989, 60) is bound up with patriarchal modes of knowing, then literary reading would seem to be a genderized activity in need of re-visioning, especially as an institutionalized object of study. Perhaps the answer lies less in re-vision than in re-hearing and re-voicing, in a theory of *stereoscopic hearing* that could incorporate the complicity theories, the oppositional theories, and the discursive theories played out in this piece.[8]

I still want it both ways—to reintegrate sensibility—to go home—and to make the world habitable within the post-tragedic stance. The knowledge that we've been placed and displaced by the hegemonic Other, and that we need to dis-place ourselves in order to be neither Othered nor Otherer, allows us to see as through a glass less darkly, but that blurring of vision makes it more difficult to speak. With the music of the spheres now in its diminished mode, what might the recovery of voice be like? It would have to transform consciousness by repositioning the reader from Steiner's female "recipient" of the text to speaker of the text in the plentitude of a self conscious of its own self-creation. Here readers could close the gap between stating and singing by becoming minstrels, wandering inside and outside the boundaries of (gendered) genre, moving from the profane place of a discursive field to the sacred space of ecstatic response, and back again.

### Leading Note (Major Seventh)

If the poetic *is* a "double," a hegemony and a liberation, and if the dialectic of literary experience and literary literacy invokes a double vision or double focus on the part of the respondent (see Chapter 10), how can readers move from the oscillating state of engagement and detachment (Chapter 5) to "the unfolding of a long and complex dialectical process" (Frye, 1982b, 226)? By taking direct response seriously enough both to politicize it and to put it first, logically as well as psychologically, I would hope readers would become embodied critics, approximating in the world of lived experience the spiritual "ecstatic state" of "pulsating inner exuberance" (Frye, 1990e, 82, 177) Frye associates with Holy Writ, the prelapsarian world of perpetual harmony, or his hypothetical third order of experience. This Longinian *ecstasis*, rooted in the reader's subjectivity, would transpose the aesthetic from the art work to the respondent. The next chapter will tell other stories of other readers and writers finding voice, discovering, exploring, and releasing this energy in ordinary existence.

# Endnotes

1. See Susan McClary, (1989, 13–62.) McClary's brilliant deconstruction of the teleological model of Baroque musical composition, of which J. S. Bach is the apotheosis, was for me a site of admiration and dread. I regarded it as both the best and worst that could be accomplished when seeking to break down the autonomy of music. By showing how the construction of Bach's cantatas simultaneously conceals and reveals a political agenda, McClary employs a musicological rhetorical analysis invoking cultural politics, viz. issues of national identity, religious belief, and gender, to demonstrate the consonance of Bach musical style with ideals of the Enlightenment. Following Adorno, McClary links the "ineffability" of Bach's music directly to the stranglehold of the Pythagorean model of music as the "correspondence between harmonious tones and numerical proportions" (15) on Western thought. In order to break out of this unproblematic articulation of the way things are into a theory of "*socially grounded [musical] meaning*" (61, emphasis original), McClary argues, we must examine why "the Pythagorean model, . . . is so seductive" (16). Though McClary can posit a correspondence between cultural values and tonally moving form by inquiring into how Bach can, for example, use the key of G minor to elicit and induce the emotional state of sadness, her analysis does not give an account of why G minor is " 'the key of sadness' " (79). "There is always, as Blake taught, 'excess' of the signified beyond the signifier" (qtd. in Steiner, 1989, 84).

2. For a discussion of the poststructuralist context of Frye's theory of reader response, see Bogdan (1990b, 1990e).

3. This is a vision that calls up, in another context, Klaus Theweleit's study of the fascist mentality in *Male Fantasies* (1987).

4. In *The Educated Imagination* (1963a), Frye emphasizes the "transfer of imaginative energy from literature to the student" (55). Reader-response theorists and researchers, on the other hand, begin with the student. Seeeespecially Susan Hynds (1989).

5. A. Ross (1989, 214) uses this phrase to describe Jean Baudrillard's stance on seduction as a metaphor for feminine "*mastery over the symbolic universe, while [male] power represents only mastery over the real universe*" (Baudrillard, 1990, 8, emphasis original). Baudrillard's gender essentialism reverses Steiner's, but the effect is no more helpful than Steiner's in either ridding theory of dichotomies or preventing women from being dragged up and down the pedestal.

6. Haraway (1988) uses the term "stereoscopic vision" to represent the partial vision of being located "in a space we hardly know how to name" (582). I use the term "stereophonic vision" to indicate the *feeling* of holism that nonetheless, I believe, accompanies recognizing partial perspective.

7. I wonder whether Robin Morgan, herself a poet, is aware that her lyrical polemic trades on her own system of noticing and un-noticing, which also leaves many things out in her case for the continuum between world and word.

8. As this book is about to go to the typesetter, six months after this chapter was written, I find myself surrounded by yet another pile of news clippings collected in the interim. "Stereoscopic hearing" seems an apt expression for describing my attempt to confront the all-at-onceness of the barrage of events that seem to demand both the immediacy of an ethical standpoint and the circumspection of a complex dialectical analysis. In the hindsight of Thomas/Hill (Bray, 1991; Goleman, 1991; MacKenzie, 1991) and the second anniversary of the Montreal massacre, I am both exhilarated and disheartened at the many changes that have occurred in increasing awareness of the blood-red continuum between word and world in the case of violence against women. The Hill/Thomas hearings, in becoming "drop everything" TV (Fraser, 1991, A23), enacted an archetypal drama that threatened to move sexual harassment from invisibility and denial to a cliché of social mythology without really being taken seriously (Galt, 1991). Yet there does seem to be hope. Two years after the Montreal massacre, the power of horror is now seen in the mainstream media as part of the poetics of ordinary existence (Sarick & Galt, 1991). As "Women Vow 'never again' " (Picard & York, 1991), and men don white ribbons, December 6th will now annually mark the scourge of passion with a victim. In a one-page pamphlet, "The White Ribbon Campaign: Breaking Men's Silence to End Men's Violence, December 1–6, 1991," Michael Kauffman and Ron Sluser confirm the cultural normalization of misogyny through the representational continuum, which these authors contend is perpetuated not by "weirdos" but "regular guys" who do not regard men's violence against women as "aberrant behavior." To wit, the white ribbon.

The white ribbon "symbolizes a call for all men to lay down their arms in the war against our sisters," urging men to work for social programs that re-educate the imaginations of professional associations, student councils, corporations, government bodies, police officers, and judges. Lest we are lulled into the illusion that this act of good will is enough, some are already skeptical about the gap between the symbolic representation and the mater-

skeptical about the gap between the symbolic representation and the material reality. As one male public affairs consultant has observed, "Notwithstanding all the attention this crisis has received, our world has yet to become one iota safer for a single Canadian female" (Caplan, 1991, B3). Even as I write, my university newspaper reports the vicious stabbing of a 22-year-old medical student by her former boyfriend (Rau, 1991, 2), and feminist groups work feverishly to redress the recent repeal of a federal rape shield law which formerly protected victims of sexual assault from being questioned about their past (Sallot, 1991a, A1). As well, the move to redefine consent at least has acknowledged "the strong male bias in the law," which has until now been blind to women's post-tragedic stance. There is now some public recognition that women "live in a different world," one suffused "with a residual fear of physical attack, particularly sexual attack" (Sallot, 1991c, A2). It is now being recognized that women in "normal" society live under a "curfew created and policed by the violence of men" (McKracken, 1991, A16). The sacrosanct taken-for-granted of judges' "objectivity" is also being interrogated, and the normative status of a "reasonable person's" standard, seen as gendered (Sallot, 1991b, D3).

At the same time, this recognition scene turns into misrecognition with the bizarre juxtaposition of two front-page articles two days before December 6th. One the left, the headline reads "Male abuse victims want to talk" (Fine, 1991, A1) and, flush against it, "AIDS revelation shakes NHL [National Hockey League]: Woman patient told doctors she had sex with 50 players" (Picard, 1991a, A1). Both these issues call for a protracted exercise in stereoscopic hearing, to be sure; my direct response, however, is that, yet again, women are othered: the first erases woman as the protagonist of her own story; the second demonizes her.

# Chapter Nine

# The Re-Educated Imagination and Embodied Pedagogy

The last chapter concluded with a note leading to a pedagogical perspective that might meet the demands of the re-educated imagination in helping to effect a shift of consciousness—an agenda perhaps as grandiose as that of mounting a "new" defense of literature education. This chapter cannot offer a pedagogical theory of literary response. My aim is only to suggest one pedagogical context for what I mean by embodied criticism, based on my own and my students' learning experiences in our efforts to politicize direct response and put it first at the same time.

The focus of Chapter 8 was a conception of embodied criticism within a feminist framework. My re-reading of my reading of Steiner used seduction as a metaphor for the continuum—and the gap—between word and world which I've been assuming underlies the meta-problem and the feeling, power, and location problems. In the first part of this chapter I want to stress the commonalities between feminist and other work being done in literature education, work which also has an emancipatory aim. That "mainstream" and feminist research in theory and practice comes together in important ways is, I think, a hopeful sign that literature will be accorded its educational value, within and outside English studies, not as cultural ornamentation, indoctrination, nor as a sub-discipline of critical thinking, but for the ethical import of its moving power, which in its promise to apprehend the world differently, can help make it a better place. The history of poetic apologetics, up to and including our own time, has shown that literary experience, of itself, can help construct the self, but not necessarily effect social change (Chapter 7). Whether we think of reading literature as the politics of engagement (literary literacy) or as a state of grace (literary experience), or as both, the case for literature as a school subject has to be remade in terms of its efficacy in producing the kind of epistemological shift that really *can* change the world.

Throughout these chapters we've encountered a number of recurring themes which have explored, directly and indirectly, the three principles of the meta-problem and the feeling, power, and location problems: the relationship between literature and life, whether and what literature says, and the autonomous reader. Once the two major hypotheses of the re-educated imagination are accepted, that is, once the primacy of engaged response is pushed up against its political implications, and once we are determined to overcome dissociation of sensibility by dissolving the dichotomy between engagement and detachment, as we've been trying to do, some further problems underlying the aims of literature education begin to surface: issues such as response development, the strictures of genre, the recovery of voice, and the influence of academic and professional commitments to the logical priority of the critical over the direct response. This chapter cannot delve into these issues in any depth; it can only point to them as indicators of change in the way we think about the relationship between the literary word and world, as it is addressed in the pedagogy of embodied criticism.

The last two chapters tried to rescue engagement in literary/aesthetic terms in the hindsight of having politicized it: Chapter 7, through the conception of literacy as a state of grace; Chapter 8, through the notion of embodied criticism. Underlying both chapters is the presupposition that the dichotomy between direct and critical response is as false as the other polarities dealt with in this book. But, as was stated at the end of the last chapter, to think our way out of this dilemma is not necessarily to speak in our own voice. Voicing voice in literary reading labors under a number of encumbrances: the new fears of giving offence and long-standing pressures, conscious and unconscious, of the order of words, of stilling our own predilections in favor of privileging sophistication. A rarely asked question in the academy is what might be the consequences for students who drop or suspend "aspects of themselves, when those aspects may in fact be essential to the processes of successful learning" (Miller, 1990, 152). Other such unasked questions concern unmasking pedagogical practice without giving up its transformational function. It is to opening up those questions that we now turn.

## First Things First: Passion Without a Victim

In the Introduction to this book, I voiced some questions I called "re-educated imagination" questions: questions asked by my students that indicated to me that they, too, were thinking about the meta-problem—the what, why, and how of teaching literature—and how the meta-problem is made more complex by the feeling, power, and location problems as the politics of engagement. This year, when I showed the film "In the Fall" (NFB, 1984) on the first evening of term, it was the second of the two principles of the re-educated imagination—the logical priority of direct response—that came into view. Below is a question asked by another student, Jeff, in his final term paper, which he drafted as a personal letter to me:

> What can we say we know, where can we start in discussing anything?. . . . [Y]ou say that "identity must be a starting point, not the end point"; and this reminds me of an encounter we had, you and I, in the first class. In answer to your question, "Is what you are saying relevant to a discussion of this text?" or words to that effect (it was a reference to the film), I said, "Of course it is, because I thought of it." [See also Booth, 1988a, 33] As I said it, I had an image of myself as a child, overstepping, but I also felt that if an individual's reaction to a text is not relevant, then perhaps I was in the wrong course. I think your reply reassured me that, as well as the fact that I had paid my fees, I really did belong there. (Reynolds, 1990)

Jeff's words bring together two qualities of the sacred in literary experience, which I've tried to stress in both my feminist and "mainstream" classes: presence and transgression. As students of embodied criticism, Jeff, his sisters, and brothers are trespassers in the order of words. Through their classroom interactions, they soon learn that the difference of their bodies, spirits, and their subject positions summon up a pedagogy of the unknowable (Ellsworth, 1989), in which voicing voice can bring in its wake absence and alienation for the Other. Living out the intensity of their difference, they aren't Longininan ecstatics, *thinking* they have produced what they have heard, but makers and remakers of boundaries, generic and disciplinary. They are *"inter alia"* in discourse, constructing their own reality. As Jeff wrote: "Perhaps the class itself, the people and their thoughts and feelings, their 'presences,' is the primary text."

The highly interdisciplinary nature of the classes at our educational "Institute"[1] is something of a mixed blessing (Chapter 6). Not everyone shares the same background or a positive predisposition to the literary. Some students have been discouraged by undergraduate experiences in English classes and are just fearful of getting it wrong yet again. Now enrolled in other departments, like Adult Education or Educational Administration, they sign up in ours (History and Philosophy of Education) for a course with literature in the title (there being no such thing at OISE as English Education) as a way of reclaiming academically a love they already espouse. Others, who come to the course, for example, from cultural studies, sociology, or critical pedagogy, often bring with them a healthy skepticism about *The* Great Tradition. Heterogeneity and "heteroglossia" (Bakhtin, 1981, 272 ff.), "cacophonous dialogic life" (Bakhtin, 1988, 56)—in intellectual training, academic conditioning, and ideological commitment—are taken-for-granteds. This concurrent co-existence of competing, multi-layered forms of discourse makes it easier to transgress and easier to get hurt, as was apparent in the encounter with "A&P" (Updike, 1962) in Chapter 6. We *start out* knowing that, if response is honored *as is*, speaking subjects are bound to be right and wrong at the same time. The very assumptions about textuality, partial truth, fragmented subject, and so on, which can construct a framework for dialoguing across discursive fields, can also widen the gap between the stating and singing of those who've been abjected by others' systems of noticing and un-noticing. This assumption of simultaneous vulnerability and sovereignty is perhaps a first step in shifting consciousness, in changing the face of *seducere* from passive complicity to active creation. It's establishing trust, claiming a victimless passion, becoming a wandering minstrel, giving ourselves permission.

Why must teachers work so self-consciously to give themselves and others such permission? As guiding principles of a classroom, presence and transgression entail rethinking what might be called *the professionalization of literary response*. Though Joseph Gold's (1990) denunciation of university English teaching as a defense against feeling is harsh (my Chapter 7), I believe he's partly right about the hegemony of interpretation in literary studies. That is, however, what literary studies is: the *study* of literature as the legacy of the educated imagination, in which response not predicated on literary knowledge is assumed to be predicated on literary ignorance (Hamilton, 1990, 221). Presence and transgression, on the other hand, are enabled by the conscious subordination of criticism to response and by the self-conscious shedding of pedagogical power, insofar as that might be possible. This is not to denigrate the interpretive process, knowledge about literature, nor to throw out lesson plans. It is to foreground theory[2] as the understanding of undergoing and the undergoing of understanding, and to structure classroom assignments as the sequencing of the aesthetic practices of reading and writing, with the knowledge that giving voice, to ourselves and to each other, is both to embrace and to trade on difference. It is to recover voice, not as Ong's homeostatic present, but as a "scene of hearing" (Kahane, 1989, 139), the acoustical counterpart to recognition of misrecognition, where people who work collaboratively and in good faith still tread on the unknowability of the Other, learning exuberantly and painfully that the same system of aesthetic noticing and un-noticing that gets me to my imaginative heaven can produce for you, if not an imaginative hell, at least a purgatory of feeling, power, and location problems.[3]

Something which the re-educated imagination accepts, especially in light of the three new, somewhat troublesome problems, is that, when feeling, power, and location are given priority, communication is likely to become difficult (Ellsworth, 1989), sometimes even impossible, hampered by what respondents might see as the tunnel vision of others. Worldviews clash or remain mysteriously incomprehensible, and offence can be committed when no offence is intended. Here the order of words, even when it is based on consummate literary scholarship, can be of little use. Sometimes it just becomes painful or impossible to speak in the face of the Other, and we breathe shallowly and squirm in our seat, as when, as a white liberal feminist, I see myself objectified as the oppressor in the poetic, or "real life" text of a woman of color; or when I know that my readerly pleasure employs a convention that makes "getting it," in the sense of participating in the culture—literacy as a state of grace—co-dependent with another's "getting it." Here the primacy of response over criticism takes on ontological weight: when readers notice the abjection of others who try not to cry while explaining why they're not laughing. Theories of textuality are simply insufficient to the task of explaining what Frantz Fanon (1970) calls a "conclusive experience," especially the experience of colonized Others who are jolted—(dis)placed—into awareness that their very being is really a "problem" for all those others who are identifying "with Tarzan against the Negroes," of whom you happen to be one (qtd. in Miller, 1990, 123). But conclusive experiences can also be of a different order: the sense of infinitude, of standing in the middle of ecstasis.

The bliss of going home aesthetically, however, is inseparable from what Edward Said has asserted in *Orientalism* (1985) is the sexualization of all knowing: "the seductive degradation of knowledge, of any knowledge, anywhere, at any time" (qtd. in Miller, 1990, [117])—one of the sub-texts of this book. "A prevailing imagery of penetration, of stamina and of the eventual discovery of the strange and the hidden at the end of a journey requiring courage and cunning serves to merge the colonising adventure definitively with the sexual adventure" (Miller, 1990, 117). Eurocentric presumption of entitlement to the "fruits" of the aesthetic object is made possible through fetishizing the feminine, whose sexuality is infinitely "available" and therefore fungible, an eternal object of exchange. And it is so precisely *because* it is already construed by its colonizer as the right to passion-with-a-victim. So it would seem that the freedom to know invokes a hierarchical relationship between the knowing subject and the object as abject, dispossessed of agency—an unreal presence.

Putting this right would involve recoding the genderized modes of aesthetic reading and writing through re-educating the imagination to the primacy of Othering and being Othered as inescapable conditions of literary reading. I believe this requires a redefinition of power as the *refusal* of power through an aesthetic theory of passion without a victim, a "sublime of nearness" (Yaeger, 1989, 195), which approaches its object with the immediacy and intensity of Romantic transcendence (Montefiore, 1987, 10) but without appropriating Otherness. A sublime of nearness takes care to preserve the integrity of ordinary existence. In contrast to traditional notions of the sublime originating in Longinus and developed mainly by Edmund Burke (1968), a sublime which annihilates its object, an alternative sublime "can include the sociable, the convivial, as well as the grandiose and the empowering," where the "*tremendum*" is absorbed and respected at the same time. "The question . . . is how one writes [and reads] . . . about an 'other' who has extra-human power the self thinks it needs, without destroying that other's alienness" (Yaeger, 1989, 195). It is about learning to be wandering minstrels singing their stating (Meek, 1990; my Chapter 8).

But how can difference be honored if readers remain awash in oceanic feelings? And how can women and other outsiders who are full of yearning (hooks, 1990) participate in the language and metaphor of empowerment without seduction into the very "grim forces of possession and domination" (Yaeger, 1989, 198) of agonistic poetics? Yaeger argues for a "prosody of transcendence, . . . in a different key" (199), which refuses power in a voluntary practice of forgetting and remembering, as the entering in of repressed libidinal forces into the writer's experience, "welcomed as a primary, healthful part of the . . . motive for metaphor" (205). Along with this entering in is an exiting out, a keeping still, a listening like a "doe in the forest," with "the delicate virtues of ambivalence—hesitation and patience" (Morgan, 1989, 342, 85–86).

How to listen (Heath, 1990, 297), though, does not just come; it has to be learned and cultivated. According to Uma Narayan (1988), those who have *not* been abjected need to conduct themselves with "methodological humility" and "methodological caution" (37). Outsiders can't just do the god trick on somebody whose feelings have grown out of a very different constellation of conditions and values. Those who have been subjugated possess (not "enjoy") "epistemic privilege" (Narayan, 1988, 34) over those not privy to their experience. "They know first-hand the detailed and concrete ways" in which "the oppression affects the major and minor details of their social and psychic lives" (36). In short, emotions of the Other need to be taken seriously. This does not mean that they are "infallible" or not amenable to revision, but that they are to be accepted as they are, as ontological and moral primary data of ordinary existence. Otherwise, we can too easily look away, avert the gaze, "go home" by ignoring the feeling, power, and location problems.

In his final paper, Jeff accused George Steiner of going home too easily, of indulging in passion-with-a-victim, "of privileging theory or biology over human feelings, over the reality of human identity in theory. [Steiner] ignores the 'Real Presences' of the female people he knows or doesn't know." In a confession of his own, Jeff expresses his good will in being sensitive to others.

> In our class I always seemed to be aware of the people and their feelings, and of their opinion of me. Is that a failing of mine? To be aware of, and eager for, the approval of others? Does it cloud my judgment, and make me say things I wouldn't? If so, it might be a negative thing. Isn't caring about others, wanting to feel part of a group (the human race) rather a natural state of mind? . . . So I have to admit that personal feelings that I had towards all the female members of the class, towards the fact that of difference in personal terms, had an impact on my reading of the course. Seeing someone's pain, seeing someone's attempts to comprehend the incomprehensible, forced me to see things in a way that I hope is more sympathetic to women. (Reynolds, 1990)

Here I think Jeff shows a coming into awareness of the "epistemic privilege" (Narayan, 1988, 34) of the Other. Yet, according to Narayan and to Ellsworth (1989; my Chapter 7), good will is not enough. There must be an accompanying social practice that can implement "methodological humility" (31). As I will describe in the last part of this chapter, I think that the re-educated imagination and embodied criticism, in which direct response is twinned with the reading of theory, can be part of that plan.

## The Professionalization of
## Literary Response and the Meta-Problem

Attempts in feminist ethics and feminist theory to shift consciousness share common cause with efforts among some professors of the New Literacy (Willinsky, 1990) in the area of literary response. Peter

Medway and Andrew Stibbs work toward instilling in students "intelligent engagement" by drawing attention to the constructed-ness of texts in terms of their cultural situatedness and social effects (1990, 81). The imagination becomes educated not only to the realms of myth and metaphor that define the relationship of literature to experience but to the conditions of textuality itself, to "the status of the text as an ingenious, but *resistible,* artefact" (82, emphasis added). Medway and Stibbs endeavor to re-educate their students' imaginations to the dialectic of assertion and hypothesis described in Chapter 4, but within the hindsight of the political consequences of literature's moving power. They "want [their] students to appreciate, as part of their routine response to new texts that all representations of the world, including those we find 'true,' are the constructions of somebody who had values and agendas, who made certain choices and could have made different ones" (82).

Aware of the consequences of upping the political ante in literary experience, Medway and Stibbs appreciate the anomalies of the engagement and detachment model of response, in which even a "passionately critical reading" (83) that tests "a pretended reality against their knowledge and experience of the actual," demands being either "in" or "out of love with literature" (Bogdan, 1990c). Their approach indirectly invokes the meta-problem and the feeling, power, and location problems. In order to avoid the censorship prob-lem, they subvert the realist bias in curriculum selection at the junior high school level by including postmodernist literary texts and by advocating pedagogical methods based on poststructuralist criti-cism. These strategies provide students with a heightened conscious-ness of the text as a construct, not just of plots and characters but of how plots, characters, and comments support individualist con-ceptions of identity and integrity at the expense of awareness of "public domain issues such as the socio-economic origin of the high-waymen, slaves, madhouses, war or whatever provide and produce the underworlds, underclasses, disruption and injustices which sen-sationalize the experiences" (Medway & Stibbs, 1990, 74). Without such an awareness, students could well "be at the mercy of the representation, and could be harmed in the way that would-be cen-sors fear" (78).

Medway and Stibbs also attend to the justification problem in their prescription to broaden the canon and diversify teaching tech-niques, to teach the literariness of literature and the political impli-cations of that literariness. It is the literature teacher as professional, as expert in "how the powerful charms of literature work, for good or ill" who is best equipped "to protect children from the dangers of literature-misunderstood-as-experience, and how to teach [them] to be disarmers for themselves of the magical powers of the texts they need to read" (83). In other words, the re-educated imagination is a life skill that can best be taught by those attuned to the politics of literary engagement. This emphasis on learning to distinguish convention from reality is valuable; but it is vulnerable to relinquishing what I have been calling the oracular aspect of literary experience, to exchanging the aural ideal of intensity for the visual one, to giving up the sacred for the profane, to limiting literature education to strategies in detachment. For me, the price of literary consciousness is too high if it demands that I reject the suspension of disbelief and am forced into seeing the lie of fiction as the *not true* rather than as the *"spiritually true"* (Frye, 1990e, 290, emphasis added). Medway and Stibbs seem mindful of the double-edged power of the spiritually true: literary works can make us "'grow'" and "by the same token . . . harm us: whether a book does good or harm will simply be a matter of *which* experiences are represented in the work" (1990, 76, emphasis original). But they have managed to avoid the trap of selecting curriculum and teaching techniques according to the "truth" of the correspondence of its content to "life." Ultimately, Medway and Stibbs justify the teaching of literature as a school subject by advocating the understanding of the undergoing of literary experience in the schools on the premise that, as readers, students do undergo texts and thus need to know how they do.

The above is, of course, a crucial aspect of cultural critique; but I would still want to allow for literary experience as a state of grace, to reclaim the literary within its sacred dimension—the self-transformation of a spiritual journey. If we credit both literary experience as a state of grace and literary literacy as worthy of school time, what yet needs to be dealt with is how to justify the inclusion of this undergoing as a priority in the curriculum, especially since direct response and centering of identities are goals literature educators continue to espouse. In light of the poetics of refusal, articulated throughout this book by the performative utterances of Judy, her sisters, her brothers, and my response to Steiner, the meta-problem and the feeling, power, and location problems will remain vexatious in classrooms. Postmodern and poststructuralist approaches to literary reading give readers more control in terms of their textual sophistication, but they do not cancel out the psychic investments in emotional engagement, where identities are still at stake. And, so long as literary texts are seen as "artifacts" to be either surrendered to or resisted, the power of literary reading will remain a double-edged sword.

Finding pedagogical ways of politicizing literary response and putting it first at the same time can bring together these sacred and profane aspects of literature education. For example, stage theories such as those propounded by Margaret Early (1960), Robert Scholes

(1985), and Jack Thomson (1987, in press) encourage response development. Underlying these perspectives is engagement and detachment as a recursive rather than alternating process. Nelms and Zancanella (1990) express their view of response development this way: the aim of a pedagogy of literature "is that the 'study' of literature grows out of and reflects back upon the 'experience' of literature and the 'experience' of literature is neither abrogated nor superseded by a premature concern for public interpretation and criticism. . . . [T]he 'lived-through' aesthetic experience is not short-circuited by the academic application of a formulaic approach to the derivation of meaning and value" (42).

Implicit here is the need to justify the logical priority of direct response on the basis of the student's own needs, desires, pleasure, and positionality. This is a stance which English education has adopted for some time (Rosenblatt, 1978, 1985; Probst, 1988); but, as I have been arguing, it has done so somewhat short-sightedly, in light of the conflicting goals of literacy as a state of grace, literary literacy as the politics of engagement, and the conservative agendas of many university English departments, in which future language arts teachers are educated. Nelms and Zancanella (1990), for example, point to the "unspoken conflicts" among student teachers about their confusions, anxieties, and guilt about "not thinking about literature in the way that they thought English teachers ought to think about literature, and wondered how they would deal with that discrepancy when they entered their own classroom" (1990, 44–45). These negative feelings are induced in large measure by the kind of the academic conditioning that grows out of the logical priority of the critical response, the subordination of the oracular/auditory to the textual/visual—the puritan work ethic about literary values. To unlearn this is to change the professional consciousness of prospective literature teachers.

Let's juxtapose Margaret Meek's (1990) lament (Chapter 8) about having to learn to sing Burns's songs in order to understand their meaning with Frye's sentiments about the oracular in poetry: "the poem, like a musical score, but unlike other types of verbal structure, is being referred back to an actual performance. If we want to know what a poem 'really means,' we have to read the poem itself aloud" (Frye, 1990b, 110). The telling difference between Meek and Frye is the difference between their respective positions on the role of criticism in literature education. Frye, of course, is unequivocal about the centrality of the critical enterprise. Meek, on the other hand, challenges two assumptions about literary response which are bound to make devotees of the educated imagination uncomfortable: first, that response must always "lead to" interpretation (sometimes "questions about . . . intertextual reference . . . [are] irrelevant"[5]); second, that one can never refuse the text (4).

Refusing the text, is, of course, what the Renaissance fundamentalists did (Chapter 4), what Judy, her sisters and brothers did (Chapter 6), and, for different reasons, what I did with George Steiner (Chapter 8). It is also, for still different reasons—educational ones— what Meek (1990) does when she asks teachers to rethink the premises of "good reading" within the context of the normative value of readerly pleasure (6), to contemplate the logical gap between the singing and the stating of literary meaning (4), in short, to consider literary experience as a state of grace. For Meek, to seek the reasons for possibly refusing a text forms a legitimate part of the literary enterprise, and redefines literary criticism itself (2). What we need now is for our pupils to

> show us how they learn the rules of the reading game; how they begin to take risks in trying out new generic forms, to tolerate uncertainty, to discover that texts have power, and to read against the grain of the writing in the spirit of the age, as we teach it. . . . [W]e still have to ask whether we are always best pleased when, as the song says, they do it our way. Would we not be better informed about literature and learning if we gave them more responsibility for texts, the undoing and remaking of them? (7)

As the next section of this chapter will show, I am not arguing for the excision of criticism from literary pedagogy. Rather, I am interested in the ways in which this "undoing and remaking of" texts can preserve the auditory ideal of literacy as a state of grace and effect a shift in consciousness at the same time. If readers are to come into their own, they must be given permission to feel and to consolidate identity sufficiently to break through the power hierarchies of the relationship between word and world that make them "parrot clichés" (Chapter 7). To be regarded as not attaining a "full response" is to be ineluctably excluded from the ethical imperative of participation in any art as a state of grace. To participate as a form of direct communion, as a feeling and falling deep into the poetic event, is to hold out hope for redefining *seducere* from the axis of surrender/ resistance to "self-subversive self-reflection" (Felman, 1982, qtd. in Penley, 1986, 140). As is being argued in the other arts, music, for example, the relationship of criticism to aesthetic experience is radically contingent. The "point of an analysis is not to *describe* what people consciously perceive: it is to *explain* their experience in terms of the *totality* of their perceptions, conscious and unconscious" (Cook, 1989, 221, emphasis original).

Here the argument is based less on the political charge of elitism than on the gap between experience and analysis. Literature, art, and music are deemed unique because of their "immediate effect" on "even the most untutored respondent" (Cook, 1989, 220); but neither accounts of structure nor of cultural production can be brought directly into line with the phenomenon of that impact. In response to literature, as in response to music, theories that attempt to derive aesthetic properties from structural features of the work result in an "aesthetic determinism" that, on the one hand, creates a list of prescriptives for entry into the canon, and, on the other, deletes the agency of the respondent (Cook, 1989, 224). This point is key in supporting the logical priority of direct response, not just as a naive neo-Romantic wish that experience *matters*, but as a necessary condition of an ethics and an ontology of literary subjectivity. I agree that the nature of the aesthetic has had to be problematized in order to challenge assumptions which privilege certain works over others and which harden the line between "high art" and "popular culture." But the flight from the category "aesthetic" (and here I agree with Steiner) often looks like a giant reaction formation, in which the willing suspension of disbelief has become the *un*willing suspension of belief.[4] Awareness of textuality is a prerequisite for conscious, humane participation in the culture, to be sure. But this new orthodoxy, essential for defending against cultural imperialism, carries with it a danger in the very efficacy of its prophylactic function: the same principle that allows us to distinguish between appearance and reality also deflects away from the reality that the "knives of saying cut deepest" (Steiner, 1989, 58).

## Girls and Boys Together: The Non-Professionalization of Literary Response

We thus come full circle to Plato, whose chief concern was that without self-conscious intervention by the "purely" ratiocinative, the power of the lie of fiction would overwhelm the soul. It seems as though current critical preoccupation with the rhetorical dimension of the poetic reinforces this fear. And so, the "simple" "granting" of permission by teachers for students "to respond freely" becomes problematic because of the contradictory nature of the whole literary enterprise, laden, as it is, with institutional expectations to perform literary interpretations and, within the exigencies of the feeling, power, and location problems. Ironically, these problems are all based on a prior presupposition which does *not* seem to be much of a problem for some: that literary experience is both ineffable because of its power (that is why only literary criticism can be taught) and an already-in-place taken-for-granted that need not be worried about in the classroom. One of our working assumptions throughout this book, of course, has been that it is precisely because literary experience is both assumed and ineffable that it is a problem teachers are dealing with all the time, and that the visibility of its problematic nature depends on the acuteness of the feeling, power, and location problems in any given teaching situation.

Assumptions about literary experience, then, especially about direct response, affect in a substantive way what goes on in classrooms full of real readers reading. Accepting the "unsayingness" of literature as an integral aspect of its spiritual dimension, recognizing that the "unspeakable" nature of literary experience, its close proximity to self-identity, forms the contradiction at the heart of the educated imagination, which allows for silent acceptance but not silent (or vocal) refusal. "The work of the imagination, . . . cannot be refuted: poetry is the dialectic of love, which treats everything it encounters as another form of itself, and never attacks, only includes" (Frye, 1971/1973, 95). A pedagogy of ordinary existence, which honors response enmeshed in the tangle of the feeling, power, and location problems, regards these problems as themselves conditions of aesthetic experience and inseparable from it, not as raw material to be corrected or refined. This reversal of priorities changes how we think about what counts as evidence for literary response, as we've seen with all the protesting readers in this book. And, it thus alters the relationship between literary literacy and literary experience.

The re-educated imagination would explicitly connect texts to readers through accepting literary response as a form of real experience in which ordinary existence is not consigned to the twilight zone of the sub-literary. To quote Meek (1990) again: "We are not absolutely sure how 'good' a reader anyone needs to be nowadays" (6). This statement is not as heretical as it may sound. Meek is not saying that schools should not be turning out competent readers, but that the relationship between being competent readers and being life-long readers has to do with satisfying reading experiences, and that satisfying reading experiences are a function of educating an imagination that is already highly competent at states of rapt attention felt as the desire to know. "Children are not awakened to understanding by learning to read. Long before they engage with books their active curiosity about the world impels them to explore it. A passion to find out is not the result of literacy but part of its cause" (1991, 166).

The job of school reading is, then, simply to provide opportunities for students to extend and reconstitute "the habit of freshly wondering" that they already possess (Meek, 1991, 170). This, of course, would mean that the education of their imaginations must take seriously what they bring to a literary text, as a *necessary* condition of interpretation. Personal response is not fodder for future, more sophisticated understandings, however useful they may be for enculturation. Personal response is part of the sacred domain of identity formation, which is also, as it turns out, an inseparable aspect of that enculturation. This point brings us back to the justification problem: the logical connection between literature and literacy is that between enculturation and self-transformation, and how they figure into the act of coming to know. Meek makes a crucial point about the relationship between literacy and the consciousness that one has come to know something:

> Readers go beyond common sense when they not only learn what hitherto they did not know, but also *discover the difference that learning makes*. Then there is a new view of the topic, a situation and the prospect of going forward. The simplest response to this awareness is 'Oh, I *see*'. For the moment at least the learner becomes a kind of visionary, someone whose thought is original. Everyone, young or old, knows what this feels like. Being literate extends this kind of activity. (1991, 167, emphasis added)

When the text is a literary text read for literary use, that is, when it is read in a satisfying way, the discovery of "the difference that learning makes" becomes embodied in acts of identification and recognition with the Other of the poem. Thus the aesthetic living-through of the literary event is precisely what is brought away efferently from the literary experience. It "stays with us," forms and informs our next reading act. We might say that in the case of the literary text, this becoming aware of the difference that learning makes can be expressed best through Maxine Greene's, "Ah, this is just how things are and I didn't know it!" (1986, 240). Hypothesis and self-assertion fold into each other as the self becomes transfigured. *Educere* as a leading out and *seducere* as the dialogue of soul with self become the conditions of enculturation in a meta-cognitive operation suffused with the powerful effect of moving from one level of consciousness to another—the "self-subversive self-reflection" (Felman, 1982, qtd. in Penley, 1986, 140) of learning who we are. A pedagogy of embodied criticism beginning with the assumption of the "self"[5] as an unconditional given to be honored, as expressed by Jeff at the beginning of this chapter, might provide readers with a language and method of "owning" a text. Embodied critics would then be those who are "part of a group that enjoys reading specially selected texts and knows how to talk about them" (Meek, 1991, 180)—a community of wandering minstrels working and playing deeply together, their epistemic power imbalances notwithstanding.

Literary interpretation, then, would be a question of "how to encourage a young reader or a would-be writer to possess a text and not simply to read it" (Meek, 1991, 181). Within the re-educated imagination, possessing the text is not occupying it or taking hold of it, but *doing* something with it, as I was ultimately forced to do with Steiner: it is Meek's "undoing and remaking" (1990, 7) of texts under the presupposition that what is done is rooted in readers' feeling, power, and location problems. Interpretation and literary literacy are concerned with understanding; response and literary experience, with undergoing. Of course, the understanding and the undergoing interrelate dialectically. But *how* they do depends upon the credence given to response on its own terms, according to how readers (including teachers) are positioned within the feeling, power, and location problems, to whether Jeff's response would count just because he "thought of it" or is dismissed as the junk data of a "precritical" response (Chapter 5).

Validating and politicizing engaged response at the same time, however, does pose a problem for the relationship between a philosophy of literary subjectivity and the demand for a "correct" response. Under the rubric of the educated imagination, there is no one "correct" reading; but that doesn't mean that just any old response would do. As we saw in Chapter 5, some responses to "A&P" (Updike, 1962) were so far off the mark in understanding that there seemed to be hardly any point to the undergoing of the story: the students just didn't seem to comprehend, to get the point. Here I'm not referring to the politics of refusal, but to those responses which were seen as incomplete or "off-line" in terms of plot or character: ("I feel that the point was that bathing suits are not allowed in stores"; "The inner meaning, that I grasped, was the fact that Sammy's job meant nothing to him and how this relates to how others feel about quitting their jobs as well"). We just don't know why these students appeared not to be engaged by the story or didn't "get it." As we saw in the work of Victor Nell (1988) in Chapter 7, engagement or the lack of it can be as much a defense against anxiety, or dissolution of self,[6] as can be refusal of a text. "Bored reading" cannot simply be dismissed as the reader's fault. If (as I've been claiming), literariness is to be defined, at least in part, as having to do with somatic consciousness as well as with concept formation, neither can "bored reading" be simply relegated to "bad teaching" or regarded unproblematically as something that just is or is not the case.

How might the re-educated imagination regard politically motivated "incorrect response" as it would stem from the poetics of ordinary existence, that is, the lived lives of readers in a state of passionately intelligent response? The students who rejected Lord of *the Flies* (Golding, 1954/1959, my Chapter 6) because of one line pejorative to blacks when experienced outside of its literary context are "wrong" in literary terms. But they are right on their own terms. Those students understood the literary context, but nonetheless refused the literary agenda of the English department of their school. If the decision had been taken to use the novel despite their protests, then the pedagogy would have had to allow their position to be accepted on its own terms. If they were to be given a chance to bridge the gap between singing and stating, they would have needed a pedagogy of refusal (Bogdan, Millen, & Pitt, 1992), for unmaking and redoing that text.

What constitutes the difference between the above and most developmental theories of reader response and pedagogy which espouse engaged response as a valid expression of the reader's subjectivity? After all, the complex intertwining of interpretation and response is not news (Rosenblatt, 1978, 1985; Probst, 1988). But, at present, that connection is generally understood within the context of feeling, power, and location, as givens, not as problems. To problematize them at the same time that we problematize the assumptions of a developmental approach to literary interpretation drastically reconfigures literature education. To challenge these assumptions is not to deny the importance of interpretation but rather to see the move from response to interpretation as only a part of re-educating the imagination. If the imagination is to be re-educated politically at the same time that it is to be authentic personally, it needs to grow out of direct response conceived as logically, not just psychologically, prior to interpretation; and that means that the premises of stock response as "immature" and not-yet are overturned to make way for a reading theory based on something other than the "*ignorance* of . . . literature" (Hamilton, 1990, 221, emphasis added). "Bored readings," politically inspired textual refusals, and double-takes on texts which were formally regarded as inoffensive can be seen as functions of the feeling, power, and location problems of real readers reading, problems which are inextricably linked to the social context of the literature classroom.

As a woman who is affected both in literature and in life by the sayingness of the patriarchal canon, I am aware that when Joseph Gold in his book discusses how reading literature can help meet the needs of feminist consciousness (1990, 294ff.), he is speaking about and for me. And it tends to make me uncomfortable. Despite his "good-will" (Narayan, 1988, 34) and his valuable contributions to the feeling problem (see especially his comments on being a Jewish high school student reader of *Merchant of Venice*, 1990, 308–310]), he doesn't have the particular power and location problems I have. And, while I wouldn't wish them on him, I would expect that, in his taking seriously literary experience as a form of real experience, he would also acknowledge my "epistemic privilege" (Narayan, 1988, 34). I am also discomfited when Frye presumes to speak for me by insisting on the absolute distinction between literature and life in all literary conventions at all times and for all people, as, for example, when he says that the "preposterous sexist ideology" of Shakespeare's *Taming of the Shrew*, which is subordinate to the "sure-fire drama" of the work, is "never taken very seriously" (Frye, 1990e, 215). Is my desire to put quotation marks around "forgiven harlot" (214), "suppliant heroines in a fix" (93), and "poetic mistresses" as "available" or "unavailable" (79), used unproblematically within the context of literary convention, something I need to "get over," or at least, "beyond"? Does the low-level anxiety I experience at the repeated metaphor of penetration (110, 112, 117) to describe the highest level of verbal revelation make me an ideologue stuck in the rut of stock response?

Like Judy, her sisters, and brothers, I *know* what I am supposed to experience within the parameters of the order of words, but like them, I don't want that experience; more important, I don't have it. With some conventions at some times (as with the rhetorical convention of the generic "he"), I am not content to follow "the wisest course," which is "to let them fossilize" (Frye, 1990e, 190) within the "natural" profession of consciousness constructing itself (298). Within the re-educated imagination, I would have to find a way to embody my criticism, to undo and remake that text into a "passionately critical reading" (Medway & Stibbs, 1990, 83) in light of my feeling, power, and location as the conditions of that passion. Otherwise, I turn into Galatea.

Embodied criticism is neither a theory of reading nor a theory of pedagogy; it is something that *happens* out of what readers do when the fact and the politics of direct response come first; when presence and transgression become guides for literary experience, and self-subversive self-reflection, a guide for literary literacy; when the aim is not to get something out of the text but to remake it as an aesthetic practice of reading and writing (Chapter 8). It is here that I would advance my defense of literature education: as the site of literary undoings and remakings, where people come together as minstrels of difference, where presence and transgression produce (s)educere as the creative critical, and the intensity of the oracular closes the gaps between stating and singing, the reading of literature and the study of it.

It is not my intention to make this a lesson in embodied criticism, which, like stasis, I don't believe can be taught. Like stasis, however, it can be taught *for* (Bogdan, 1990c). To put it another way, certain principles, classroom conditions, and sequenced structures of reading and writing that encourage the presence of direct response and the transgression of expectations set up by literary genres and interpretive agendas can be subverted so that something other than digging out meaning can occur. This does not deny the importance of literary interpretation. It simply reinforces that, if we are serious about changing consciousness, about giving up addiction to the assumption that Enlightenment notions of truth and knowledge, including the educational value of literature, entail passion with a victim, we need ways of starting over.

In her critique of Robert Scholes's (1985) erotics of reading, Susan Winnett (1990) suggests two principles of starting over by advancing a meta-cognitive theory of reading. Readers should, above all, learn *how* it is that they read; first, by interrogating the ways in which any interpretive community comes into existence historically, and, second (taking her cue from Freud himself) by recommending that readings be geared to beginnings and birthings rather than endings and dyings. This would involve a Barthesian "textual hedonism" (Bogdan, 1990b, 155 ff.) that could reverse the logic of the relationship between the premises and analyses of how texts read readers. By reading backwards from response to the conditions that produced it, both within the text and within our lives, readers possess their feelings of inevitability, irresistibility, and synthesis, as they are produced by the power of genre to make some readers notice some things and not others, and then disrupt those feelings. I would add to Winnett's transgressive prescriptives the suggestion that the disruption of readerly pleasure serve as the entry point for why readers read as they do in light of their feeling, power, and location.

Winnett's plea for starting over joins with the other voices in this book which have spoken to the need for complexity, disruption, and diversity in justifying the logical priority of direct response in literature education. Replacing negative images of the Other with positive ones is no way out for those affected by grave location, power, and feeling problems. That is a trap that simply perpetuates the cycle of potential exploitation, reinforces content as the arbiter of literary reading, gets us right back into the meta-problem, and enshrines Plato's banishment of the poets. We would do better to trust diversity and complexity in thinking about identities (Miller, 1990, 164). But we can still refuse the text without being accused of censorship, self-censorship, or agnosis (my Chapter 6). The institutional path of permission granted or not granted by educational establishments, which has been influenced by the ethos of the educated imagination, has traditionally devalued direct response as hovering somewhere between stasis, kinesis, and stock, because it is not "literary" (Chapter 5). I suggest that by starting over, we can work toward explicit pedagogical strategies honoring the primacy of *human witness*.

Until the power of literary naming becomes the conscious awareness of the reading act itself as always situated within a nexus of each reader's feeling, power, and location problems, the power of naming *for ourselves* will remain elusive. It seems strange that the corporeality of readers is a point that needs to be stressed within a profession that makes extravagant claims about changing readers' lives for the better. Jane Miller (1990) makes opaque an assumption that harkens back to why reading is a genderized activity. Like the feminine seducee, "a reader is a person in history, a person with a history. Like literature itself, readers have been idealised, and this idealisation has depended on a peculiar privileging and therefore unsexing of reading as one version of the aesthetic encounter, which is essentially available to anyone who makes a certain sort of effort" (Miller, 1990, 154). This is a long way from not caring "a tinker's curse what a student thinks and feels about literature until *he* can think and feel, which is not until he passes the stage of stock response" (Frye, 1970, 83, emphasis added, my Chapter 5). Caring means starting over: undoing and remaking texts and embodying our criticism to name for ourselves.

## Dissonant/Dissident Behaviors: From Transgression to Transfiguration

How can gendered subjects make themselves knowable, to themselves and to others? What are the options available to Others who would be knowable on their own terms, particularly given the enormous power of literary naming as we have been discussing it throughout this book? Perhaps an answer would make literary reading one of Haraway's (1988) "situated knowledges" (579) of partial vision, but, I would hope, an ecstatic one. I base this claim on the hypothesis that this kind of epistemological shift *can* take place in literary reading, when the reading of "self" is accompanied by the reading of theory and in a classroom with a collaborative setting.[7] In this section I try to illustrate how one form of embodied criticism, what we might call *the pedagogy of transgression*, was designed to give permission to respond directly within the interstices of each student's feeling, power, and location, and to reflect on those responses as a way of making theory and writing literature.

What follows is a description and analysis of student response journals in a graduate seminar in women's literature and feminist criticism, in which we studied the feminist critique of Romanticism, what has been called the "moribund aesthetic" of "crisis, confrontation, and renewed domination."[8] Our explicit reason for doing so was my need for a block of time to focus on the subject in order to write a paper of my own; the students agreed to help me by exploring the topic with me. My implicit reason, which I can see more clearly now, three years later, was to provide an exercise in the re-educated imagination, in which the main purpose was to try to break through the impasse of "good" and "bad" images of and theories about women in literature by studying the influence of Romanticist poetics as one powerful way our culture has come to understand itself. Because of its historical distance from current sensibilities that would precipitate acute feeling, power, and location problems, this unit of study provided a safer space for dealing with issues of gender than literature closer to the bone of today's political concerns. Some might think this a failure on my part to help meet the need for strategies dealing with the politics of engaging more controversial literature. I acknowledge this limitation. My purpose in this chapter, though, is to argue for direct response as a philosophical basis for developing such strategies, to show that direct response is not just a "first step" toward interpretation, but that it anticipates, in the passion of its presence and its transgressive authority, the multiplicity, complexity, and intellectual rigor of literary critical positions that have been worked out from a more intellectualized stance by scholars and critics. But my intent goes further: to give one example of reader response when students share the agenda of a pedagogical enterprise in which the "teacher" is in fact little more of an "expert" on the topic than the "students."

I do not trumpet this study as unique, particularly revolutionary, or even wholly successful. But I detail it here to give some idea of how being given academic permission to possess the texts in Meek's sense of undoing and remaking them, by moving back and forth and through them (see Appendix), along with the overlay of the self-conscious reading of theory, helped the students close the gap between stating and singing. The result, which I may have well romanticized because of my memories of the sheer joy of that class, causes me to make yet another grandiose claim: that those students turned seduction into (s)educere as the creation of criticism. Coming from highly diverse disciplinary backgrounds, including history, philosophy, psychology, sociology, adult education, curriculum theory (there were even some English majors), these eleven *inter alia* in discourse became a chorus of yearners within their post-tragedic stance. Amid their ontological shocks, they worked through difference by crossing boundaries with little emotional distance, but much reflective thought.

## Ways in to William Wordsworth

This classroom experiment came about as a result of my involvement in a session at the NCTE Conference in 1988, sponsored by the Association of Departments of English of the Modern Language Association, part of whose mandate is to help break down barriers in English studies existing across the levels: elementary, secondary, postsecondary. In choosing the topic, "Engaging Wordsworth Today" the ADE was interested less in devising other approaches to teaching Wordsworth's poetry, which already exist (see Hall, 1986), than in discovering new modes of learning it, in finding "ways in" for contemporary non-specialists whose sensibilities might be out of tune with the major themes of Wordsworthian Romanticism, such as the continuity between the natural and the human, and the transcendence of the poet's moral vision.[9]

The task of the panel was to find ways that could offset a common problem in literature education: students' reluctance to encounter a poem on its own terms, as "an *alien* structure of imagination, set over against [us], strange in its conventions and often in its values" (Frye, 1970, 77, emphasis original). I set out to discover how students might be encouraged to approach Wordsworth's poetry as something other than a "textoid" (Vipond & Hunt, 1987, 179), the kind of text which is deemed artificial, fragmentary, and inane by its readers, totally unrelated to the social context in which it is read, in other words, to explore the problem of student ownership of literature texts (Meek, 1991, 180–181). The poetry of William Wordsworth can seem as much of a textoid to members of an interdisciplinary graduate class in feminist literary criticism, who have very different ideas about what they want to read and why, as it can to junior or senior high school students. Both groups would probably question its "relevance" to their immediate concerns.[10] Thus from the outset, the issue of engaging with Wordsworth became a problem with exciting possibilities for feminist pedagogy as well as for literature education. I decided to approach the task by focusing on the relationship between Dorothy Wordsworth, author of journals and "secondary" poetry of the picturesque, and her brother, William, poet of the sublime and acknowledged architect of Romantic poetics.

The ground for a theoretical inquiry into the relationship between feminism, Romanticism, and literary engagement has already been broken by a number of scholars. In *Feminism and Poetry: Language,*

*Experience, Identity in Women's Writing* (1987), Jan Montefiore identifies Wordsworth's poetics, ironically enough, as the "father" of radical feminist aesthetics, in that Wordsworth's "Preface to the Lyrical Ballads," with its credo of poetry as the spontaneous overflow of powerful feelings, validates the experiential in literary response, in contrast to the intellectualized aesthetic values of Samuel Johnson and the neo-classicists. In spite of the unwitting sexism of Wordsworth's "definition of the poet as 'a man speaking to men,' " and of "the myth of Romantic transcendence," (10) which has posed difficulties for women writers and readers to this very day (Chapter 8), Montefiore credits Wordsworthian poetics with forming the basis for two canons of radical feminist aesthetics: the belief that poetry is a way in to the poet's own experience and that poetry's capacity for compressing linguistic power is a way in to understanding human existence.

In my reading and re-reading of Steiner in Chapter 8, I repeatedly indicted the poetics of Romanticism as an ideology responsible in part for demanding that passion have a victim, and it seems odd that I should now use that very subject as the topic of my pedagogy chapter to show that passion need *not* have a victim. But this paradox of resistance and complicity underlies my whole defense of literature education. It is the social nature of reading—responding, and studying literature and theory as a group, where voicing voice with each other allows the dialogic nature of language (Bakhtin, 1981) to transmute individual self-reflecting dispositions to the text into altered dispositions to the world. The feminist critique of Romanticism has challenged the myth of the poet as single (male) genius speaking to his brothers as a redemptive vision which, despite its universal claim to ward off mortality by "mastering" experience through the poetic imagination, is heavily coded with gendered systems of noticing and un-noticing that exclude as much as they include (Diehl, 1990). Romanticism is perhaps the paradigm case for a seduction theory of teaching reading and criticism: its tenets serve as a reference point for the literary conventions and criteria of poetic quality by providing the intellectual context within which poetry is read and studied in classrooms. *Whether* certain poetry engages readers and *how* it does so, then, becomes an educational issue that can be traced back to William Wordsworth and his sister, Dorothy.

This entire book has been concerned with whether and how poetry engages readers as an educational problem. The connection between engagement as a theoretical issue and Romantic poetics is salient. John Willinsky has charted the correspondences between the shift in English studies from a transmission to a transactional model of reading and nineteenth-century Romantic poetics (1990,

175–204; see also 1987). Locating current received wisdom about the New Literacy within the history of ideas, he sees commonalities between the nineteenth century's privileging of a "theory of organicism and a reverence for the imagination and the self" (1987, 267), in reaction to neo-classical literary conventions, and the "use of expressive . . . whole language . . . psycholinguistics . . . and interactive, transformative and constructive models of [reading] comprehension" (268), in reaction to the "Old Literacy," with its stress on decoding and *explication de texte* in literary interpretation.

In *Radical Literary Education* (1987), Jeffrey Robinson presents an affecting chronicle of his undergraduates' movement from uncritical engagement to engaged reflection throughout an entire term devoted to a single Wordsworth poem, the *Intimations Ode*. By means of class discussion, journal writing, and the sequenced study of the literary, historical, biographical, psychoanalytic and compositional contexts of this poem, Robinson led his students to challenge liberal humanist presuppositions of engagement without dismissing its literary or educational value. I intended that my project would add the variable of gender to a similar kind of investigation, in which the main focus was the constructive and constructed nature of a woman's self as reader and writer. Our major objective was, through as direct a response as could be afforded by journal writing, to integrate literary literacy with literary experience, to understand our undergoing so as to increase awareness of the influence of literary theory on reading, and to provide a space for the knitting up of literary and critical reading with personal history as a way of coming to terms with subjectivity. The relationship between Dorothy and William in its many aspects seemed an apt starting point.

## The Singing School[11]

### The Assignment and the Journals

Our first assignment consisted of two parts. The first was a "free response" to two poems, William's "I wandered lonely as a cloud" (1954a) and Joyce Peseroff's "Adolescent" (1988), a parody of that poem (see Appendix). For the second, the students were asked to write again about the two poems after having read William's "Preface to the Lyrical Ballads" and the excerpt from Dorothy's journals which is generally regarded as having furnished her brother with the controlling image of his poem. The response journals became a valuable way in to the feminist critique of Romanticism and its implications for the educational value of engaging with literature generally.

In reading these journals, I identified two main categories of responses. The first group tended to focus on "common sense" interpretation (Belsey, 1980), in which the slide from literature to life is made more or less directly. These responses contained reminiscences about the students' own adolescence, which Joyce's[12] poem allowed them to recollect in Wordsworthian tranquillity. For example, Joyce's opening lines, "I wandered lonely as a dog/avoiding trouble,/and others of her species" evoked obvious points of contrast between the loneliness of a "dog" in an urban landscape of alienation and the "cloud" of Wordsworth's bucolic bliss. As one student put it, "Peseroff is expressing the decline of William Wordsworth's world almost two hundred years later." This contrast was recognized by most students as recapitulated in the final invocation to William, "O William, what common/memories stir our yelps in the dark?" where the reservoir of "common memories" has been displaced by the cacophonous "urban music" of a disposable society. The central image of the daffodils, the source of inspiration for William, was seen to have degenerated into the tawdry "gold stars" of conformist behavior and the "civic displays" of bureaucratic control.

The second group of papers was more meta-critical, providing ways in to discussions about the relationship between Romanticism, feminism, and English studies. These readings centered on three characterizations of Joyce's image of the poem's persona as a "dog"— as woman, adolescent reader, and adolescent writer. For one student, Clare, the phrase "lonely as a dog" betokened the alienation experienced by man's best friend—woman, and his appropriation of the feminine echoed in the poem's "phallic clusters" of daffodils. Clare disliked what she saw as the Romantics assuming they had proprietorial rights over the feminine. Another student, Marion, was much more positive in her celebration of a woman writer coming into her own. She saw admiringly the poet as a "real bitch," who, feeling no pain of "male defined reality," keeps her "nose to the curb [kerb]." Marion felt that through looking "into commonly ignored or misapprehended places—i.e., 'the sewer-grate' of her own mind, Joyce finally came out of the broom-closet and into the streets." For her, the poet spoke "with poetic authority and distinction," refusing "to pay obeisance to old forms" (e.g., the stanzaic triplet or metric iambic tetrameter), dropping "all guise of parody . . . to pose the question directly" in the final invocation "to a world (albeit dark) where, together, men and women might seek truth."

These negative and positive perceptions—of woman as victim and woman as exuberant transgressor—were echoed in other journal entries about the poem's persona. Karen, an English teacher, focused on the plight of the typical high school English student as a dog or a hobo, prevented from engaging with Wordsworth directly. Corraled by stultifying pedagogical approaches into traditional interpretations through the "civic display" of "policed" meaning that tended to keep Wordsworth untouchable, Karen envisaged the student reader "forced to wander from the experience of the poem." Jane, however, interpreted the persona's angst in trying to find her voice as that of Joyce herself, who, holding up William's poem as her ideal product, resplendent in its organic unity, could only keep her nose to the curb of process, rebuked by the daffodils of her own muse. As a sociology student who was unaware of Wordsworth's original poem but steeped in the assumptions of the social construction of knowledge, Jane confessed that her interpretation was probably a result of her outsider status in the literary interpretive community; but it was only after she encountered William's theory of poetry in his "Preface to the Lyrical Ballads" that she could articulate how and why she felt.

In the second part of this assignment, students were invited to respond again to both poems as well as to Dorothy's journal entry, within the hindsight of William's critical manifesto, in his "Preface." They were then asked to comment on the significance to themselves of engaging in the exercise. Here the main aims were to provide a reference point for their initial responses, to serve as a means of comparing the poetic values of William's and Dorothy's writing, and to indicate the degree to which this self-conscious attention to process might have precipitated change in their perceptions about the texts and about themselves. I have organized my analysis around three major contexts in which these embodied criticisms struck me. The first was the recursive and self-scrutinizing quality of their written thoughts about their initial responses. The second was a preoccupation with engagement as a literary critical issue. The third was a lack of agreement as to whose writing, William's or Dorothy's, was the more successful in achieving the goals stated in William's "Preface."

I was surprised at how much all these students, regardless of their background in literature or literary theory, enjoyed reconsidering Joyce's and William's poems in the light of the "Preface." Here their writing became remarkably fluid and bold. Some used William's critical canons to see commonalities in the two poems. Others saw Joyce's poem as directly challenging those canons. Some even saw "Adolescent" as a better example of William's poetics than his own daffodil poem. What stood out was the students' interest in deploying Wordsworth's poetic principles to clarify their understanding of their reading. Clare subjected the principles of the "Preface" to Belsey's critique of commonsense theories of language

(Belsey, 1980). For Clare, William was operating under the misapprehension that "poetry reflects the real world" and that "those who read poetry will respond the same way," thus gaining access to "universal truth." She thought that William would probably have classified Joyce's poem as a textoid, as possessing, in his words, "matter . . . [that is] contemptible. . . . This wants sense; it is neither interesting in itself, nor can lead to anything interesting" (W. Wordsworth, 1954b, 29). But for Clare, a city woman, the politicized content of "Adolescent" was far more exciting than the moment of beauty recaptured, however successfully, in William's poem. By contrast, Jane's examination of William's "Preface" led her to prefer his poem. While she challenged his assumptions that "'the language of men,' 'common life,'" and transcendent experience produce timeless poetic truth (W. Wordsworth, 1954b, 8, 3–4, 15, 44), she nevertheless luxuriated in precisely the kind of aesthetic pleasure that William's poetic method intended to evoke, finding this a welcome relief from self-consciously ferreting out a meaning for "Adolescent."

This awareness of self-consciousness brings me to my second and third points: engagement as a poetic value, and who was better at eliciting it, William or Dorothy. Another student, Ruth, cited William's own reference to the poet's " 'act of writing in verse' " by which he " 'makes a formal engagement . . . [to] gratify certain known habits of association,' " (W. Wordsworth, 1954b, 2) noting that both poems "fly in the face of [Wordsworth's] 'savage torpor'(7) by calling up images which deny and defy acquiescence to uniformity." Ruth saw both poems as deliberate intentions by both poets to engage the reader actively. Gayle, on the other hand, complained that "Wordsworth expects his reader to be a mere passive recipient of what is already known to be 'true,' " while Joyce let her into the text as a collaborator in reconstructing the cityscape. For Gayle, as for Liz, the problem with William was "that he is a little guilty of the very thing he accuses other 'lesser' poets of. He speaks from a 'poet's' perspective . . . rather than translating "the feelings of us mere mortals." Liz blamed William's failure to engage her on the self-consciousness he brings to the poet's mandate to engage through the deliberate act of remembering. She wrote that perhaps William was correct in his assertion that the poet's task is to bind humankind together by " 'passion and knowledge' " (W. Wordsworth, 1954b, 18); but, for her, instead of achieving this emotional immediacy, William attenuated the effect through the very philosophical contemplation thought necessary to bring it about. She acknowledged that theoretically "it may well be that the . . . act of remembering is more significant than the emotions stirred by the memories"; but in the end, instead of dancing with the daffodils, William "just wrote a poem about it." This stance, what Marion called the poet as "magus," the poet as Wordsworth's "man of 'livelier sensibility,' in possession of 'a greater knowledge of human nature, and a more comprehensive soul' " (1954b, 13), whose "self-claimed preserve is none other than 'truth' " (15), was thought to be counterproductive to the evocation of powerful feeling in the reader, the assumption of the poet's priestly mantle actually working against itself in achieving specific effects. For her, William's credo that a poem has determinate meaning resulted, paradoxically, in a more diffused poetic effect than Dorothy achieved by her simple description. She saw William's poem as an exhalation whereas "Dorothy's daffodils draw air into the lungs; they inspire and conspire to cut cleanly through the persona of the poetic genius looking down at himself as poetic genius."

It would be a misrepresentation of the students' journals to see them as having given William's poetry and poetics short shrift. On the contrary, William pre-dominated throughout, his centrality as theoretician and supreme practitioner of poetic language and effect incontestable. To look at him directly, backwards at him through Joyce, or obliquely at him through Dorothy, meant inevitably encountering his paramountcy in generating the very premises upon which a course in personal and creative identity might be structured. When this identity is interwoven with the reader's poetic engagement as a powerful reception of/connection with powerful feeling, *how* that feeling registers *matters*. Here is where the journal responses to Dorothy's excerpt became invaluable as what I would claim is the theory-making activity of this class. In having to account for—even merely record—poetic effect (or "impact," as the students chose to call it), in engaging in reflection about their original response, they necessarily tangled with issues of poetic quality and method.

The journals disclosed a real division among the students on the question of Dorothy and William as "literary engagers." The English specialists tended to prefer William, and those who were "Other," Dorothy.[13] Karen, an English specialist, found William's poem more imaginatively satisfying and emotionally intense than Dorothy's "drawn out and uninspiring" prose, and accounted for her response in terms of Dorothy's distance from nature, her outsider status, as a woman in society and as a poet. She also noted Dorothy's absence from the scene she is describing, an absence, according to William, that is crucial to the communication of powerful feeling. Dorothy's lack of poetic persona was precisely what for Liz, a non-specialist, rendered Dorothy's daffodils more vivid and immediate. Their specificity was a product of simple memory or direct observation rather than the long reflection recommended by William (W.

Wordsworth, 1954b, 16). Ruth also found Dorothy's multi-layered, nuanced descriptions three-dimensional, all the more active and complex for their being less removed, less intentionally poetic; and Clare was prompted to question William's claim in the "Preface" that poetry *qua* poetry elicits our most passionate responses. Dorothy's directness of perception was for Jennifer paradigmatic of "a female presence equally as sensitive [as William's] to the world around her." Ann described this as a presence which expresses through "the language of women speaking to women," the universal vision William longed for "but failed to convey."

With respect to the final layer of the exercise, which invited the students to reflect on the entire process, Gayle wrote:

> I enjoyed reading and analyzing the poems in their own right, looking at the text and seeing how it worked as a New Critic would, but I still could not get away from the "common sense" reading of the poem, which is also important to me. In fact, it is the common sense reading, the emotional connection with the poem, that gives me the incentive to reread the poem in a different way. I saw both narrators in the poems as men, and because of the nature of this class, I was aware that I was doing that even though Joyce Peseroff is a woman. I wondered why I did this (conditioning, perhaps, which comes from reading more male than female poets). Then I realized that I was stereotyping a young male as one who does not do well in school, who gets into trouble, who would see himself as a dog, who would be preoccupied with the size of his genitals. I let William speak as a man, yet his sister was with him on this walk as we can see from her journal, and so he could have been speaking through her although it has not been my experience that men can do this well. Was gender an important issue here? The question of the gender of the narrators was brought home further with a rereading of the "Preface," where the poet is clearly male, where there is reference to "manly style" (whatever that is), and this failure to acknowledge women as poets or subjects or readers annoyed me. It seemed to me to be specific. Dorothy's journal reminded me that there is a female presence equally sensitive to the world around her. This made me read the Peseroff poem one more time.
>
> Now I see this poem "Adolescent" as male/female, and the question at the end about "common memories" takes on another meaning. Perhaps this is a cry for the unification of the sexes, for the creation of an organic whole.

The response journals of these students turned out to be a learning tool that extended beyond the breaking down of potential resistance to William's poetry as a textoid. The combination of direct response, the movement back and forth between the juxtaposed texts—poetic and theoretical—as a sequenced activity, I believe, helped to loosen

their critical categories, integrated literary theory with literary experience, and encouraged reinterpretation of their responses in the first
half of the assignment. As we can see from the above, Gayle used her
insights about Dorothy and William at the end of the process to
challenge and rethink her own gender stereotyping—and to go back
to the poems. The exercise also provided the basis for a more systematic inquiry into substantive theoretical issues in Wordsworthian
criticism itself, which we pursued in subsequent meetings. The juxtapositioning of the three primary texts, the sequenced readings, and
combining the free response technique with studying the "Preface to
the Lyrical Ballads" resulted in the students foreshadowing at a
deeply intuitive level the major critical positions we explored later
in some of the most richly rewarding recent criticism on gender in
Romanticism (see especially Mellor, 1988; Homans, 1980, 1986).

These students were engaging in an "alternative sublime": their
direct responses were transgressive, passionate, but neither victimiz-
ing nor engulfing their subjects. Rather, they wandered around like
minstrels, singing and stating, mindful of the conditions of their own
seduction, in whichever way they seemed to be led by these texts,
embodying their criticism, entering their libidinal forces, their noticings and un-noticings, into their writing experience, not as a system,
but as a series of forgettings and rememberings of *their* "motive for
metaphor" (Yaeger, 1989, 205).

The writing described above is not unique to this class; it is
merely one example of the kind of writing that is embraced by some
research in feminist pedagogy and by proponents of the New Literacy
(see especially Beach, 1990; Bleich, 1988, 1978; Hynds, 1990). The
use of reader response journals is certainly not new in the schools
and is gaining increasing acceptance in universities. But it is a practice that is still resisted in many sectors of the academy as being
sophomoric and anti-intellectual—even romantic. As a practice in
the schools, it is just now coming to be accepted at the level of
"metacomprehension." Jack Thomson's work (1987, in press), for example, "suggests very powerfully that a reflexive awareness of their
own processes of response can lead adolescents to achieve greater
control over their reading—and greater appreciation of the books
they read" (Durrant, Goodwin, & Watson, 1990, 211). The collaborative nature of this exercise (we shared each other's papers, including
the one I wrote on the experiment), as well as other features of this
endeavor—putting response first and structuring the readings of the
poetry and the theory—helped integrate and embody literary literacy
and literary experience into "the unfolding of [the] long and complex
dialectical process" Frye speaks of in The Great Code (1982b, 226).
Embodied pedagogy validates a conception of literature education as

enacting, through the social context of a classroom, with an awareness of gender as an informing principle the poetics of ordinary
existence, what in Chapter 7 we called literacy as a state of grace, in
which direct response as response can be justified on grounds other
than the ignorance of literature (Hamilton, 1990).

This pedagogical shift has implications for a defense of literature
education, primarily in terms of revealing the dialectical nature of
what it means to come to know anything. The kind of knowing these
journals disclose freely explores the relationship between intuited
knowledge and the continual testing of that knowledge within an
intellectual framework or theoretical construct at the same time that
the knower authenticates knowledge by taking responsibility for the
very process of coming to know. As such, it is not a rehearsal for
life but the real thing. Through direct response to poetry and the
sequenced reading of theory, readers "come to know" by reflecting
on literary texts in an especially fertile discourse that both honors and interrogates their knowledge as "experiential realization"
(Woodman, 1985, 157). This dialectic between literary literacy and
literary experience, I believe, contains elements of the oracular in
some of these writings, expressed as ironic musings (William's poem
as a substitute for his dancing with the daffodils), analogical play
(William's poem as an exhalation and Dorothy's fragment as drawing
air into the lungs), and metaphorical flights (the woman writer coming out of the broom-closet). But it is the oracular of the alternative
sublime, in which the knower is both sovereign, as the commitment
to the process of knowing, and vulnerable, as tentativeness about the
certitude or finality of any single act of coming to know.

The importance of being ambivalent—of avoiding closure—was
manifest throughout this project. To be ambivalent is to engage with
language reflectively without having to repress or kill the signified.
To be ambivalent is to be at once accepting and critical. It is to
embrace Otherness without self-abnegation in an alternative sublime. It is to dissolve the distinction between the sacred and the
profane in the ability to say, "I stand here, but am willing to move
there." It is to leave the self open to transfiguration. This is an
intensely personal affair, which the educated imagination has
regarded as the business of the private act of devotion. But it is also
what happened in this class, where these students embarked on a
pedagogy of the unknowable through the sharing of interiorities by
giving themselves over to a process and a person they did not know
but were willing to trust. To be ambivalent is to attempt transcendence without appropriation, to disengage from the spontaneous
overflow of powerful feeling long enough to recognize absence in
presence, difference in oneness. To undertake such an enterprise

with both presence and transgression makes real claims in the lives of real readers reading—from kindergarten to graduate school—claims that *can* change the world .

Recent research into the relationship between Dorothy and William Wordsworth, Dorothy's ambivalence about her own poetic identity and her acceptance of a "fragmented self" is sometimes interpreted as a counterbalance to the poetics of engagement typified by the "unitary self" of William's poetic genius (Levin, 1987; Wolfson, 1988). Dorothy's "resistance to poethood" (Homans, 1980, 41), her amateur status, not only grounds her brother's apocalyptic language and transcendent vision in a way which allows them both to test their process of coming to know, but serves to challenge the criteria of poetic quality now being reconsidered in attempts to dissolve the boundaries between high art and popular culture, literature and "women's literature."[14] The deep but ambivalent intuitions embodied in these journals brought to consciousness these critical concerns for these students, who voiced their voices, first, by lighting out, and then by listening like does in the forest. Their transgressions became beginnings that interrupted the inexorable march of genre towards the production of endings; their listenings to the texts, to each other, and to themselves, within the context of each other, gave them control by helping them relinquish control. In the process they were displaced by the lack of literary context and displaced themselves by creating their own.

Not all my feminist classes have been as willing as this one to spend their time on what in the age of post-humanism has been characterized as this "moribund aesthetic" (Weiskel, 1976, qtd. in Yaeger, 1989, 197). I argue, however, that it is important to confront, undo, and remake the conditions of the cultural history that frames our consciousness. I also argue that the theoretical unseating of an unproblematic transcendence does not, and should not, necessarily negate the desire for it. The aim of this project was like the aim of this book: to participate in and at the same time to disrupt a cultural tradition. When I next take up the Wordsworths unit, I would want to concentrate more on issues of epistemic and political privilege as they are played out in the relationship between Dorothy and William, and how that study would implicate the feeling, power, and location problems of members of the class. The harmonic dissonance of the experiences we shared in this group was tuneful. I do not expect it always to be so. For one thing, I have to be accountable to the logic of inclusion and exclusion, which dictates that studying "a moribund aesthetic" eclipses more pressing issues of literary and cultural concern related to how a course in literature can more directly address marginalizations of race, class, and sexual orientation. Yet I would hope that, whatever the content, the use of direct response and theory together would enable a different class under different circumstances to come to terms with both the positive and negative expression of the kinds of "conclusive experience[s]" (Fanon, 1970, qtd. in Miller, 1990, 123) I saw in these journals through moments of mutuality: real presence as pure utterance, sites of transfiguration as the poetry of ordinary existence.

# Endnotes

1. The Ontario Institute for Studies in Education, University of Toronto.

2. By theory I do not mean just literary theory and practical criticism, but newspapers, magazines, television, and all the texts that help in the understanding of the undergoing of literary experience.

3. Some might notice that when speaking of the quasi-religious dimension of the re-educated imagination, I sometimes combine the vocabulary of Catholicism with the evangelical fervor of low-church Protestantism. My thanks to David Bleich for this observation.

4. My thanks to Mike Hayhoe for this phrase, which he coined in private conversation during the International Conference on Language and Literacy at the University of East Anglia, Norwich, England, in April of 1991.

5. Poststructuralist critiques of an unchanging, universalist "self" (Weedon, 1987) have been needed and valuable, but they do not give me license to question the validity of your experience when it's offered on your terms, even when that experience is literary experience.

6. My thanks to Alice Pitt for this observation.

7. In her moving address titled "Feeling like a Fraud," delivered as the R. Freeman Butts Lecture at the Annual Meeting of the American Educational Studies Association in Toronto, November 4, 1988, Margaret Means McIntosh called for the humanizing of class assignments at the post-secondary level. In order to increase students' feelings of authenticity about their own knowledge, more college and university classrooms should adopt the principles of the decentered classroom, writing as process, and students' accounts of their own learning experiences, in contrast to soloistic "hierarchical academic products," such as the term paper and its outline. See also Bleich, 1988.

8. Patricia Yaeger borrows the term "moribund aesthetic" from Thomas Weiskel (1976). See Yaeger, 1989, 197, 198, 202.

9. In private conversation with David Laurence, Chair, Association of Departments of English, Modern Language Association.

10. Trying to work with the relevance issue, not evade it, is, I believe, also a way of forging "the critical path." I leave to the reader's judgment whether the pedagogy in the account below was taking "the slithering downward way

of mindless educators" in relating "the subject to the student," taking "the flinty uphill path of relating the student to the subject" (Frye, 1971/1973, 156), both, or neither.

11. "The Singing School" is the title of the second chapter of Frye's *The Educated Imagination* (1963a). The original citation is from Yeats's "Sailing to Byzantium" (qtd. in Frye, 1963a, 12).

12. To avoid the condescending and implicitly sexist practice of referring to "Dorothy" and to her brother as "Wordsworth," and to avoid the stylistic encumberment of "Dorothy Wordsworth" and "William Wordsworth," I shall refer throughout to "Dorothy" and "William." In order to preserve stylistic continuity I'll henceforward refer to Joyce Peseroff as "Joyce."

13. I am not an ethnographer, and I make no empirical claims here. "Proving" something about academic or professional literary conditioning was never part of the intent of this project. But I wonder whether this division in the students' preferences for Dorothy or William was coincidental. If this experiment can be considered substantive in any way, it would reconfirm presuppositions about the specific effects of education on the history of taste and canon formation (Widdowson, 1982).

14. Smith (1988) expresses her suspicion of "better" and "worse" responses as they apply to aesthetic experience on the basis of enjoyment. Proceeding from "Bourdieu's analysis that all normative theories of culture, . . . serve vested tastes and vested interests" (76), she repudiates "the suggestion that *certain* people (such as high-culture publics or, as in [I.A.] Richards, those who are neurologically well organized) "get more" from the art they prefer than *other* people (such as low-culture publics or those with "inadequate impulses"). . . . For not only does the question of what they get more *of* remain unanswered or begged, but the facile allusions to "measuring" and "comparing" the "content" of different people's aesthetic "rewards" must sooner or later confront the classic epistemological conundrum of how to determine the quality of other people's experiences. Is my airplane-neighbor reading *Rebecca* enjoying it less than I am enjoying *Emma*? Is there any way (by the difference in our EEG-waves? rates of heartbeat? muscle tone?) it could be demonstrated that the teenager listening to Pink Floyd is not feeling as good as I do when I listen to *Parsifal*?" (82, emphasis original).

# Chapter Ten

# Toward an
# Alternative Sublime

## The Poetics of Ordinary Existence and Pure Utterance

I ended the last chapter with the suggestion that conclusive experiences—positive and negative—happen to people all the time in the course of their routine existence. Personal experiences that change lives and, by extension, the world are not necessarily related either to literary literacy or literary experience in the way in which we've been using these terms. So now we must ask why writing or reading this book should make any difference to the attainment of literacy in its broader context: as a state of grace or as cultural critique. Gayatri Spivak (1988), in arguing for questioning the ideology of " 'literary studies,' " has ruefully pointed out that the " 'world' " continues to read itself without us (95). For Spivak, the discipline of literature alone cannot redress this situation. "One must fill the vision of literary form with its connections to what is being read: history, political economy—the world. And it is not merely a question of disciplinary formation. It is a question also of questioning the separation between the world of action and the world of the disciplines" (95). In other words, the received wisdom of the discipline, what here we've been thinking of as the sharp distinction between the worlds of ordinary existence and imaginative experience, is the very factor that "refuses to allow us to read. As a result, even as in classroom and article we mouth the freedom of the aesthetic, in bulletin and caucus and newspaper and meeting we deplore our attenuation and betrayal by society" (Spivak, 1988, 95).

In the last two chapters I've been attempting to make a case for the poetics of ordinary existence, and thus reduce the polarity between life as "brute fact" and aesthetics as that which is "free and transcends life" (Spivak, 1988, 95). In continuing our case, let's go back to the testimony of Jeff, the wandering minstrel, whose final paper I excerpted at the beginning of Chapter 9. Following his sentence in that paper about the importance of "knowing someone's pain, seeing someone's attempts to comprehend the incomprehensible," he writes:

> My family just came in from a party, and I interrupted this to help the kids to bed. But a crisis developed when my son, Jamie, saw some library books I had gotten for him. Hallie, my daughter, asked if I got any for her. I hadn't. I hadn't even thought of it. Forty-five minutes of reassuring, of reading her the old library book, of hugging and kissing and singing and flossing of teeth comforted her, and she sleeps. But is that slight, that failure of mine to fully consider her, now a permanent part of her psyche? Perhaps I am being overly dramatic (she doesn't read yet; perhaps the exclusion was based on that, not on gender). But there was no denying the reality of her pain. I have realized in this course not only the residual and unexamined linguistic impediments to equality, and the various losses that I have experienced or will have to experience as a result, but the ways in which I participate in patriarchy. I had never heard the term before the first class. I had thought that feminism was passé, that the real work had been done and, in due course, the wrongs of male chauvinism would be righted. But I am no longer so sure. And here's the point: if the class had been peopled by men alone, the discussion would have been different. Awareness of people's difference is a radicalizing, liberating experience. And isn't this what a good literature course could include? If studying literary theory can mean what it did for me, how could that not help students not only to read as more fully formed human beings, but also to relate to their classmates in a more compassionate, empathic way? (Reynolds, 1990)

Now, what are we to make of this? Is it assertion, hypothesis, literary experience, ordinary existence, "going home," not "going home," being eccentric, partial vision, material for deconstruction, aesthetic living-through, moral judgment, parental concern, the spontaneous overflow of powerful feeling, methodological humility, engagement, detachment, desire for community, literary literacy, "pure utterance," recognition of misrecognition, fragility of goodness, good will, "a genuine epistemological shift" (de Lauretis, 1987, 10)? Because I feel that I *know* Jeff, I think I can safely say that it isn't just "masculine guilt" or "trying to get an A." But perhaps something in the writing makes it unnecessary for me to guarantee that. Is the directness of this response—which is political and theoretical, too, this intensification of mind, expansion of spirit, writing of the body—a result of the educational value of poetry, the poetic value of education, or simply a matter of devotion?

Throughout these chapters I have used the above terms within a particular context; but I have also tried to reconfigure that context by relating the terms to each other in order to articulate a conception of the educational value of literature that stresses the transformational process of literary experience as the poetics of ordinary existence. In a way, we've come full circle to Plato, for whom true art was the art of living the moral life. Juxtaposing Jeff's statement and the songs of the Singing School has left me standing in a space between what seemed like the pure utterance of a single voice speaking in the plenitude of a unitary (male) self and the dissonant ambivalence of a (female) chorus. The women in the Dorothy and William Wordsworth class and Jeff were all singing their stating. They were also bearing witness to the primacy of human witness as the ground for a defense of the educational value of poetry and of the poetic value of education. By putting the gender of Jeff and the Singing School in parentheses, I don't wish to denigrate its importance, but rather, as I hope will become clear, to stress gender as a factor that is perpetually open to personal transformation and social reconstruction in the ongoing process of shifting human consciousness.

That the single voice happens in this instance to be male, however, and the chorus, female, is perhaps emblematic of the way in which I have approached gender in this book: masculine as solitary, in the Romantic tradition of the sublime; and feminine as communal, as the alternative sublime. Yet I hope my formulations present themselves as a sign of yet another category to be blurred, transposed, and transfigured. These crossings over—from masculine to feminine, from prosaic to poetic, from imaginative experience to ordinary existence, from philosophy to literature, from the schools to the universities, from text to reader, from reading to writing, from literature education to "education for life," from identification to recognition, from misrecognition to a state of grace, from dissociation of sensibility to the singing of stating—and back again—all are markers of the terrain of this journey.

I understand my undergoing in these pages in part as traversing a path between two traditions of response to literature: the Aristotelian mimetic tradition, with its stress on coherence, unity, and representation; and the Longinian aesthetic tradition, with its stress on intensity, immediacy, and experience (Longinus, 1965; Frye, 1963c, 114–115). It is the connection between them which I see as metaphorical of the connection between the educated imagination and the re-educated imagination. The latter is not a rejection of the former but rather a transvaluation of it from an alternative perspective which involves a different set of values and a different system of noticings and un-noticings: transferring imaginative energy from life to literature rather than the other way round. Of course, this energy always moves both ways, but it's the latter direction we're emphasizing here. Frye himself has indirectly contrasted these two stances as that between the spatial and structural, typified by architecture, and the temporal and processual, symbolized by music (Frye, 1990a, 94). The context within which I've tried to do this has politicized literary response at the same time that it has tried to make the phenomenon of response itself, that is, the *fact* that someone responds in one way rather than another, logically prior to what that response might ultimately mean. (Recall Jeff's question to me about the "relevance" of his reaction to the film on the first evening of class [Chapter 9].)

My journey also has had to do with emphasizing the oral-aural dimension of the poem as pure utterance and what that can say about the religious quality of direct response as it relates to the world of ordinary existence. In hindsight, I realize that, in covering this ground, I have created a kind of chaos out of which I hope readers can sort out some order for their own lives, an order having the character of subjective knowledge, which, according to Mary Warnock (1970/1988), "is identical with faith" because of the element of paradox inherent in it (9). Subjective knowledge is necessarily emotional and "concrete, not abstract. This is because it must necessarily be related to the actual concrete existence of a living individual" (9–10).

In creating my own subjective knowledge, I find myself in the paradoxical position of the traveller who, despite having ended up in a different place from where she intended, has really never left home. For it is this chaos that marks the tradition which I have been exploring and challenging but of which I recognize I am still very much a part. It seems that I do share the sensibility of Frye and the defenders of poetry who precede him, after all: the sensibility of English Romanticism, which "is passionate, biblical, and marked by a sense of the sheer confused variety of things" (Prickett, 1986, 212). Out of this multiplicity I invite readers to make their own connections and to ask their own questions. But I would also like to offer some noticings and un-noticings of my own within the logic of what I've attempted to accomplish in the project as a whole.

In the excerpt from Jeff's final paper reproduced above, I found an example of the oracular language of recognition—Jeff's recognition of a primary datum of ordinary existence—his *mis*recognition of himself as someone who is complicitous in patriarchy. In this sense I would claim that his text, an example of the aesthetic practice of self-disclosure, manifests a kind of transfiguration. Embedded in his narrative of direct address is a series of utterances, the urgency, imagery, and immediacy of which speak and bespeak the language of poetry. It is the language of a powerful internal coming to know, a feature of what Margaret Meek (1991) sees as the heart of literacy itself, that is, the self-consciousness of discovering "the difference that learning makes" (167).

I suggest also that it could be valid evidence of what Spivak (1988) might include in her prescription when she refers to the need to redefine practical criticism as "readings and discussions" of the ideological underpinnings of the discipline (102). As part of fulfilling the requirements of the course in the philosophy of literature and literature education, Jeff had conducted an incisive analysis (yet another example of the poetics of refusal) in *his* reading of Steiner's *Real Presences* (1989), where he accused Steiner of mistaking the locus of the power of aesthetic transformation. For Jeff, himself a professional musician, Steiner had misguidedly privileged music over human existence. Steiner's was an "onanistic art," an example of the god trick that traded on the compensatory function of art, Othering, and an existential dread of aloneness.

I believe that the misrecognition scene Jeff experienced regarding his daughter and the library books, recounted in his final paper, resulted from a conviction about the poetics of ordinary existence: that an ontology of art cannot be divorced from life. This is a belief he already held from his life experience before coming to the course; but his interaction with feminists and feminist ideas in the class had transmuted it into what we've been calling literary literacy. In class, Jeff and I went on to present our Steiner papers in dialogue form, he having written his before reading mine, the two of us consulting with each other beforehand. Class discussion had centered on the commonalities and divergences between his "mainstream" and my expressly feminist analysis.

Though I would not call Jeff's statement or the songs of the Singing School Sidney's "poetry strictly speaking" (Sidney, 1966, 26), I did suggest that something in the writing manifestly exhibited the authenticity of his poetic/literary transfiguration. What might this be? For both Jeff and the Singing School, the expressions of their recognitions and misrecognitions, their languaged awarenesses of the process of knowing, are distinguished by the fragmented yet psalmic quality of the lyric, redolent of the English Romantic tradition, the tradition, ironically, of course, out of which Frye's whole *modus operandi* arises. This epiphanic element of direct address is expressive of what we earlier referred to as a "conclusive experience" (Fanon, 1970, qtd. in Miller, 1990, 123, my Chapter 9), of which the poetics of refusal is one negative form. But in this chapter we are concerned with its positive manifestation and how it can clarify the significance of the poetics of ordinary existence to our defense of literature education, how it might help the profession to read the world in a way that the world can care about.

I would characterize what Jeff did as transfiguration: working on his literary literacy in and out of the class opened a space for literary experience as an embodied response in his final paper. The work of The Singing School was, though, more like transposition—the undoing and remaking of texts (Meek, 1990, 7) through the students' presence and their transgression. Both presence and transgression involve active participation in literacy as a state of grace, and both share in the legacy of the Romantics in reconceptualizing transcendence, not as the world of imaginative experience that would "go beyond" ordinary existence, but as the intensified perception of the quotidian.

These literary transfigurations and transpositions presuppose certain redefinitions of the language of poetry and of the imagination which have to do with shortening (not collapsing altogether) the distance between the literary and the nonliterary, art and reality, the extraordinary and the ordinary, literary convention and reality, the poetic and the religious, the sacred and the profane, the natural and the supernatural, the carnal and the spiritual, subject and object, literature education and other disciplines. They also work toward reclaiming a neo-Romantic privileging of the lyrical, self-expressive function of language, with the very practical aim of making the oracular into forms of attention, ways of being-in-the-world which demand no victims (Chapters 8 and 9). This would in the end comprise my defense of the poetics of ordinary existence as an alternative theory of the sublime (Yaeger, 1989; my Chapter 9).

Colin Falck (1989), whose book I read after coming to my own determinations about these issues, asserts that "reality is ontologically revealed to us in our most ordinary experience—if it is not revealed to us there, it is not revealed to us anywhere. . . . [T]here is a kind of 'imagination' at work in our most ordinary perception which is continuous with, and not self-declaringly distinguishable from, the kind of imagination which is at work in our more innovative or 'creative' perceptions of form or significance" (67). Falck goes on to demystify the poetic. Rather than sweeping it clear of the felt experience of daily life, he returns the poetic to the context of its origin (in contrast to Ellis, 1974; my Chapter 7):

> No subjects are more appropriate to poetry than any others, and the
> revelations, or luminous details, or epiphanies, of poetry must be

thought of as capable of occurring, or as liable to occur, almost anywhere in our experiencing. . . . These are the lessons which Romanticism has given us overwhelmingly convincing reasons for accepting. . . . Nor, . . . is poetry a particular kind or quality of language, distinguished by the presence of particular linguistic properties such as "irony," or "tension," or—except in an unfamiliarly general sense—"ambiguity." Any kind of language-using—any spoken sentence, any snatch of journalism, any passage from a scientific textbook, any entry in a diary, any note to a local delivery man—may be poetry if they have the right (which is to say an ontological or expressive) kind of interest for us. (82–83)

In light of the above, I would want to claim that the transpositional utterances of the Singing School and the transfigurative ones of Jeff and so many others like them qualify as poetry on the grounds of their "expressive" and "ontological" "interest for us." That is, their very utterance interests us as a prior question to whether what they say is "true" or "false," "subjective" or "objective"; and that fact alone exhorts us to listen to them like "does in the forest" (Robin Morgan, 1989, 342, my Chapter 8). Because their utterances, I believe, signify a "genuine shift in consciousness" (de Lauretis, 1987, 10), they are not "merely" self-expressive, but expressive of something fundamental to the human condition—that human consciousness is capable of change and growth and that the dissolution of the ego and the notion of the self as intricately interconnected with social reality are preconditions for understanding the human condition. But, more fundamental than this, and more to the point of this book, that they are *self*-expressive connects the ontological order with the ethical inasmuch as that these utterances are indicative of the "pre-subjectivity" (59) of what Falck calls "mood" and "gesture," both of which speak to the "necessities of human embodiment which lie at the base of language" (Falck, 1989, 25). This is something to which I have been referring throughout as a primary datum of ordinary existence. Here gesture and mood are not "about" anything: they are pre-conceptual metaphysical necessities from which spring the need for human beings to speak at all.

It is this category of human experience which I had in mind when I introduced the idea of the poetics of ordinary existence in Chapter 8 and to which I think the reader responses of both the Singing School and Jeff belong. It is what I think Steiner was aiming for but misappropriated, and why, despite its insight, Falck's account of the spiritual dimension of poetry is incomplete (see p. 294). And the reason it is so brings us back to Frye and the educated imagination. The schema for our discussion will be, as stated at the end of the last chapter, a modification of the meta-problem with which we began and its three underlying premises: the response problem (the autonomous reader); the censorship problem (whether and what literature says); and the justification problem (the relationship between literature and life).

Now, at the end of this journey, I see that the feeling, power, and location problems have transposed and transfigured the premises of the meta-problem into three re-visionings of this problem. The premise of the autonomous reader becomes that of the embodied reader; whether and what literature says becomes the doubleness of seeing, hearing, speaking, and living; and the relationship between literature and life becomes the interplay between literary literacy and literary experience, seen more broadly as that between culture and literacy in general. In this chapter, I will try to come to some kind of closure, however tentative, about what the re-educated imagination stands for: the defense of literature education within an interdisciplinary context. The first part of this chapter will deal with the relationship of Frye's notion of the embodied reader to the poetics of ordinary existence, particularly as it invokes the gendered nature of his spiritual vision and its relationship to how we read. Later we address the transposed premises of the censorship and justification problems. But, just as these principles were seen as overlapping in the meta-problem, as it was first configured, so are they in their transfigured form. And so, "doubleness" opens up into a consideration of the continuum and the gap between word and world; and literary experience and literary literacy doubles back into new forms of doubleness, transposition, and transfiguration that promise change for the world.

## Double Mirror: Frye, Process, and Embodiment

If we accept the poetics of ordinary existence as testimony to the triumph, not the failure, of experience, we might be persuaded that, contrary to Frye's claim, poetry or literature is not necessarily made out of itself (1957, 97). We might also concede that the revelatory aspects of language that go to make up the literary can have their genesis in the secular and the mundane, without recourse to the special pleading of Holy Writ or the utopic "third order" of hypothetical experience. But we already know that the poem is pure utterance (Frye, 1990b, 110, my Chapter 9).[1] The poetry of William Blake, of course, is the apotheosis of the religious aspect of this poetic self-consciousness. What is curious about Frye's devotion to the Blakean ideal in poetry is that he lived it more than he spoke or wrote about it, at least in quantitative terms. While he revered the reality of literary experience, what he wrote about, for the most part, was criticism and poetry as the *product* of the poetic imagination. It was mainly in his later works, particularly *The Great Code* (1982b) and *Words with Power* (1990e), that he concentrated on the oral aspect of the Word. Yet in rereading his early writings I have noticed his emphasis on the oracular and the performative in the *teaching* of poetry, especially at the school level.

For Frye, poetic language, not prose, *is* "natural" language. His recognition of the associative, rhythmic quality of poetic language ranges throughout his writings but was eclipsed by his interest in the more "visual scholarship" of literary criticism. This left him with, according to Howard D. Weinbrot, an impoverished conception of literary reading as process (1990/91, 176). Weinbrot alleges that Frye had a relative lack of appreciation for affective aesthetics (this in contrast to Frye's devotion to and claims for the alteration of consciousness that literary experience can bring about). "Frye seems to assume that the mind left to its subconscious state lacks order and connection and reverts to the uncivilized psychology of, say, *Lord of the Flies*; or perhaps to the apparent wanderings of Sterne's Tristram Shandy, or Joyce's Bloom or Faulkner's Benjy" (192). In short, the mind might succumb to the wandering images of desire (Frye, 1976a, 30) if it is not shored up by the epistemological strength of the educated imagination, which, as we recall, if it is not interfered with, will, for Frye, produce conceptual thought (1976a, 36).

After *The Great Code* (1982b), however, the domain of affective aesthetics seems less dichotomous with Frye's anatomizing. The reason, I think, is partly historical, partly personal. Historically, his main mission of legitimating the forms of literature as autonomous, distinct from historical and biographical criticism, and criticism itself as a discipline in its own right had been accomplished. Personally, one might say there seemed to be a "transfer value" from working on Holy Writ to the secular scripture in terms of Frye's conception of response. It is as though his schematizing overtook and became a refuge from the intensity of his own direct responses—until his later works on the Bible, which somehow permitted him to concentrate more on embodiment of response. But his notion of the embodied reader, even in his later writing, as we'll see shortly, is still a hypothetical taken-for-granted.

Elsewhere I have written in more detail about the effect of the study of the Bible on Frye's relaxing of the tension between engagement and detachment in literary response (Bogdan, 1989a). This, I argued, is directly related to changing the metaphor for literature from "the stubborn structure" (Frye, 1970) to "the double mirror" as the types and antitypes of biblical typology, "each reflecting the other but neither the world outside" (Frye, 1982b, 78). With the writing of *The Great Code,* the poetic and the religious attain a closer proximity. As a result, the reader is "protected" from the wandering images of what in Chapter 4 we referred to as "centrifugal" or "extra"-literary meaning (Frye, 1971/1973, 32). Though this is not the place for a full argument, I think it necessary to juxtapose Frye's move in his latter years toward embodiment, the oracular process, and what we might call the sacralization of the reader with my notion of the poetics of ordinary existence, literary experience, literary literacy, and gender as an essential element in the need for re-educating the imagination.

Part of Frye's motivation in writing *The Great Code* was to reiterate his dedication to the communicative power of literary language: "It is a futile manoeuvre to retreat from words into some body language of gesture or similar forms of implied understanding that short-circuits the verbal" (1982b, 226). Frye's refusal to short-circuit the verbal in confronting the intransigence of reality has directly to do with his conviction "that a transformation of consciousness and a transformation of language can never be separated," (1982b, 226). In contrast to the stress on the visual scholarship of criticism, *The Great Code* discloses a commitment to the temporal nature of the participating response, to the actual rather than the virtual literary event, and, by extension, to experience itself. As literature, the Bible, of course, is something "other" than the hypothetical imaginative construct; it is less the insulation from nature represented by the images of the stubborn structure, the fugue, or the cultural envelope, than simply an irrepressible force of energy, "a vision of upward metamorphosis, of the alienated relation of man [sic] to nature transformed into a spontaneous and effortless life. . . . " (1982b, 76; see also 124, 167). It is not that Frye renounced the spatial dimension of language. He still spoke of "freezing" myth (1982b, 63, 71), as was described in Chapter 4; but now the spatial becomes a necessary but not sufficient condition for describing biblical typology. This different angle of his vision suggests a consciousness of response that demands a consciousness of "creative time." If "[the] real world is beyond time," it nevertheless "can be reached by a process that goes on in time" (76). And so we observe a downplaying, if not outright rejection (at least within the context of the sacred), of the critical response separate from direct response. Instead of engagement followed by detachment, the double response fuses into the single act of reading as "the unfolding of a long and complex dialectical process" (226). What Milton termed criticism of the "heart" (Frye, 1982b, 138) somehow confers a certain infallibility on the interpretive process, and, by extension, the liberation of the reader, who now inherits the moral and aesthetic inviolateness formerly reserved for the poet: "The reader completes the visionary operation of the Bible by throwing out the subjective fallacy along with the objective one. The apocalypse is the way the world looks after the ego has disappeared" (138). Here his conception of language emphasizes a "scholarship of the ear" rather than that of the eye so prominent in literature conceived as a stubborn structure (my Chapter 4).

Literature, then, is no longer only what the eye can see but what the ear can hear, for the images of the wandering of desire have now become the container of the thing contained (Frye, 1957, 145), the anagogic phase of The Word has been made incarnate. Paralleling the shift from spatial to temporal, from detachment to engagement, from *poeisis* to rhetoric, from literacy to oracy, from unity to diversity, from dissociation to reintegration of sensibility, and finally from literary criticism itself to just plain reading, is a change in the controlling myth of Frye's own theory and of his role within that myth: from consciousness to love (1982b, 231-233).

In keeping with the subsumptive power of time over space in *The Great Code*, Frye comes close to a sense of Longinian *ecstasis* which does stress process and intensity, values about which, as we've already noted throughout this book, he had been particularly cautious because of his misgivings about the world of ordinary existence. Though ecstasy can signify genuine participation in as paradisal a reality as we can get on earth, it is nonetheless a reality in time, and as such, very much subject to the gambling machine of an ideal experience and thus a monument to the failure of experience. Nonetheless, Frye saw the aesthetic as the gateway to the religious. As he asserted in an interview with me in 1986: "I don't think that the aesthetic experience is in a separate category from the religious experience. I think that, if anything, it's the other way round, that it's the experience that I've got of literature and music, and to a lesser degree of the other arts, which has given me the sense of what Kierkegaard calls ethical freedom, and it seems to me that it's the aesthetic attitude that made me break away from the objectivity of literature as 'out there' " (Frye qtd. in Bogdan, 1986/1991, 339).

After *The Great Code*, Frye continued to emphasize the proximity of the religious and the aesthetic mainly through his reiteration of the principle of the literal as the metaphorical meaning, enunciated in that book (1982b, 24, 62, 64, 65). In "The Dialectic of Belief and Vision" (1990a), written in 1985, he explains again that literal meaning, as, for example, in "the newspaper type of reaction," applies only "to the sense of a verbal structure in itself," whereas metaphorical meaning refers to what leads to transformative experience. "In reading the Bible we find ourselves following a verbal structure intensely metaphorical in its language and full of events that seem to have no counterpart in actual history or in ordinary experience" (97). The Bible, then, can be thought of as "pure centripetality," where there is no distinction between literal and metaphorical meaning.

The powerful religious/literary vision of Frye's later years went a long way toward approximating the unification of mind and spirit as a kind of embodiment. In a lecture given to medical doctors in 1989, entitled "Literature as Therapy," he spoke of literature as "controlled hallucination . . . where things are seen with a kind of intensity with which they are not seen in ordinary experience" (1989/1991, 31); of catharsis as "a response of emotional balance, a kind of self-integrating process" (28); and of "the immense recuperative power that literature, along with the other arts, could provide in a world as crazy as ours" (32). (Northrop Frye, a bibliotherapist?)

Here we find an instance of unmistakable *ecstasis* in the convergence of physicality, the oracular, and pedagogy, captured graphically through a personal anecdote about Milton's *Paradise Lost*. It was through teaching it with "considerable intensity" that he found that "those tremendous lines tended to detach themselves from their context and [became] individual beings chasing themselves around inside [his] head" (Frye, 1989/1991, 31). When one line became so overpowering that it caused insomnia, he "examined the contents of [his] brain" for a more peaceful one to contemplate, "and was asleep in no time" (32). This kind of self-irony was an attribute of Frye's basic sense of humanity, and was combined with a generosity that radiated outward from the academy to classroom teachers. In what was one of the last interviews of his life about the teaching of poetry to secondary school students, on December 10, 1990, he returned again and again to the body as the locus of response to the "language of poetry."[2]

Whereas Frye's earlier work was a defense of criticism, *Words with Power* answered a different historical challenge, that of defending poetry—"the integrity of literature and other traditional verbal enclaves" (1990e, xviii) in the face of conflicting and competing critical schools, under which, Frye believed, there lies the assumption of a coherence that would eventually surface once the differences were worked out. The re-educated imagination regards as part of its work reconfiguring the system of noticing and un-noticing that determines what is coherent and what possesses integrity, as challenging the concept of a verbal enclave, and as subverting the hierarchy Frye set up between the poetic and the ideological upon which the existence of such an enclave is made possible. This is not to deny the existence of literature but to expand the discussion of its relationship to consciousness.

Grounding this work has been my belief that the spiritual dimension of the literary imagination—its oracular, ecstatic element—as the poetics of ordinary existence, rests in the endless recognition and misrecognition scenes taking place within classrooms full of embodied readers. These readers offer their readings and writings as aesthetic practices of self-disclosure, which are shared by their peers, and heard by their teachers within a democratic educational environment that values the primacy of human witness. This is no monument to the failure of experience, especially when this grounded base is trebly cleft by the feeling, power, and location problems. In this chapter, my questions arise from my reading and rereading of Frye's later work and from my effort to locate myself in these works, in particular, his last two major books, *Words with Power* (1990e) and *The Double Vision* (1991a).

## Double Vision, Double-Take: Mythology, Ideology, and Gender

Doubtless the most mystical of his works, *The Double Vision* (1991a) is a last testament to Frye's actual movement into the hypothetical "third order of experience" (1971/1973, 170) during the final year of his life. In these four lectures he recapitulates the major themes of the major texts and fulfills to a degree the promise of embodiment, the message of love, and the revelatory quality of the oracular and the ecstatic expressed in *The Great Code* (1982b). Locating himself within a brand of Christianity attracted less to "doctrine" than to the intensity of "*religious experience*" (1991a, 3, emphasis added), *The Double Vision* begins with a focus on the integration of the natural and spiritual worlds through the image of the body, where there is no "separation from one's natural and social context, except insofar as a greater maturity includes some knowledge of the conditioning that was formerly accepted uncritically" (14). It ends: "In the double vision of a spiritual and a physical world simultaneously present, every moment we have lived through we have also died out of into another order. Our life in the resurrection, then, is already here, and waiting to be recognized" (85).

Here Frye proffers a reconciliation of the kinds of dualities that have formed a sub-theme of the re-educated imagination: the literal and the metaphorical, ordinary existence and imaginative experience, the sacred and the profane, the aesthetic and the religious, the literary and the literate. The double vision succeeds in recovering the unification of the religious and the aesthetic through the incarnation of the Word by "the restoring of a 'pure speech'" [Zephariah 3:9]" (1991a, 83). This is not logic, descriptive accuracy, nor "simply a creative element in the mind, but a power that recreates the mind, or . . . an autonomous force" (83). Frye's double vision really is Blake's "third stage of development, one in which the vision of gods comes back in the form of a sense of identity with nature, where nature is not merely to be studied and lived in but loved and cherished, where place becomes home. . . . [And] we should be gods or numinous presences ourselves" (83–84).

Yet the integration of the natural and the spiritual in Frye (like the integration of his other distinctions, such as ordinary existence and imaginative experience, and primary and secondary concern) turns on maintaining the absolute hierarchy between mythology and ideology, upon which his conception of anagogy (Chapter 3), the theoretical basis of his justification for literature as the informing verbal discipline, devolves. This hierarchy also accounts for the "unsayingness" of literature, that is, its hypothetical nature (Chapter 4), as the theoretical basis of his central argument against censorship. I hope to show that, just as the theoretical distinction between the direct, participating response and the critical response spills over into the *division* between them when real readers read, especially in classrooms (Chapters 5 and 6), so the hierarchy between mythology and ideology dismisses the feeling, power, and location problems. This, in turn, has consequences in the lives of real readers and how they not only draw distinctions, but live the dissonances—and the consonances—between literary convention and reality.

I have already developed the position that the hierarchy between mythology and ideology (Bogdan, 1990b, 1990e, 1990f) has crucial implications for the feminist reader. Now I want to extend this argument to show how upsetting the hierarchy laid out explicitly in "The Dialectic of Belief and Vision" (1990a) and later reiterated in *Words with Power* (1990e) is related to my defense of literature education as an interdisciplinary enterprise. I will argue that, though Frye's double vision does not entail a victim, it does invoke a patriarchal worldview, out of which the re-educated imagination would climb in its attempt to formulate the poetics of ordinary existence, where feeling, power, and location are problematized, not taken-for-granteds. But I will conclude with the hypothesis that by typologizing *ecstasis* as the oracular, revelatory element of " 'pure speech' " (Frye, 1991a, 83), Frye's double vision does open up a space for the primacy of human witness as an alternative sublime, which can help come to terms with what we've been calling the continuum and the gap between world and word that affects the power of literature to influence for ill as well as for good.

"Double-take" can be thought of as what happens when double vision, a concept predicated on the subordination of ideology to mythology, is seen within the context of the feeling, power, and location problems, particularly from a feminist standpoint. "Double-take" is what I did in Chapter 7 when I put quotation marks around certain literary conventions in *Words with Power* (1990e) that indicated to me how the non-recognition of the material effects of their genderization tended to affect me for ill. I also suggested that my reaction to this was not something I necessarily needed to "get over" or "work through" to a "higher interpretation." But I want to show, as I did through my reading of Steiner (1989) in Chapter 8, that I need to go beyond resistance to seduction (Miller, 1990) by a theory of the transformational or spiritual value of literature, to which I still passionately adhere, but which, as I argued in Chapter 7, I believe needs a counterpart in literary literacy or the re-education of the imagination into the politics of engagement in order to effect any real social change. What I continue to be laboring at here is a case for the transformational process of teaching and learning literature premised less on distinctions, especially hierarchical ones, than on the tangible and tangled messiness of situated readers with feeling, power, and location problems growing out of their lived experience, the grounds for which there exists no consensus about what counts as normal in a world "as crazy as ours" (Frye, 1989/1991, 32), especially if experience is regarded as largely unreal. The experience of the single mother waiting her turn in a legal-aid lineup is certainly real enough in a world that thinks that abrogation of paternal responsibility is, well, maybe not quite right, but, nevertheless, a certain taken-for-granted.

Surely, though, I have made a huge category mistake here. I'm supposed to be talking about criticism and literature, not life. Shouldn't I be adopting a "broader" perspective? Yet, whether one regards experience as real or unreal directly affects conceptions of the normal and the ironic, which in turn influence what is deemed "convention" and what "reality." As Frye asserts: "The world itself is so much more ironic a place than any kind of ironic construction [writers] themselves could dream up. In a way, their work has all been done for them" (1989/1991, 29). In literature "we recognize a certain action to be grotesque or absurd or evil or futile or whatever, and it is that sense of normality in the audience that enables irony to make its point as irony" (1989/1991, 29). That there *is* no such consensus in a world "as crazy as ours" (1989/1991, 32), but that the power of language, especially in the intensity of its poetic form, continues to turn strings of words into lives of their own that can rob us of sleep turns on whatever system of noticing and un-noticing our social conditioning, our "ideology" brings to bear on the matter. One might say it has to do with how we are situated with respect to our feeling, power, and location problems. (I suspect that David Perry also lost some sleep over the two hundred repetitions of "nigger" in *The Adventures of Huckleberry Finn.*)

As we have seen in previous chapters, all readers deploy their own systems of noticing and un-noticing in terms of their ideological commitments and how they affect the enmeshment of the fictional and the real in constructing attention during reading (Nell, 1988; Walton, 1990). This affects what is put into the text proper and what gets consigned to parentheses, to footnotes, and etceteras. When those texts are read within an educational context, the process of noticing and un-noticing has to do with what David Bleich calls the "affective dependency" (1988, 94) of readers on other readers in social, especially pedagogical, situations and how they help or hinder the power of literature to transpose and transfigure.

Near the beginning of *Words with Power* (1990e) Frye reiterates the importance of distinguishing "where we cannot divide, in order to preserve the unity of the whole, and the distinctiveness of the parts" (26). He then goes on to characterize many contemporary critics as still being stuck in "the ideological stage in dealing with literature, because they are less interested in literature than in the relation of literature to some primary ideological interest, religious, historical, radical, feminist, or whatever" (27). Frye didn't want "to deny the ideological relations of literature, or belittle their importance, but to ascertain more clearly what it is that is being related"(27). He speaks of the difference between the literary and the rhetorical, reiterating his conception of criticism as "language that expresses the awareness of language" (27), what we've been calling the "sayingness" of literature: "All intensified language sooner or later turns metaphorical, and that literature is not only the obvious but the inescapable guide to higher journeys of consciousness" (28). Literature, in its Arnoldian version as a " 'criticism of life' . . . is at its most inclusive in the imaginative mode," but this is not the highest mode of consciousness. Beyond the critical, its Arnoldian or Virgilian phase, there is "Beatrice, who represents among other things a criticism or higher awareness of the limits of the Virgilian vision" (28). Criticism can take us to "the limit of what words can do for us. But what looks like a limit from a distance often turns out to be an open gate to something else when we reach it" (28–29).

Regarding biblical "images of women," Frye wryly observes that no Council of institutionalized religion has ever actually declared the traditional ones: "[m]other, bride, virgin," the equivalent of a blessed trinity ("They are only female figures after all" [1990e, 203]). This is obviously an ironic criticism of the systemic sexism endemic to Christianity as a male preserve. He also acknowledges that, because of the close proximity between the Bible and literature, images of the female have been given short shrift within the discipline of literary criticism. So it would seem that Frye sees there is a lot of work still to be done here. I expect that in the future this work will go hand-in-hand with work on the religious basis of Frye's liberally educated imagination (Denham, 1991). According to his own summary in *Words with Power* (1990e), Frye expands the discussion of biblical images of the feminine into "(a) woman as one of the two human sexes, (b) woman as representative of human community, (c) woman as symbol of the fact that humanity cannot be redeemed in isolation from nature" (203–204). And, he does refer to the possibility of a utopic "spiritual kingdom" of equality of the sexes (204, 215–216), while recognizing the fact that the male-dominated literary tradition claims countless female victims "from the ferocity of Medea to the quiet self-obliteration of Ophelia" (222). Juxtaposed with these awarenesses appears this powerful image, central to the book:

> I think of a poet, in relation to his society, as being at the center of a cross like a plus sign. The horizontal bar forms the social and ideological conditioning that made him intelligible to his contemporaries, and in fact to himself. The vertical bar is the mythological line of descent from previous poets back to Homer (the usual symbolic starting point) which carries him into our own time. (47)

What I am at pains to show is that even a quasi-mystical double vision of a perfectly integrated humanity, one that makes of taxonomizing a profound spiritual exercise, trades on a system of noticing and un-noticing that is itself stuck within the very patrilinearity it recognizes. Frye's last major work presents an anagogic recognition scene of the religious basis of the order of words, which he acknowledges is patriarchal, and which would posit the feminine as what Richard Rorty (1982) refers to as the point "when *we* [have] passed beyond [verbal] hypotheses" (166). But what is first required is a *mis*recognition scene—that such a statement presents feeling, power, and location problems for women and other Others adversely affected by words with power. In writing this, I identify with Jeff, who felt like a child transgressing sacred text on that first evening of class. But, for me, the most important part of Frye's quotation above is the throwaway line in parentheses; and my impulse to remake and redo this text would be to say that for women and women writers the center of the cross is more like a minus sign. My "kinetic response" to this would be to perform a category change on Beatrice, to transfigure her from silent partner to languaged ecstatic, for whom other lines take on the character of epiphanies under different contexts, depending on how they are embodied within their readers' and speakers' particular feeling, power, and location problems.

## Literary Convention and Reality

In theory, the embryo of such a misrecognition scene *is* there, within Frye's own concept of *The Double Vision*. Here he sees the "passing of experience into knowledge" in terms of a post-tragedic stance, as "part of a reality in which at every instant the still possible turns into a fixed and unalterable past. We feel partly released from this tragic vision when we are acquiring skills, getting an education, or advancing a religious life: there we are exploiting the memory of our past to give direction along the present" (Frye, 1991a, 53). Regarding the moving out of experience as tragic, not comic, is a look in the right direction toward embodiment as a necessary condition of a rehumanized humanism. The problem is, though, that when one speaks from the center as a white, privileged male, the mind-body split comes into gear somewhat more freely than otherwise might be the case: "I pass over the more pathological and racist forms of [literalist] attitudes, merely saying that hysteria, by insisting that an inner state of mind is united when it is actually divided, is bound to project its frustrations sooner or later on some outward scapegoat who symbolizes the objecting inner self. The assertion 'I believe that' is not simply meaningless but actively dangerous when we still don't know who 'I' is or what 'that' is" (Frye, 1990a, 98).

While projections certainly are half-truths and while our "selves" and "reality" are continually being discovered, created, produced, or whatever metaphor fits one's discourse community, faith is not a matter of certitude, but of leaping into the abyss of one's deepest un-knowing—and of standing there anyway. But my point here is that the comparative freedom with which one notices but can pass over the pathological enactment of racist, sexist, and homophobic attitudes is, in this case, won mainly by reasserting the hierarchy between mythology and ideology, a position which makes it fairly easy to be able to say "merely say." This hypothetical gaze in turn informs the relationship among the genres, which in turn influences the relationship between convention and reality, which, in its turn, bears upon whether justification, censorship, and response are deemed problems worth worrying about.

How projections work, whether one's belief is a species of psychic split in which division of mind has been wrought by abjection, is a problem that concerns the re-educated imagination. What constitutes "hysteria" (a term which is itself implicated with female myths and stereotypes) and under what circumstances depends, I would contend, on the two premises of the re-educated imagination: accepting responsibility for the politics of engagement (the feeling, power, and location problems) and formulating an ontology of literary subjectivity in which direct response is logically prior to critical response (whether the "I" of the "that" would be taken seriously by interlocutors even if the person attached to it is at a "stage" of stock response). The lived result of these principles is not an either/or choice between the preservation or the loss of faith (Frye, 1990a, 98), but, as we saw in Chapter 8, the keeping of faith in the face of having been cleft by the post-tragedic stance.

The system of noticing and un-noticing which goes to make up what the world regards as normal is radically contingent on the luxury, or lack of it (depending upon people's embodied situatedness), of being able to separate themselves from what they have probably already distinguished, as, for example, Judy and her sisters, David Perry, and the single mother in the legal aid queue. They know all too well about the *distinctions* between good faith and the social effects of the educational and bureaucratic welfare systems, both of which are dedicated to improving "the human condition" but which in fact produce victims of their own teleology. There are some who just cannot afford to regard these obscenities in terms of slippages between primary and secondary human concern, mythology and ideology, convention and reality. The question for teachers of literature is whether taking responsibility for these slippages should be considered part of their mandate, and, if it should, how literary theory might bear on the issue. These questions are all part of the larger question of the conditions upon which it might be possible to revive the ideal of a liberal education, which at present espouses unproblematic goals of freedom and autonomy in preparing students "for an unfree existence, one where they will be functions and not whole, integrated persons" (la Brecque, 1990, 486–487). Part of this emancipatory project is implementing integrative studies and appraising "critically the purposes of existing institutions" (494).

One of the achievements of *Words with Power* is to have located contemporary culture as one in which there seems to be an equal sign between *mythos* and *logos* (Frye, 1990e, 105). In other words, we've been living in an ideological age ever since Plato supplanted mythology with rational dialectic (Frye, 1991a, 77). Part of Frye's mission here, a continuation of that of *The Great Code* (1982b), is, through the power of the creative poetic imagination fortified by love, to go beyond the literary imagination to the realm of "imaginative literalism," where judgment is no longer suspended, gratification no longer delayed, and where myths and metaphors *do*

become guides to "a vision of spiritual life that continues to transform and expand our own" (1991a, 17). Imaginative literalism allows
everything to "fall into place" (17). Whereas "[d]emonic literalism
seeks conquest by paralyzing argument," imaginative literalism
"seeks what might be called interpenetration [sic], the free flowing of
sprirtual life into and out of one another that communicates and
never violates" (18)—passion without a victim.

This stark contrast between the paradisal and demonic forms of
imaginative literalism begs the question of verbal power, and of feeling and location as problems the imagination should care about.
Imaginative literalism invokes "the continuous paradox of experience in which whatever one meets both is and is not oneself" (Frye,
1991a, 17). Re-educating the imagination entails, in part, regarding
the ways in which this paradox is experienced as a gendered activity;
and this, in turn, requires accepting taxonomical categories and
conceptions of convention and reality as designations that are not
value-neutral. For Frye, to experience the fictional as a construct
which is not happening but which can be experienced imaginatively
as though it were, for example, presumably enables the reader to
move *through* the literary convention from "the *inadequacy* of ordinary experience" to literary experience, which, though "imperfect,"
can be improved with "incessant practice" until there is an integration of ordinary experience with the "analogical structures" of criticism pointing "to some kind of union between the imaginative and
the actual that we have not yet identified" (1990e, 90, emphasis
added). This union depends upon our going beyond the identification of *logos* with *mythos* (105).

The equating of *logos* with *mythos* is something that Frye would
like to see changed back to putting first things first (mythology before
ideology). And I would agree with him inasmuch as primary concern
is related to the moral *imperative* behind moral action, which can
only literally "proceed" from such an imperative. Part of the project
of the re-educated imagination, however, as we've been noticing, is
to understand what happens to real readers reading now, when *logos
is mythos*, that is, when literary interpretation tends to be literal
rather than metaphorical. Putting first things first must thus involve
acknowledging that the patriarchal structure of the mythological universe literally affects the lives of women and other Others, and that
the ethical demand to change the way things are, rather than wait
around for "patriarchal ascendancy eventually [to reverse] itself"
(Frye, 1990e, 216), entails the consideration of gender as inextricably
bound up with the primary categories themselves, "of humanity,
food, sex, possessions and freedom of movement" (307).

It would be more comfortable for me to pass over this, to admit to
having made a category mistake rather than to contest the hierarchy

between mythology and ideology. But subsuming ideology under mythology can have grave consequences in the world for many readers reading. Within the mythological framework, virgin-baiting (the theme of both the beer ad discussed at the beginning of this book and the Montreal massacre), for example, is a literary convention that, within the ethos of the educated imagination, is a condition of imaginative freedom. As A.C. Hamilton writes:

> The consummate scholarship acquired through wide reading that led Sidney [in writing his Arcadia] to his imaginative grasp of a central romance convention, and thereby to demonstrate the unity of his critical insight and creative power, may be applied to Frye's comment on the motto's significance: 'deep within the stock convention of virgin-baiting is a vision of human integrity imprisoned in a world it is in but not of' (R 86)[3]. Such criticism may be called creative because it makes reading creative: having been made consciously aware of the archetype, the reader may understand Sidney's romance and connect it with all other romances. In fact, once posited, this motif serves to connect a multitude of literary works which offer some such vision by treating a particular crisis of identity central in the life of any reader: of losing or having lost, of preserving, gaining, or regaining identity. Then the reader may relate and evaluate the whole of literature to the earlier mythology (or ideology) in which personal identity is a key concept. (1990, 199)

There is no such thing as "any reader," and even readers with "consummate scholarship" can relate convention to reality for ill as well as for good. Virgin-baiting is a literary convention deeply implicated in the misogynistic structure of civilization, still largely invisible, whose habitual mode of thought has been grounded in taking violence against women as an invisible given. Most women live in the twilight zone of convention *as* reality. The conventional—what is *not* supposed to be "actually" happening—that women are in fact baited daily and suffer for it—is being acted out as a taken-for-granted of sexual harassment in the culture all around them (Hossie, 1991; Mitchell, 1991). And so are its corollaries: maternal nurturer, eternal goddess, exotic Other, and all those other images descended from *mythos* as a "blood-red thread" (Wolf, 1984, 296). We might say that the attention constructs influencing what is regarded as fictional and what, real (Nell, 1988), become skewed when *logos* is mistaken for *mythos*. Part of getting them straight, I submit, involves making gender a marker of the permeable boundaries between ideology and mythology.

That reading is a gendered activity is a point already made in previous chapters, and by many other feminist critics. But what needs to be emphasized within the context of the spiritual dimension of aesthetic response, the central concern of this chapter, is that the distinction between convention and reality is directly bound up with what in Chapter 7 we saw as the dialectic between reading sovereignty and vulnerability, and how that relates to the feeling, power, and location problems. Not every reader remains unthreatened by the structure of literary convention, which is predicated on co-optation of the feminine. The double vision is "flexible enough for us to feel that the same man may actually *get* both heroines, one in his imaginative and the other in his everyday life" (Frye, 1990e, 269, emphasis added). And even at this "highest" level, some of us are not content to just let "patriarchal ascendancy eventually [reverse] itself . . . into a society where love makes everyone equal" (216). Only hypothetical readers read hypothetically. Real readers engage "the paradox of experience" (Frye, 1991a, 17) in every reading act according to the interplay of sovereignty and vulnerability in their reading selves; and these in turn are structured by their lived lives as those lives are constructed by the complicity between word and world, a dialectic that leaves the integrity of some lives rent more than it does others.

As a woman deeply drawn to the spirituality of Frye's double vision, I appreciate his interest in primary concern and the value he places on "the drive toward peace and freedom in our time [a]s an impulse toward love growing out of a new immediacy of contact" (1991a, 34). And I take as a mark of good faith his self-disclosure about the Montreal massacre: "It is difficult not to feel some involvement even with the fantasies of a psychotic murdering women who want to be engineers" (34). But good faith, as we've already seen, is not enough. To be added to it is acknowledging our feeling, power, and location as problems. While I respect Frye's authorial intention, which I take to be his effort to identify with the alien Other (" 'We must love one another or die,' as W.H. Auden says" [34]), my feeling, power, and location problems prevent me from being an "imaginative literalist" (17) when I read those lines.

So I am compelled to ask how we are to interpret what feeling "some involvement with the psychotic fantasies" of Marc Lepine might mean. Might it mean that love for the Other will unite humanity in the third world of experience? Might it signify a misrecognition scene of shared responsibility for violence against women? Might it mean both? Is this a "genuine epistemological shift" (de Lauretis, 1987, 10) that can help change the world? It may be that Frye is referencing the demonic form of virgin-baiting, the demon lover writ large; but what is missing are the bodies of those dead women. Though I am willing to grant all the ambiguity of the doubleness, all the polysemy that would allow for a misrecognition scene at the level of *mythos*, I read those lines, not as an example of imaginative literalism, but as an effect of a system of noticing and un-noticing that, in taking refuge in the verbal construct of Auden, has swept clear of "the world of facts" (Frye, 1991a, 18) too easily and too soon.

It would be easier for me to remain silent in the face of my transgression and, instead, internalize the sin of my category mistake, if in fact I have made one; but I don't think that I have. I would say rather that here Frye has been seduced by the breadth of his own theory, by his disbelief in experience, by his failure to distinguish what we cannot separate—the continuum between word and world that begins with the "blood-red thread" (Wolf, 1984, 296) of *mythos* and *logos* and ends with the dissolution of misogyny into "universal brotherhood." In responding to Frye's response, I follow the principles of the re-educated imagination—to put response first and politicize it at the same time. Again, there is always somewhere to go in criticism, but one can only be where one is. So while I accept his response unconditionally as a manifestation of the ontology of literary subjectivity, I must also submit it to scrutiny under the feeling, power, and location problems.

If, indeed, Frye is right that "transformation of consciousness and a transformation of language can never be separated" (1982b, 226), then what we need is a transformation of language that moves from the *reality* to the *convention* so that what "falls into place" is not abjection for the Other. But here I take refuge in theory. Wearied by yet another ontological shock, I somehow see through a glass less darkly "from below" (Haraway, 1988, 584) and provide my own consolation: first, by using abjection as a condition for the literary, and second, by locating Frye as having a location problem that needs to be recognized. As to the first, I open a slim volume titled simply *The Montreal Massacre* (Malette & Chalough, 1991), a book of poems, letters, pensées, newspaper articles, and remembrances, sent to me as a birthday gift by my daughter, the architecture student, who in her medium is also trying to language Beatrice. It was the real turned literary, but not *only* literary, where ordinary existence became, for me, not just imaginative experience but conclusive experience, the kerygma of Holy Writ:

> On December 7, 1989, I learn that a man has just killed fourteen women. The man, they say, separated the men and the women into two groups. The man called the women feminists; he voiced his hatred toward them. The man fired. The women dropped. The other men ran away. Suddenly,
> I/they are dead
> felled by a
> break in meaning.
> A WOMAN WHO IS CRYING OUT IN PAIN CAN SHE HEAR

AT THE SAME TIME THE CRY OF ANOTHER WOMAN AND OF
ANOTHER AND THE CRY OF ANOTHER WOMAN AND DO THEY
COME TOGETHER COLLIDE IN SPACE AND TIME, THE DEEP
CRY OF THE REBEL AND THE WAILING CRIES OF THE DOCILE
DO THEY COME TOGETHER COLLIDE SO THAT IT WOULD
SEEM ONE HEARS ONLY ONE IMMENSE LONG HORRIBLE
SOUND? (Brossard, 1991, 93–94)

Here Brossard assumes the persona of the *connata*, for whom the
ecstatic is not a "state" nor the ideological, a "stage." As to my second
strategy for survival—redressing Frye's location problem—I would
say that in the very act of realizing his own meaning, Frye's perspective was partial, subject to his own mythological conditioning, an
effect of the logic of inclusion and exclusion; but it is spoken *ex
cathedra*, from above. As such, it conflates the categories of the
mythological and the ideological. Yet, I would argue, it is the very
blurring of these boundaries, in the knowledge that each subject
position is self-interested, that is a requirement for attaining the
mature society he envisions in *The Double Vision* (1991a). I would
also suggest that, in order to ameliorate the potential harm of the
"knives of saying [and unsaying]" (Steiner, 1989, 58), the Shelleyan
vision of love, of which Frye is a direct descendant, needs supple-
menting with some lessons in literary literacy, the kind of lessons
that the "affective dependency" (Bleich, 1988, 94) of the Singing
School can give.

My discussion of the problematic nature of the relationship
between convention and reality within the educated imagination,
even within Frye's movement toward embodiment and the profun-
dity of his double vision, suggests that his passion for integrating the
natural and the spiritual worlds is still his monument to the failure
of experience. It is not that I want to belittle this kind of ultimate,
hypothetical dimension of criticism (after more than a dozen years of
education within the Roman Catholic church, it was only after reading *Fearful Symmetry* [Frye, 1947] that I came to any glimmering of
understanding about Christian views of salvation and the love of
God). It is that there are some critics who, despite their conditioning
by and passion for the entire tradition of Western thought, continue
to be abjected by its detritus as it tends to be inscribed through
powerful texts, literary and nonliterary, in the world. And, if those
critics are like me, they also tend to be what Marion Woodman (1990)
calls "father's daughters" (73, 111–115; see also Benjamin, 1988),
women who are particularly marked, through their very aspiration to
the intellectual and creative life, by the savagery of Cartesian dualism. And we need to tell about it: to relate it to man-made theory, to

follow out the lines of our induction into and our seduction by it (Miller, 1990).

In hindsight, I believe that it is neither coincidence, oversight, nor indolence that prompted me to postpone reading Wayne C. Booth's *The Company We Keep: An Ethics of Fiction* (1988a) until after I'd finished this book. Having dipped into it sufficiently to realize that Booth's ethical stance was consonant with many of my concerns, I carted that thick volume across a continent and an ocean, confident that here was a friend. Yet, even its sympathy of temper with my own threatened to diminish the integrity of my lived-through theorizing over time. In the very act of using Booth to support some of my claims,[4] I risked re-constellating the incest taboo, erecting yet another father figure to approve/disapprove, eroticizing my knowing, compromising the precious "aloneness" of my empowerment (Woodman, 1990, 117), its roots in sorority. It is this resistance to agreement with Booth, and disagreement with Frye, this "anxiety of influence" (Harold Bloom, 1973), that brings us to the principle of the continuum and the gap informing the censorship problem, and, ultimately, the relationship between literary word and world.

## The Continuum and the Gap

What do I mean by the continuum *and* the gap? Isn't it one or the other? To address this, let's return to the examples of the war crimes trial and the beer ad poster introduced in Chapter 1. The way in which I posed the question about who was right, the judge who trusted the juror to be able to distinguish between fact and fiction in *Music Box,* or the MediaWatch representative who lobbied for removal of the offensive beer ad poster was in terms of either/or. Implied in my question was the assumption that to support the judge would be to adhere to "the gap" position on the relationship between word and world, and to endorse MediaWatch would be to subscribe to "the continuum" theory. I then went on to complicate the issue by noting that the problem could not be solved by invoking the distinction between art and non-art; nor could it be approached satisfactorily by appealing to the presumed greater indoctrinatory power of images over print, because the beer ad had co-opted the subtleties of verbal ironic distance in making its point. I also suggested that a wide range of responses and interpretations besides my own was possible.

I do not know how to solve this problem; nor do I think recourse to theory alone, though it can lend insight, can do so either. What I *can* do is to outline briefly some positions and problems I think are further invoked by these examples, beginning with two positions which I think are untenable. The first is the "pure" anti-censorship stance, which I think has been sufficiently detailed, along with my reservations about it, in Chapters 4 and 6. It just will not do to merely say that a "man is defiled by what comes out of him and not by what goes into him [sic]" (Frye, 1990e, 263). Simply to assert the power of language to influence for good but not for ill would be to subscribe to a "pure" "gap theory," which begs the questions raised in this book. And, though I agree with the *principle* that freedom of expression ceases to exist "[w]ithout the freedom to offend" (Rushdie, 1990b, 6), the censorship problem is not that simple either. The very "liberal formulation of liberty as a right" is called into question by a "post-masculinist, post-bourgeois, post-colonial politics of freedom," which inserts "power and responsibility" as "two terms most strikingly absent" from current discussions of the subject (Brown, 1991, 3).

The case for a "pure" "continuum theory," on the other hand, is also problematic. Advocates of this position most often tend to argue their case on the basis of a cause-and-effect chain reaction (like Plato and the magnet metaphor in the *Ion* and Gosson in *The School of Abuse* [1579]). This stance is tenuous from empirical, logical, and political standpoints. Empirically, it implies that issues of censorship are to be adjudicated on the basis of the "content" of the message (whether the representation represents "positively" or "negatively"). Logically, it means that, once standards of "correct content" are determined, then certain people with "right values" can police the content. Politically, policing the content sets up a totalitarian structure that decides who is offending whom and on what grounds, thus reinscribing Plato's banishment of the poets. Additionally, the content argument can easily be reduced to its absurd conclusion, as is often done, by right wing groups who want to control what is read in schools (Chapter 4) and by those who would trivialize the psychic and social harm *felt* by those who are abjected by what they regard as offensive representations.

For example, in a follow-up article to the beer ad controversy, a newspaper journalist wrote a scathing satire characterizing Media-Watch as an organization that would endorse scotch drinkers rather than beer drinkers on the basis that MediaWatch classified the women in the beer ads as "sex objects" and in the scotch ads, as "decision-makers" (Kastner, 1990, D2). This co-opting by journalism, advertising, and other forces, of the serious bid for women and minorities to fight for their emergent political identities is part of the censorship problem in the schools, within feminism, and within the academy (Bernstein, 1990), where contemporary literary theory has rendered so contingent language, the "self," the "I," representation and the representable, and how representations reinscribe the very thing they seek to excise that any hope of a "solution" seems remote.

The feminist literature on censorship is vast (see especially Chester & Dickey, 1988), and positions are multiple. On the issue of censorship and pornography, they range from a compelling continuum theory based on the *structure* of representation (*not* a cause-and-effect chain reaction based on content) and the complicity of the arts and literature with the history of misogynous pornography, in which women are robbed of their agency (Kappeler, 1986), to a complexly argued "gap" theory calling for the abolition of gender as an ontological or normative category (Butler, 1990b). Neither position advocates censorship. For example, Kappeler emphasizes intersubjectivity based on a greater sense of ethical responsibility within literature, the arts, and the academy in a world which accepts blasphemy against women (1986, 24–25) through the tacit conspiracy of word, deed, and gesture. She would dismantle what Spivak calls "sentimental humanism" (1988, 100) as the culture of men based on "the individualist perspective on the 'human condition'" (Kappeler, 1986, 217). In *Gender Trouble: Feminism and the Subversion of Identity*, Judith Butler argues persuasively for redeploying the tool of critical analysis, in which "[t]he question is not: what meaning does that inscription carry within it, but what cultural apparatus arranges this meeting between instrument and body" (1990b, 146). She advises a closer look at the systems of noticing and un-noticing that construct the constructions we seem to be constructed by.

I appreciate the merits of both stances, and would locate Kappeler's position more within the domain of what we've been calling literary experience and Butler's within literary literacy. Ultimately, my actions as a teacher would be guided by the two major premises of the re-educated imagination: the logical priority of direct response and the politicizing of literary engagement. But premises are not strategies, and I would still have to ask myself whether I would "teach" "A&P" (Updike, 1962) using the theories and strategies referred to in Chapter 7, or skip it and do something else that would speak more cogently to the feeling, power, and location problems of the students in my class. It's a tough question, one which I hope readers of this book will see as a problem and not something we shouldn't lose sleep over. For, one of those epiphanies that tend to take on a life of its own is, "If you prick us, do we not bleed?"

The conundrum of the sayingness and unsayingness of the word, particularly the Word, at the heart of the censorship problem, as we said earlier, cannot be resolved any more than can the paradox of the continuum and the gap between word and world, at least not in "purely theoretical" terms, because of the sheer incommensurability of human experience underlying the power of language to name things, and—if we still believe in literature—to name them literarily. In the end, one has to make a decision to try to get that poster removed, or not, and to allow the juror to remain in the jury after having seen that film, or not. This book is not about what should have been done but about the basis for making the decision. But I would say that lobbying for removing the poster doesn't *necessarily* mean that those who do so posit "a logical or causal continuum among fantasy, representation, and action" (Butler, 1990a, 109) under the assumption that all representations must be "positive." I agree with Butler that "a call for censorship . . . is a restriction which can only displace and reroute the violence it seeks to forestall" (119). On this argument, the strategy for interrupting the "'sign-chain'" (119) would not be to remove the poster, but to exploit its positive possibilities for further redoings and remakings of the gap between word and world. Focusing on the Mapplethorpe case, she writes: "It is important to risk losing control of the ways in which the categories of women and homosexuality are represented, even in legal terms, to safeguard the uncontrollability of the signified." To censor is to assert rather than to delegitimize. Rather, we should produce an ongoing chaotic "multiplicity of representations" (121) in order to keep definitions open.

The above argument is analogous to the principle of transgression discussed in Chapter 9, where the border crossings of the Singing School reworked the power relations and the conditions of the powerful texts of Dorothy and William Wordsworth. Proliferating chaotic representations would also certainly erode the reductive anti-feminist attack of the Kastner (1990) article. Butler regards states such as Kristeva's abjection and Foucault's interiority in terms of the drive for coherence, all of which are effects and functions "of a decidedly public and social discourse" (1990b, 135, 136). I would respond that, all of this notwithstanding, abjection and interiority continue to exist as the *felt* products of the feeling, power, and location problems.

The assumptions of this book would not deny the linguistic ground of emotional states. Yet the very uncontrollability of the signified, the gap between the "real" and the represented speaks not just to the uncontrollability of discourse, but to the *fact* that different words affect people differently. *How* they are affected changes, to be sure; and exploring those changes through the redoing and remaking of texts is one of the practices encouraged by literary literacy. That they *do* is what my emphasis on the feeling, power, and location problems as demanding more recognition within the terms in which they are *expressed as felt* would make the phenomenon of human witness ontologically and ethically prior to how it is linguistically constructed. The understanding of the undergoing of experience, the tracing of the seduction, is an infinitely ongoing process. But to push the infinite regress of signification to the point of making it yet another "first principle" shifts the ground of discussion again to a kind of content, and this risks falling back into the humanist trap of devaluing the very exclusions that awareness of a politics of engagement seeks to remedy.

Experience has had to be problematized but not rendered so contingent that it becomes, yet again, just a "stage" or "state" for the pursuit of "higher" knowledge, in which the "pain of learning" can be too easily reduced to a taken-for-granted. We need to preserve the tension between transgression and presence: transgression as the redoing and remaking of texts, and presence as unconditional acceptance of interiorities, felt and shared as they are given, only then to be transfigured and transposed within a dialectical intersubjectivity. Working to remove the poster could be itself interpreted as the expression of a felt presence of women whose post-tragedic stance expresses their loss of spirit (Sethna, 1990), both real and symbolic, in a world in need of many misrecognition scenes to interrupt the continuum. It is this tension which I have been attempting to describe as the dialectic between literary literacy and literary experience. And I believe that both the personal and political expressions of identity that would eliminate the poster and preserve it for analysis of the possibilities for new positionings within the representation encoded in it can be accommodated by a comprehensive theory of literature education.

## Girls and Boys Together Again?
## Literary Experience and Literary Literacy

The contribution of the gap-continuum problem to the re-educated imagination is the awareness that enacting doubleness—the double of the poetic, of language, of vision—is easier from positions of comparative sovereignty than it is from positions of vulnerability. Bringing that to light has been the point of the feeling, power, and location problems. The very act of reading creatively—resisting rather than complying—depends itself upon how any one reader deals with internalizing oppression, in not accommodating one's self-esteem "to what is actually experienced" (Weigel, 1985, 80). When it comes to literary reading, of course, this has a bearing upon the comparative regnancy of one's reading "self" in individual reading acts (Nell, 1988). The latent schizophrenia in any woman who wants to hang on to her "senses, [her] reason, and [her] feelings" in face of what the world thinks is normal can turn double vision into a *"double life* of living by the pattern set by the dominant images *and* in the anticipation of the emancipated woman" (Weigel, 78, 71, emphasis original). Until then, there can be no seeing life steadily and seeing it whole, through literature or anything else; for our eyes have been crossed by the minus sign between mythology and ideology. In the end, however, Haraway's "seeing from below" may still be the best vantage point (1988, 584).[5]

This is where the ambivalent readings of the Singing School come again to the fore: their voluntary split gaze has helped them "live through this transitional space between the *no longer* and the *not yet* without going mad" (Weigel, 1985, 73, emphasis original). In doing this they have articulated what we have been calling an alternative sublime—passion without a victim. Here they tread the path of their foremother, Virginia Woolf, who prefigured the "inanity of Being" (Kristeva, 1977/1980, 146) over fifty years ago by recognizing the impossibility of a victimless passion, of synthesizing the physical and the spiritual without first acknowledging the inextricability of the private and the public, the personal and the political—and the ideological and the mythological. Let's return to Woolf in moving from the censorship problem back to the justification problem by looking at the transfigured version of the last of the principles of the meta-problem: the relationship between literary literacy and literary experience.

### Can Literature Education Change the World?
### Woolf and Three Guineas

One way of answering Spivak's exhortation for literature education to read the world in a way that the world cares about is to reconsider the quotation from Woolf's *Three Guineas* (1938/1966, 35–36) cited in Chapter 6, which I used to support Judy and her sisters in their refusal of John Updike's "A&P" (1962). In addressing the underlying premise of the justification problem—the relationship between literature and life—I now want to ask, in the hindsight of all the versions of doubleness we've been discussing, How can the dialectic between literary literacy and literary experience be said to change the world? Given the events of the past year and the media prominence of the war of words to the war in the Persian Gulf, we might ask whether literature education can be said to be a form of peace studies.[6] In

*Three Guineas* Woolf asserts that the very fabric of "human nature, the reasons, the emotions of the ordinary man and woman [that] lead to war" can be changed by education, that "men and women . . . are able to exert their wills," that "[t]hey are not pawns and puppets dancing on a string held by invisible hands," and that "they can act and think for themselves. Perhaps even they can influence other people's thoughts and actions" (6). For Woolf in 1938, education was the peaceful alternative to war, and "the profession of literature," the only exemption from war. There was, she maintained, no literary "battle of Grub Street" (89).

Thinking for ourselves, exerting our wills in light of new visions, influencing others in the direction of making the world a better place—all were for her elements of the larger question of the relationship between literature and life, language and reality. Within the parameters of this book, we might say that the issue of literature education as peace education was also a function of the relationship between enculturation and self-transformation, between consolidating and extending identity, on the one hand, and between the honoring of difference and freedom from psychological and social conditioning, on the other.

The quotation from *Three Guineas* (1938/1966) in Chapter 6 invokes the double-bind of forced compliance with the structures of oppression in order to transcend them. Knowing that in order to prevent war, women must be educated to earn their living while abhorring the "blood-red thread" (Wolf, 1984, 296) of competition invoked by privilege and hierarchy, like all the protesting readers in this book, Woolf eschews the indirection of the literary for the direct rhetorical address of the polemicist in the heat of a justified anger. Abandoning the technique of the ever-shifting multiple perspectives that mark her supreme achievement as a novelist of modernism, Woolf takes refuge in "the unitary self," railing against the post-tragic stance of an educated woman dedicated to the prevention of war, a reality which she saw as inevitably bound up with the impossibility of being a woman under patriarchy.

Woolf's cry, "Let it blaze! Let it blaze!" arises out of her recognition of the gap between word and world, a gap that was always a mark of the paradox of human consciousness itself. Despite the fervency of her faith in the near magical capabilities of language and her stunning artistry in exploring linguistic possibilities, she was ambivalent about the power of words to "say"; and her oscillation between orality and writing, between direct and indirect discourse, witnesses her belief that meaning lies "on the far side of language" (Woolf, 1966, 55; qtd. in Bishop, 1986, 410). Even at the point of uttering "Let it blaze! Let it blaze!" Woolf found herself within Weigel's double focus (1985) and she knew it; for in the very next sentence, she recants, in the desultory realization that "there is something hollow about [her cry], as is shown by a moment's conflict with fact" (Woolf, 1938/1966, 36), that fact being the logical and material enmeshment of gender with the preventing of war. And so, Woolf ultimately complies and does "send a guinea to the honorary treasurer of the college fund, [to] let her do what she can with it" (36).

Holding the tension between presence and transgression, Woolf declares that educated women need not necessarily "follow the old road to the old end" (1938/1966, 36). But, for her, the new way depended, of course, on the degree to which the personal could become the political. Only then would the ability to think for ourselves, exert our wills, and influence others in the prevention of war take hold. Despite her awareness of the split gaze and the unsayability of language, in the plenitude of her regnant reading self, Woolf shouts:

> Take this guinea then and use it, not to burn the house down, but to make its windows blaze. And let the daughters of uneducated women dance round the new house, the poor house, the house that stands in a narrow street where omnibuses pass and the street hawkers cry their wares, and let them sing: 'We have done with war! We have done with tyranny!' And their mothers will laugh from their graves, 'It was for this we suffered obloquy and contempt! Light up the windows of the new house, daughters! Let them blaze!' (83)

Here the image of new windows signals the creative construction of the daughters of uneducated women, as Woolf's vision of the new order supplants the old one of the daughters of educated men, the father's daughters who can choose only from alienation, refusal, and destruction. Until Beatrice speaks, the fullness of meaning will continue to lie there—in metaphor or political action—"on the far side of language."

It is this possibility of overcoming either/or categories that promises escape from the double-bind of living in a world "as crazy as ours" (Frye, 1989/1991, 32) expressed by Woolf in *Three Guineas* (1938/1966) and by Frye in *The Double Vision* (1991a). This seems to me another way of describing the dialectic between Nell's sovereignty and Nussbaum's vulnerability that we said earlier (Chapter 7) is required to preserve the interplay of control and the relinquishing of control, between literary literacy as cultural critique and literary experience as a state of grace. For windows to blaze with the passion for peace, literature education must learn to speak in the way the world cares about.[7]

## Old Myths, New Myths

The reformulation of the educated imagination evident in Frye's *Words with Power* (1990e) and his *The Double Vision* (1991a) is a synthesis of *Anatomy of Criticism* (1957) and *Fearful Symmetry* (1947). What he gave us in his last years was another map of the order of words, one within the spiritual kingdom proceeding to redemption: the edenic vision of sexual equality (Frye, 1990e, 204). It is only in that world that words can truly transform without being a monument to the failure of experience. But if we are to ensure that the verbal incarnation of "the third order of experience" (Frye, 1971/ 1973, 170) doesn't replicate the patriarchal one we already have, then there's still much work to be done in continuing the project of Woolf's *Three Guineas* (1938/1966). This means toppling some myths and creating others.

The first myth to go is the myth of equal sexual categories. Violence against women is not a "species" of violence as a "genus." Even though violence against women may involve violence towards others, it must remain a category of its own (McKracken, 1991)—not a logical or ontological category but one socially constructed by the gap and the continuum between word and world—until the fact of misogyny is recognized as something other than just the way things are. That is why the "organic whole" of sexual unity (recall Gayle of the Singing School at the end of Chapter 9) as things stand now, can only be part of the hypothetical "third order of experience." At present, while *mythos* is still *logos*, the myth of the sexes as an organic whole produces headlines such as, "Man pleads guilty to killing wife: Former auxiliary RCMP officer shot woman, mutilated body," with an accompanying photograph of each of them captioned "TROUBLED COUPLE" (Mascoll, 1991, A8). It also produces "not guilty" verdicts for rapists because gender-blind judges don't yet "get" that "a 'reasonable person' is not necessarily male" (Sallot, 1991b, D3).

The next myth to go is the Dead Poets Society as a "members only" club that claims no victims. Metaphorically, making the Dead Poets Society co-educational would be to implement Woolf's bid for truly a democratic theory of education. And that, in turn, means disabusing literature of both its privilege and its marginalization. Literally (and, if we are to take Frye at his word, the literal is the metaphorical), it is to see the feeling, power, and location problems less as an ideological subset of myth than to regard them positively as a form of "applied mythology" (Frye, 1990e, 23), an application which, contrary to Frye's claims, does do something other than adhere to belief in an ideology.[8] I agree with

Frye that "there is a strong resistance within an ideology to placing its excluded initiative, the myth it lives by, into focus and examining it in a broader perspective" (24). But I suggest that the excluded initiative of the educated imagination as the silent Beatrice, the hypothetical level of the unsayingness of literature, which, in the tradition of Sidney and Shelley, "asserts nothing but simply holds up symbols and illustrations" (24), might be examined within its broader context of the feeling, power, and location problems.

To do so, of course, would be to language Beatrice, and thus to transfer the feeling, power, and location problems out of the footnotes and into the text: to rethink the myth that literature only influences for good. That it just might not is taken seriously by Wayne Booth, another proponent of the educated imagination, whose anguish over the unresolvable dilemma about the sayingness and un-sayingness of literature and its relation to "extra-literary" considerations, such as the poem's relation to "truth" and the politics of its author, spills onto every page in his continual reiterations of "on the one hand" and "on the other" (see especially 1988a, 380–381). Colin Falck (1989) also recognizes the feeling, power, and location problems, but, less worried about them than Booth, consigns them to a footnote in his book. Putting them into his text would have radically altered his conception of a "religion of full experiencing" (170), and, in my view, rendered it a more viable poetics of ordinary existence.[9]

## Double Perspective: The Pedagogy of Ordinary Existence

That the foreshortening of ordinary existence and imaginative experience, along with the admixture of other disciplines into reading and writing as a practice, is not just an uncritical belief is evidenced in some work now being done in the radical theoretical and pedagogical restructuring of the relationship between literature and language at the post-secondary level. For example, David Bleich indicts the academy's ethical irresponsibility with respect to its "intra-masculine interests" (1988, 17). His The Double Perspective: Language, Literacy, and Social Relations (1988) provides another critique of the kind of privileged individualism I pointed to earlier in Dead Poets Society, whether it shows up as the surface performatives of the language game or conceptions of "religious transcendence" as an intense but secret affair (18).

By dismantling the dichotomy between the personal and the social, private and public (variants of that between the mythological and the ideological), Bleich joins with Woolf in Three Guineas (1938/

1966). Bleich's "double perspective" would not deny "the moving power" of poetry; it would mobilize it in classrooms full of real readers reading into something other than a technique for meditation —as the very condition of cognitive and emotional interdependency that transfigures and transposes students who are *inter alia*. The "double perspective," which Bleich defines on a number of levels as the generic marking of a social event (1988, 118), is not just about the plurality of literary meaning, but about the multi-layered awareness of how doubleness constitutes the dynamic interplay of the personal and the social of "how language works all the time" (xi). It is also about taking ethical responsibility for the effects of affective aesthetics (19) and about the contingent role a given work of literature might play "in a culturally and politically situated living person" (xiii). It's about the "impurity" of the English class where other subjects disrupt the autonomy of the literary enclave. It's about the "new" and "used" nature of all language (120), seen as both a name and a context with a history, and about regarding the *tremendum* of transformation less as the *mysterium* and more as the aggregate of "the double perspectives of individual minds and the unified perspectives of several" (120). But it is most decidedly not about the literary imagination as a monument to the failure of experience. It's about presence and transgression. And it works toward a theory of an alternative sublime which would combine redoing and remaking of texts with awareness that your imaginative hell might be a condition of my imaginative heaven.

## Transformations and Transfigurations

If literature is so privileged in the academy (Bleich, 1988, 25), why is it so marginalized in the schools? And, what can be done about it? In ending this book, I want to juxtapose two texts taken from my own cultural and professional context, texts which at first seem disparate but which presage the confluence of forces that speak to the re-educated imagination. The first is taken from the last formal address given by Frye before his death, and the second, from the final paper of another student outside the Singing School, a feminist historian enrolled in my "mainstream" course in the philosophy of literature and literature education. In both these texts we see glimpses of presences and transgressions, of locating boundaries and crossing them. These excerpts attest to the politics of engagement and the ethical demand of human witness, and they are both critical in the highest sense—as the pure utterances of the English major and the "non" English major, both of whom seem transfigured and transposed as they speak them.

In addressing the Social Sciences and Humanities Research Council of Canada, Frye spoke movingly about boundaries— among countries and among the genres of literature—and how important it is for them to be porous, "open to influences from any- where in the world" as a safeguard against ossification and authori- tarianism. "The more vigorous the literature, the more it thrives on cross-pollenization" (1991b, A13). Though these statements were not particularly new for Frye, they contained, for me, one utterance that assumed a self-propelling life of its own. It was a comment about the relationship between education and culture that went beyond the stubborn structure (Chapter 4), about a culture without boundaries as "the social manifestation of the educational system" (1991b, A13; see also 1991a, 38). Given the scope and shape of Frye's own prescrip- tives on education—his criticism of its lack of rigor, his preference for the four-year honor degree in The Great Tradition, his insistence on skill in the order of words and practice in the anagogic world- view—I did another double-take at this:

> A central and very important aspect of education, and probably the part that stays with us the longest, is what comes not from what we are taught or what we read, but from what we learn from one another. The more homogeneous and provincial the community, the more of what we learn in this way is simply the repeated preju- dices of our friends, backed up by similar repetitions in the news media.
>
> Canada has now become cosmopolitan to a degree that would have been incomprehensible 50 years ago. If Toronto is a world- class city, it is not because it bids for the Olympics or builds follies like the Skydome, but because of the tolerated variety of the people in its streets.[10] (1991b, A13, emphasis added)

If this statement can be taken as testimony to Frye's own belief in the poetics of ordinary existence (and I think it not unreasonable to assume that it can), it is also evidence of what he has always said about the benefits of living in a country that, while still searching for its identity, creates it daily through the strength of its imagination. (It was this very point in this very article used by my other daughter in her crossing of borders. Enrolled in a design history program which focuses on the material and social analysis of cultural artifacts, she presented a seminar in London, England, on the Canadian literary imagination!)

Against Frye's literary transposition, let's put the final paper of Christabelle, feminist historian. Christabelle was a colleague of Jeff's in the class that prompted his "literary transfiguration" quoted at the beginning of this chapter. But her role there was not that of just another "ground" for male "enlightenment." If Jeff came to a redefinition of aesthetic experience by having improved his literary literacy through cross-pollenization with feminist theory, Christabelle came from the other direction, offering her feminist theory to defend the aims of literature education, not as a masculinist territorial prerogative (Bleich, 1988, 31), but as a shared wealth and a shared burden. Using her knowledge of the history of women in teaching, Christabelle framed her critique of the meta-problem within the genderization of forms of knowledge—who is doing the work and to what ends—in terms of the patriarchal structure of what counts as knowledge in the Western cultural tradition, past and present (see also Stuckey, 1991). Beginning with Plato's characterization of poetry not just as feminine, but as feminizing—making men womanish—she proceeded to consider the legacy of Cartesian dualism in contemporary educational values. Literature, she suggested, "as perhaps the apotheosis of the soft side of the classroom curriculum, is a convenient target for attack. Despite the fact that mathematics, chemistry and physics are as, or even more, sexist, racist, and classist than English could ever hope to be, the essence of these disciplines is rarely questioned."

Though Christabelle's critique of the meta-problem addressed all three of its aspects—justification, censorship, and response—I found most compelling her remarks on the enmeshment of the censorship problem with the gap between enculturation and self-transformation:

> Because I speak also of the symbolic loss of spirit many women experience, I can sympathize with those black parents who wanted *Lord of the Flies* banned, but I do not believe that the answer lies in banning such books from the curriculum. . . . The answer lies in expanding the enculturation and self-transformation process into other disciplines which have traditionally not assumed responsibility for this process. Once we . . . acknowledge the gap between enculturation and self-transformation, . . . we, as educators, administrators and legislators are all responsible for bridging this gap. (Sethna, 1990)

As the symbolic grand-daughter of Virginia Woolf, Christabelle rages in the regnancy of her reading and speaking self, one rent by all those ontological shocks, but nonetheless rising in a calling to account about the conditions and responsibilities for literacy:

> Despite the increasing tension in the classroom, literature, in its dual goals of enculturation and self-transformation, has come to represent [a] "haven in a heartless world." And who better to tend the hearth than the woman teacher? . . . [i]f healthy and viable

citizens can be enculturated and transformed in the "private sphere" of the English studies classroom, there is little need to tackle the "public" sphere of mathematics, chemistry and physics. Or, business, the law and medicine. . . . Allowing literature to continue to represent this haven . . . means adding to women's work. . . . Literature cannot remain the only means whereby students' enculturation and self-transformation are realized. If we believe in the value of a re-educated imagination, then . . . [i]t is time to kill the Angel in the English studies classroom.

I propose that teachers' colleges and curriculum guidelines . . . encourage all teachers to work in tandem not only to achieve the dual goals of enculturation and self-transformation but to narrow the gap. . . . I call for physics teachers to project a model of the Bohr atom on screen while their students come face to melted face with the Canadian-made and American-banned film, "If You Love This Planet." I call for chemistry teachers to direct their students to combine oil and water in a test-tube, shake well, remember the Exxon Valdez and bake under the 48 C. [sic] degree temperature of the Persian Gulf. I call for geography teachers to have students cast British Columbia and Bangladesh in papier maché, mold stumps for felled trees, and wait for the Flood. I call for computer literacy teachers to permit their students to peer into the brains of a monitor, tear aside the confusion of the red and blue wires and make space for the women with failing eyesight on Mexican assembly lines. (Sethna, 1990)

Christabelle, it seems, would language Beatrice, too. I reproduce this text here not because I necessarily endorse her literature-across-the-curriculum program as "the answer" to the meta-problem, but as an example of embodied criticism within an expressly educational context. Hers is just one of a multiplicity of possible solutions that emerged in a course explicitly addressing the meta-problem, but it is one that particularly advocates the need for integrative studies (la Brecque, 1990) and a socially responsible context for literary studies (Levine, 1986, 164–170). In the directness of her pure utterance, she transposes the gender designations of single (male) and plural (female) that began this chapter. As Beatrice speaks—and is heard— the single mother of literature education becomes the communal parent of cultural literacy. There will be those, of course, who will regard the statements of Christabelle and Jeff as naive, even romantic. Within the educated imagination, Jeff's confession and Christabelle's polemic could be seen as embryonic literary forms. Within the re-educated imagination, they represent the kind of "genuine epistemological shift" (de Lauretis, 1987, 10) that grows out of politicizing engagement and making direct response, the ethical demand of human witness, logically as well as psychologically prior in criticism. It is hoped that this might open the gate beyond criticism (Frye, 1990e, 29) "so that the word criticism expands until it is practically synonymous with education itself" (Frye, 1991a, 38). Here "the third order of experience" (Frye, 1971/1973, 170) is transfigured from a chorus of yearners to the practitioners of ordinary existence, and the imagination, transposed from the order of words to the dailiness of life.[11]

# Endnotes

1. Falck (1989) is quick to point out Frye's association of the lyric with the expressly musical aspects of poetry (60).

2. I would like to express my gratitude to Barbara O'Byrnne, a high school English teacher and graduate student at The Ontario Institute for Studies in Education for permission to listen to this tape and to refer to it here. On January 25, 1991, two days after his death, Frye was scheduled as keynote speaker for a conference, "The Body/The Text," at his own Victoria College, University of Toronto, with a paper on "Bodies and Non-Bodies, or Where the Body Stops."

3. This abbreviation refers to Frye's *The Secular Scripture: A Study of the Structure of Romance,* (1976a).

4. Particularly pertinent to the spirit of this book are Booth's definition of "coduction" as what we do whenever we compare our literary experience with others (1988a, 72–73), the blurring of the line between censorship and teaching (27), the perils and joys of submission to Otherness (70–71), the logical priority of direct response as a "primary intention" (32), the broad definition of literature to include "all narrative" (14), and, of course, the enmeshment of the ethical with the aesthetic, seen most tenuously as the possibility that literature might influence for ill (40).

5. A comprehensive theory of literature education, what in Chapter 8 we saw as stereoscopic hearing, would have to cope with the contradictions involved in dealing with the relationship between ethical stance and the infinite regress of redoing texts in light of seeing from below. As I made my final revisions to this chapter, two more newspaper articles compel me to call attention to the tension between the making and remaking of art and the possibility that such art may be sweeping clear of "the world of facts" (Frye, 1991a, 18) too soon.

The first example castigates the audience at a ballet for failing to make the very connections between art and life which the judge in the war crimes trial (Chapter 1) would have us ignore. A member of the board of the Ottawa Ballet resigned her post in protest against the production of *The Lesson*, a ballet based on Eugene Ionesco's play, in which "a dance teacher strangles a young girl and enlists his female pianist as an accomplice." Though the intended allegorical meaning was the relationship between Hitler, "the Gestapo and the SS machinery," the resisting reader extended the continuum of the sign-chain by noting that the "themes of fascism and domination are part of what violence against women is all about." She also objected to the alleged lack of the audience's sensitivity to what in this book would be called a feeling, power, and location problem: "the wild applause of the audience . . . led her to believe '*they couldn't see beyond the art* and see the message being portrayed' " (Ballet's violence toward women is deplored: Board member resigns over The Lesson's depiction of murders," *The Globe and Mail*, Toronto, ON, December 4, 1991, C1, emphasis added). Here the respondent's proximity and vulnerability to the events of Montreal discloses the gap between message sent and message received, the message in this case being less a matter of knowing what evil lurks in the hearts of men (sic) than the conviction that this is a story which has lasted long enough. Of course, there is the distinct possibility that the enthusiastic audience applause signaled that it had indeed caught the moral, and anti-violent message of the work, in which case the objector entirely missed the message sent by the audience.

Ironically, "Une Aussi Longue Histoire" is precisely the title of an installation in a Montreal department store, one that could be interpreted as the commercial appropriation of the very poem by Nicole Brossard cited earlier. For me and for others, Brossard's poem had become more than a consolation for the massacre. It was Beatrice screaming the power of horror; now it was selling dresses at Jacob's on St. Catherine Street. Yet this commodification was orchestrated by artist Christine Horeau, who drew "the blood-red thread" (Wolf, 1984, 296) in neon, competing with the peep shows, strip joints, and sex cinemas (Sher, 1991, C1) that serve as the co-dependent underbelly of an upright citizenry. Is this literature or is this life? Does it matter? One journalist sees it as a poem of ordinary existence (Sher, 1991, C1); a philosophy professor sees its challenge to censorship and pornography laws as a way of distinguishing between freedom of speech and hate literature. The artist says that it's about the "suffering that women all too often live with in silence, shame, and humiliation" (Picard, 1991b, A5). The re-educated imagination would say, of course, that they are all right, that what's important is to talk about it, but that where any of us chooses to stand is really a matter of devotion in terms of the feeling, power, and location problem. The question is, how to negotiate the impossible all-at-onceness of stereoscopic hearing.

6. The topic, "Is Literary Research on Education 'Research on Preventing War'?: Virginia Woolf's *Three Guineas* (1938/1966) 50 Years Later," organized by Susan Laird of the University of Maine, was presented on November 5, 1988 at the Conference of the American Educational Studies Association, Toronto, Ontario, November 2–6. Some of the ideas from this section are taken from my participation in that session.

7. Here I note the connection between literature education as peace studies and the history of education and misogyny. For two studies that take up the relationship of the Montreal massacre to the history of women in education, see A. Prentice (1991) and Lykke de la Cour et al. (1990).

8. "Last December [1990] OCUFA [Ontario Confederation of University Faculty Associations], with support from the Council of Ontario Universities, the Ontario Federation of Students, and the Confederation of Ontario University Staff Associations, had proposed an Ontario Memorial Fund to End Violence in the memory of the women students murdered the previous December 6 in Montreal. The proposal called for funding of campus projects such as workshops and programmes on violence against women, support services for women, and physical improvements such as extra lighting." The four projects announced by the Ontario government were Campus Safety for Women Project, Women in Engineering Project, Date Rape Prevention and Awareness Project, and the Wife Assault Project (Preventing violence against women: Ontario launches programs to improve women's safety on campus. OCUFA Forum, May/June, 1991, 1).

9. "The question of *who* finds art worth attending to and in what ways is of course an important one, but it is also one which does not undermine the argument being developed here. It is an aspect of the traditional 'problem of ideology,' and is a problem which needs to be re-structured in cultural and social-historical terms; it is a problem which relates not just to art, but to science, philosophy, and the whole structure of human reason in general" (Falck, 1989, 83, emphasis original).

10. Frye, 1991b, A13. This quotation is also in marked contrast to the excerpt from *The Educated Imagination* (Frye, 1963a) cited in Chapter 3 about the woman "who . . . learned to talk like the Declaration of Independence" even though she never got past grade six as the *exception* to the rule that most people lack what literature has to give (64).

11. Such a vision involves the "other" tradition of Plato studies, which read him as a "normative strategist" not as "an ontological foundationalist," as one who uses "convictions of value that serve as humanly formulated criteria for critically judging the world of experience" (la Brecque, 1990, 485; see also Benne, 1990; Bogdan, 1983; Randall, 1970; Reich, 1906). But to have started there would be to have written a different book.

# Postlude

My Introduction spoke of the retrospective and prospective nature of this project. As part of the prospectus, I still need to point to important work and issues this book has not had room for: the thorny question of literary quality (Booth, 1988a, 50, 56) and the many issues now being dealt with in feminist pedagogy (Grumet, 1988; Lather, 1991), popular culture (Giroux & Simon, et al., 1989), philosophy of the emotions (de Sousa, 1987), and philosophy of education, not least of which is the feminist critique of the one who started it all, Plato. This latter new area of inquiry involves exciting philosophical and much heated debate about Plato's theory of equality of education and its relationship to reading his dialogues (see especially J.F. Smith, 1990). I also need to reference the increasing rapprochement between philosophers of education and philosophers of literature education (Arcilla, 1990; Burgess, 1989), those who do not regard the feeling, power, and location problems as a case of either an "instrumental" view of literature or the "affective fallacy." The ways in which poetry and philosophy are coming together would turn the banishment into a figment of Plato's imagination. Each conference I attend generates so much energy between borders that I am coming to believe that there is no place to be home, and that home is everywhere.

The final chapters of this book were written during my first sabbatical year, "on location" in two places, which I now realize I must have chosen quite unconsciously as sites of my own cultural conditioning. The first was California, USA, that paradise of my ordinary existence; the second, London-of-the-world, that heaven of my imaginative experience. Reared, as I was, on the novels of The Great Tradition and the fantasies of Beverley Hills, how could I possibly have escaped the conviction that someday my Prince would come?

Within the same week of my arrival in Santa Cruz, the Persian Gulf War had broken out and Northrop Frye had died. I was on page 87 of Words with Power (1990e). While finishing that book, I took notes on a war that made the conventions of "hero" and "villain" reality in an archetypal misrecognition scene, and clipped more newspaper articles for my files. Each underlining in red and highlighting in BOLD became sign of *my* system of noticing and un-noticing. Most readers of this book will have similarly stuffed folders. At Santa Cruz, I witnessed an entire university, students and faculty, putting their personal and professional lives on hold to become activists for peace. I also saw people speaking and acting across their difference—from Arab-Israel relations to pornography—in their efforts at a victimless passion. Pondering these and other issues, from the debate over identity politics in the California social studies curriculum (Kirp, 1991) to the absence of a universal health care system, rendered surreal the blazing sunsets, whispering surf, and my long walks along the magnificent coastal expanse stretching outside my one-room sublet.

"Whilst" in London, I was struck by the teaming diversity of the urban scape. As I puzzled over my new electric kettle, which came, as these things do in Britain, innocent of a plug, I found a young man in a video shop who fitted those mysterious wires into their rightful place, while musing how no one in that country could be considered literate who couldn't perform this task. In London, you can hear chamber music for the price of a movie but can't take your bookbag into the university library. As I made my nightly trek to the Wigmore Hall, I thought about the British National Curriculum, less emancipatory than it could be (O'Hear & White, 1991).[1] I thrilled to concerts that brought me to the interstices between stasis, kinesis, and the whole gamut of the taxonomies. When octogenarian Vlado Perlemuter gave a recital of monumental proportions, with the kind of pianism that left you wondering whether you were in the right century, I couldn't tell why I felt what I felt. Was it the Chopin ballades, his performance practice, my knowing beforehand that he'd been badly bruised in a fall at the airport, or his being overwhelmed at the audience being overwhelmed? But I do know that it was a state of grace! And when Chiharu Sakai, the only female out of four finalists, won the inaugural London World piano competition, all I knew was that Beatrice had begun to sing, not *only* because the winner was female, but also because the sheer grace of her musicality had belied "the blood-red thread" (Wolf, 1984, 296) of the *agon*, and been a recognition scene for so many. But neither scene was easily locatable on either a continuum or a gap between imaginative experience and ordinary existence.

In closing, I find myself grateful for my own recognition scenes, but, more so, for misrecognition scenes that are inescapably, and perhaps the better part of, any coming to know, where the dance of sovereignty and vulnerability is inextricably linked to the recognitions and misrecognitions of others around me, with whom I may or may not share these interiorities but who will experience theirs with others in their own way and in their own time. It is this gratuitousness and immediacy of life that the poetics of ordinary existence would celebrate, in schools and outside them. If that makes me a romantic, I trust that it is not of the "moribund kind" (Weiskel, 1976, 6, qtd. in Yaeger, 1989, 197, my Chapter 9); for that insists on engulfing resolutions. In order for literary literacy and literary experience to inter-play into making us "numinous presences ourselves" (Frye, 1991a, 84) but not "gods" in order for them to be able to create what Maxine Greene calls "renewal of . . . a 'common world,' " we must risk the pain of incommensurability. As Greene continues to remind us, human beings live in but also "against their own life worlds and in the light of their lives with others, able to express, to call, to say, to sing. And, using their imaginations, tapping their courage, to transform" (1990a, 16, 17). Perhaps re-educating the imagination can lend the hope of a "more generous view of the ways in which we come to know ourselves" (Nussbaum, 1986, 390).

By thus ending with Nussbaum, I indicate my resistance to the very position I have argued myself into; for I still want to accord to the construct of the poem and of art, as she does, its privileged status in effecting transformation. To repudiate it completely would be to deny the very premises upon which a book such as this can be written. So the dialectic continues. Here I find myself in the company of those other explorers in poetic apologetics, who resist closure on the ethical, social, and political relationship between the literary word and world. In his review essay of some of those authors (Bersani, 1990; Booth, 1988a, 1988b; Eldridge, 1989; Poirier, 1987; Watkins, 1989), William E. Cain (1991) reinforces the phenomenon of poetic power even as he reiterates the importance of preserving critical distance on it: "It should be possible to remain skeptical about the power of literature while continuing to believe that this power is not always harmful or repressive, and that it *can* [not *does*] function as a force for the liberation of men and women. Perhaps we remain uneasy about acknowledging the power of literary texts to do good for us because we know how dependent we are upon them" (476, emphasis added). This shift from the indicative to the subjunctive mood about the moving power of poetry, literally and metaphorically, signifies that the re-education of the imagination is already underway. It is a re-education that is both wordless and wordful. And so I end not with assertion, denial, or equivocation, but in the sacred space between recognition and misrecognition, literary experience and literary literacy, the triumph of experience and the sanctuary of art—extraordinary forms of ordinary existence, in which

Beatrice suspends singing her stating, and advances, not regresses, to the silence of listening between *educere* and *educare*, between what she knows and what she can hope to know.

# Endnote

1. Philip O'Hear and John White, a classroom teacher and philosopher of education, have written a critique of the British National Curriculum which calls for a broader, more democratic, curriculum based on scientific, social, and personal knowledge and understanding, experience of the arts, and practical competencies, with increasing emphasis on student choice. See P. O'Hear and J. White (1991),

# Appendix

### I Wandered Lonely as a Cloud

I wandered lonely as a cloud
That floats on high o'er vales and hills,
When all at once I saw a crowd,
A host, of golden daffodils;
Beside the lake, beneath the trees,
Fluttering and dancing in the breeze.

Continuous as the stars that shine
And twinkle on the milky way,
They stretched in never-ending line
Along the margin of a bay:
Ten thousand saw I at a glance,
Tossing their heads in sprightly dance.

The waves beside them danced; but they
Out-did the sparkling waves in glee:
A poet could not but be gay,
In such a jocund company:
I gazed—and gazed—but little thought
What wealth the show to me had brought:

For oft, when on my couch I lie
In vacant or in pensive mood,
They flash upon that inward eye
Which is the bliss of solitude;
And then my heart with pleasure fills,
And dances with the daffodils.

—William Wordsworth

### Adolescent

I wandered lonely as a dog
avoiding trouble,
and others of her species,

while daffodils like gold stars
(for good behavior)
rebuked me, and lilac buds

in phallic clusters,
doubling size each day.
I kept my nose to the curb,

307

never to the grindstone,
like someone looking for money
down a sewer-grate. Depressing,

isn't it, when buses grind past—
not one going where you're going,
the crowd at your back

revving its discontent
as if you were leader of the pack.
A Coke bottle tinkles, hurled

rocks ripple the civic
display of daffodils.
You watch Coke drip

into the gutter, livening
a party of ants,
their frenzied dancing—

better to wander, quickly,
away, before the soft
wow of police cars

climbs rapidly up the scale
of urban music . . .
O William, what common

memories stir our yelps in the dark?

—Joyce Peseroff

(I would like to thank the author and the *Harvard Magazine* for permission to reproduce this poem which appeared in the July/August 1988 issue of the magazine.)

When we were in the woods beyond Gowbarrow park we saw a few daffodils close to the water side. We fancied that the lake had floated the seeds ashore, and that the little colony had so sprung up. But as we went along there were more and yet more; and at last, under the boughs of the trees, we saw that there was a long belt of them along the shore, about the breadth of a country turnpike road. I never saw daffodils so beautiful. They grew among the mossy stones about and about them; some rested their heads upon these stones, as on a pillow, for weariness; and the rest tossed and reeled and danced, and seemed as if they verily laughed with the wind, that blew upon them over the lake; they looked so gay, ever glancing, ever changing. This wind blew directly over the lake to them. There was here and there a little knot, and a few stragglers a few yards higher up; but they were so few as not to disturb the simplicity and unity and life of that one busy highway. We rested again and again.

—Dorothy Wordsworth

# Works Cited

Abrams, M.H. (1953). *The mirror and the lamp: Romantic theory and the critical tradition.* London: Oxford University Press.

'Aggressive' tot ruling up-held in B.C. sex case. (1990, January 14). *The Toronto Star,* A24.

Alter, R. (1989). *The pleasures of reading in an ideological age.* New York: Simon & Schuster.

Althusser, L. (1969). *For Marx.* (B. Brewster, Trans.). Harmondsworth, England: Penguin.

———. (1971). *Lenin and philosophy and other essays.* (B. Brewster, Trans.). London: New Left Books.

Apple, M. (1979). *Ideology and curriculum.* London: Routledge & Kegan Paul.

Applebee, A. N. (1978). *The child's concept of story: Ages two to seventeen.* Chicago: University of Chicago Press.

Arcilla, R.V. (1990). Edification, conversation, and narrative: Rortyan motifs for philosophy of education. *Educational Theory, 40* (1), 35–39.

Aristotle. (1965). On the art of poetry. In T. S. Dorsch, (Ed.), *Aristotle, Horace, Longinus:* Classical literacy criticism. Harmondsworth, England: Penguin.

Atkins, J. W. H. (1934). The attack on poetry: Plato. *Literary criticism in antiquity,* Vol. 1. Cambridge, England: Cambridge University Press.

Atwood, M. (1986). English teachers speech. *indirections, 11* (1), 6–14.

Bakhtin, M. M. (1981). *The dialogic imagination: Four essays.* (M. Holquist, Ed. and Trans., C. Emerson, Trans.). Austin, TX: University of Texas Press.

———. (1988). Discourse in the novel. (N. Mercer, Ed. and Trans.). *Language and literacy from an educational perspective.* Milton Keynes, England: Open University Press.

Ballet's violence toward women deplored: Board member resigns over The Lesson's depiction of murders. (1991, December 4). *The Globe and Mail,* Cl.

Bartky, S.L. (1979). Towards a phenomenology of feminist consciousness. In S. Bishop & M. Weinzweig, (Eds.) *Philosophy and women.* Belmont, CA: Wadsworth Publishers, Inc.

Bate, W.J. (Ed.). (1970). *Criticism: The major texts.* New York: Harcourt, Brace, Jovanovich.

Batsleer, J., Davies, T., O'Rourke, R., & Weedon, C. (1985). *Rewriting English: Cultural politics of gender and class*. London: Methuen.

Battin, M.P. (1977). Plato on true and false poetry. *Journal of Aesthetics and Art Criticism, 36*, 163–174.

Baudrillard, J. (1990). *Seduction*. (B. Singer, Trans.). Montreal: New World Perspectives; Culture Text Series. [1990].

Bauer, M.D. (1985). The censor within. In N.J. Karolides & L. Burress (Eds.), *Celebrating censored books*. Urbana, IL: NCTE.

Beach, R. (1979). Issues of censorship and research on effects of and response to reading. In J. Davis (Ed.), *Dealing with censorship*. Urbana, IL: NCTE.

———. (1990). The creative development of meaning: Using autobiographical experiences to interpret literature. In D. Bogdan & S. Straw (Eds.), *Beyond communication: Reading comprehension and criticism*. Portsmouth, NH: Boynton-Cook/Heinemann.

Belsey, C. (1980). *Critical practice*. London: Methuen.

Benjamin, J. (1988). *The bonds of love: Psychoanalysis, feminism, and the problem of domination*. New York: Pantheon.

Benne, K. (1990). Plato's divided line: A dramatistic interpretation. *Philosophy of Education: 1989. Proceedings of the forty-fifth annual meeting of the Philosophy of Education Society*. Normal, IL: Illinois State University, 363–373.

Bergvall, A. (1989). *The 'enabling of judgement': Sir Philip Sidney and the education of the reader*. Uppsala: Distributor Almqvist & Wiksell International.

Berkin, C.R. (1979). Private woman, public woman: The contradictions of Charlotte Perkins Gilman. In C.R. Berkin & M.B. Norton (Eds.), *Women of America: A history*. Boston: Houghton Mifflin.

Bernstein, R. (1990, October 28). Academia's fashionable orthodoxy: The rising hegemony of the politically correct. *The New York Times*. (Section 2), 1, 4.

Bersani, L. (1990). *The culture of redemption*. Cambridge, MA: Harvard University Press.

Bishop, E. (1986). Writing, speech, and silence in *Mrs. Dalloway*. *English Studies in Canada, 12* (4), 397–423.

Bleich, D. (1975). *Readings and feelings: An introduction to subjective criticism*. Urbana, IL: NCTE.

———. (1978). *Subjective criticism*. Baltimore, MD: Johns Hopkins University Press.

———. (1988). *The double perspective: Language, literacy, and social relations*. New York: Oxford University Press.

Bloom, A. (1987). *The closing of the American mind*. New York: Simon & Schuster.

Bloom, H. (1973). *The anxiety of influence: A theory of poetry*. London & New York: Oxford University Press.

Bogdan, D. (1980). *Instruction and delight: Northrop Frye and the educational value of literature*. Unpublished doctoral dissertation, University of Toronto.

———. (1982). Northrop Frye and the defence of literature. *English Studies in Canada, 7* (2), 203–214.

———. (1983). The censorship of literature texts and Plato's banishment of the poets. *Interchange, 14* (3), 1–16.

———. (1984). Pygmalion as pedagogue: Subjectivist bias in the teaching of literature. *English Education, 16* (2), 67–75.

———. (1985a). The justification question: Why literature? *English Education, 17* (4), 238–248.

———. (1985b). Literary criticism in the classroom. In K.B. Whale & T.J. Gambel (Eds.), *From seed to harvest: Looking at literature*. Ottawa: Canadian Council of Teachers of English.

———. (1986a). Literary response as dialectic: Modes and levels of engagement and detachment. *Cuadernos de filologia inglesa, 2*, 45–62.

———. (1986b). The rhetorical fallacy: Values as literary representation. Part Two of D. Bogdan & S. Yeomans, School censorship and learning values through literature. *The Journal of Moral Education, 15* (3), 197–211.

———. (1986c). Sidney's defence of the "lying" Greek poets: The argument from hypothesis. *Classical and Modern Literature: A Quarterly, 7* (1), 43–54.

———. (1986d). Virtual and actual forms of literary response. *The Journal of Aesthetic Education, 20* (2), 51–57.

———. (1986/1991). Moncton, mentors, and memories: An interview with Northrop Frye. *Studies in Canadian Literature, 11*, 246–269. Reprinted in R.D. Denham (Ed.), (1991). *A world in a grain of sand: Twenty-two interviews with Northrop Frye*. New York: Peter Lang.

———. (1987a). From the inside out: On first teaching women's literature and feminist criticism. Popular Feminism Papers of the Centre for Women's Studies in Education. May 4, 1987. Toronto: Ontario Institute for Studies in Education.

———. (1987b). Literature, values, and truth: Why we could lose the censorship debate. *English Quarterly, 20* (4), 273–284.

———. (1987c). A taxonomy of literary responses and respondents. *Paideusis: Journal of the Canadian Philosophy of Education Society, 1* (1), 43–54.

———. (1988a). A case study of the selection/censorship problem and the educational value of literature. *Journal of Education, 170* (2), 39–56.

———. (1988b). The censorship of literature texts: A case study. In B.F. Nelms (Ed.), *Literature in the classroom: Readers, texts, and contexts*. Urbana, IL. NCTE Forum Series.

————. (1989a). From stubborn structure to double mirror: The evolution of Northrop Frye's theory of poetic creation and response. *The Journal of Aesthetic Education, 23* (2), 33–43.

————. (1989b). Judy and her sisters: Censorship and the poetics of need. In J. Giarelli (Ed.), *Philosophy of Education: 1988. Proceedings of the forty-fourth annual meeting of the Philosophy of Education Society*. Normal, IL: Philosophy of Education Society, 66–77.

————. (1990a). Censorship, identification, and the poetics of need. In A. Lunsford, H. Moglen, J. Slevin (Eds.), *The right to literacy*. New York: The Modern Language Association of America.

————. (1990b). From meditation to mediation: Breaking out of total form. In D. Bogdan & S. Straw (Eds.), *Beyond Communication: Reading comprehension and criticism*. Portsmouth, NH: Boynton-Cook/Heinemann.

————. (1990c). In and out of love with literature: Response and the aesthetics of total form. In D. Bogdan & S. Straw (Eds.), *Beyond Communication: Reading comprehension and criticism*. Portsmouth, NH: Boynton-Cook/Heinemann.

————. (1990d). Joyce, Dorothy, and Willie: Literary literacy as engaged reflection. *In R. Page (Ed.) Philosophy of Education: 1989. Proceedings of the forty-fifth annual meeting of The Philosophy of Education Society*. Normal, IL: Philosophy of Education Society, 168–182.

————. (1990e). Reading and 'The fate of beauty': Reclaiming total form. In D. Bogdan & S. Straw (Eds.), *Beyond Communication: Reading comprehension and criticism*. Portsmouth, NH: Boynton-Cook/Heinemann.

————. (1990f). The re-educated imagination and the power of literary engagement. *The Journal of Educational Thought, 24* (3A), 83–109.

————. (1990g). Total form as a moveable feast: A response to Walsh. *Paideusis: Journal of the Canadian Philosophy of Education Society, 3* (2), 43–44.

Bogdan, D., Millen, K.J., & Pitt, A. (1992). Feminist approaches to teaching John Updike's 'A&P.' In E. Evans (Ed.), *Young readers, new readings*. Hull, England: Hull University Press.

Bogdan, D. & Straw, S. (Eds.). (1990). *Beyond communication: Reading comprehension and criticism*. Portsmouth, NH: Boynton-Cook/Heinemann.

Bogdan, D. & Yeomans, S. (1986). School censorship and learning values through literature. *The Journal of Moral Education, 15* (3), 197–211.

Booth, W.C. (1988a). *The company we keep: An ethics of fiction*. Berkeley, CA: University of California Press.

————. (1988b). *The vocation of a teacher: Rhetorical occasions, 1967–1988*. Chicago: University of Chicago Press.

Borch-Jacobsen, M. (1991). *Lacan: The absolute master*. (D. Brick, Trans.). Stanford, CA: Stanford University Press.

Borovilos, J. (1985). The English myth debunked. *OCTE Newsletter, 4* (2), n.p.

————. (1990). *Breaking through: A Canadian literary mosaic*. Scarborough, ON: Prentice-Hall Canada, Inc.

Boullart, K. (1988). *Tragic action and aesthetic contemplation.* Unpublished paper delivered at the International Congress of Aesthetics. University of Nottingham, England, September 1, 1988.

Bousson, J. B. (1989). *The empathic reader: a study of the narcissistic character and the drama of the self.* Amherst, MA: University of Massachusetts Press.

Boyd, D. (1991). One man's reflection on a masculine role in feminist ethics: Epistemic vs. political privilege. In D. Ericson (Ed.), *Philosophy of Education: 1990. Proceedings of the forty-sixth annual meeting of the Philosophy of Education Society.* Normal, IL: Philosophy of Education Society, 286–299.

Bray, R. L. (1991, November 17). Taking sides against ourselves. *The New York Times Magazine,* 56, 94, 95, 101.

Britton, J. (1982). Shaping at the point of utterance. In G.M. Pradl (Ed.), *Prospect and retrospect: Selected essays of James Britton.* Portsmouth, NH: Boynton/Cook.

———. (1984). Viewpoints: The distinction between participant and spectator role language in research and practice. *Research in the Teaching of English, 18,* 320–331.

Brossard, N. (1991). December 6, 1989 among the centuries. In L. Mallette & M. Chalough (Eds.), *The Montreal massacre.* M. Wildman, Trans.). Charlottetown, PEI: Gynergy Books.

Brown, W. (1991). Deregulating women: The trials of freedom under a thousand points of light. *Sub/versions—Feminist Studies—Work-in-Progress.* Santa Cruz, CA: University of California. March 24, 1985.

Bruffee, K. (1984). Collaborative learning and "The Conversation of Mankind." *College English, 46,* 635–652.

Buchanan, R. (1985). Unpublished position paper on Margaret Laurence's *The diviners,* presented by the Peterborough County Board of Education English Department Heads, March 24, 1985.

Burgess, T. (1989). Liberal ironists and English teachers: The philosophy of Richard Rorty. *English in Education, 23* (3), 1–11.

Burke, E. (1968). *A philosophical enquiry into the origin of our ideas of the sublime and beautiful.* (J.T. Boulton, Ed.). Notre Dame, IN: University of Notre Dame Press.

Burress, L. & Jenkinson, E.B. (1982) The students' right to know. Urbana, IL: NCTE.

Butler, J. (1990a). The force of fantasy: Feminism, Mapplethorpe, and discursive excess. *differences: A Journal of Feminist Cultural Studies, 2* (2), 105–125.

———. (1990b). *Gender trouble: Feminism and the subversion of identity.* New York: Routledge.

Byatt, A.S. (1990). *Possession.* London: Bloomsbury Press.

Cain, W.E. (1991). The ethics of criticism: Does literature do any good? *College English, 53* (4), 467–476.

Cairn, W. (1984). *The crisis in criticism.* Baltimore, MD: Johns Hopkins University Press.

Campion-Smith, B. (1989, December 3). Many judges unaware of devastation sex attacks cause women. *The Toronto Star,* B13.

Canadian Broadcasting Company. (1989). The great teacher: Northrop Frye. December 25. Directed and produced by H. Rasky.

Caplan, G. (1991, December 8). Beneath white ribbons men's power trip goes on. *The Toronto Star,* B3.

Cavarnos, C. (1972). *Plato's theory of fine art.* New York: Astir Publishing Co.

Cavarnos, C. (1977). Fine art as therapy according to Plato. *Philosophia, 7* (Athens), 266–288.

Chereb, S. (1990, July 16). Album sparked suicide pact, court told. *The Globe and Mail,* C4.

Chester, G. & Dickey, J. (Eds.). (1988). *Feminism and censorship: The current debate.* Bridport, Dorset, Great Britain: Prism Press. Distributed in the USA by Avery Publishing Group, New York.

Christian, B. (1987). The race for theory. *Cultural Critique,* 6, 51–63.

City of tears to bury dead at Notre Dame. (1989, December 9). *The Toronto Star,* A13.

Cleroux, R. & McInnes, C. (1989, December 8). Opposition MPs demand long-promised gun control amendments. *The Globe and Mail,* A13.

Collingwood, R.G. (1925). Plato's philosophy of art. *Mind,* n.s., 34, 154–172.

Connell, D. (1977). *Sir Philip Sidney: The maker's mind.* Oxford: Clarendon Press.

Cook, N. (1989). *A guide to musical analysis.* London: J.M. Dent & Sons.

Cornford, F.M. (Ed.). (1941/1945/1975). *The Republic of Plato.* London: Oxford University Press, Oxford University Press Paperback.

Corrigan, P. (1989). *Why are Muslims treated differently? A commentary on the so-called "Rushdie affair" and ethnic nationalism.* Unpublished paper to 'OPEN SEMINARS' Centre for Research in Ethnic Relations, University of Warwick, Coventry, England.

Cudjoe, S.R. (Ed.). (1989). The world, the text, and the jug: Salman Rushdie and his verses. *Salman Rushdie and his verses: A discussion at Wellesley College.* Wellesley, MA: Calaloux Publications.

Czarnecki, M. (1985, October). Margaret Laurence and the book banners. *Chatelaine,* 55, 186–191.

D'Angelo, F.J. (1982). Luria on literacy: The cognitive consequences of reading and writing. In J.C. Raymond (Ed.), *Literacy as a human problem.* University, AL: University of Alabama Press.

Davis, J.E. (Ed.). (1979). *Dealing with censorship.* Urbana, IL: NCTE.

Dead Poets Society [Film]. (1989). S. Hart, T. Thomas, & P. J. Witt (Producers), & P. Weir (Director). USA: Touchstone Pictures, in association with Silver Street Partners.

de la Cour, L., Dubinsky, K., Forestell, N., Kelm, M.E., Marks, L., & Morgan, C. (1990). "'Here's where we separate the men from the boys': Comments on women's experiences as students in graduate history programmes in Canada." Paper presented jointly to the Canadian Women's Studies Association and the Canadian Historical Association, University of Victoria, BC, May 26–29, 1990.

de Lauretis, T. (1984). *Alice doesn't: Feminism, semiotics, cinema.* Bloomington, IN: Indiana University Press.

———. (1986). Feminist studies/critical studies: Issues, terms, context. In T. de Lauretis (Ed.), *Feminist studies/critical studies.* Bloomington, IN: University Press.

———. (1987). *Technologies of gender: Essays on theory, film, and fiction.* Bloomington, IN: University Press.

———. (1990). Eccentric subjects: Feminist theory and historical consciousness, *Feminist Studies, 16* (1), 115–150.

de Man, P. (1983). Criticism and crisis. In P. de Man, *Blindness and insight: Essays in the rhetoric of contemporary criticism.* 2nd edition, revised. (W. Godzich, Intro. & Ed.). *Theory and History of Literature, Volume 7.* W. Godzich & J. Schulte-Sasse. (Gen. Eds.) Minneapolis, MN: University of Minnesota Press.

Denham, R.D. (1978). *Northrop Frye and critical method.* University Park, PA & London: The Pennsylvania State University Press.

———. (1991). The religious basis of Northrop Frye's liberally educated imagination. Unpublished paper presented to the International Convention on Innovation in Higher Education, Budapest, Hungary, June, 1991.

Derrida, J. (1981). *Dissemination.* (B. Johnson, Trans. and Intro.). Chicago: University of Chicago Press.

de Sousa, R. (1987). *The rationality of emotion.* Cambridge, MA & London: MIT Press.

Diamond, A. & Edwards, L.R. (Eds.). (1977/1988). *The authority of experience: Essays in feminist criticism.* Amherst, MA: University of Massachusetts Press.

Diehl, J.F. (1990). *Women poets and the American sublime.* Bloomington & Indianapolis, IN: Indiana University Press.

Dixon, J. (1985). Teaching English 1984. In S.N. Tchudi (Ed.), *Language, schooling, and society.* Portsmouth, NH: Boynton/Cook.

Dixon J., Stratta, L., & Wilkinson, A. (1973). *Patterns of language: Explorations of the teaching of English.* London: Heinemann.

Donovan, J. (Ed.). (1975). *Feminist literary theory: Explorations in theory.* Lexington, KY: University of Kentucky Press.

Doran, M. (1964). *Endeavors of art: A study of form in Elizabethan drama.* Madison, WI: University of Wisconsin Press.

Dorter, K. (1973). The Ion: Plato's characterization of art. *Journal of Aesthetics and Art Criticism, 32,* 65–78.

D'Souza, D. (1991). *Illiberal education: The politics of race and sex on campus.* New York: Free Press; Toronto: Collier Macmillan.

Durrant, C., Goodwin, L., & Watson, K. (1990). Encouraging young readers to reflect on their processes of response: Can it be done, is it worth doing? *English Education, 22* (4), 211–219.

Eagleton, T. (1983). *Literary theory: An introduction.* Oxford: Blackwell.

———. (1990). *The ideology of the aesthetic.* Oxford: Blackwell.

Early, M. J. (1960). Stages of growth in literary appreciation. *English Journal, 49,* 161–167. Reprinted in D. W. Burton & J.S. Simmons (Eds.). (1965/1970). *Teaching English in today's high schools.* New York: Holt, Rinehart and Winston.

Ecker, G. (Ed.). (1985). *Feminist aesthetics.* (H. Anderson, Trans.). London: Women's Press.

———. (1988). Anger and play: Strategies of feminist writing. Unpublished paper presented at the Symposium, "Women writing across borders," The Ontario Institute for Studies in Education, Toronto, June 20, 1988.

Edelstein, L. (1949). The function of the myth in Plato's philosophy. *Journal of the History of Ideas, 10,* 463–481.

*Educating Rita* [Film]. (1983). L. Gilbert (Director and Producer) & W.R. Cartlidge (Co-producer). Great Britain: Columbia Pictures, Acorn Production.

Eldridge, R. (1989). *On moral personhood: Philosophy, literature, criticism, and self-understanding.* Chicago: University of Chicago Press.

Eliot, T.S. (1975). The metaphysical poets. In F. Kermode (Ed.), *Selected prose of T.S. Eliot.* London: Faber and Faber.

Ellis, J. (1974). *The theory of literary criticism: A logical analysis.* Berkeley, CA: University of California Press.

———. (1989). *Against deconstruction.* Princeton, NJ: Princeton University Press.

Ellsworth, E. (1989). Why doesn't this feel empowering? Working through the repressive myths of critical pedagogy. *Harvard Educational Review, 59* (3), 297–324.

Evans, M.N. (1989). Hysteria and the seduction of theory. In D. Hunter (Ed.), *Seduction and theory: Readings of gender, represention, and rhetoric.* Urbana & Chicago: University of Illinois Press.

Falck, C. (1989). *Myth, truth and literature: Towards a true post-modernism.* Cambridge, England: Cambridge University Press.

Fanon, F. (1970). *Black skin white masks*. London: Paladin.

Fausto-Sterling, A. (1985). *Myths of gender: Biological theories about women and men*. New York: Basic Books.

Felman, S. (1982). Psychoanalysis and education: Teaching the terminable and interminable. *Yale French Studies, 63*, 21–44.

Felperin, H. (1985). *Beyond deconstruction: The uses and abuses of literary theory*. Oxford: Clarendon Press.

Felski, R. (1989). *Beyond feminist aesthetics: Feminist literature and social change*. Cambridge, MA: Harvard University Press.

Ferguson, M. (1979). Sidney's *Defence of Poetry*: A retrial. *boundary 2, 7*(2), 72–75.

Fetterley, J. (1978). *The resisting reader: A feminist approach to American fiction*. Bloomington, IN: Indiana University Press.

Fine, E. (1989). Collaborative writing: Key to unlocking the silences of children. *Language Arts, 66* (5), 501–508.

Fine, S. (1991, December 4). Male abuse victims want to talk. *The Globe and Mail*, A1, A11.

Fischer, M. (1985). *Does deconstruction make any difference? Post-structuralism and the defense of poetry in modern criticism*. Bloomington, IN: Indiana University Press.

Fish, S. (1980). *Is there a text in this class? The authority of interpretative communities*. Cambridge, MA: Harvard University Press.

Foot, P. (1972). Morality as a system of hypothetical imperatives. *The Philosophical Review, 81*, 305–316.

Foucault, M. (1982). The subject and power. *Critical Inquiry, 8*, 777–795.

———. (1986). *The use of pleasure*. (R. Harley, Trans.). New York: Vintage.

Fraser, M.B. (1991, October 17). Great TV, but what's the theme? *The Globe and Mail*, A23.

French, O. (1990, March 1). Pacific rim curriculum offered: East York responding to immigrant flux. *The Globe and Mail*, A9.

Frye, N. (1947). *Fearful symmetry: A study of William Blake*. Princeton, NJ: Princeton University Press.

———. (1949). The function of criticism at the present time. *University of Toronto Quarterly, 19*, 1–16.

———. (1957). *Anatomy of criticism: Four essays*. Princeton, NJ: Princeton University Press.

———. (1963a). *The educated imagination*. The Massey Lectures. Toronto: CBC Publications.

———. (1963b). *Fables of identity: Studies in poetic mythology*. New York and London: Harcourt, Brace, Jovanovich.

———. (1963c). *The well-tempered critic*. Bloomington, IN: Indiana University Press.

————. (1965a). *A natural perspective: The development of Shakespearian comedy and romance.* New York: Harcourt, Brace and World, Inc.

————. (1965b). *The return of Eden: Five essays on Milton's epics.* Toronto & Buffalo, NY: University of Toronto Press.

————. (1966). Reflections in a mirror. In M. Krieger (Ed.), *Northrop Frye in modern criticism.* New York: Columbia University Press.

————. (1967). *The modern century.* Toronto: Oxford University Press.

————. (1968). *A study of English romanticism.* (Studies in language and literature). NY: Random House.

————. (1970). *The stubborn structure: Essays on criticism and society.* London: Methuen.

————. (1971). *The bush garden: Essays on the Canadian imagination.* Toronto: Anansi.

————. (1971/1973). *The critical path: An essay on the social context of literary criticism.* Bloomington, IN: & London: Indiana University Press.

————. (1972). *On teaching literature.* New York: Harcourt, Brace, Jovanovich.

————. (1976a). *The secular scripture: A study of the structure of romance.* Cambridge, MA: Harvard University Press.

————. (1976b). *Spiritus mundi.* Bloomington, IN & London: Indiana University Press.

————. (1980). *Creation and recreation.* Toronto, Buffalo, & London: University of Toronto Press.

————. (1982a). *Divisions on a ground: Essays on Canadian culture.* (J. Polk, Ed.). Toronto: Anansi.

————. (1982b). *The great code: The Bible and literature.* Toronto: Academic Press Canada.

————. (1983). Preface. In *The myth of deliverance: Reflections on Shakespeare's problem comedies.* Toronto: University of Toronto.

————. (1988). *On education.* Markham, ON: Fitzhenry & Whiteside.

————. (1989/1991). Literature as therapy. The Chris Moranis Lecture on Science and Culture, presented at Mount Sinai Hospital, November 23, 1989. Transcribed from a tape provided by John Roder. Reprinted in the *Northrop Frye Newsletter, 3* (2), 23–32.

————. (1990a). The dialectic of belief and vision. In R.D. Denham (Ed.), *Northrop Frye: Myth and metaphor, selected essays, 1974–1988.* Charlottesville, VA & London: University Press of Virginia.

————. (1990b). Expanding world of metaphor. In R.D. Denham (Ed.), *Northrop Frye: Myth and metaphor, selected essays, 1974–1988.* Charlottesville, VA & London: University Press of Virginia.

————. (1990c). The journey as metaphor. In R.D. Denham (Ed.), *Northrop Frye: Myth and metaphor, selected essays, 1974–1988.* Charlottesville, VA & London: University Press of Virginia.

———. (1990d). Literature as a critique of pure reason. In R.D. Denham (Ed.), *Northrop Frye: Myth and metaphor, selected essays, 1974–1988*. Charlottesville, VA & London: University Press of Virginia.

———. (1990e). *Words with power: Being a second study of 'the Bible and literature.'* Harmondsworth, England: Penguin.

———. (1991a). *The double vision: Language and meaning in religion*. Toronto: University of Toronto Press.

———. (1991b, April 15). Northrop Frye's Canada. Address presented to the Social Sciences and Humanities Research Council of Canada. *The Globe and Mail*, A13.

Fulford, R. (1989). *Literature and literacy: The future of English studies*. Jackson Lecture 1989. Toronto: The Ontario Institute for Studies in Education.

Gallop, J. (1982). *The daughter's seduction: Feminism and psychoanalysis*. Ithaca, NY: Cornell University Press.

Galt, V. (1991, December 4). 48% in poll say victims invite sexual harrassment. *The Globe and Mail*, A11.

Gambell, T.J. (1986). Response to literature [Special Issue]. *English Quarterly, 19* (2), 83–176.

Gilbert, A. (1939). Did Plato banish the poets or the critics? *Studies in Philology, 36*, 1–19.

Gilbert, S.M. & Gubar, S. (Eds.). (1977). *The Norton anthology of literature by women: The tradition in English*. New York: Norton.

———. (1979). *The madwoman in the attic: The woman writer and the nineteenth-century literary imagination*. New Haven, CT: Yale University Press.

Giroux, H.A. (1988). *Schooling for democracy: Critical pedagogy in the modern age*. London: Routledge.

Giroux, H.A., Simon, R.I., & Contributors. (1989). *Popular culture, schooling and everyday life*. Foreword by H.A. Giroux and P. Friere. Granby, MA: Bergin & Garvey.

Godzich, W. (1983). Introduction: Caution! Reader at work! In P. deMan, *Blindness and insight: Essays in the rhetoric of contemporary criticism*, 2nd edition, revised. (W. Godzick, Ed.). *Theory and History of Literature, Volume 7*. W. Godzich & J. Schulte-Sasse. (Gen. Eds.). Minneapolis, MN: University of Minnesota Press.

Gold, J. (1990). *Read for your life: Literature as a life support system*. Markham, ON: Fitzhenry & Whiteside.

Golding, W. (1954/1959). *Lord of the flies*. New York: Capricorn Books.

Goleman, D. (1991, October 26). Harrassment: Not about sex, but power. (New York Times Service) *The Globe and Mail*, D10.

Graff, G. (1979). *Literature against itself*. Chicago: University of Chicago Press.

———. (1987). *Professing literature: An institutional history.* Chicago & London: University of Chicago Press.

Graham, B. (1990). Only men can stop violence against women: From the President. *OCUFA Forum: (The Ontario Confederation of University Faculty Associations), 6* (9), 2–3.

Gramsci, A. (1971). *Selections from the prison notebooks.* London: Laurence.

*(The) Great Teacher: Northrop Frye* [Film/Video]. (1989). H. Rasky (Director & Producer). Canada: Canadian Broadcasting Company. First broadcast, December 25, 1989.

Greene, M. (1986). Toward possibility: Expanding the range of literacy. *English Education, 18,* 231–243.

———. (1990a). Multiple voices and multiple realities: A re-viewing of educational foundations. *Educational Foundations, 4* (2), 5–19.

———. (1990b). The passion of the possible: Choice, multiplicity, and commitment. Second Annual Lawrence Kohlberg Memorial Lecture. *The Journal of Moral Education, 19* (2), 67–76.

Greer, G. (1981). *The obstacle race: The fortunes of women painters and their work.* London: Pan Books.

Gribble, J. (1983). *Literary education: A revaluation.* Cambridge, England: Cambridge University Press.

Griffith, P. (1987). *Literary theory and English teaching.* Philadelphia, PA & Milton Keynes, England. Open University Press.

Grumet, M. (1988). *Bitter milk: Women and teaching.* Amherst, MA: University of Massachusetts Press.

Gutteridge, D. (1988). *Truth and consequences: Principles for selecting literature in grades 7–12.* Unpublished manuscript.

Hall, R.W. (1990). Art and morality. *The Journal of Aesthetic Education, 24* (3), 5–13.

Hall, S. (Ed. with J. Ramsey). (1986). *Approaches to teaching Wordsworth's poetry.* New York: The Modern Language Association of America.

Hamilton, A.C. (1990). *Northrop Frye: Anatomy of his criticism.* Toronto, Buffalo, New York, & London: University of Toronto Press.

Hamilton, E. & Cairns, H. (Eds.). (1961/1980). *Plato: The collected dialogues, including the letters.* (L. Cooper, Trans.). Bollingen Series LXXI. Princeton, NJ: Princeton University Press.

Haraway, D. (1988). Situated knowledges: The science question in feminism and the privilege of partial perspective. *Feminist Studies, 14* (3), 575–600.

Harper, T. (1989, December 9). Minister resists call for fast bill on gun use. *The Toronto Star,* A12.

Havelock, E.A. (1963). *A history of the Greek mind, volume one: Preface to Plato.* Cambridge, MA: Belknop Press of Harvard University Press.

———. (1986). *The muse learns to write: Relections on orality and literary from antiquity to the present.* New Haven, CT: Yale University Press.

Hawkes, T. (1977). *Structuralism and semiotics.* Berkeley, CA: University of California Press.

Hayhoe, M. & Parker, S. (Eds.). (1990). *Reading and response.* English, Language, and Education Series. (A. Adams, Gen. Ed.). Buckingham, England: Open University Press.

Hearn, J. (1986, August 4). Letter to the editor. *The Globe and Mail*, A6.

Heath, S. (1983). *Ways with words: Language, life, and work in communities and classrooms.* Cambridge, England: Cambridge University Press.

———. (1990). The fourth vision: Literate language at work. In A. Lunsford, H. Moglen & J. Slevin (Eds.), *The right to literacy.* New York: The Modern Language Association of America.

Heidegger, M. (1971). *What are poets for? Poetry, language, thought.* (A. Hofstadter, Trans.). New York: Harper & Row.

Heintzman, R. (1978). Liberalism and censorship. *Journal of Canadian Studies, 13* (4), 1–2, 120–122.

Heninger, J. K. (1983). Sidney & Serranus' *Plato. English Literary Renaissance, 13* (2), 146–161.

Henley, D. & Young, J. (Eds.), (1990). *Canadian perspectives on critical pedagogy.* Canadian Critical Pedagogy Network, Occasional Monograph, No. 1. Winnipeg: The University of Manitoba Printers.

Herman, E.S., & Chomsky, N. (1988). *Manufacturing consent: The political economy of the mass media.* New York: Pantheon.

Hirsch, E.D. (1987). *Cultural literacy: What every American needs to know.* Boston: Houghton Mifflin Co.

Hobbs, M. (1987). The perils of 'unbridled masculinity': Pacifist elements in the feminist and socialist thought of Charlotte Perkins Gilman. In R.R. Pierson (Ed.), *Women and peace: Theoretical, historical and practical perspectives.* London: Croom Helm.

Homans, M. (1980). *Women writers and poetic identity: Dorothy Wordsworth, Emily Brontë, and Emily Dickinson.* Princeton, NJ: Princeton University Press.

———. (1986). Building refuges: Dorothy Wordsworth's poetics of the image. In M. Homans, *Bearing the word: Language and female experience in nineteenth-century women's writing.* Chicago: University of Chicago Press.

Hooks, B. (1990). *Yearning: race, gender, and cultural politics.* Toronto: Between the Lines.

Hossie, L. (1991, October 16). Men often deny harassment charges: Inquiries face common dilemma. *The Globe and Mail*, A8.

Hunt, R. (1983). Literature is reading is writing. *Inkshed: Newsletter of the Canadian Association for the Study of Reading Writing, 2* (6), 5–8.

Hunt R. & Vipond, D. (1984). *The reader, the text, the situation: Blocks and affordances in literary reading.* Unpublished manuscript.

Hutcheon, L. (1988). *A poetics of postmodernism: History, theory, fiction.* New York & London: Routledge, Chapman & Hall.

————. (1989). *The politics of postmodernism.* London & New York: Routledge.

Hynds, S. (1989). Bringing life to literature and literature to life: Social constructs and contexts of four adolescent readers. *Research in the Teaching of English, 23,* 30–612.

————. (1990). Reading as a social event: Comprehension and response in the text, classroom and world. In D. Bogdan & S. Straw (Eds.), *Beyond communication: Reading comprehension and criticism.* Portsmouth, NH: Boynton-Cook/Heinemann.

*In the fall.* [Film/Video]. (1984). D. Brinton (Executive Producer), S. Thomas (Producer), & A. Kroeker (Director). Canada: CKND Television with the assistance of the Canadian Film Development Corporation, Manitoba Dept. of Education, and the National Film Board, Prairie Region.

Iser, W. (1974). *The implied reader: Patterns of communication in prose fiction from Bunyan to Beckett.* Baltimore, MD: John Hopkins University Press.

Jacobsen, T. (1976). *The treasures of darkness: A history of Mesopotamian religion.* New Haven, CT & London: Yale University Press.

Jaeger, W. (1943/1969). *Paideia.* (G. Highet, Trans.). London: Oxford University Press.

Jameson, F. (1981). *The political unconscious: Narrative as a socially symbolic act.* Ithaca, NY: Cornell University Press.

Jauss, H.R. (1982). *Aesthetic experience and literary hermeneutics.* (M. Shaw, Trans.). Minneapolis, MN: University of Minnesota Press.

Jaynes, J. (1976). *The origin of consciousness in the breakdown of the bicameral mind.* Boston: Houghton Mifflin.

Jensen, J.M. (1989). *Stories to grow on: Demonstrations of language learning in K-8 classrooms.* Portsmouth, NH: Heinemann.

Jowett, B. (Ed. & Trans.). (1892). The dialogues of Plato. 5 vols. Vols I & III: *Symposium, Ion,* and *Republic.* 3rd Ed. London, New York: Oxford University Press.

————. (Ed. & Trans.). (1955). *The dialogues of Plato.* (J.D. Kaplan, Ed. & Intro). New York: Pocket Books.

Kahane, C. (1989). Seduction and the voice of the text: *Heart of darkness* and *The good soldier.* In D. Hunter (Ed.), *Seduction and theory: Readings of gender, representation, and rhetoric.* Urbana, IL & Chicago: University of Illinois Press.

Kappeler, S. (1986). *The pornography of representation.* Minneapolis, MN: University of Minnesota Press.

Karolides, N. J. & Burress, L. (Eds.). (1985). *Celebrating censored books*. Urbana, IL: NCTE.

Kastner, S. (1990, September 9). Has sexism crept into your home? *The Toronto Star*, D1, D2.

Kauffman, M. & Sluser, R. (1991). *The white ribbon campaign: Breaking men's silence to end men's violence, December 1-6, 1991*. Pamphlet. Toronto, ON.

Kearney, R. (1988). *The wake of imagination: Toward a postmodern culture*. Minneapolis, MN: University of Minnesota Press.

Kermode, F. (1979). *The genesis of secrecy: The interpretation of narrative*. Cambridge, MA: Harvard University Press.

———. (1985). *Forms of attention*. The Wellek Library Lectures at the University of California, Irvine. (F. Lentricchia, Series Ed.). Chicago: University of Chicago Press.

Kirp, D.L. (1991, February 24). The battle of the books. *Image. San Francisco Examiner*, 17–25.

Kolodny, A. (1985a). Dancing through the minefield: Some observations on the theory, practice, and politics of a feminist literary criticism. In E. Showalter (Ed.), *The new feminist criticism: Essays on women, literature, and theory*. New York: Pantheon.

———. (1985b). A map for re-reading: Gender and the interpretation of literary texts. In E. Showalter (Ed.), *The new feminist criticism: Essays on women, literature, and theory*. New York: Pantheon.

Krieger, M. (1956). *The new apologists for poetry*. Minneapolis, MN: The University of Minnesota Press.

———. (1966). Northrop Frye and contemporary criticism: Ariel and the spirit of gravity. In M. Krieger (Ed.), *Northrop Frye and modern criticism: Selected poems from the English Institute*. New York: Columbia University Press.

Kristeva, J. (1977/1980). *Desire in language: A semiotic approach to literature and art*. (L. S. Roudiez, Ed. & Trans., T. Gora & A. Jardine, Trans.). New York: Columbia University Press. *Polylogue* Copyright, 1977, Editions du Seuil.

———. (1982). *Powers of horror: An essay in abjection*. (L. S. Roudiez, Trans.). Oxford: Blackwell.

———. (1986a). Stabat mater. In T. Moi (Ed.), *The Kristeva reader: Julia Kristeva*. Oxford: Blackwell.

———. (1986b). Women's time. In T. Moi (Ed.), *The Kristeva reader: Julia Kristeva*. Oxford: Blackwell.

———. (1986c). Word, dialogue, and novel. In T. Moi (Ed.), *The Kristeva reader: Julia Kristeva*. Oxford: Blackwell.

La Brecque, R. (1990). Liberal education in an unfree world. *Educational Theory*, 40 (4), 483–494.

Landsberg, M. (1986, July 26). Schoolyard pain outweighs value of teaching some classics. *The Globe and Mail*, A2.

Langer, S. K. (1942/1982).*Philosophy in a new key: A study in the symbolism of reason, rite, and art.* (3d Ed.). Cambridge, MA: Harvard University Press.

———. (1953). *Feeling and form: A theory of art developed from 'Philosophy in a new key.'* New York: Charles Scribner's Sons.

Lather, P. (1991). *Getting smart: Feminist research and pedagogy with/in the postmodern.* New York: Routledge.

Laurence, M. (1964). *The stone angel.* Toronto: McClelland & Stewart.

———. (1966). *A. Jest of God.* Toronto: McClelland & Stewart.

———. (1974). *The diviners.* Toronto McClelland & Stewart.

———. Letter to the *Peterborough Examiner*, April 26, 1985; Reprinted in *An anti-censorship kit* prepared by The Book and Periodical Development Council for its annual "Freedom to Read Week," Toronto, ON, October 19–26, 1986.

Leavitt, D. (1990, August 19). Fears that haunt a scrubbed America. *The New York Times*, Section 2H, 1, 27.

Leeies, R. D. (1986, August 4). Letter to the editor. *The Globe and Mail*, Toronto, A6.

Levin, H. T. (1958). *Contexts of criticism.* Cambridge, MA: Harvard University Press.

Levin, S. (1987). *Dorothy Wordsworth and romanticism.* New Brunswick, NJ: Rutgers University Press.

Levine, K. (1986). *The social context of literacy.* London: Routledge and Kegan Paul.

Lewis, C. S. (1954). *English literature in the sixteenth century, excluding drama.* Oxford: Clarendon Press.

Lipking, L. (1983/1984). Aristotle's sister: The poetics of abandonment. In R. von Hallberg. (Ed.), *Canons.* Chicago: Chicago University Press.

Liptrot, B. (1986). In with the new. *indirections*, 11 (2), 55–59.

Livingstone, D.W. & Contributors. (1987). *Critical pedagogy and cultural power.* (H.A. Giroux & P. Friere, Intro.). Toronto: Garamond Press.

Longinus: (1965). On the sublime. In T.S. Dorsch (Ed.), *Aristotle, Horace, Longinus: Classical literary criticism.* Harmondsworth, England: Penguin, 99–158.

Lyotard, J. (1979/1989). *The postmodern condition: A report on knowledge.* (G. Bennington & B. Massumi, Trans.). (F. Jameson, Foreword). *Theory and History of Literature, Vol. 10.* W. Godzich and J. Schulte-Sasse. (Gen. Eds.). Minneapolis, MN: University of Minnesota Press.

Macherey, P. (1978). *A theory of literary production.* (G. Wall, Trans.). London: Routledge & Kegan Paul.

MacKenzie, C. (1991, October 16). Thomas squeaks by in senate: Judge confirmed for seat on U.S. supreme court. *The Globe and Mail*, A1.

MacLeod, A. (1976). In the fall. In A. MacLeod, *The lost salt gift of blood*. Toronto: McClelland & Stewart.

Mahowald, M. B. (Ed.). (1983). *Philosophy of woman: An anthology of classic and current concepts*. (2nd ed.). Indianapolis, IN: Hackett.

Malette, L. & Chalough, M. (Eds.). (1991). *The Montreal massacre*. (M. Wildeman, Trans.). Charlottetown, PEI: Gynergy Books.

Martin, J.R. (1981). The ideal of the educated person. *Educational Theory, 31* (2), 97–109.

Martindale, K. (1987). On the ethics of 'voice' in feminist literary criticism. *Resources for Feminist Research/Documentation sur la rechereche feministe, 16* (3), 16–19.

Mascoll, P. (1991, February 19). Man pleads guilty to killing wife: Former auxiliary RCMP officer shot woman, mutilated body. *The Toronto Star*, A8.

McAuley, E.P. (1985). Rationale for teaching *The catcher in the rye*. Unpublished manuscript prepared for the Textbook Review Committee of the Peterborough County Board of Education, March 1986.

McCarthy, T. (1989/90). The politics of the ineffable: Derrida's deconstructionism. *The Philosophical Forum, 12* (1–2), 146–168.

McClary, S. (1989). The blasphemy of talking politics during Bach year. In R. Leppert & S. McClary (Eds.), *Music and society: The politics of composition, performance and reception*. Cambridge, England, New York & Melbourne: Cambridge University Press.

McIntosh, M.M. (1988). Feeling like a fraud. R. Freeman Butts Lecture, delivered at the conference of the American Educational Studies Association, Toronto. November 4, 1988.

McKeon, R. (1936). Literary criticism and the concept of imitation in antiquity. *Modern Philology, 34* (1), 1–35.

McKracken, G. (1991, December 16). A call to arms for women? *The Globe and Mail*, A16.

McMurtry, J. (1989). *A case against censorship in literature education: The 1976 and 1985 school text controversies in the county of Peterborough, Ontario*. Unpublished doctoral dissertation, University of Toronto.

Medway P. & Stibbs, A. (1990). Safety and danger: encounters with literature of a second kind. In M. Hayhoe & S. Parker (Eds.), *Reading and response*. Buckingham, England: Open University Press.

Meek, M. (1990). Why response? In M. Hayhoe & S. Parker (Eds.), *Reading and response*. Buckingham, England: Open University Press.

Meek, M. (1991). *On being literate*. London: The Bodley Head.

Meese, E. (1986). *Crossing the double-cross: The practice of feminist criticism*. Chapel Hill, NC: University of North Carolina Press.

Mellor, A. K. (Ed.). (1988). *Romanticism and feminism.* Bloomington and Indianapolis, IN: Indiana University Press.

Meynell, H. (1990). The justification of 'English.' *The Journal of Aesthetic Education, 24* (4), 5–15.

Miall, D.S. (in press). Constructing the self: Emotion and literary response. In S. Straw & D. Bogdan (Eds.), *Constructive reading: Teaching beyond communication.* Portsmouth, NH: Boyton-Cook/Heinemann.

Miles, S. (1986). (Ed. and Intro.). *Simone Weil: An anthology.* London: Virago.

Miller, J. (Ed.). (1984). *Eccentric propositions: Essays on literature and the curriculum.* London: Routledge.

Miller, J. (1990). *Seductions: Studies in reading and culture.* London: Virago.

Minter, M. (1991, April). Letter to the editor. *off our backs: A women's newsjournal, 12* (4), 26.

Mitchell, A. (1991, October 16). Harassment still hidden issue: Employers' awareness of problem low, legal experts say, *The Globe and Mail*, A8.

Moffett, J. (1988). *Storm in the mountains: A case study of censorship, conflict, and consciousness.* Carbondale & Edwardsville, IL: Southern Illinois University Press.

————. (1990). Ways of teaching literature. In D. Bogdan & S. Straw (Eds.), *Beyond communication: Reading comprehension and criticism.* Portsmouth, NH: Boyton-Cook/Heinemann.

Moffett, J. (Ed.). (1973). *Interaction, a student-centred language arts and reading program, K-1.* Boston: Houghton Mifflin.

Moi, T. (1985). *Sexual/textual politics: Feminist literary theory.* London: Methuen.

Moi, T. (Ed.). (1986). *The Kristeva reader: Julia Kristeva.* Oxford: Blackwell.

Montefiore, J. (1987). *Feminism and poetry: Language, experience, identity in women's writing.* London: Pandora.

Moorhouse, A. (1989). *Art, sight and language: A reading/writing of some contemporary Canadian art.* Kapuskasing, ON: Penumbra Press.

Morgan, Robert. (1987). *English studies as cultural production in Ontario, 1860–1920.* Unpublished doctoral dissertation, University of Toronto.

————. (1990). The 'Englishness' of English teaching. In I. Goodson & P. Medway (Eds.), *Bringing English to order.* London: Falmer Press.

Morgan, Robin. (1989). *The demon lover: On the sexuality of terrorism.* New York & London: W.W. Norton.

Morrison, T. (1987). *Beloved.* New York: Alfred A. Knopf.

Mouré, E. (1989). Watching the watchwords. *Books in Canada,* November, 3, 4.

Mullin, D.F. (Ed.). (1990). *Third text: Third world perspectives on contemporary art and culture. Beyond the Rushdie affair.* (Special issue), vol. 11.

Murdoch, I. (1977). *The fire and the sun: Why Plato banished the artists: Based upon the romanes lecture 1976*. London: Oxford University Press.

*Music Box* [Film]. (1989). I. Winker (Producer), & C. Costa-Gavras (Director). USA: Carolso Pictures.

Nabokov, V. (1980). Good readers and good writers. In V. Nabokov, *Lectures and literature*. New York & London: Harcourt Brace Jovanovich.

Narayan, U. (1988). Working together across difference: Some considerations on emotions and political practice. *Hypatia, 3* (2), 31–47.

Nawawi, A. M. (1989). Infuriating and tragic verses. In S.R. Cudjoe (Ed.), *Salman Rushdie and his verses: A discussion at Wellesley College*. Wellseley, MA: Calaloux Publications.

Nell, V. (1988). *Lost in a book: The psychology of reading for pleasure*. New Haven, CT & London: Yale University Press.

Nelms, B. & Zancanella, D. (1990). The experience of literature and the study of literature: The teacher-educator's experience. In M. Hayhoe & S. Parker (Eds.), *Reading and response*. Buckingham, England: Open University Press.

Nelson, C. (Ed.). (1986). *Theory in the classrooom*. Urbana, IL: University of Illinois Press.

Nussbaum, M.C. (1985). 'Finely aware and richly responsible': Moral attention and the moral task of literature. *Journal of Philosophy, 82*: 516–529.

––––––. (1986). *The fragility of goodness: Luck and ethics in Greek tragedy and philosophy*. Cambridge, England: Cambridge University Press.

––––––. Nussbaum, M.C. (1990). *Love's knowledge*. New York: Oxford University Press.

Oakley, A. (1981). *Subject women*. New York: Pantheon.

*Off our backs: A women's newsjournal*. (1991, February). *12* (2).

O'Hear, P. & White, J. (1991). A national curriculum for all: Laying the foundations for success. London: Institute for Public Policy Research.

Olsen, S.H. (1978). *The structure of literary understanding*. Cambridge, England: Cambridge University Press.

Ong, W.J. (1988). Some psychodynamics of orality. In E. R. Kintgen, B.M. Kroll & M. Rose, (Eds.), *Perspectives on literacy*. Carbondale & Edwardsville, IL: Southern Illinois University Press.

Ontario Ministry of Education. (1977). *English curriculum guideline for the senior division*. Toronto: Ontario Ministry of Education.

––––––. (1987). *English curriculum guideline for the intermediate and senior divisions (grades 7–12)*. Toronto: Ontario Ministry of Education.

Otto, R. (1950/1968). *The idea of the holy*. (2nd Ed.). (J.W. Harvey, Trans.). London: Oxford University Press Paperback. (Original work published in 1923).

Ozick, C. (1980, May 26). The Shawl. *New Yorker, 56*, 33–34.

Partee, M.H. (1972). Plato's theory of language. *Foundations of Language, 8,* 113–132.

———. (1981). *Plato's poetics: The authority of beauty.* Salt Lake City, UT: University of Utah Press.

Peacock, T.L. (1965). The four ages of poetry. In J.E. Jordan (Ed.), *A defence of poetry/The four ages of poetry: Shelley and Peacock.* Indianapolis & New York: The Bobbs-Merill Company, Inc. (Original work published in 1820).

Peart, P. (1989). A moral drama for our times must never be censored. *OCTE Newsletter, Directions,* Supplement to *indirections, 14* (2), 1–2.

Penley, C. (1986). Teaching in your sleep: Feminism and psychoanalysis. In C. Nelson (Ed.), *Theory in the classroom.* Urbana, IL: University of Illinois Press.

Peseroff, J. (1988, July/August). Adolescent. *Harvard Magazine, 50.*

Picard, A. (1991a, December 4). AIDS revelation shakes NHL: Woman patient told doctors she had sex with 50 players. *The Globe and Mail,* A1, A2.

———. (1991b, October 11). Fighting sexism proves profitable. *The Globe and Mail,* A5.

Picard, A. & Lalonde, M. (1990, September 26). Killings of women are 'routine'. *The Globe and Mail,* A1, A6.

Picard, A. & York, G. (1991, December 7). Women vow 'never again': Services, vigils mark second anniversary of murders in Montreal. *The Globe and Mail,* A1, A2.

Platiel, R. (1990, May 28). Defence wanted Finta juror disqualified over film visit. *The Globe and Mail,* A12.

Plato. (1961/1980). *Ion.* In E. Hamilton & H. Cairns (Eds. and Trans.), *Plato: The collected dialogues.* Princeton, NJ: Princeton University Press.

———. (1961/1980). *Protagorus.* In E. Hamilton & H. Cairns (Eds. and Trans.), *Plato: The collected dialogues.* Princeton, NJ: Princeton University Press.

———. (1961/1980). *Republic.* In E. Hamilton & H. Cairns (Eds. and Trans.), *Plato: The collected dialogues.* Princeton, NJ: Princeton University Press.

———. (1961/1980). *Symposium.* In E. Hamilton & H. Cairns (Eds. and Trans.), *Plato: The collected dialogues.* Princeton, NJ: Princeton University Press.

———. (1973). *Phaedrus.* In W. Hamilton (Ed. and Trans.), *Phaedrus and the seventh and eighth letters.* Harmondsworth, England: Penguin.

Poirier, R. (1971). *The performing self: Compositions and decompositions in the languages of contemporary life.* New York: Oxford University Press.

———. (1987). *The renewal of literature: Emersonian reflections.* New York: Random House.

Popper, K.R. (1945/1966). *The open society and its enemies.* (Vols. 1 & 2). London: Routledge & Kegan Paul.

Postman, N. (1985/1986). *Amusing ourselves to death: Public discourse in the age of showbusiness.* New York: Viking Penguin.

Postman, N. & Weingartner, C. (1961). *The soft revolution: A student hand-book for turning schools around.* New York: Dell Publishing Co.

Pradl, G. M. (Ed.). (1982). *Prospect and retrospect: Selected essays of James Britton.* Portsmouth, NH: Boynton-Cook/Heinemann.

Prentice, A. (1991). Bluestockings and other difficult truths: The early history of women's employment at the University of Toronto. Paper presented to the Canadian Historical Association, Queen's University, Kingston, ON, June, 1991.

Preventing violence against women: Ontario Launches programs to improve women's safety on campus. (1991). *OCUFA* 6 (29), 1.

Prickett, S. (1986). *Words and 'The Word': Language, poetics, and biblical interpretation.* Cambridge, England: Cambridge University Press.

Pritchard, D. (1984). The English myth. *OCTE Newsletter,* 4 (1), n.p.

Probst, R.E. (1988). *Response and analysis: Teaching literature in junior and senior high school.* Portsmouth, NH: Boynton-Cook.

Purves, A. (1991). The aesthetic mind of Louise Rosenblatt. In J. Clifford, (Ed.), *The experience of reading: Louise Rosenblatt and reader-response theory.* Portsmouth, NH: Boynton-Cook Heinemann.

Randall, J.H., Jr. (1970). *Plato: Dramatist of the life of reason.* New York: Columbia University Press.

Randall, M. (1989, December 12). "Men cannot know the feelings of fear": Yet an anti-feminist backlash has been intensified by the massacre in Montreal. *The Globe and Mail,* A7.

Rau, K. (1991, December 10). Survives brutal attack. Woman stabbed at U of T. *The Varsity,* University of Toronto, 2.

Reich, E. (1906). *Plato as an introduction to modern criticism of life.* London: Chapman & Hall.

Reither, J. (1989). Teaching reading and writing: Texts, power and the transfer of power: Or, what if they had a revolution and nobody came? *Inkshed: Newsletter of the Canadian Association for the Study of Reading Writing,* 8 (4), 3–13.

Renaissance Peterborough. (1977, February). Unpublished position paper on "Aspects of the teaching of English literature." Presented to the Peterborough County Board of Education.

Reynolds, J. (1990). Final term paper. Course 1484: Philosophy of Literature and Literature Education, December, 1990.

Rich, A. (1979). *On lies, secrets and silence: Selected prose, 1966–1978.* New York: Norton.

Richler, M. (1959). *The Apprenticeship of Duddy Kravitz.* Harmondsworth, England: Penguin.

————. (1990, June 29). The censoring of Duddy Kravitz. *The Globe and Mail*, C1.

Ricoeur, P. (1976). *Interpretation theory: Discourse and the surplus of meaning*. Fort Worth, TX: The Texas Christian University Press.

Rilke, R. M. (1989). *Letters to Merline (1919–1927)*. (J. Bower, Trans.). New York: Parson House.

Roberts, M. (1966). The pill and the cherries: Sidney and the neo-classical tradition. *Essays in Criticism*, 16 (22), 22–31.

Robinson, J. C. (1987). *Radical literary education: A classroom experiment with Wordworth's "Ode."* Madison, WI: University of Wisconsin Press.

Rorty, R. (1979). *Philosophy and the mirror of nature*. Princeton, NJ: Princeton University Press.

————. (1982). *Consequences of pragmatism*. Minneapolis, MN: University of Minnesota Press.

Rose, J. (1983). Femininity and its discontents. *Feminist Review*, 14, 5–21.

Rosenblatt, L. M. (1978). *The reader, the text, the poem: The transactional theory of literary work*. Carbondale, IL: Southern Illinois University Press.

————. (1985). Literature, language, and values. In S. N. Tchudi (Ed.), *Language, schooling, and society*. Upper Montclair, NJ: Boynton/Cook.

Rosenwald, L. (1989). Notes on the Ayatollah Khomeini's proclamation by a western liberal. In S. R. Cudjoe (Ed.), *Salman Rushdie and his verses: A discussion at Wellesley College*. Wellesley, MA: Calaloux Publications.

Ross, A. (1989). Baudrillard's bad attitude. In D. Hunter (Ed.), *Seduction and theory: Readings of gender, representation, and rhetoric*. Urbana & Chicago: University of Illinois Press.

Ross, M. (1988). Romantic quest and conquest: Troping masculine power in the crisis of poetic identity. In A. K. Mellor (Ed.), *Romanticism and feminism*. Bloomington, IN: Indiana University Press.

Ross, S. (1971). The painted door. In A. Lucas (Ed.), *Great Canadian short stories*. New York: Dell.

Rushdie, S. (1981). *Midnight's children*. London: Picador.

————. (1989). *The Satanic verses*. New York: Viking.

————. (1990a). *Haroun and the sea of stories*. London: Granta.

————. (1990b). *In good faith*. London: Granta.

Ruthven, K. K. (1984). *Feminist literary studies: An introduction*. Cambridge, England: Cambridge University Press.

Ryan, M. (1982). *Marxism and deconstruction: A critical introduction*. Baltimore, MD: Johns Hopkins University Press.

Said, E. (1985). *Orientalism*. London: Penguin.

Salinger, J. D. (1951). *Catcher in the rye*. Boston: Little, Brown.

Sallot, J. (1991, November 21). Planned law may revive rape shield: Campbell hears women's plea for fresh approach in sex cases. *The Globe and Mail*, A1, A2.

――――. (1991b, December 14). Redefining reasonable: Justice removes her blindfold. *The Globe and Mail*, D3.

――――. (1991c, December 12). Sexual-assault law will define consent: 'Mistaken belief, to be unnacceptable. *The Globe and Mail*, A1, A2.

Sang, B. A. (1981). Women and the creative process. *Arts in Psychotherapy*, 8, 43–48.

Sarick, L. & Galt, V. (1991, December 7). Breaking the silence on assault: Activists take to subways, boardrooms to demand end to violence against women, *The Globe and Mail*, A10.

Scahill, J. H. (1989). Education policy studies. Review of *Teachers as intellectuals: Toward a critical pedagogy of learning*, by H. A. Giroux. *Educational Studies*, 20 (1), 91–99.

Schmalz, P. F. (1986, August 4). Letter to the editor. *The Globe and Mail*, A6.

Scholes, R. (1979). *Fabulation and metafiction*. Urbana, IL: University of Illinois Press.

――――. (1985). *Textual power: Literary theory and the teaching of English*. New Haven, CT: Yale University Press.

――――. (1989). Protocols of reading. New Haven, CT: Yale University Press.

School board rejects bid to ban novels. (1988, July 1). *The Globe and Mail*, A4.

School board votes to continue using novels by Laurence. (1985, April 26). *Peterborough Examiner*, 1.

Schweickart, P. P. (1986). Reading ourselves: Toward a feminist theory of reading. In E. A. Flynn & P. P. Schweickart (Eds.), *Gender and reading: Essays on readers, texts, and contexts*. Baltimore, MD: Johns Hopkins University Press.

Scribner, S. (1988). Literacy in three metaphors. In E. R. Kintgen, B. M. Kroll & M. Rose (Eds.), *Perspectives on literacy*. Carbondale & Edwardsville, IL: Southern Illinois University Press.

Sethi, S. (1989). Talk at Wellesley College, March 9, 1989. In S. R. Cudjoe (Ed.), *Salman Rushdie and his verses: A discussion at Wellesley College*. Wellesley, MA: Calaloux Publications.

Sethna, C. (1990). Final term paper. Course 1484: Philosophy of Literature and Literature Education. December, 1990.

Shelley, P. B. (1965). A defence of poetry. In J. E. Jordon (Ed.), *A defence of poetry/The four ages of poetry: Shelley and Peacock*. Indianapolis, IN & New York: The Bobbs-Merrill Company, Inc., (Original work published 1821).

Sher, E. (1991, November 28). Addressing the issues: Emil Sher argues for the word on the street. *The Globe and Mail*, C1.

————. (1977). *A literature of her own: British women novelists from Brontë to Lessing*. London: Virago.

Showalter, E. (Ed.). (1985). *The new feminist criticism: Essays on women, literature, and theory*. New York: Pantheon.

Shugert, D. P. (Ed.). (1983). *The Journal of the Connecticut Council of Teachers of English*, 15 (1). Urbana, IL: NCTE.

Shusterman, R. (1989). Postmodernism and the aesthetic turn. *Poetics Today: International Journal for Theory and Analysis of Literature and Communication*, 10 (3), 605–622.

Sidney, P. (1966). *A defence of poetry*. (J. A. Van Dorsten, Ed.). London: Oxford University Press. (Original work published 1595).

Smith, B. H. (1988). *Contingencies of value: Alternative perspectives for critical theory*. Cambridge, MA & London: Harvard University Press.

Smith, J. F. (1990). Plato, irony and equality. In A. Y. al-Hibri and M.A. Simons. (Eds.). *Hypatia reborn: Essays in feminist philosophy*. Bloomington, IN: Indiana University Press.

Smith, S. E. (1986, August 4). Letter to the editor. *The Globe and Mail*, A6.

Souchard, M. (1990). On the concept of the aesthetic/An interview with Terry Eagleton. *Recherches sémiotiques/semiotic inquiry*, 10 (1–2–3), 163–174.

Spender, D. (1984). *Invisible woman: The schooling scandal*. London: Writers and Readers.

Spivak, G. C. (1988). *In other words: Essays in cultural politics*. London: Routledge.

Steiner, G. (1974). *Nostalgia for the absolute: The Massey lectures*. Toronto: CBC Publications.

————. (1989). *Real presences*. Chicago: University of Chicago Press.

Stierle, K. (1980). The reading of fictional texts. In S. R. Suleiman & I. Crosman (Eds.), *The reader in the text: Essays on audience and interpretation*. Princeton, NJ: Princeton University Press.

Strauss, M. (1990, July 19). TTC calls beer ad sexually exploitive: Molson poster of "long-haired fox" will be pulled from Toronto subways. *The Globe and Mail*, A1.

Straw, S. & Bogdan, D. (1990). Introduction. *Beyond communication: Reading, comprehension and criticism*. Portsmouth, NH: Boynton-Cook/ Heinemann.

————. (Eds.). (in press). *Constructive reading: Teaching beyond communication*. Portsmouth, NH: Boynton-Cook/Heinemann.

Street, B. (1984). *Literacy in theory and practice*. London: Cambridge University Press.

————. (1988). A critical look at Walter Ong and the 'Great divide'. *Literacy Research Centre of the University of Pennsylvania*, 4 (1), 3–5.

Stuckey, J. E. (1991). *The violence of literacy.* Portsmouth, NH: Boynton-Cook/Heinemann.

Sullivan, J.M. (1989a, July 1). Censorship cries heard as province changes textbooks. *The Globe and Mail,* C3.

———. (1989b, June 21). Stirring up Newfoundland's cultural pot: Artists join committee to redesign provincial policies. *The Globe and Mail,* C9.

Sutherland, R. (1971). The Calvinist-Jansenist pantomine. In his *Second image: Comparative studies in Quebec/Canadian literature.* Toronto: New Press.

Sweet, L. (1989, December 9). Inside the mind of a mass murderer. *The Toronto Star,* A12.

Tate, J. (1928). Horace and the moral function of poetry. *Classical Quarterly, 22* (2), 65–72.

Taylor, B. (1989, December 8). Hundreds in Toronto mourn killing of 14 women. *The Globe and Mail,* A13.

Textbook Review Committee. (1985). Unpublished brief. Peterborough County, ON.

Theweleit, K. (1987). *Male fantasies. Volume 1: Women, floods, bodies, history.* (S. Conway, in collaboration with E. Carter & C. Turner, Trans.). Minneapolis, MN: University of Minnesota Press.

Thomson, J. (1987). *Understanding teenagers' reading: Reading process and the teaching of literature.* Melbourne, Australia: Methuen Australia.

———. (in press). Helping students to control texts: Contemporary literary theory into classroom practice. In D. Bogdan & S. Straw (Eds.), *Constructive reading: Teaching beyond communication.* Portsmouth, NH: Boynton-Cook/Heinemann.

Tom and Huck still required reading: But you can't teach the word 'nigger' without being offensive, blacks complain. (1990, December 7). *The Globe and Mail,* C8.

Tompkins, J. (Ed.). (1980). *Reader-response criticism: From formalism to post-structuralism.* Baltimore, MD & London: The Johns Hopkins University Press.

Treichler, P. (1986). Teaching feminist theory. In C. Nelson (Ed.), *Theory in the classroom.* Urbana, IL: University of Illinois Press.

Tuve, R. (1968). Imagery and logic: Ramus and metaphysical poetics. In P. O. Kristeller & P. P. Weiner (Eds.), *Renaissance essays from the 'Journal of the History of Ideas'.* New York: Harper & Row.

Updike, J. (1962). A&P. In his *Pigeon feathers and other stories.* New York: Alfred A. Knopf.

Verdenius, W. J. (1971). Plato's doctrine of artistic imitation. In G. Vlastos (Ed.), *Plato: A collection of critical essays II: Ethics, politics, and philosophy of art and religion.* Notre Dame, IN: University of Notre Dame.

Vincent, I. (1990, March 9). 'Violent' kids' book on restricted list in school libraries. *The Globe and Mail*, C6.

Vipond, D. & Hunt, R. (1984). Point-driven understanding: Pragmatic and cognitive dimensions of literary reading. *Poetics, 13*, 261–277.

———. (1987). Aesthetic reading: Some strategies for research. *English Quarterly, 20* (3), 178–183.

Von Franz, M. L. (1981). *Puer aeternus*. (2nd Ed.). Zurich: Sigo Press.

Walton, K. (1990). *Mimesis as make-believe: On the foundations of the representational arts*. Cambridge, MA: Harvard University Press.

Warnock, M. (1970/1988). *Existentialism*. Oxford: Oxford University Press.

———. (1973). Towards a definition of quality in education. In R. S. Peters (Ed.), *The Philosophy of Education*. Oxford: Oxford University Press.

———. (1976). *Imagination*. London: Faber & Faber.

Warry, J. C. (1962). *Greek aesthetic theory: A study of callistic and aesthetic concepts in the works of Plato and Aristotle*. London: Methuen.

Watkins, E. (1989). *Work time: English departments and the circulation of cultural value*. Stanford, CA: Stanford University Press.

Weedon, C. (1987). *Feminist practice and poststructuralist theory*. Oxford: Blackwell.

Weigel, S. (1985). Double focus: On the history of women's writing. In G. Ecker (Ed.), *Feminist aesthetics*. London: Women's Press.

Weil, S. (1949). *L'Enracinement: Prélude à une declaration des devoirs envers l'être humain*. Paris: Gallimard.

———. (1952a). *Gravity and grace*. London: Routledge & Kegan Paul. Ark Paperbacks, 1987.

———. (1952b). *The need for roots: Prelude to a declaration of duties toward mankind*. New York: Routledge & Kegan Paul.

Weinbrot, H. (1990/91). Northrop Frye and the literature of process reconsidered. *Eighteenth-Century Studies, 24*, 173–195.

Weiskel, T. (1976). *The romantic sublime: Studies in the structure and psychology of transcendence*. Baltimore, MD: Johns Hopkins University Press.

Widdowson, P. (Ed.). (1982). *Re-reading English*. London: Methuen.

Willinsky, J. (1987). The seldom-spoken roots of the curriculum: Romanticism and the new literacy. *Curriculum Inquiry, 17* (3), 267–285.

———. (1990). *The new literacy: Redefining reading and writing in the schools*. New York & London: Routledge, Chapman & Hall.

Wimsatt, W. K., Jr. & Brooks, C. (1957). *Literary criticism: A short history*. Chicago & London: University of Chicago Press.

Winnett, S. (1990). Coming unstrung: Women, men, narrative, and principles of pleasure. *PMLA, 105* (3), 505–518.

Wolf, C. (1984). *Cassandra: A novel and four essays*. (J. V. Heurck, Trans.). New York: Farrar, Strauss, Giroux.

———. (1985). *A letter, about unequivocal and ambiguous meaning, definiteness and indefiniteness; about ancient conditions and new viewscope; about objectivity*. (J. van Heurch, Trans.). In G. Ecker (Ed.), *Feminist Aesthetics*. London: Women's Press. Excerpted from C. Wolf. (1984). *Cassandra: A novel and four essays*. (J. van Heurck, Trans.). New York: Farrar, Strauss, Giroux.

———. (1989). *Accident/A day's news*. (H. Schwarzbauer & R. Takvorian, Trans.). New York: Farrar-Straus-Giroux.

Wolfson, S. (1988). Individual in community: Dorothy Wordsworth in conversation with William. In A. K. Mellor (Ed.), *Romanticism and feminism*. Bloomington and Indianapolis, IN: Indiana University Press.

Woodman, M. (1985). *The pregnant virgin: A process of psychological transformation*. Toronto: Inner City Books.

———. (1990). *The ravaged bridgegroom: Masculinity in women*. Toronto: Inner City Books.

Woods, J. & Coward, H.C. (1979). Reflections on a liberal education: Out of the vortex of slush and nonsense. In J. Woods & H. G. Coward (Eds.), *Humanities in the present day*. Waterloo, ON: Wilfrid Laurier University Press.

Woolf, V. (1938/1966). *Three guineas*. New York: Harcourt.

———. (1966) *Collected Essays* (Vol. 1). London: Hogarth Press.

Wordsworth, D. (1985). The Grasmere journals. In S. Gilbert & S. Gubar (Eds.), *The Norton anthology of literature by women: The tradition in English*. New York: Norton.

Wordsworth, W. (1954a). I wandered lonely as a cloud. In C. Baker (Ed. & Intro.), *William Wordsworth's 'The prelude,' with a selection from the shorter poems, the sonnets, 'The recluse', and 'The excusion' and three essays on the art of poetry*. New York: Holt, Rinehart & Winson, Inc.

———. (1954b). Preface to the lyrical ballads. In C. Baker (Ed. & Intro.), *William Wordsworth's 'The prelude,' with a selection from the shorter poems, the sonnets, 'The recluse', and 'The excusion' and three essays on the art of poetry*. New York: Holt, Rinehart & Winson, Inc.

Yaeger, P. (1989). Toward a female sublime. In L. Kauffman (Ed.), *Gender and theory: Dialogues on feminist criticism*. Oxford & New York: Blackwell.

Zita, J. (1988). From orthodoxy to pluralism: A postsecondary curricular reform. *Journal of Education, 170* (2), 58–76.

# Index

"A&P" (Updike), 114–125, 131,
  134–135, 140, 144, 147, 150, 151,
  162–164, 242, 287
Abjection, 196, 206, 211, 214, 283, 288;
  defense of poetry and, 221–222;
  seduction and, 217
Abrams, M. H., 22
Adolescent fiction, 91
"Adolescent" (Peseroff), 250–253,
  307–308
Adventures of Huckleberry Finn, The
  (Twain), 97, 157, 205, 276
Advertising: censorship problem and,
  4–5, 8; moral issues and, 33–34;
  sexism in, 4–6, 285, 286
Aesthetic: literary response and,
  200–205; literature and, 68; morality
  and, 111
Aesthetic education: critical thinking
  and, 60
Aesthetic engagement. See
  Engagement
Aesthetic experience: dual effect of,
  202–203; as engagement, 177–178,
  185; literary experience as, 68, 165;
  literature and, 170–174; reading as,
  68; shock and, 178–179; stasis and,
  168
Aesthetic pleasure, 111
Aesthetic reading: cultural factors and,
  187–188; language arts curriculum
  and, 60, 108
Aesthetics of total form, xxvii. See also
  Total Form
Affective dependency (Bleich), 276
Affliction (Weil), 196
Agnosis, 75, 136–137, 140, 150; in ludic
  readers, 187
Aha! response, 164–165, 167, 178. See
  also Stasis
Allegorical imagination, 24–26, 32, 42
Alternate texts, 154
Alternative sublime, 266, 274, 290
Ambivalence, 257–258

Amusing Ourselves to Death (Postman),
  18, 50
Anagnorisis, 54, 113, 114
Anagogic perspective, 47, 53–57, 274
Anatomy of Criticism (Frye), 87, 293
Anxiety: ludic reading and, 188;
  ontological, 185
Apologetic essay, 23
Apologie for Poetrie (Sidney), xxxvi, 2,
  23, 26–32
Apprenticeship of Duddy Kravitz
  (Richler), 106
Arimneste, 142, 144
Aristotle, 186, 188, 191, 263;
  anagnorisis, 54, 113, 114; Greek
  tragedy and, 179–181, 183;
  imagination, 56; as inventor of text,
  24; sacred quality of literary
  experience and, 165; stasis and, 175
Arnold, M., 52
Art: social value of (Frye), 50–51
Atwood, M., 63–64
Auden, W. H., 282
Auditory hallucination, 14
Auditory ideal: defined, 168; harmony
  as, 167–169; visual ideal and, 172–173
Author-reader relationship. See also
  Reader response; Text-reader
  relationships; allegorical imagination
  and, 25
Autonomous reader, 102, 120;
  censorship and, 149–150; defined,
  111; educated reader and, 112–120;
  real readers and, 123–125

Barthes, R., x, 63, 169
Bartky, S. L., 139, 156
Bate, W. J., xxv–xxvi
Baudrillard, J., 220, 226n
Beach, R., 71
Beatrice, 283, 292, 294, 298, 304, 306
Beauty: Plato's concept of, 7–8, 16–17;
  poetry and, 39–40; Renaissance
  concept of, 24

*Beloved* (Morrison), 221
Belsey, C., 66–67, 252–253
Bergvall, A., 27
Berkeley, Bishop, 37
Betrayal, 214. *See also* Seduction
Bible: Frye and, 269–273, 276–277
Bibliotherapy, 174, 272
Bicameral mind, 14, 17, 18
Blake, W., 88, 268
Bleich, D., 160n, 171–173, 194n, 276, 294
Bloom, A., 2
Booth, W., 285, 294
Bored readings, 242, 243
Borovilos, J., 61, 62
Britton, J., 63
Brooks, C., 23
Brossard, N., 283–284
Brown, W., xxxix
Burke, E., 233
Butler, J., 287–288
Byatt, A. S., xiii

Cain, W. E., 305
Canadian Broadcasting Corporation, 45
Cassandra, 196, 205
Castlevetro, 23
*Catcher in the Rye* (Salinger), 80, 95–96
Catharsis, 179
Cave metaphor: Plato, 7
Censorship: alternate texts and, 154; assumptions about, 73–78; continuum theory and, 286–287; discomfort and, 149; educated imagination and, 92–99; enculturation and, 152, 156, 297; feminist criticism and, 135–136, 138–143, 146, 286–287; gap theory and, 286–287; independent thinking and, 93; literature education and, 75–78; morality and, 85; poetics of pluralism and, 136–140; political context of, 153–154; pornography and, 79–80, 287; principles related to, 77–78; regional culture and, xxv; school texts and, xxi–xxii; stubborn structure and, 89–90; teaching with sensitivity and, 97; transformation and, 156, 157; truth-of-correspondence and, 81–82, 98

Censorship problem, xxiv; advertising and, 4–5; autonomous reader and, 149–150; court system and, 4; defense of poetry and, 48; doubleness and, xliv; educated imagination and, xxxvii–xxxviii, 73–99; justification problem and, 38–40; literary criticism and, 97; literary experience and, 163; literature as stubborn structure and, 85–92, 94; Plato and, 11–13; poetics of total form and, 55; politics of engagement and, 94; professionalization of literary response and, 235; response problem and, 92; Shelley and, 39–40; Sidney and, 31
Centrifugal fallacy, 120
Centrifugal meaning, 87–88, 270
Centripetal meaning, 87–88
Children: response to poetry by (Plato), 15
Christian, B., 200
Classics: as literature, 60
Closed mythology, 119, 144
*Closing of the American Mind, The* (Bloom), 2
Co-creation, 211
Collingwood, R. G., 6
Common memories response, 251
Common sense response, 251
Communication: literary language and, 270; problems of, 232; skills, need for, 61–62
*Company We Keep, The: An Ethics of Fiction* (Booth), 285
Complicity: seduction and, 217
Concerned truth, 157
Connata(e): Canadian women as, 206; defined, 139, 205; feminist critic as, 145; mothers as, 207; women readers as, 145
Consciousness: literacy and, 241; raising, literary experience as, 165; transformation of, 283
Continuum theory: censorship and, 286–287; doubleness and, 289–290; gap and, 285–289
Control: Other and, 221
Counter-creation (Steiner), 207, 211
Counter-society, 207
*Creation and Recreation* (Frye), 53
Creative reading, 289

Creativity: in women, motherhood
  and, 203–204, 207
Critical consciousness, 105, 109;
  engaged reader and, 109
*Critical Path, The* (Frye), 45
Critical response, 120, 121–122. *See
  also* Literary response; Reader
  response; Response; educated
  imagination and, 109–112; literature
  and, 68–69
Critical thinking: approaches to,
  162–164; literary criticism and, 60;
  vs. poetry, 16–17
*Criticism: The Major Texts* (Bate),
  xxv–xxvi
Cultural envelope, 53, 270
Cultural literacy, 173
*Cultural Literacy* (Hirsch), 2
Culture without boundaries, 296

D'Angelo: F. J., 60
Dante, 38–39
*Dead Poets Society*, 35, 42, 45, 46, 85,
  105, 120, 138, 180, 294
Defense of poetry, xxxv, xxxvi, xxxvii,
  2, 21–23, 26, 28; abjection and,
  221–222; bibliotherapy and, 174;
  censorship problem and, 48; in
  *Educated Imagination, The* (Frye),
  xxii–xxiii; Frye and, xxii–xxiii,
  xxxv, 47–48, 57–58, 272–273;
  Kristeva and, 206; as meta-problem,
  24–26; Morgan (Robin) and,
  221–222; response problem and, 48;
  Shelley and, xxxvi, 2, 36–37, 41, 90;
  Sidney and, 26–32; Steiner and,
  200–203
*Defense of Poetry* (Shelley), xxxvi, 2,
  36–37, 41, 90
de Lauretis, T., xl, 138, 196, 222, 223, 224
de Maupassant, G., 113
Demonic literalism, 279–280
*Demon Lover, The: On the Sexuality
  of Terrorism* (Morgan), 220
Desire: thwarted, 196
Detachment: censorship and, 94;
  pedagogy of, 163;
  professionalization of literary
  response and, 235; reader-response
  theory and, 110; self-conscious, 171
Dialectic: total form as, 119–120
Dialectical reader: stages of, 120–122
Dialectician: Plato and, 8

*Dianoia*, 88, 113, 115
Direct response, xlii, 247–250
Disempowering power, 220–221
Disidentification, 151–155
Dissonant/dissident behaviors,
  246–250
Divided Line parable: Plato, 7
Divine child (*puer aeternus*), 219
Divine inspiration, 9, 79
*Diviners, The* (Laurence),
  xxxvii–xxxviii, 80–84, 86, 91, 98,
  155
Dixon, J., 63, 70
Double mirror: literature as, 269–270
Doubleness, xliv, 289–290
Double ontological shock. *See also*
  Ontological shock; of feminists, 139;
  of minorities, 56
Double perspective, 294–295
*Double Perspective: Language,
  Literacy, and Social Relations*
  (Bleich), 294–295
Double-take, 275
Double vision, 273–285
*Double Vision, The* (Frye), 273–278,
  284, 292, 293

Eagleton, T., 67, 68, 165
Early, M., 120, 236–237
Eccentric subject (de Lauretis), 222–223
*Ecstasis*, 112, 225, 271–272
*Educare*, xxii, 241
Educated imagination. *See also* Frye,
  Northrop; censorship problem and,
  xxxvii–xxxviii, 73–99; critical
  response and, 109–112, 121;
  defined, 1–2; evaluating, 1; issues,
  xxviii; justification problem and,
  xxxvii, 45–72; language arts
  education and, 57–63; literary
  literacy and, 130–135;
  meta-problem and, xxxvi–xxxviii,
  130–135; overview, xxxii,
  xxxv–xxxviii; premises of, 75; reader
  response and, 99, 126; re-educated
  imagination and, 263–264; response
  problem and, xxxviii, 102–127; skill
  and, 65–66
*Educated Imagination, The* (Frye),
  xxii–xxiii, 45, 65–66, 226n
Educated reader: autonomous reader
  and, 112–120
*Educating Rita*, 112–113

Education. *See also* Literature
　education; aesthetic, 60; as *educare*,
　xxii, 241; as *educere*, xxii, 244, 247; as
　enculturation, xxii, xxiii, xxix–xxx;
　liberal, 49; as personal development,
　xxii, xxiii; poetry as, 10–16, 31,
　49–53; through art (*paideia* ), 11, 13
Educational policy: response problem
　and, 102–109
*Educere*, xxii, 244, 247
*Eikasia*, 7, 42
Eliot, T. S., 47, 220
Ellis, J., 67–68, 170–171, 177, 182
Ellsworth, E., 199–200, 203, 234
Embattled Books Conference, 195, 212
Embodied criticism: defined, 244;
　education and, 298–299; "ownership"
　of texts and, 241; pedagogy of, 241;
　re-educated imagination and,
　xlii–xliii, 195–225; seduction and,
　216–225; teaching for, 245
Embodied pedagogy, xliii, 228–259
Embodied reading, xi, 200–205, 268–273
Embodied vision, 218–219
Embodiment, 268–273
Emotional response: distrust of, 164
Empowering power, 220–221
Enculturation. *See also* Regional
　culture; censorship and, 152, 156,
　297; education as, xxii, xxiii,
　xxix–xxx; through poetry, 13–14,
　16–17; transformation and, 164,
　168–169
Engagement: aesthetic experience as,
　177–178, 185; in alternative sublime,
　256; bored reading and, 242;
　censorship and, 94, 95; cultural
　exchange and, 186; as double-edged
　sword, 202–203; educational
　problems and, 249–250; identity and,
　192; intelligent, 235; language arts
　curriculum and, 106–108; literary
　experience as, 162, 165; ludic readers
　and, 184–185; model of literary
　education, 105–108; Other and, 185;
　poetics of, 258; as poetic value,
　253–254; political context of, 153,
　229; professionalization of literary
　response and, 235; reader-response
　theory and, 110–111; real reader and,
　109–110; re-educated imagination
　and, 235–236; reflective, 250;
　spirituality and, 194; student

response journals and, 254–259;
　tragedy and, 178, 183–184
*L'Enracinement* (Weil), x
Epistemological shift, 212, 282
Eros: Logos and, 206, 208
Ethical behavior: literary experience as,
　179–181
Ethical freedom, 176–177
Ethical import: of literature education,
　xxxiii
Evans, R., 61
Existential imagination, xxxi
Experiential realization, 212

Falck, C., 266–267, 294
Fanon, F., 232
*Fascinans*, 201
Father's daughters (Woodman),
　284–285, 292
*Fearful Symmetry* (Frye), 284, 293
Feeling: fear of, 174; literary experience
　as, 174–175, 189; mortification of, 97
Feeling problem, xxxiii, 97, 140–143,
　212, 215; communication and, 23;
　myths and, 294; reader response and,
　243
Felman, S., 144
Felperin, H., xl
Female: as ground, xxix
Feminine identity: reconstruction of,
　221–222
Feminism. *See also* Gender; Women;
　alternative sublime and, 263;
　censorship and, 135–136, 138–140,
　286–287; double vision and, 274,
　276–285; embodied criticism and,
　243–244; embodied pedagogy and,
　xliii; fear of, 195; Montreal massacre
　and, 195–197, 200; poststructuralism,
　xxxix; Wordsworth and, 249
*Feminism and Poetry: Language,
　Experience, Identity in Women's
　Writing* (Montefiore), 248–249
Feminist consciousness: embodied
　criticism and, xlii–xliii
Feminist criticism, 138–140;
　censorship and, 141–143, 146;
　connatae and (in)connatae and, 145;
　poetics of pluralism and, 138–139,
　144–145; response journals and,
　250–256; of Romanticism, 246–250;
　social imagination and, 139; Steiner
　and, 203–205

Feminization of total form, xl
Fetterley, J., 144
Fiction. *See also* Literature; Poetry;
  misrecognition and, 182
Final vocabularies, xii
Foot, P., 173–174
Foucault, M., 162, 288
*Four Ages of Poetry, The* (Peacock), 36
Fragmented self, 258
Freedom: flight from, 132
Frost, R., 35
Frye, N., xxi, xxxi, 193, 194. *See also*
  Educated imagination; anagogic
  perspective, 47, 53–57, 274;
  *Anatomy of Criticism*, 87, 293; Bible
  and, 269–273, 276–277; closed
  mythology, 119, 144; concerned
  truth, 157; *Creation and Recreation*,
  53; *Critical Path, The*, 45; culture
  without boundaries, 296; defense of
  poetry and, xxii–xxiii, xxxv, 47–48,
  56–58, 272–273; *Double Vision, The*,
  273–278, 284, 292, 293; *Educated
  Imagination, The*, xxii–xxiii,
  xxxv–xxxviii, 2, 45, 65–66, 226n;
  educational value of poetry and,
  49–53; embodiment and, 268–273;
  esoteric knowledge and, 35; *Fearful
  Symmetry*, 284, 293; *Great Code, The*,
  xxvii, 112, 126, 131, 256, 269–271,
  273, 279; humanism and, 52–53;
  imagination and, xxxii; imaginative
  literalism, 84; interdisciplinary
  context and, xliv; involuntary
  journey, xxxiv, xxxv; justification of
  poetry, 22; literary criticism and,
  xli–xlii; literary experience and,
  163–166; literary literacy, 133;
  literary reality, 56–57; literature as
  double mirror, 269–270; literature as
  stubborn structure, 85–92, 269;
  meta-problem and, xxxvi–xxxviii,
  47–53, 130–135; Montreal massacre
  and, 282; moral values of literature,
  71–72; mythology and, 293–294;
  *Natural Perspective, A*, 126; oracular
  in poetry, 237; Plato and, 48; poetic
  language as natural language, 269;
  poetics of total form, 55–57; poetry as
  "rhetorical analogue," 25, 27;
  reader-response theory, 109–112;
  reading literarily and, 182;
  re-educated imagination and, 264;

  regional as universal, xxviii;
  Romanticism and, 36, 265; sacred
  quality of literary experience and,
  165–166; *Secular Scripture, The*, 110;
  sexism and, 244; Shelley and, 41, 42,
  45–46; *Spiritus Mundi*, 45, 85; stock
  response and, 141; *Stubborn
  Structure, The*, 45, 85–92, 109–112;
  third order of experience, 57, 268,
  273; verbal imagination, xxiv; voice
  and, 225; *Words with Power*, 269,
  272–273, 274–277, 279, 293,
  303–304
Fulford, Robert, 64–65, 66, 83
Functional readers, 108

Gap theory: censorship and, 286–287;
  continuum and, 285–289;
  doubleness and, 289–290
Gender. *See also* Women; approaches
  to, 162–164; literature and, xl–xli;
  poetics of, 203; poetics of ordinary
  existence and, 262–263; poetry and,
  43n; reading and, 280–282
*Gender Trouble: Feminism and the
  Subversion of Identity* (Butler), 287
Gilbert, S. M., 138
Gilman, C. P., 204
God trick (Haraway), 218–219, 233–234
Goebbels, J., 50
Gold, J., 174, 175, 180, 181, 231,
  243–244
Golding, W., 155, 157, 158
Gosson, S., 26, 32, 35, 286
Graff, G., 74
*Great Code, The* (Frye), xxvii, 112, 126,
  131, 256, 269–271, 273, 279
*Great Teacher, The: Northrop Frye*, 45
Greek tragedy, 178–181
Greene, M., 142, 241, 305
Gribble, J., 93
Gubar, S., 138

*Hamartia*, 178
Hamilton, A. C., 132–133, 134, 281
Haraway, D., 218–219, 220, 226n, 246,
  290
Harmony: as auditory ideal, 167–169
*Haroun and the Sea of Stories*
  (Rushdie), xii
Havelock, E., xxxv, 11, 12, 13, 18
Heath, S., 173
Hegemony, 176–177

Heidegger, M., 165, 200
Heintzman, R., 80–81
Hemingway, E., xxv
Heraclitus, 132
Heterogeneity, 231
Heteroglossia, 231
Hirsch, E.D., 2
Homeostatic present (Ong), 172–173, 175
Homer, 9, 36
Homeric mind, 17, 18, 22, 172
Horizontal perspective: stubborn
  structure and, 85
Horror: power of (Kristeva), 195–200
Humanism, xxxix; Frye and, 52–53; use
  of term, xlivn–xlvn; values, xxiii–xxiv
Hume, D., x
Hunt, R., 62, 115, 128n

Idea of the Holy, The (Otto), 178
Identity and identification, 151–155;
  educated imagination and, 131;
  enculturation and, 156–157;
  excessive, xxix; feminine,
  reconstruction of, 221–222; Other
  and, 199–200; personal response and,
  241; relocating, 222–223
Ideology: mythology and, 133, 273, 274,
  278–284, 293–294; partial response
  and, 118–119
Illiteracy: culture of, 64–65
Illusion (eikasia), 7, 42; bent-stick
  example, 13
Imagination. See also Educated
  imagination; Re-educated
  imagination; Uneducated
  imagination; allegorical, 24–26, 32,
  42; Aristotle and, 56; defined,
  xxxi–xxxii; evaluating, 1; existential,
  xxxi; literary, xi; Plato's view of, 7;
  Romantic, 23, 34–41, 46; social, 139;
  uneducated, xxxii, 1–19; verbal, xxiv
Imaginative identity: stasis and, 113
Imaginative literalism, 84, 279–280
Imitations Ode (Wordsworth), 250
Immoral literature, 55
(In)connata(e). See also Connata(e);
  feminist critic as, 145
Independent thinking: censorship and,
  93
Indoctrination: literature as, 94–95
"In the Fall" (MacLeod), xxvi–xxx, 230
Information-driven readers, 115
Interaction (Moffet), 78

Interdependence, 211, 213
Interiority, 165, 168, 182, 209, 288
Involuntary journey, xxxiv, xxxv
Ion (Plato), xxxvi, 9, 26, 31, 40, 202, 286
Iser, Wolfgang, 209
"I Wandered Lonely as a Cloud"
  (Wordsworth), 250, 307

Jackson, R. B. W., 64
Jaeger, W., 11
James, H., 137
Jameson, F., 113
Jaynes, J., 14
Jest of God, A (Laurence), 80
Johnson, S., 249
Jouissance of being, 169
Journal of Canadian Studies, 80–81
Justification problem, xxiv; censorship
  problem and, 38–40; educated
  imagination and, xxxvii, 45–72;
  identity and, 241; language arts
  education and, 57–63; literary
  experience and, 163–164; Plato and,
  13–16; poetics of total form and, 55;
  professionalization of literary response
  and, 235–236; reader response and,
  92; response problem and, 111;
  Shelley and, 37–41, 42; Sidney and,
  31; transfer-value from literature to
  life, 50; Woolf, Virginia and, xliv

Kappeler, S., 287
Kastner, S., 288
Kearney, R., xxxi, xxxii, xxxv–xxxvi,
  12, 20n, 37
Kermode, F., ix
"Killers, The" (Hemingway), xxv
Kinawha County, West Virginia:
  censorship in, 78
Kinetic response: partial form and, 116,
  117–118
Kolodny, A., 138
Krieger, M., 21–22
Kristeva, J., 162, 195, 206, 208, 217, 223,
  288

Language: literary, communicative
  power of, 270; mistrust of by Plato, 8;
  reality and, 81–82
Language arts. See also Literature
  education; curriculum, 60, 103;
  educated imagination and
  justification problem in, 57–63;

Language arts (*continued*)
  integrated curriculum, 103–109;
  literature and, xxi, xxiv, 58–63, 95–96
Laurence, M., xxxvii, 79–84, 86, 91, 98,
  155
Lepine, M., 196, 282
Levin, H., 22
Lewis, C. S., 26
Life-long readers, 240
Lipking, Lawrence, 140
Listening, 233–234
Literacy: D'Angelo's definition of,
  60–61; literary and, xxiv; orality and,
  173–174; as primary need, 61–62; as
  state of grace, 108, 185, 187
Literalism: imaginative and demonic,
  279–280
Literariness, 177–178
Literary: literacy and, xxiv
Literary conventions: censorship and,
  84; reality and, 86, 278–285
Literary criticism, xli–xlii. *See also*
  Literary response; censorship and,
  96–97; as container, 109; education
  and, 298–299; Frye and, 87–89;
  justification problem and, 97;
  language arts and, 60; literary
  experience and, 113; vs. reading,
  133–134; response problem and, 215
Literary education. *See also* Language
  arts; Literature education; as poetic
  knowledge, 64; use of term, xlivn
Literary experience: as aesthetic, 68,
  165; alphabetizing of, 171, 172;
  bibliotherapy and, 174; censorship
  problem and, 163; conditions of, 162;
  as consciousness raising, 165; as
  cultural critique, 186–190; defined,
  xxx, 111; educational value of, 162; as
  engagement, 162, 185; as ethical
  behavior, 179–181; ethical demand
  of, 176–177; as feeling behavior,
  174–175, 189; gender issues and,
  162–164; harmony as auditory ideal,
  167–169; as holistic, 69; justification
  problem and, 163; literary criticism
  and, 113; literary literacy and, 240,
  289–299; as literate behavior,
  177–179; as ludic behavior, 184–185;
  meta-problem and, 69–70; as
  misrecognition, 181–184; moral
  values and, 70–72, 165; as real

experience, xxxiii, 174, 189; real
  experience and, 171; real readers and,
  239–240; recognition scene as,
  176–177; re-educated imagination
  and, xlii, 161–194; sacred and
  profane qualities of, 165–170,
  175–176, 236–237; self and Other in,
  169–170; shock and, 178–179; social
  change and, 165, 190–191; spiritual
  quality of, 165; stasis and, 164–165,
  167, 168; as a state of grace, 175–176,
  236; as stereophonic vision, 170–185
Literary imagination: text and, xi
Literary language: communicative
  power of, 270
Literary literacy: as cultural critique,
  186–190; defined, xxx, 139; educated
  imagination and, 130–135;
  engagement and, 162; Frye's
  definition of, 133; language arts
  curriculum and, 105; literary
  experience and, 240, 289–299;
  misrecognition and, 181–184;
  pluralism and, 152–153; poetics of
  need and, 161–162; re-educated
  imagination and, xli, 135–136; stasis
  and, 167, 168
Literary reading, 290; critical skills and,
  108; language arts curriculum and, 104
Literary reality, 56–57
Literary response, xxx, xli–xlii,
  131–132. *See also* Critical response;
  Literary criticism; Reader response;
  Response; correct and incorrect
  modes of, 79; as dialectic, 119–120;
  direct, xlii; educational value of,
  131–133; as embodied form of
  knowledge, xxxiii; embodied reading
  as, 200–205; non-professionalization
  of, 239–246; partial form, 115–119;
  professionalization of, 231, 234–239;
  stasis and, 112–115; total form as
  dialectic, 119–120; total form as
  stasis, 112–115
Literary subjectivity: ontology of, 206,
  219
Literary texts: concepts of, 67–68
Literary use, 177–178; of language, 68,
  171; learning and, 241
Literate behaviors: literary experience
  as, 177–179; social context of, 173
Literate person, 60–61

Literature. *See also* Poetry; aesthetic and, 68, 170–174; assumptions of power in, 83; centripetal and centrifugal meaning in, 87; "classics" as, 67–68; conditioning of, 66; defining, 67–68, 170–174; as double mirror, 269–270; educational value of, 55, 57, 131–133; as engagement, 106–108; as holistic experience, 69; as indoctrination, 94–95; influence of, 152; language arts and, xxi, xxiv, 58–63, 95–96; as literature, 14, 67–68, 96; as male-dominated, xl–xli; moral values of, 55–56, 70–72; as musical voice, 172–173, 175; order of words in, 82, 85, 87; as *ostranenie*, 143; "ownership" of texts and, 242; plurality of, 95; politicizing, xxxiv–xxxv; power of, xxv, 64–65, 105–108; reality and, 83–84, 86; Renaissance concept of, 24; sayingness and unsayingness of, 85–87, 96–98, 180, 274, 276, 287–288; selection of, censorship and, 95; social value of, 48; as a survival skill, 174–175

Literature education. *See also* Education; Language arts; aim of, 75–76; censorship and, 75–78; defense of, 49–50; direct response and, 237; in interdisciplinary context, xliii–xliv; sacred and profane aspects of, 165–167, 175–176, 236–237; use of term, xlivn

Location problem, xxxiii, 97, 142, 147–148, 212, 215; communication and, 23; locating location, 218–219; myths and, 294; reader response and, 243

Logos. *See also* Order of words; Eros and, 206, 208; logical structure and, 89; mythos and, 279–283, 293; as power of horror, 199

Longinus, 111, 112, 263; *ecstasis*, 112, 225, 271–272; transport, 111

*Lord of the Flies* (Golding), 116, 155, 157, 158, 242–243

*Lost in a Book: The Psychology of Reading for Pleasure* (Nell), 184

Love: of beauty, 7; Eros, 206, 208; order of, 206; of poetry, 7; of reading, 240–241

Lucretia, 29–30, 33

Ludic reading, 192–193; anxiety and, 188; cultural factors and, 187; literary experience and, 184–185; reality and, 190

Lyotard, J., xl

McAuley, E. P., 96

*Macbeth*, 54, 176

McClary, S., 225n

McKeon, R., 10–11

MacLeod, A., xxvi

Mapplethorpe case, 288

Martin, J. R., 146

Mazzoni, 23

Meaning: centrifugal, 87; centripetal, 87; readers and, 66–67

Media: violence in, 5

Media literacy, 18, 104–105

MediaWatch, 4–5, 6, 8, 285, 286

Medway, P., 235–236

Meek, M., 15, 215, 237–238, 240–242, 247, 265

Mendelssohn's *Octet*, 202, 205, 211, 223

*Merchant of Venice, The*, 76–77

Meta-cognitive theory of reading, 245

Metaphor: cave (Plato), 7; ludic reading and, 188; poetry as, 42; realism and, 85

Meta-problem. *See also* Censorship problem; Justification problem; Response problem; defense of poetry as, 24–26; defined, xxiv–xxvi, xxxiii; educated imagination and, xxxvi–xxxviii, 130–135; educational policy and, 102–109; expansion of, 155–159; Frye and, 47–53, 134; integrative studies and, 298; literary experience and, 69–70; newspaper stories pertaining to, 2–5; Plato and, 3, 10–18, 31–34; pluralism and need and, 148–151; politics of engagement and, 230; professionalization of literary response and, 234–239; re-visioning of, 268; Shelley and, 35, 37–41; stubborn structure and, 85–92

Miller, J., xi, 216, 217–218, 222, 246

Milton, J., 38, 52, 270, 272

*Mimesis*, 6, 203

*Mimesis as Make-Believe: On the Foundations of the Representational Arts* (Walton), 189

Mimetic representation: theory of, 106
Minturno, 23
*Mirror and the Lamp, The* (Abrams), 22
Misogyny, 196, 212–213, 221
Misrecognition scene, 198, 207,
  213–214, 264–265, 277. *See also*
  Recognition scene; literary
  experience as, 181–184;
  post-tragedic, 203; thwarted desire
  and, 196
Modernism: use of term, xlivn–xlvn
Moffett, J., 63, 78, 136–138, 140, 141,
  144, 158
Moi, T., 138
Montefiore, J., 249
Montreal massacre, 195–197, 206–207,
  212–214, 220, 226n-227n, 281;
  feminism and, 195–197, 200; Frye
  and, 282
*Montreal Massacre, The (Malette and
  Chalough)*, 283
Moorhouse, A., 168–169, 170
Moral values: advertising and, 33–34;
  aesthetics and, 111–112; censorship
  and, 85; Frye and, 55–56; language
  and, 79–80; literary experience and,
  165; literature and, 70–72, 96; poetry
  and, 31, 32–34, 39–41; reality and,
  81–82; social value of literature and,
  48
Morgan, Robert, 66, 168–170, 176
Morgan, Robin, 220, 221
Morrison, T., 221
Mortification of feeling, 97
Motherhood: creativity and, 203–204,
  207; idealization of, 220–221
Motherless father, 220–221
Mouré, E., 210–211, 213–214
Multiculturalism, 152
Munsch, R., 106
Murdoch, I., 11, 16
Music: augmented sub-mediant,
  223–224; diminished mediant,
  220–221; imperfect dominant, 223;
  major seventh, 224–225; minor
  second, 218–219; perfect
  subdominant, 221–222; poetry and,
  202, 211, 213; of the spheres, 200,
  216–218
*Music Box*, 3, 5, 10, 29, 285
Myth: allegorical interpretation of, 15;
  Frye's definition of, 54; ideology and,
  133, 273, 274, 278–284, 293–294;

ludic reading and, 188; open, 144;
  realism and, 85; sexual, 293; victims,
  293–294
*Mythos* (plot), 88, 113, 115; logos and,
  279–283, 293; reader as mental
  traveler, 134

Nabokov, V., 116
Narayan, U., 233–234
National Endowment for the Arts, 48
*Natural Perspective, A* (Frye), 126
Nature: Frye's definition of, 53
Nearness: sublime of, 233
"Necklace, The" (de Maupassant),
  113–114, 115
Need: pedagogy of, 151–155; poetics of,
  140–148, 150
*Need for Roots, The* (Weil), x
Nell, V., 184–185, 186–189, 190, 192,
  212, 213, 242, 292
Nelms, B., 237
Neo-Platonism, 24–25, 35
Neo-Romanticism, xxxvii
New Critical textualism, 106
New Literacy, 234–235, 250, 256
Newspapers: stories pertaining to
  meta-problem in, 2–5
Nonliteracy, 60–61
*Northrop Frye: Anatomy of His
  Criticism* (Hamilton), 132–133
Noticing and un-noticing, 220–221,
  224, 231–234, 275–276, 278–279,
  287, 304
Numinous, 201
Nussbaum, M., 178–181, 183, 185, 192,
  193, 214, 292, 305

*Oedipus Rex*, 177
Ong, W., 168, 169, 170, 172–173, 175,
  177, 190, 193, 232
Ontario Institute for Studies in
  Education, 64
Ontario Ministry of Education
  *Guideline for English*, 102–109, 165,
  167
Ontological anxiety, 185
Ontological shock: double, of
  minorities, 56; double, of feminists,
  139; post-tragedic stance of, 218;
  triple, 196, 198
Ontology of literary subjectivity, 206,
  219
Open mythology, **144**

Orality: ideal, 172–173; literacy and,
    173–174; quality of, 264
Order of love, 206
Order of words. *See also* Logos;
    censorship and, 82, 85, 87, 89;
    re-educated imagination and, 201,
    299; response problem and, 89;
    stubborn structure and, 85–87
Ordinary existence: pedagogy of, 240,
    294–295; poetics of, xxxii, 206–210,
    214, 261–268, 296
*Orientalism* (Said), 232
*Ostranenie*, 85, 143, 180
Other: aesthetic engagement and, 178;
    aesthetic experience and, 203;
    ambivalence and, 257;
    communication problems and, 23;
    control and, 221; cultural exchange
    and, 186; desire for and fear of, 198,
    199, 203, 205, 207–210; engagement
    and, 185; identity and, 199–200; in
    literary experience, 169–170; ludic
    readers and, 187; noticing and
    un-noticing, 220–221, 224, 231–234;
    pluralism and, 158, 198; power of
    horror and, 199; recognition scene
    and, 176; refusal to embrace,
    207–208; violence and, 212; women
    as, 205, 207–210, 212, 214, 217
Otto, R., 178
Ownership of texts, 241–242
Ozick, C., 180

*Paideia*: Plato and, 11, 13, 14, 17
"Painted Door, The" (Ross), 123
*Paradise Lost* (Milton), 272
Partee, M., 11, 12
Partial form, 115–119
Partial response, 115–119
Passion: victims and, 221, 230–234;
    without a victim, 249, 256, 280, 290
*Patio: patere*, 137, 150
Peacock, T. L., 90; irrelevance of poetry,
    38; Shelley and, 35–37
Peart, P., 76–77
Pedagogy: of detachment, 163;
    embodied, xliii, 228–259; of
    embodied criticism, 241; of need,
    151–155; of ordinary existence, 240,
    294–295; of refusal, 243; of
    transgression, 246–250; of the
    unknowable, 199–200
Penley, C., 144

Perlemuter, V., 304
Perry, D., 97, 157, 205, 276, 279
Personal development: education as,
    xxii, xxiii
Personal response, 241. *See also*
    Response
Peseroff, J., 250–251, 307–308
Peterborough County, Ontario:
    censorship in, 74, 78–85, 89–91,
    95–96, 98, 106, 135
Peters, R. S., 146
*Pharmakon*: poetry as, 27
Plato, xxiii, xxxix, 37, 57, 58, 66, 69, 93,
    99, 126, 152, 193, 197, 201, 202, 263,
    303; avoidance of self-conflict by,
    8–9; banishment of poets, xxxiii,
    xxxv–xxxvi, 2, 6–12, 16–19, 43*n*;
    bent-stick example, 13; bicameral
    mind and, 14, 17, 18; cave metaphor,
    7; censorship problem and, 11–13;
    defense of, 31–34; divided line
    parable, 7; engagement as
    double-edged sword, 202–203; Frye
    and, 48; imagination and, 7; *Ion*,
    xxxvi, 9, 26, 31, 40, 202, 286;
    justification problem and, 13–16;
    meta-problem and, 10–18; mistrust of
    language by, 8; *paideia*, education
    through art, 11, 13, 14, 17; poetry as
    educational, 10–16, 31; poetry as
    *eikasia*, 42; poetry as good and
    evil/truth and lies, 22, 25, 27, 51, 166,
    173, 182, 224, 239; recognition scene
    and, 176; *Republic X*, 27, 38; response
    problem and, 16–18; sacred quality of
    literary experience and, 165–166;
    "Stone of Heraclea," 9; *Symposium*,
    112, 120; uneducated imagination
    and, xxxvi, 1–19
Pleasure: aesthetic, 111; reading for,
    184–185
Pluralism: literary literacy and,
    152–153; meta-problem and,
    148–151; Other and, 158, 198; poetics
    of need and, 150; poetics of, 136–140,
    144–145
*Poeisis*, 175
Poetic apologists, xxxv. *See also*
    Defense of poetry
Poetic apologetics, 21–22
Poetic image, 88
Poetic knowledge, 64
Poetic language: Plato and, 8

Poetic response. *See also* Response; dangers of (Plato), 15–16; Shelley and, 40–41
Poetics of engagement, 258
Poetics of gender, 203
Poetics of need: feeling problem, 140–143; literary literacy and, 161–162; location problem, 147–148; pluralism and, 150; power problem, 143–147
Poetics of ordinary existence, xxxii, 206–210, 211, 214, 261–268, 296
Poetics of pluralism, 136–140, 144–145
Poetics of refusal, 165, 265
Poetics of total form, 55–57. *See also* Total form
Poetic truth, 66, 182
Poetry. *See also* Defense of poetry; Literature; beauty and, 39–40; vs. critical thinking, 16–17; double-edged, 10–16, 31, 49–53, 202–203, 209–210; educational value of, 10–16, 49–53; enculturation through, 13–14, 17–18; good and evil/truth and lies, 22, 25, 27, 30–33, 166, 224; as imitation, 27, 33; influence of, 197–198; as irrelevant, 36, 37; justification of, 13–16; morality and, 25, 32–34, 38, 39–41; music and, 202; as *pharmakon* (poison and cure), 27; Plato and, xxxiii, xxxv–xxxvi, 2, 6–19, 25, 42; power of influence on, 197–198; reader response to, 26–31; reality and, 12, 16–17, 26–28; response of children to, 15; as "rhetorical analogue," 25, 27; Romantic view of, 35–37; Shelley and, 42; Sidney and, 42; as speaking picture, 26–31; transvaluation of in Renaissance, 24; uneducated imagination and, 1–19
Poets: allegorical imagination and, 30; banishment of, 43n; best, 38–39; changing concept of, 66–67; justification of, 22; moral issues and, 23, 25, 30–31, 38, 41; philosophical, 33; Plato's banishment of, xxxiii, xxxv–xxxvi, 2, 6–12, 16–19; second-string, 38
Point-driven readers, 115
Poirier, Richard, 50

Political consciousness: embodied criticism and, xlii–xliii; literary literacy and, xli
Politically correct: use of term, xlvn
Politically inspired text refusals, 155, 157, 158, 242–243
Politicizing literature, xxxiv–xxxv
Politics of engagement: censorship problem and, 94
Politics of referentiality, 82
Pope, A., 36
Pornography: censorship and, 79–80, 287
Possession, xiii, 241–242
Postcritical response, 120
Posthumanism, xlivn–xlvn
Postman, N., 18, 50
Postmodernism, xxxix, xlivn–xlvn
Poststructuralism, xxxix–xl
Post-tragedic stance: misrecognition scene, 203; of ontological shock, 218; of women, xl, 195–197, 224, 278
Power: of choice, 223; (dis)empowering, 220–221; reclaiming, 221–222; as refusal of power, 233
Power problem, xxxiii, 97, 142, 143–147, 212, 215; communication and, 23; myths and, 294; reader response and, 243
Powers of horror, 195–200, 206
*Powers of Horror* (Kristeva), 208
Pre-conscious mind, 14
Precritical response, 120–121
Predictors: partial response and, 118
"Preface to the Lyrical Ballads" (Williams), 250, 252–253
Presence, 230, 231, 289
Presubjectivity, 267
Pritchard, D., 61
Probst, R., xli
Pure utterance, 262–268
Purves, A., 69
Pythagoras, 216

Racism: *Huckleberry Finn* and, 97, 157, 276; *Lord of the Flies* and, 116, 155, 157, 158, 242–243
*Radical Literary Education* (Robinson), 250
Reader response: educated imagination and, 99; feminist criticism and, 139–140; student response journals,

247–259; subjectivity and, 243; taxonomy of, 112–120; to poetry, 26–31; value of, 92

Reader-response theory: development of, 23; dialectical stages of, 120–122; educated imagination and, 126; Frye and, 109–112; real readers and, 123–127; stages of, 120–122

Readers: ambivalent, 257–258; autonomous, 102, 111, 112–120, 123–125, 149–150; awareness by, 142, 241, 246, 256–257; competent and life-long, 240; educated, 112–120; embodied, xi, 200–205, 268–273; encouraging, 240–246; engagement of, 106–108; functional, 108; information-driven, 115; life-long, 240; ludic, 184–185, 187–189; point-driven, 115; as producers of meaning, 67; real, 108–110, 239–240; understanding by, 242

Reading: as bibliotherapy, 174, 272; creating, 289; vs. criticism, 133–134; Frye's theory of, 87–92; as a gendered activity, 280–282; interactive, xi; inward and outward motions during, 87; literary, 290; literature as literature, 67–68; meaning and, 66; meta-cognitive theory of, 245; models of, 223–224; for pleasure, 184–185; purposes of, ix–xiii

Reading ego: regnant, 185, 186, 188, 189, 192; repressed, 188, 212, 213

Reading self, 185, 187

Reading sovereignty, 185, 187, 192

Read for Your Life (Gold), 174

Realism: approaches to, 91; censorship and, 91

Reality: Frye's definition of, 53–54; literary, 56–57; literary convention and, 278–285; literature and, 83–84, 86; poetry and, 12, 16–17, 26–28

Real Presences (Steiner), 200–221, 234, 265

Real readers: engaged reader and, 109–110; literary experience and, 239–240

Reclaiming power, 221–222

Recognition scene, 176–177; Frye and, 277; misrecognition and, 181–184, 196, 198, 207, 213–214, 264–265, 277; oracular language of, 264–265

Redoing and remaking texts. See Undoing and remaking texts

Re-educated imagination: defined, xxxii–xxxiii; distancing and, 193; educated imagination and, 263–264; embodied criticism and, xlii–xliii, 195–225; embodied pedagogy and, xliii, 228–259; feminist critique of Romanticism and, 246–250; Frye and, 272–273; identity and, 192; imaginative literalism and, 280; issues, xxviii; literary engagement and, 235–236; literary experience and, xlii, 161–194; literary literacy and, xli, 135–136, 158–159; literary response and, 240; love of reading and, 240–241; ludic readers and, 185; need for, 6; Other and, 191; overview, xxxviii–xliv; poetics of ordinary existence and, 208–210, 274; politically inspired text refusals and, 242–243; possession of texts and, 242; power of embodied horror and, 195–200

Reflective engagement, 250

Refusal: pedagogy of, 243; poetics of, 165, 265

Regional culture. See also Enculturation; ensorship and, xxv; universality and, xxviii

Regnant reading ego, 185, 186, 188, 189, 192

Regressed reading ego, 188, 212, 213

Religion: Frye and, 269–273, 276–277, 284

Relocating identity, 222–223

Remaking texts. See Undoing and remaking texts

Renaissance Peterborough, 80–84, 86, 93, 94, 96, 155

Republic (Plato), 14, 27, 38

Research in the Teaching of English, 62

Response. See also Critical response; Literary response; Poetic response; Reader response; development, 151–155, 213; kinetic, 116, 117–118; language arts curriculum and, 103; model, xxi, 92, 103; moral issues and, 34; stock, 116–118; student response journals, 247–259

Response journals: feminist critique of Romanticism and, 247

Response problem, xxiv, xxv;
censorship problem and, 92; defense
of poetry and, 48; educated
imagination and, xxxviii, 102–127;
educational policy and, 102–109;
justification problem and, 111; Plato
and, 16–18; self-disclosure and, 215;
Shelley and, 40–42; Sidney and, 31
Rich, A., 138
Richler, M., 106
Ricoeur, P., 171
Rilke, R. M., 202, 206
Robinson, J., 250
Romantic imagination, 23; Frye and, 46;
Shelley and, 34–41
Romanticism: feminist critique of,
246–250; recognition and
misrecognition and, 265
Rorty, R., xii, 277
Rosenblatt, L., 67–70, 108, 188, 215
Ross, S., 123
Rushdie, S., xii, 73–74
Ruthven, K. K., 149, 162
Ryan, M., 151

Said, E., 232
Sakai, C., 304
Salinger, J. D., 80, 95–96
Sartre, J.P., xxxi
*Satanic Verses, The* (Rushdie), 73–74
Sayingness and unsayingness, of
literature, 274, 276, 287–288;
censorship and, 96–98; stubborn
structure and, 85–87; tragic action, 180
Scholes, R., 236–237, 245
*School of Abuse, The* (Gosson), 26, 286
School text censorship, xxi–xxii
Schumann, M., x
Scribner, S., 175
*Secular Scripture, The* (Frye), 110
*Seducere*, 241, 244, 247
Seduction: abjection and, 217; betrayal
and, 214; complicity and, 217;
embodied criticism and, 216–225;
reading, 212–216; Romanticism and,
249
Self: fragmented, 258; in literary
experience, 169–170; reading, 185,
187; unitary, 258
Self-conflict: Plato's avoidance of, 8–9
Self-consciousness, 171–172, 253
Self-disclosure: response problem and,
215

Self-displacement, 223
Self-sufficient reader, 185
Self-transformation, 297
Sensibility: reader-response theory and,
110
Sexism: in advertising, 4–6, 8, 285, 286;
in literature, 124–125, 128n; stock
response and, 141
"Shawl, The" (Ozick), 180
Shelley, P. B., xxiii, 2, 21, 34–42, 56, 61,
66, 69, 70, 106, 158, 193; censorship
problem and, 39–40; *Defense of
Poetry*, xxxvi, 36–37, 41, 90; Frye
and, 45; justification problem and,
37–41, 42; meta-problem and, 35,
37–41; poetry as Romantic ideal, 42;
response problem and, 40–42;
Romantic imagination and, 34–41
Shock: in aesthetic/literary experience,
178–179; ontological, 56, 139, 196,
198, 218; of recognition, 122
Showalter, E., 138
Sidney, P., xxiii, 2, 21, 37, 39, 40, 42,
43n, 54, 56, 61, 69, 86, 88, 90, 106,
177, 183, 193, 265; allegorical
imagination and, 24–26, 32; *Apologie
for Poetrie*, xxvi, 23, 26–32;
censorship and, 82; defense of Plato,
31–34; defense of poetry, 26–32;
meta-problem and, 31–34; poetry as
feigning, 42; reader response, 26–31
Singing School, 250, 263, 265–267, 288,
290
Smith, B. H., 186, 213
Social change: literary experience and,
165, 190–191
Social imagination, 139
Social value: of art, 50–51; of literature,
48
*Soft Revolution, The* (Postman), 50
Sound: centering effect, 172
Sovereignty, in reading, 185, 187, 292
Speaking picture: poetry as, 26–31
Spirituality, 194
Spiritual truth, 236
*Spiritus Mundi* (Frye), 45, 85
Spivak, G., 261, 265, 287, 290
Stasis. *See also* Aha! response; abjection
in, 214; autonomous response and,
123–124; defined, 112, 113, 115–116;
literary experience and, 164–165,
175; literary literacy and, 168; literary
response and, 114–115; partial form

and, 119; recognition scene as,
176–177; repudiating, 218–219;
sacred and profound and, 168–169;
state of grace and, 175; teaching for,
245; total form and, 112–115,
167–168; as transparency, 166–167
State of grace: literary experience as,
175–176, 236
Steiner, G., 50, 200–221, 234, 265, 267,
275
Stereophonic vision, 219; literary
experience as, 170–185
Stereoscopic hearing, 224, 226n
Stereoscopic vision, 226n
Stereoscopy: cognitive, 194n
Stibbs, A., 235–236
Stierle, K., 84
Stock response, 124, 127, 131, 137, 187;
partial form and, 116–118; sexism
and, 141
Stone Angel, The (Laurence), 80
"Stone of Heraclea" (Plato), 9
Storm in the Mountains: A Case Study
of Censorship, Conflict, and
Consciousness (Moffett), 78,
136–137
Story-driven readers, 115
Street, B., 173
Stubborn structure, 269–270;
architectural motif of, 88, 89;
censorship and, 85–92, 94; literature
as, 85–92, 269; order of words and,
85–87; reader response and, 109–112
Stubborn Structure, The (Frye), 45,
85–92
Student response journals, 247–259.
See also Response
Subjectivity, 264; literary, ontology of,
206, 219; presubjectivity, 267; reader
response and, 243
Sublime: alternative, 274, 290; of
nearness, 233
Symposium (Plato), 112, 120

Taming of the Shrew, The, 244
Tasso, 23
"Teaching with sensitivity" approach,
97
Text: allegorical imagination and, 25;
literary imagination and, xi;
possession of, 241–242; undoing and
remaking of, 238, 245–246, 247, 266,
288–242

Textbook censorship. See also
Censorship; Censorship problem; in
Peterborough County, Ontario, 78–85
Text-reader relationships, 6, 25, 66–67
Textual hedonism, 245
Thomson, J., 237, 256
Thoreau, H. D., 35
Three Guineas (Woolf), 144, 290–293,
294
Thwarted desire: power of horror and,
196
Toronto Transit Commission, 4
Total form: aesthetics of, xxvii; as
dialectic, 119–120; feminization of,
xl; poetics of, 55–57; stasis and,
112–115, 167–168
Tragedy: Greek, 178–181; literary
engagement in, 183–184; recognition
scene in, 176–177, 178; sayingness
and unsayingness and, 180; stasis
and, 175
Tragic response, 178–181; aesthetic
engagement and, 178
Transfiguration, 246–250, 295–299;
defined, 266, 267
Transformation, 152, 283, 295–299;
censorship and, 156, 157;
enculturation and, 164, 168–169
Transgression, 230, 231, 246–251, 288,
289; defined, 289; pedagogy of,
246–250
Transparency: stasis as, 166–167
Transposition, 266–267
Tremendum, 196, 198, 201, 209, 233
Trent University, 79
Trickster-as-Coyote (Haraway),
218–219
Truth: concerned, 157; Plato's concept
of, 7; poetic, 66, 182; spiritual, 236
Truth-of-correspondence: censorship
and, 81–82, 98; Frye's rejection of,
88–90, 92; imaginative literalism
and, 84; interpretation and, 87

Undoing and remaking texts, 238, 242,
245–246, 247, 266, 288–289
"Uneducated" imagination: Plato and,
xxxvi, 1–19
Unitary self, 258
Unity: concept of, xl
Universality: regional culture and,
xxviii
Unknowable: pedagogy of, 199–200

Un-noticing. *See* Noticing and
    un-noticing
Updike, J., 114–115, 116–118, 121–123,
    140, 162
Utterance: pure, 262–268

Vertical perspective: stubborn structure
    and, 85
Victims: passion and, 221, 230–234,
    249, 256, 280, 290; women as, 251
Vida, 23
Violence. *See also* Montreal Massacre;
    against women, 195–197, 293; in
    media, 5
Vipond, D., 115, 128n
Virgin-baiting, 281, 282
Visual ideal: auditory ideal and,
    172–173
Visual literacy, 104
Voice: recovery of, 232; voicing,
    223–224, 230
Vulnerability, of readers, 183–184, 192

*Wake of Imagination, The* (Kearney),
    xxxii, 12, 20n
Walton, K., 188–189
Warnock, M., xxxi–xxxii, 264
"Watching the Watchwords" (Mouré),
    210–211
Weedon, C., 138
Weigel, S., 292
Weil, S., x, 196, 203
Weinbrot, H. D., 269
Weingartner, C., 50

Weir, P., 35
Whitman, W., 35
"Why Doesn't This Feel Empowering?"
    (Ellsworth), 199
Williams, R., 35
Willinsky, J., 249
Wimsatt, W. K., Jr., 23
Winnett, S., 245
Wolf, C., xli, 196
Women. *See also* Feminism; Feminist
    criticism; Gender; Montreal
    Massacre; biblical images of,
    276–277; as exuberant transgressors,
    251; as father's daughters, 284–285,
    292; female as ground, xxix;
    misogyny and, 196, 212–213, 221; as
    mothers, 203–204, 207, 220–221;
    post-tragedic stance of, xl, 195–197,
    224, 278; power and, 222;
    reconstruction of feminine identity,
    221–222; as victims, 251; violence
    against, 195–197, 293
Woodman, M., 284
Woolf, V., xliv, 144, 290–293, 294
Words: order of. *See* Order of words
*Words with Power* (Frye), 269, 272–273,
    274–277, 279, 293, 303–304
Wordsworth, D., 248, 250–258, 288, 308
Wordsworth, W., 36, 248–258, 288, 307
Writing: language arts and, 59, 62–63

Yaeger, P., 233
Young, G. P., 65, 66

Zancanella, D., 237